Steven Berkoff

Steven Berkoff was born in Stepney, London. After studying drama and mime in London and Paris, he entered a series of repertory companies and in 1968 formed the London Theatre Group. His plays and adaptations have been performed in many countries and in many languages. Among the many adaptations Berkoff has created for the stage, directed and toured, are Kafka's *Metamorphosis* and *The Trial*, *Agamemnon* after Aeschylus, and Poe's *The Fall of the House of Usher*. He has directed and toured productions of Shakespeare's *Coriolanus*, while also playing the title role in *Richard II*, *Hamlet*, and *Macbeth*, as well as Oscar Wilde's *Salomé*.

Berkoff's original stage plays include *East, West, Messiah: Scenes from a Crucifixion, The Secret Love Life of Ophelia, Decadence, Harry's Christmas, Massage, Acapulco,* and *Brighton Beach Scumbags*. He has performed his trilogy of solo shows, *One Man, Shakespeare's Villains,* and *Requiem for Ground Zero*, in venues all over the world.

Films Steven has acted in include *A Clockwork Orange, Barry Lyndon, Octopussy, Beverly Hills Cop, Rambo, Under the Cherry Moon, Absolute Beginners* and *The Krays*. He directed and co-starred with Joan Collins in the film version of his play *Decadence*.

He has published a variety of books on the theatre such as the production journals *I am Hamlet, Meditations on Metamorphosis,* and *Coriolanus in Deutschland*. Berkoff's work has led him to traverse the globe, and his love for travel is apparent in his book *Shopping in the Santa Monica Mall: The Journals of a Strolling Player.*

www.stevenberkoff.com

First published in the UK in 2026 by SUPERNOVA BOOKS
(an imprint of Aurora Metro Publications Ltd) 80 Hill Rise, Richmond, TW10 6UB www.supernovabooks.co.uk
Shouting at Night: From East End Rebel to Hollywood's Master Villain

Editor: Mark Gunn

Printed and bound in Great Britain by Short Run Press Ltd, Exeter
on paper that has been sustainably resourced.

ISBN: 978-1-913641-59-7 (print)
ISBN: 978-1-913641-60-3 (ebook)

FSC www.fsc.org
MIX
Paper | Supporting responsible forestry
FSC® C014540

SHOUTING AT NIGHT

From East End Rebel to Hollywood's Master Villain

by

STEVEN BERKOFF

SUPERNOVA BOOKS

ACKNOWLEDGEMENTS

I would like to thank Keiron Pim for his help with the book, as well as my partner Clara Fischer, my agent Joanna Marston, my assistant Sacha Tanyar, and editors Mark Gunn and Cheryl Robson.

Me and my partner Clara at Chelsea Flower Show, 2016

CONTENTS

PROLOGUE

The Blitz – 7 Septempter 1940 – 57 straight nights

It was a balmy autumn evening at 124 Whitechapel Road, when we heard a huge and terrifying sound through the air, as if some vast and mysterious beast was on the rampage – the sirens of the Second World War. Each night, Ma and Pa would gather us up, me and my sister Beryl, and trundle down the stairs from our rented first-floor rooms to join the hordes in Whitechapel Road scurrying to the local Underground station. This we did for fifty-seven straight nights. But each morning as we crawled out of the station blinking and coughing into the bright sunlight, we all gave thanks that for another night we were spared.

I believe it was on the fiftieth night, when the dinosaurs were screeching that they were on the warpath and Mum jumped up to perform the nightly ritual, that Dad, seeing that I was still half-asleep, said, 'Look, it's the first time he's been able to sleep even through this nightmare – let's just risk it for one night, Polly. They've been dropping these bombs for fifty nights and it's always the docks that have taken the brunt of it.' Ma was not one for taking that kind of risk and just grabbed a blanket, wrapped me in it, and made her way down the stairs. We all poured into the Underground, which was fast filling up. There was lots of noise and animated chatter – some old biddy was even singing some ancient cockney tune while her neighbours were begging her to put a sock in it. We half dozed through the night waiting for the all-clear, but even when we heard it, most of us just waited for daylight.

At last, we stepped out onto the wide, grim Whitechapel Road just opposite the great Royal London Hospital – but the air was dusty and full of smoke. When we reached number 124, we saw that it was no longer there. A direct hit had decapitated the house.

That's how Ma remembered it. Days later we were evacuated to Luton in Bedfordshire and for the first time in our lives became country folk.

Me at Manor House, aged 13

PART 1

CHAPTER 1

In the Beginning

I was born Leslie Steven Berks on 3 August 1937 at Mother Levy's Nursing Home just off Vallance Road, which was a short walk from our top-floor flat on Whitechapel Road, Stepney. I have vague and misty memories of the flat – a small pram on the first-floor landing – but that is about all. My mother, Pauline (otherwise known as Paula, Polly, or Poll), was the youngest of ten brothers and sisters who had mostly scattered to America. She was born in Odessa, Russia, and her maiden name was Hyman. My father, Alfred, was born in England, but both my paternal grandparents were from Romania. On arriving in England, my grandfather anglicised the family name from Berkowitz to Berks.

After our home was blown up in 1940, my sister and I were evacuated to mysterious environs north of London. My sister went at first to Crewe, right up north in Cheshire, which she loved so much that she never stopped talking about it and the wonderful woman who cared for her, Miss Meachum. I was deposited in the small Bedfordshire town of Luton. All I can remember to this day is a giant hall, which was obviously a refugee centre. I recall one of the staff offering me, as Ma left, a large, bitter green apple. It is as clear to me as if it happened yesterday. I held the apple in my hand, but it meant little to me – Mum had disappeared.

That consumed me utterly. It was the very first time that my darling, warm-hearted mum wasn't immediately on tap for me. She had dissolved into the ether. I remember howling my head off without stopping. Endlessly, ceaselessly, and still holding this vile green apple. I don't recall eating or sleeping; I only recall the endless howling which was consuming me. Somehow, the staff managed to contact her to say that it wasn't possible to keep me there and so she was obliged to collect me, and soon she materialised out of the very mist from whence she had dissolved. Time passed until memory becomes more vivid.

***

In 1943 I was five. My sister Beryl had joined me in Luton and then our parents were reunited with us there. We had found temporary rented accommodation at 25 Grantham Road, a small, gentle country road, indistinguishable from thousands of others in small country towns. The houses looked as if they had been constructed on assembly lines.

What I remember then so very clearly, since memory must have a vital clue which hooks itself into your mind, is examining the small gate, which was the entrance to our tiny front garden and as is children's wont, thrusting my head through the wooden struts so I was unable to pull myself out. Eventually, a kind neighbour produced a saw, and I was soon put out of my misery, to everybody's relief. Later I was to discover that it was the very first day in our new home – so it seems that I could only demarcate time if a serious event scored an impression; otherwise, time would pass without rhyme or reason.

Now my memory is beginning to store up images I recall so clearly. From our back room, I could stare out of the window and see in the distance a beautiful group of swaying cedar trees. I was sure that their tips would soon touch the sky, and I remember them so clearly because each morning I would ask my sister if they had yet touched the base of the clouds. 'Nearly,' she always lied, 'but not quite yet.' But as it was obvious something was in transition, I would not hesitate to ask her again the next morning and got virtually the same response.

Beryl and I shared a small bedroom, as I wasn't considered old enough to be unsupervised. For me, each day was a new adventure, and I was glad to get up early in the morning while it was still dark. I came downstairs early one morning. Ma already had a roaring fire in the grate, the wireless was on, and the BBC news was telling us how many Messerschmitts our glorious air force had shot down since yesterday. I knew that we had to be winning the war because we were the good guys and they were the devil.

I had not yet begun school, and my great pleasure was to ride my red three-wheeled bike round and round the room. Once, as I left my little upstairs bedroom, I bumped into Dad just as he was leaving his. Suddenly, impulsively, he grabbed me under my armpits and lifted me high in the air. I can remember it so clearly because he had never done this before and never did it again.

The days passed quite uneventfully. I remember very clearly my first day at Maidenhall Primary School in 1943. Again, it was a bit of a shock, so I recall it vividly. Ma and I strolled round the corner to the school, which was just off the main Dunstable Road. I was deposited at a small wooden desk, which I had to share with another boy. Ma stood at the doorway of the classroom watching this historic occasion and waving goodbye to me as all the children streamed in and took their seats. Then, almost as soon as we were seated, the teacher began the first lesson by talking about the alphabet. And just like that, I was suddenly absorbed by this new lady in front of us, writing squiggly letters on the blackboard with her piece of chalk, that I hardly noticed that my mother was no longer a fixture in my life. Then the teacher drew the letter 'H'. Why do I remember that letter? Surely, she must have started with 'A', must have, but I only remember 'H' so well. We all had little blackboards and small pieces of chalk and simply copied her. In those days, all the desks had small porcelain inkwells, and we were allocated pens with nibs, though on occasion this would encourage the beast sitting next to you to take some bizarre pleasure in stabbing you on the back of your hand, which from time to time I reciprocated.

After about an hour, we were given a break to drink from a small milk bottle. This was quite pleasant and took at least twenty minutes off the morning. Then suddenly it would be lunchtime, and a flock of mothers would be gathered outside to rescue their newly initiated fledglings and take them home for lunch. I saw Ma at the door again to pick me up, and I felt reassured to see the familiar, warm, motherly face. The boy sitting next to me exclaimed as she stood with the other mothers at the entrance, 'Hey, that's a fat one!' I accepted the comment, making no claim to know the 'fat one' in my cowardly shame – yes, maybe she was a tad plump then – but then I dashed quickly out of the room so he might be absolved from any guilt if he saw me greeting her.

Some of the children would stay for school dinner, for which their parents had paid sixpence. I tried that once or twice but didn't like it too much, so Ma picked me up instead. That became the routine for all those years; it must have been very tiring for Ma to try and cook up something interesting each and every day. After a couple of weeks, I was allowed to walk home alone since it wasn't far to go.

I enjoyed the school in the main, some lessons more than others. But what I particularly loved were the 'acting classes', which to me were less classes than playtime when Miss Hammond would have us play out scenes from *Brer Rabbit and Brer Fox*. I liked this class so very much and totally threw myself into it; Miss Hammond always cast me as Brer Rabbit, since it came to me so easily. Each Friday, the day when she used to read us the story, she would cast her eye around the class and would ask which character we'd like to play. I, of course, would invariably reply 'Brer Rabbit, Miss.' I entered the game as if I were actually the character.

Now, one day – and this was after many weeks of playing – she asked me, 'OK, Leslie, who would you like to play today?' (Leslie was my first name, which I jettisoned a few years later and opted from then on to go by my middle name – Steven.) And I said, 'Brer Fox,' since I was a little self-conscious about taking the lead each week and thought some other boy should have a chance. Suddenly, and this I have never forgotten, Miss Hammond stared at me and even, I have to admit, looked a little crestfallen. She obviously really liked and maybe even looked forward to my jolly impersonations of Brer Rabbit. However, after that one time of personal sacrifice, I naturally returned to Brer Rabbit (and we all lived happily ever after).

I liked Miss Hammond so much. I have always carried her in my heart. There was not a great deal I enjoyed about the school, although I do remember loving spelling and learning the exact order of the letters. One day, we had a special spelling exam. The teacher spoke clearly the words which we would then write down. I recall getting every answer correct and being very proud. I even brought my sheet of paper with all my correct answers home to show my mother with my proud ticks by each word.

***

The years slowly passed by. We had to move to another address much further down the road and for a while Mother would walk me to the same school, until I reached the royal age of eight, when I was confident enough to go alone. Every so often, say about once every two weeks, Ma gave me a shilling to give to the barber, who would give me a haircut. Well, it said on the list of services pinned to the wall: **CHILDREN'S/BOYS' HAIRCUTS TEN PENCE.** After I gave him his shilling, I always wondered why he never gave me my twopence change. Sometimes my mother didn't bother to explain those finer details of life to me. But eventually, when questioned, she did confess that those two pennies were what came to be known as a tip.

Now, I had been at school for a few months when Ma decided to enrol me at Hebrew classes so I could be indoctrinated into our ancient history. These were held two evenings a week and once on Sunday, and I started to identify myself as a Jew for the very first time. Ma used to keep the Passover ritual each year, when I had to stuff myself with matzos and avoid bread for a whole week. I found the Hebrew language quite fascinating, and I was studying a mystical text that none of my schoolmates at Maidenhall would have the slightest clue about. Also, I loved the biblical stories that a lovely young teacher would enchant us with on the Sunday morning class as we all gathered round her desk. I quite fell in love with her. I attended the midweek Hebrew classes in order to acquaint myself with finer aspects of my religion, and the wondrous stories there gripped me thrillingly and chilled me to the bone.

We felt safe from the war but now and then worries would creep in, prompted by some snatch of news or gossip. A strange boy named Baxter who lived on our street once informed me that if Hitler conquered England, he would kill all the Jews. I didn't believe that the Germans would win the war, because we were the goodies and good would always overcome evil; but still, something changed within me. The smallest incident could throw me into a fit of anxious trembling. Being singled out by a teacher for some minor misdemeanour would make me shake with fear. Or if my sister said light-heartedly on an overcast day that the sky was falling down, I would succumb to profound dread. Gradually, I changed from being a relatively carefree boy into one who lived in a state of doubt and fear.

Of course, I was at an age when the infinite mysteries of the world began to torment me with desire, especially when I saw so many young men and boys my age bestride those glorious machines called bicycles. Oh, how I craved one. I craved one so badly. I recall mounting one of those magical machines and being transported so easily with a simple thrust down of my foot. So this became my first and lasting obsession, and I could hardly let a day pass without dreaming about my triumphant Pegasus. I begged, I caterwauled, I whined, I pleaded to my dad but all to no avail, all fobbed off with simple responses like 'streets round here are far too dangerous', 'you're far too young', 'maybe when you're a little older', when actually what were truly dangerous were the snatched moments when I would beg a neighbour's son to allow me to ride his bike round the block a few times. I knew no Highway Code and so would just tear down the hill and brake at every junction and feebly ride across the road and then cycle until I came to the next junction, when I would stop again. I could so easily have been killed. How sensible it would have been to at least teach me some of the laws of the road, but as the time passed my desires were dismissed or ignored.

Well, as it happens, my father would bring back from one of his frequent visits to London a large bag of groceries, and our favourites were the crispy and moreish circles of dough called beigels, an ancient Jewish bread roll. We'd heat them up and smother them with swathes of cream cheese and, when we could afford it, smoked salmon. Nowadays, for some unknown reason, these beigels have been anglicised and are pronounced 'bagels', but in my young days the word was emphatically pronounced 'beigels' like the 'i' in 'bicycle'. I remember to this day that I was in the garden doing not so very much, as usual, when I saw my dad at the kitchen window. He tapped the windowpane, and I heard him shout out 'Beigels!' I froze. All I heard was the first syllable, 'bei', and in my mind I heard the whole word 'bicycle'. Perhaps Dad, I thought, had actually given in to my heartfelt longings? As soon as I heard the word, I dashed to the kitchen. I then saw the beigels and immediately knew I had misheard. I briefly glanced at this man, who was so absent in my life that he was more stranger than father, and left the kitchen.

Now Dad was getting fed up with my constant whining, so he made a deal with me. He promised he would get me a bike if I would be on my best behaviour for forty days straight. Forty days… With discipline and restraint, this was something that I could surely do; however, on the twentieth day I dropped the baton and the demon flew out of me, probably to do with the grub that Mum cooked up from her Eastern European ancestors, which made me gag. For this misdemeanour, I was set back to day one. So, I started again from the beginning; I would not give up. My determination to have that gleaming bike under me was too compelling to be put off by the odd hindrance. However, even after I concentrated like fury for forty days without a blemish, I never saw my longed-for bicycle. But I did learn something… I would never, ever trust him again.

Now, it came to pass that once a week at Maidenhall School, a teacher gave us 'religious instruction' and, of course, much of it centred around the life of Jesus and how he was persecuted by 'the Jews', and since the class was only too aware that I had been identified as one of those whose ancestors were believed to have had him nailed to a cross, I was picked on in the playground as the 'Jew boy'. Their favourite method was to tie their woollen scarves into a knotted end and attack me joyously with them. So I chose to tie my scarf in an equal manner and give back as good as I got. Curiously this didn't bother me at all; it was as if we were playing Cowboys and Indians and I was the Indian. I didn't even feel any sense of bullying; I just accepted it as a jolly game. Soon, as we returned to class, it was swiftly forgotten about and after a few days, the kids got bored with it and sought out other distractions. Regrettably, we had hardly any music study except for idly banging tambourines. Frankly, I saw very little point in them.

We now moved for a third time, this time to Highfield Road just about a quarter of a mile further down Dunstable Road. It was a smallish house in one of those pre-war developments where each house was an exact replica of the next with a miserable patch of back garden. However, it came with a beautiful black cat called Peter, which I immediately fell in love with. Nevertheless, the original owners, who had rented the house before us, would eventually come to collect him. I had my own bedroom and no longer had to share with my sister – a great relief since I was now reaping the benefits of growing up. There was a slightly larger back garden to play in, but the main difference from the previous house was that I made friends with two charming children who lived just across the road from me. They were John and Janet Ellis. I believe these were the first friends I made. We were always finding adventures together, walking and exploring and collecting beautiful firm and shiny conkers that lay in proliferation in Wardown Park. They were like hard, round amber jewels, and I could never get enough of them. A simple piece of string threaded through, and one had yet another toy, which could be endlessly used to thrash an opponent's conker. Thinking back, I can almost taste it.

Sometimes the three of us would explore a large factory called Fricker's which was just round the corner. Once inside, we'd watch in amazement the wonders of the industrial age – those huge cylinders trembling and shaking, although we hadn't a clue as to what they were. Or we'd scramble over the wasteland at the back of the factory and build a little shack using rusty old oil drums and even tried unsuccessfully to cook a potato as if we had been exiled to some desert island. Meanwhile, Peter the cat returned looking thin and bedraggled from his long hike all the way from Dunstable. We were so overjoyed to see him that we happily watched him drag a large piece of fish from a plate that Ma had fried for our supper.

My best friend, John Ellis, made me deeply value those early bonds of friendship. I missed him and Janet so much after my family decided to uproot us for our big adventure, the dream of our lives, our planned trip to the New World which was New York. Ma and Pa had, in fact, along with at least half a dozen brothers and sisters, emigrated to New York in the early 20s. This was made possible by

Ma's intrepid brother Sam. He had made the trip a few years earlier and had certainly feathered his nest by becoming a bootlegger. He became very rich and consequently financed the entire Hyman family to make the trip to New York. In fact, my parents got married there in 1923 and lived there quite happily until my father felt that he had to return to London so he could take care of his parents. However, as luck would have it, just when they had decided to return to New York, war broke out and then we were stuck in the East End of London, where I was born. So now, two years after the war had ended, Ma was determined to resume the glorious life amid her close family in the Big Apple.

Meanwhile, I had only just begun to discover the sheer mystery of the female of the species, and I recall wondering frequently how I could ever tell my inamorata, Janet, how much I loved her. Alas, I never did; even while I tied myself in little knots, I was still unable to make my feelings known to her. Consequently, because we now were leaving England forever, or so I thought, I lost all connection with my two dear friends and never found such a loyal pal as John again. I still think of him seventy-five years later and so wish I could see him and his sister, Janet, his sweet, lovely sister. I find it strange that as I dip into old age, the memories of the past carry with them such a desperate sweetness and poignancy that the present has no hope of comparison. I almost want to gather them all in my arms and howl, 'Forgive me! Forgive me!'

My American cousin Morris Nathan, who was drafted into the forces that were most fortunately stationed in England, used to visit us on the weekend. I always looked forward to seeing him; he used to tell me tales of army life and even taught me to tell the time. All the things that my own father never bothered about.

The weeks in between visits slowly crawled by while I scrabbled round the garden full of giant cobwebs and spiders, or I went to the local recreation ground and played on the swings and slides and delighted in the profusion of butterflies that danced around the abundance of flowers. (They had totally disappeared when I visited the park fifty years later in an attempt to savour the sweet nostalgia of my past.) There was a shed at the park's edge where a nice elderly gentleman sat all afternoon, just watching the comings and goings, and when I thought it might be time to be getting back home for my supper, I would approach him with my perpetual question: 'Have you got the time, please mister?' Very patiently, he would dip his fingers into his waistcoat pocket, pull out his old and no doubt precious pocket watch and answer me.

I asked him so often and not once, or for even a second, did he show the slightest impatience with me, until I began to see him as an official timekeeper for the kids in the park, especially as he was there every day without fail. One day I noticed that he was not at his usual perch, but there was another man there who seemed to have taken his place, and so I asked him and he answered me in the same patient way as the previous old man, whom I never saw sitting on his usual seat again. I had to assume that he was now watching us from a higher place.

I continued quite happily at my two schools, and I was able to supplement my weekly pocket money by selling the brightly coloured American comics which my divine cousin Morris, now back in America, sent me each week without fail. This was a kind of rite of passage for me. I sold these comics in my Hebrew classes. I truly loved them, even the smell of them. They smelled of America – *Captain Marvel, Superman, Batman, Mickey Mouse, Dick Tracy*, and *Bugs Bunny* – and I would devour them cover to cover. Since the price of the comic was ten cents, I converted that to five pence and a short while later to sixpence, which felt a bit tidier. This meant that on a good day I might sell six comics, which would reward me royally with three shillings!

I was rich and yet, apart from my friend John Ellis across the road, I had few friends, and my main adventure was Hebrew classes three times a week and a fortnightly trip to Bluebell Woods, where we were encouraged to pick flowers and press them in a special book and title them.

The war was drawing to its pathetic, pitiless end. The small house we rented at 25 Grantham Road was comfortable and now I had my own bedroom; this is where my memory starts, apart from the small shards I have already mentioned.

Our landlady, a Mrs Everett, came once a week to collect the rent. She kept the front room of the house always locked, as it was her private office, and would only unlock it once a week when she came to collect the rent. Mrs Everett was what you might call a grand old Victorian lady. One rent day, when she arrived and opened the door to the front room where she would collect the rent, I dashed in with my mother and discovered a wondrous piece of furniture. A piano – a beautiful, gleaming, black upright piano. Oh, how very exciting! I opened the lid and almost threw myself onto the keys. I wasted no time in playing it, thumping keys up and down. Ma told me to be quiet, but Mrs Everett was a benign old lady and made no objections, saying: 'Oh let him play with it...'

So now, while we were on school holidays, I would wait for her to come and open the room with the magic piano, which I would happily thump. I was drawn to it as if I had been waiting for it all my life, and from that day I could only dream of possessing my own piano. There seemed to be a little imp inside me that was howling for it.

But, like the bike, it was not to be – ever. Ma told me that one day when the war was over, we were going to America, so this was not a suitable time to pursue costly hobbies. This was a rather thoughtless decision, since she herself had been something of a prodigy when she was my exact age of eight years old. Her older brother, boxer Uncle Alf, had bought her a piano from his blood-soaked earnings. Ma picked up the piano swiftly and within two years, she proudly told me, was playing for the school at morning assembly.

However, when she reached the age of fifteen her father, a grumpy old patriarch, decided it was time for her to go to work and bring some money into the home. He sent her out to an office job as a copy typist and the piano was sold off. There was no illustrious fortune to be made except to bide your time until you were scooped up for marriage and children: the usual route for all Jewish girls. There was no doubt in my mind that, in the mysterious way the brain functions, I had inherited some elements of her old passion. Even more than that, the fact that this had been torn away from her as a child, leaving her with a wounded soul, and my crazed passion for the piano at such an early age was a *cri de cœur* to repair the wound. But it remained inside me and would never let me go until I had fulfilled that great hunger. I was sure that, somehow, I would.

The summers seemed endless and each day was spent at the Luton Lido. During the long summery walks there and, even better, walking back, I felt baptised and fulfilled. Guided by my yellow water wings, I learned to swim in just a few hours. Some days I went with Mum, who never swam but just loved to watch me leaping from the top board and sometimes diving, even if a warning sign announced: **EXPERT DIVERS ONLY!**

***

The war was over, had been over for two years, but at last came a sign that Britain's wounded flanks were gradually healing – the glorious neon lights of Piccadilly Circus were about to be switched back on for the first time since the Blitz.

Obviously, this was not an event to be ignored. So, when we had returned to the East End, Mum and I took the number 15 bus from Stepney to the West End to witness that magical moment when the switch is flicked on. The crowd grew a little hushed, as news of the event had infected everybody, and they were waiting with heightened anticipation. London was, as usual, a dirty grey. Suddenly shazam! The whole of Piccadilly Circus exploded into light. It was magical, as if rivers of sheer, unadulterated joy had poured into the streets. The crowds stomped, wept, and cheered. Little children wobbled on their fathers' shoulders, and at that very moment Mum felt that the only way she could express her buoyant girly happiness was to plant a big kiss on my cheek. Dad wasn't there – God knows where he was. It didn't matter; the evening was just me and Mum and the gigantic crowd of beaming faces. It was 1947, and I was ten years old. We stared at the glorious lava flow of lights – all the grey had disappeared; the light had washed it away.

The time had come that Ma had been thinking about, dreaming about, hoping for, and which, this time, had arrived at last. We were going to America! That's what Ma told me, and I even had to tell my teacher that I was going away for just three months; Ma had that in her mind just in case it didn't work out and after three months we would return. But this was never, ever on the agenda. We were meant to be going to America for the rest of our lives.

The excitement was mounting, yet there was one fly in the ointment, of course – the man of the house. He would be joining us later, *blah blah blah*, he just needed to sort things out, *blah blah blah*, earn a bit more cash etc.

Blah blah blah.

So the day came in October 1947 when we packed our bags and Dad booked a car to take us to Southampton, to set out on the biggest adventure of my life!

Me and my sister Beryl, c.1947

CHAPTER 2

Going to the Promised Land

When we arrived at the Southampton docks, it took quite a while for me to interpret that gigantic wall in front of us as being the side of a ship called the *Queen Elizabeth,* the largest vessel, at that time, on Earth. How glorious it was to walk up the gangway to enter the ship: me, Mum, and Beryl, but, of course, no Dad. But what did we care? What a day it was! I was smartly dressed in a new blue serge suit from our local store in Luton. A steward escorted us to our small cabins. Ma was below and I was above in one cabin, while Beryl, who was now eighteen, shared a cabin with another single voyager. Oh such excitement, such thrills, such bewilderment!

After settling in, it was time to explore the ship. We soon found the huge tourist dining room and our table, where we sat chatting excitedly to our neighbours, for whom this journey was as life-changing as it was for us. We had a boisterous waiter who liked to impress us kids by showing how he could ram his fist into the highly polished teak woodwork without hurt himself. That was a stunt he would do nearly every mealtime because he knew we enjoyed watching him so much. After our sumptuous dinner, even in tourist class we were asked to depart for the lounge, where coffee and drinks would be served, and then desserts. Oh God, we were such a happy family. We were in a future world. We were in a demi-paradise.

Then, once this utterly wondrous ship had been loaded with umpteen tons of fuel, its endless sacks of spuds and veg and meat and salad and everything needed in this vast and astonishing floating world, we would set sail. We didn't feel it. We didn't even sense it. But when we woke early in the morning, we saw behind us the distant line of the shore and ahead and around us the endless, mysterious sea. I can only say that for me it was all a dream.

For the first hours and days, I kept close to Ma, but after a while I was tempted to explore the bowels of the ship and walked endless corridors until I passed by tourist land and entered the new, spruced world of first class, and there I discovered the pool! That was quite wonderful and the pool staff simply assumed that I was a first-class passenger, having just arrived by myself, and allowed me to swim whenever I liked.

And so each day I would walk through the mysterious entrails of this gigantic monster, swim, and then find my way back to the tourist deck for lunch; it was a constant adventure. I explored the ship from top-to-toe and from left to right, and on sunny days I played quoits on deck; unfortunately, I clipped a lady tourist with one of my throws but was most apologetic. Strange that Ma didn't bother to keep an eye on me, to keep me under control. I suppose she was fantasising about what it would be like being back in New York, especially now she was going alone, except for me and my sister. When not at breakfast, lunch, or dinner, most passengers would just sit in the lounge and pleasantly while away the time. It was a journey of about five glorious days and, being October, the weather was not yet rough enough to send us to the sick bays. These were five happy and carefree days, the likes of which we hadn't experienced for many years.

The time had come to prepare ourselves to disembark, having just sailed across that almighty ocean, and we were full of excitement and anticipation. That night I could barely sleep, and so when we arrived, I rushed from my bed while it was still dark, although the sky was growing lighter as we steamed into Manhattan to Pier 93. I could never forget those names or numbers. Suddenly, I witnessed views the likes of which I had barely even dreamed about. Before me stretched a most improbable fantasy: the skyscrapers of downtown Manhattan lit up in all their heavenly glory! It was as if I was living a dream, seeing things I could never have even imagined; the sky was still a canopy of stars, but the city ahead seemed like some mysterious future world.

I stayed watching for what seemed like hours as more people clambered onto the deck to transport themselves to this new and almost satanic universe. I ran back to my cabin and poured everything that I had just seen out to Ma.

There was still time to have breakfast – it would take the best part of a day to disembark. I dressed in my blue serge suit and joined the queue. Eventually, we descended the gangway, and they were all waiting for us: Ma's beloved family. There was a huge limo on the concourse. Ma's sister Doris and her husband, Sol, were waiting first, and then there was hugging and kissing and weeping and laughing as the Hyman family was reunited once again. I got into the back seat, and my Aunty Doris slipped a *Hershey* bar into my hands; I tore it open and had my first taste of America, and I have to say it tasted sublime.

The limo, or probably a rented taxi, took us to a pleasant suburb in the Bronx where Aunt Doris lived with Uncle Sol and their daughter, Blanche. As we got out of the car, I saw Blanche pacing along the street carrying a large brown paper bag. It was the bag I always saw in American movies. Everything fitted. We all raced up the stairs and entered their simple flat. Food was already laid upon the table, and we piled in with great excitement. There was so much talk, and more and more talk, and I know that Ma could not have been happier. She was with her own – her blood – her beloved family who hadn't been together since their childhood in Batty Street, off Commercial Road in the East End of London. After dinner, Sol entertained us all with his conjuring tricks and soon it was time to crash out. They had a room for all of us, and I slept like the dead.

The next day, we had the utmost pleasure of linking up with my beloved cousin Morris, whom I had last seen when he visited us in Luton on his leave from the army. Mum had looked after him well on his few periods of leave. He had always been happy to visit us and I had been equally happy to spend time with him, remembering how he taught me how to tell the time and that nobody had ever bothered at home to show me anything. He had always been glad to educate me and tell me lots of thrilling stories about life in the American army.

Now, he was picking us up to take us to Mum's other sister, Aunt Ray, his mother, and so we drove across the great and glorious

George Washington Bridge to the small bucolic town of Nyack in upstate New York. It lay some 25 miles north of Manhattan and quite soon we were swiftly driving through the idyllic autumn countryside of New York State, passing the charming clapboard houses, until at last we came to Nyack. It was everything I had ever seen in every movie about suburban American life. We were just yards from the Hudson River. Wonderful!

Now, for the first time, I was meeting Ma's family, and my Aunt Ray was the grand matriarch. She was the eldest and a very fine figure of a woman. Rather haughty, with a strong, determined face, she was obviously the leader of the pack. The only thing missing for Ma was her husband. Nobody seemed to care or even talk about him. But I know that Ma was missing him badly and I suspect even felt some degree of shame that her husband was not behaving like a mensch, especially at such a major event in our lives. I found my Aunt Ray rather stern and not overly affectionate, unlike my Aunt Doris in the Bronx. After washing up, she poured me a chilled glass of milk, and I was shocked by how cold it was. I had never had anything from a fridge before, and I rather enjoyed it.

After a couple of hours, Morris drove me into town to introduce me to the drugstore he owned with his brother, Sol Nathanson. It was everything a country drugstore should be, and it smelled exotic – a smell that was becoming familiar to me, the smell of modern America. As you entered on the left side was a food counter where you sat on those small stools facing the staff. 'What would you like?' the waitress asked. Well, after the far more modest fare in war-torn Britain, everything was utterly scrumptious. I ordered a toasted cheese and salad sandwich with mayonnaise and could not have been happier; at last my tongue was being seduced by the most exotic flavours. I always loved that enticing American aroma that lingered in the air.

After that Morris took me across the road to a men's store which also catered to young men, and I tried on a beautiful rust-coloured suit with long pants – the first time I had ever tried on long pants! I stared at myself in the mirror and thought, *'Yes, I am entering a new world'*. I felt quite wonderful. My carefully bought blue serge suit with its short pants was fit only for the garbage. Now I was a man! Then

Morris suggested I try on a very elegant double-breasted grey suit and that was even more perfect. The trouser legs were pinned up to the appropriate length and my dearest, sweetest cousin bought both of the suits for me. Both! Later that day, I picked up my treasures and had never been so happy, never; I don't think I have been so happy in my entire life.

The next morning, I slowly slipped into my adult trousers. I was now grown up at age ten and a half and felt every bit of it – so strange to feel that cloth around my calves, signifying I was no longer a child. He even bought me a trilby hat to go with it. How astounding was this new world of America. Each day held a revelation. I felt like I was living a dream that I hoped I would never wake up from.

Every morning Morris would get up and dress and I would see him, as I slept in the same room. He had probably given up his bedroom to Ma and Beryl for our sadly all-too-short visit. After a cold glass of milk, I would get into Morris's beautiful Buick car and wait for him and then he'd drive me into town. Once in the store, I'd order my delicious 'Breakfast in America' at the counter and then spend most of the day hanging around or doing odd jobs for Morris, but I never once was bored. In the evenings after supper, we would all gather in the lounge and turn on the small black-and-white TV, which started at 6 p.m.! First there was an image of the Empire State Building. Then the only things on were fake wrestling matches, so we'd patiently watch those – more impressed with the sensation of TV than anything we were watching.

After a few days, it was obvious that Aunty Ray couldn't house the three of us and feed us and entertain us indefinitely and neither was she expected to. We had had a glimpse of paradise and now we would have to face the much more demanding life with Ma's brother Joe in his boarding house in the Bronx. The decision had been made that when we arrived, we were to stay at Uncle Joe's (Mum's elder brother) in the Bronx, 308 East 173rd Street – an address I have never forgotten. Joe had, smartly, bought an old Victorian rooming house and let cheap rooms to working people. For us, he had set aside half of an attic. I was a little sad to leave Nyack, however the prospect of a new adventure soon excited me enough to arouse my interest as to what we could expect. We arrived at this marvellous old scabby Victorian house and mounted the few steps to the entrance. There we met Uncle Joe and his wife, Alice, and daughter, Sandra, with her thick red hair. Again, hugs and laughter and tears and giggles and more hugs, and then we all sat down to tea, beigels, and cream cheese.

Eventually we were introduced to our new lodgings. We were all rather expectant and just a little wary as Joe led us up the stairs to the attic. The last stairs were very much narrower than the rest of the house and wound in a circle to the top floor. Ma and Beryl started to laugh almost hysterically. We just could not believe where they had decided to house us. I didn't mind; it was something new. We had one large room with a double bed for Mum and Beryl and a single one for me. The middle area held a kitchen and a small toilet. The other half was let to a hospital porter called Chris, a pale and out-of-shape man with watery blue eyes and blond hair. He was an ordinary guy and had a simple job. The one small joy was the radio which he played all day, and there were some marvellous programmes, especially at 7 p.m. on Mondays. We loved listening to a horror programme called *The Creaking Door*. He seemed glad of the company.

Ma and Beryl unpacked and washed, and then we all trundled downstairs again. The others sat and gossiped about old and new times, but I wandered around the house making friends with the tenants.

I really enjoyed sitting in Uncle Joe's main living room, where his family used to hang out. It was a bit scrappy but really cosy. There was a phone there and Joe taught me the right etiquette in answering it: 'This is Mr Hyman's residence; can I help you?' I think he got a few laughs out of that considering that many of his chums were ex-longshoremen, as was he. He also had a small record player which I liked to use, but I always played the same record – I think he only had two. It was called *Peg O' My Heart*, and I played it over and over again and never got tired of it.

Now Ma thought it was time to get me out of the house and into a school. First, I needed to show them a doctor's certificate to prove I was free of the thousand and one bugs the immigrants were bringing over from war-torn Europe, so Alice took us to a local doctor and embarrassed me no end when she had to bargain with him to knock off a few dollars. Then we went to the school, Public

School 70 (or PS-70), which was just around the corner on 174th Street. As we strolled down the corridor, I was amazed to see a New York policeman carrying a gun in his holster! I entered the classroom and was briefly introduced before sitting down. I was astonished to see that the girls were all wearing stockings and make-up, even lipstick.

I really enjoyed the classes. Before we began the school day, we'd all gather in the great auditorium and recite 'Ode to America' and then someone would sing a patriotic song. I recall a teacher one day telling us the story of a Japanese woman who had escaped to America and in thankfulness wrote a moving tribute to her American rescuers. I have never forgotten it. The song starts, 'I love life – and I want to live'. It was very moving. Then we would all march down to the gym and get into our class groups.

We began with a system of exercises, then we played American football, mainly passing the ball swiftly to each other. After that came the hard one: the pull-ups. Your two hands gripped the wooden bar behind you, and you tried to bring your chin up to the bar. Very tough. Following that daily routine, we would all return to the classroom and begin our day's instruction. Quite suddenly, I realised that I had had the same mathematical exercises the previous year in my old school in Luton. Oh, how fortunate, since now, with a smidgeon more concentration, I thought I would catch up on all those peculiar tests that I found so irksome. Lunchtime was downstairs, which I partook in, there being little point in going home to an empty house – Ma had to go out as much as she could to escape the loneliness as she waited like Penelope for the man called my father.

One image has never escaped me. It was so sad. Each morning when I left our drab little attic to go to school, I crossed the road and walked up to PS-70. One morning I just happened to turn my head to look back towards the attic front window that faced the street. Ma was standing there looking down. Normally, she couldn't do this in that half of the attic, as it was occupied by Chris, the hospital porter. I suppose he must have left early that morning, so Ma was able to see me from the front window. When I turned and saw her, I swiftly waved and walked on. Suddenly, all the unfairness of the situation hit me. The loneliness, the disappointment with our wretched living conditions, the utter boredom of waiting around in that bleak house – what did she do all day? Wait patiently for Dad while I had a full, purposeful day at school.

Just seeing her up in the attic, a face in the window, set a dozen bitter thoughts in motion, and I've never forgotten that image. Maybe she squeezed just a few drops of joy, as she stared down, from watching me cross the road, and wouldn't she have been surprised to see me turn my head, stare back, and wave. Maybe she carried that thought, as I did, far beyond its real worth, wondering as she looked down how I was coping with my lack of new friends and my shabby home. But in fact, I was happy, so happy: I was engaged, alive, being taught bright new things, excited every minute of the day, and discovering the world of America. I remember standing in the PS-70 classroom, looking out the window and seeing the Chrysler building in the distance. It looked to me like an Aztec temple. I was besotted by the skyscrapers of NYC; they were the essence of America. Whenever we drove into the city, my eyes would be on stalks when I glimpsed the Empire State Building. No other occupant of the car's back seat, be it my sister or an elderly aunt, was safe from being scrambled over in my attempts to get a better look!

Sometimes after school I might, as a rare treat, cross the road to Nathan's deli and buy a burger for only 12 cents. Can you imagine anything so cheap? It came with sauerkraut and mustard and was utterly delicious. On the weekends when we were all gathered in our little cubby hole together, Ma and Beryl might ask me to go down the road and pick up hot dogs and burgers for us as a special treat, and I was only too happy to oblige.

I had made a good friend in the owner of a tiny jewellery and watch shop just a few yards after you turned onto 174th Street when I went to buy a stretch elastic band for my wristwatch, thinking that would be cool. As the young owner, who was maybe in his early thirties, changed the strap, he started talking to me and before long I felt compelled to tell him the story of my life as he fired one question after another at me. From then onwards, especially after school, I would just pop in for a chat, which he said he didn't mind in the least. We both enjoyed telling our mutual stories. That was great – someone I could always pop in for a chat with when passing. Having a friend was so important to me. Up to now, I had only had ageing relatives to communicate with in America, and at my new school I never found my soulmate, but now I actually had a human being to whom I could open my heart and confess my dreams.

Well, the weather was getting chilly and the severe New York winter was on its way. We wrapped up warmly when we went out, which was mostly just shopping on the weekend, and on Sundays we had a special treat. Cousin Morris and his mother, Ray, would pick Ma and me up and take us for a short drive around Central Park, as I remember. The trick was never to drive too fast so you could catch every green light.

After that adventure he would take us to a Chinese restaurant in the exotic Chinatown – something we very much looked forward to. We'd always enjoy our Chinese feast, but I do remember one time when the waiter ran after us because Morris had committed the unforgivable sin of failing to leave a tip. He looked somewhat shamefaced as he was held up for forgetting this valuable service, yet Morris was a very generous man, and I have never forgotten the overwhelming treats – those two suits he had bought me in Nyack for starters. For more sightseeing, we would drive to the slums of the Lower East Side and there he'd show us the scores of men lying flat out on the pavement, stone cold drunk. The place was called The Bowery. I'd never seen anything like it in my whole life. Then he'd drive us back to the Bronx to our beloved hovel.

One afternoon, Morris was driving a little bit too slow for Aunty Ray, when she pointed out that as it was Sunday, she didn't wish to miss her favourite TV show. That remark didn't go amiss. Morris sped up and took us home, and Ma and I sulkily trundled up the stairs to our den of misery, where at least we had the lively radio. I think Beryl had graduated and made friends by this time, and she was smart enough to find a part-time job in a deli. She was good at making friends. She knew, maybe only too well, that friends are vital to your mental health – in fact to your very existence.

The weeks oozed past, each one similar to the one before, and Christmas came and we were invited to a small country house in an area called Great Neck, but I don't recall too much about it. A few days later, of course, it was New Year's Eve: 31 December 1947. The family weren't celebrating, so after a bite and some entertainment from our favourite radio stations, we all just tumbled into bed.

But New York was celebrating. Suddenly there was a knock on our door. It was about 9.30 p.m., I think. Beryl got up and a shrill female voice said, 'What are you doing, Beryl? Come on and get up, all of you. It's New Year's Eve and we are going out!' This was a friend from the deli where Beryl worked. Beryl must have told her that we weren't doing anything for New Year except wrapping up the loneliness in blankets of sleep, although I'm sure she didn't say those exact words! Somehow, I was even feeling a mite ashamed. This very sweet girl, thinking about us, had decided to sacrifice her own plans, if she had them, for New Year and travel all the way over to us in the Bronx. She sent a spirit of love through us like a lightning bolt, and we all crawled a bit sheepishly out of our beds and followed our liberator down the stairs and into the street.

We were all suddenly so alive and happy. She took us to a local diner, just a short walk away, and we were transformed into a joyful family. What a lovely girl, what a generous, full-hearted gesture. I have never ever forgotten that evening. A night marked in grace and love. Where are you now, nice lady? Gone like all of them, maybe long gone, but never forgotten. You are a saint in my repertoire of saints.

Meanwhile, and I remember this so well, Ma waited anxiously for this mysterious man called my father to write that he was on his way, but all the letters repeated the same worn-out slogan that he was very soon on his way but that he was waiting for – and this is the big joke – he was waiting for a 'big win'! Letters about how much he missed her – he even dared to confess how much it upset him too – but begging her to be patient. And what was the address on the letterhead? The Piccadilly Club – a mainly Jewish spieler round the corner from the Regent Palace Hotel just off Piccadilly Circus. And how do I know all this? Because Ma kept all these shabby, phoney letters, which I later inherited.

As I read them, the shamefulness of his behaviour became apparent. I'm sure he loved Ma and even had a smattering of love for me and my sister, but his love of freedom was even more powerful. In one he tells Ma to 'make the most of it, it's only a matter of days now so try and make a holiday of it'.

In another he writes:

Please don't think what I am going to say is blaming you, but I must say that with the house and home gone and conditions as they are here is like being blitzed out in the war & we have to take it like that. Now the position is as follows, I have considered it carefully. If I find anything suitable or reasonably possible to live in, you come back – otherwise hold on and I will come over. I am trying hard to get something and to get hold of some cash if I have to come out there ...

Keep your chin up and keep writing. I will phone you as soon as I get a winning turn ... The clothing trade is at a standstill at the moment but that would not deter me if I could find something decent for you. I would like to have a good win and buy a house – it would not require such a lot down and then you could come back and forget all the unpleasantness and unhappiness you had ... Every day if you are hurt or blue, say to yourself "Al would do anything for me, and he loves me like life itself". I hope that will make you feel good again ...

Also why doesn't Beryl write & Les too? Have I been so bad to them? It's as though they are not my children. I am enclosing six dollars (I wish it were 6000).

With all my love & kisses to you as long as I live,

Your loving husband
Al

God bless & keep you my darling

So day after day, Ma waited in that godforsaken attic until one day, one totally unexpected day, when I returned home from school and walked into my Uncle Joe's parlour, as I always did before ascending to my attic, whom did I see sitting there but 'he' himself – Dad! He was sitting opposite Uncle Joe, Alice, and Ma, and they all looked cosy and were playing cards, probably just for cents to while away the time. It felt, and even looked, strange and, even to my young eyes, vaguely unwholesome. After all, I had spent the day learning, studying, singing 'Ode to America', exercising in the gym, and at the end of the day, I returned to a group of old people sitting in a cloud of cigarette smoke playing cards. I can barely remember Dad's greeting to me. Did he cuddle me? Did he welcome me? Did he even kiss me? No, nothing, but he was here. Now, surely, he would eagerly search for a job – tailors were always needed – and then we could afford to rent a decent apartment. Dad had been a tailor all his life; I can never forget all the knickknacks of his trade that littered our dining room table. However, I don't recall holding even one conversation with him about it – not one.

I seem to remember that same evening all of us sitting in a roomy old car, maybe Uncle Joe's, and driving round the Bronx, and one sentence stuck out and remained in my brain forever. Dad spoke out in something approaching joyful enthusiasm as he saw all the bright, neon-lit streets: 'Hey, it looks a bit like Broadway!' That was his memory of living in New York with my Ma in the late '20s, so as he happily declaimed his amazement at the transformation of the world he had once known, I remember feeling just a little bit proud, since maybe in some way this was now my city.

I saw little of him in the next few days, but I do recall one occasion most especially. I was asked to sleep in one of the small bedrooms downstairs. I thought little of it and just went to bed – at that age you just do as you're told. But suddenly during the night, I awoke feeling very uneasy and dizzy and felt that I was so isolated from the world, and lonely, and so I cried out, cried out for help, cried out in the darkness. There was a tap on the door, and it was my cousin Paula, my Uncle Alf's daughter, who was staying with Joe while struggling to make a career for herself in New York as an actress. She was a sprightly young woman and she had heard me cry out, since her room was not far from mine. She came in and asked me, 'Oh what is it, darling, what's the matter?' She stayed with me, comforting me until the horror of that moment slowly passed and I settled back into my bed. Of course, later I reckoned that I had been shifted, as had my sister probably, so that my parents could have a night or two together.

One day, when I came back from school and asked, 'Where's Dad?' I learned that he had just returned to London! How sad, if not rather pathetic, that he made not the slightest effort to find work; it would have helped him, it would have given him purpose. Instead, he just packed his bags and left us in limbo. Not even a goodbye, zero, nothing... I know how poor Ma was suffering.

Some months later, after we had returned to England, I happened to come across those pathetic letters from my dad; they had been opened and were just lying on the kitchen table. Mum must have been going over them. Being the snooper I am, I had to acquaint myself with them. In all the letters, he must have been answering Mum, since he was always pleading with her to be patient, saying that he was absolutely dying to see her, that he didn't even want to confess how much he missed her in case she rushed on the next ship to England. But, of course, she couldn't – he didn't have a flat for us to go to. He added, 'Please, please, darling, be patient, it won't be long,' and then he said, as a distraction, how disgusted he is with her family's shocking neglect of us in New York and how dare they provide us with such primitive accommodation.

Each letter more or less repeated that theme: begging her to be patient and not to do anything rash like booking tickets to return – of course until he has in some distant future found a sanctuary. But no matter how much he missed her, he always said, 'Just hold on for a little while longer…' etc., etc., etc. All while he bathed in freedom and whatever that brought him – we were not to know; all while he was staying at the Regent Palace Hotel where they did all his laundry and everything else. That must have been costing a few bob.

Our American relatives, in spite of what Dad said, had done what they could, probably thinking that a man called Dad would swiftly get a job and look for a cheap flat in the neighbourhood. That if they found us some beautiful, expensive flat that they would obviously be paying for, we might stay there forever. They hoped they were helping us get our feet back on the ground and they never caused her the grief that my dad did. To call them neglectful was so hypocritical when his lies and neglect were causing her more grief than she had ever experienced, and I was witness to it.

My Aunty Ray in Nyack, NY, 1947

CHAPTER 3

Returning to London

The heavy winter settled over New York City and the snow was thick in the Bronx. Our Sunday treats continued with Morris and Aunty Ray, and I continued to enjoy America. I was becoming an American and even making one or two friends. But Ma was getting so desperate that one day when Chris suggested that we all go to the movies one night – I'm sure that he was lonely too – she willingly accepted. The way he phrased it was weird, though: 'Steve can sit in the middle and I'll be on the side.' He was trying to demonstrate in his awkward way how proper he could be.

So we went out that night to the local movie house, which was quite an experience. First, there was a live show before the movie came on, and, from what I recall, there were a couple of acrobats performing intricate pirouettes and then a comedian. Then it was the film, which I believe was a comedy but not quite good enough to make a dent in my brain cells. This was the first time I had been to a movie in America. Ma could not cope for much longer, though, as what gave her life and purpose was no longer part of her world. She enjoyed her family and relished going to the stores and shopping for food, then cooking for her family and having a husband to love and care for, yet these elements were no longer part of her life. Her life here was simply to endure and make do with waiting: waiting for me to return from school, waiting for the odd letter from her husband, waiting to be called back to London.

Eventually it had to come to an end. She could not sit and rot in that stinking attic. One day I got up as usual, dressed to go to school, and Ma said, 'You're not going to school today, we are going back to Nyack for a few days' holiday.' At last, Ma found some purpose in her life. We took the bus, since Ma was now more familiar with the routes, and as it slithered in the snowy slush past Public School 70, I felt a deep sense of guilt about being absent from my familiar classroom and about how much they would all wonder what on earth had happened to me.

We stayed in Nyack for about three days, which gave Ma time enough to book tickets on that other massive Cunard ship, the *Queen Mary*. I had just enough time to visit my closest friend in his little jewellery shop on 174th Street. He was sad to lose his new English friend and presented me with a small gift: a miniature silver penknife, which I treasured. There was quite a severe snowstorm on the night we were meant to travel, and few cabs were prepared to risk it to the docks, but eventually Joe was able to persuade one to drop us off for an enormous fare. We made our brief farewells. Beryl was determined to stay in New York; good for her. She had a good job where they seemed to like her, and she earned a good wage.

Before I forget, the day before we were to depart, Ma decided not to just sit and wait in our grim attic but to go out and celebrate, go to Broadway and see the latest movie. So we did and I'll never forget that day. We took the bus to Manhattan and walked in that thrilling network of streets until she decided we should see a movie called *The Gangster*, which had only just opened, and then afterwards go to a diner for supper. Starring in the film was an actress known by a single name: Belita. Apparently, she was once a famous figure skater. Ma and I enjoyed the film immensely. Oh my gosh, we were at last having fun – all the more because it was the first time we had gone out on the town.

The next day, the cab took us to the *Queen Mary* and once on board all problems, all stress, just seemed to dissipate. Peace reigned. The great monstrous ship absorbed us and all our petty problems. We would have five long, anguish-free days in the next best thing to heaven on earth. The days of the attic were over, over, that nightmare for Ma was well and truly over. And what was it replaced with? A piece of heaven.

That night we sat in the glorious tourist lounge and had dinner. Mother was smiling again; she was happy. She was waited on. She had neighbours to talk to and new adventures. We ordered our food and enjoyed everything and just sat with our eyes wide open, amazed at the wonders of the world. We slept, but the next day the sea was heaving like some colossal animal twitching to shake us off its back. I wandered as usual around the boat, almost walking on a diagonal as the boat dipped violently left and then to the right. By evening I was violently seasick and the next day I was no better. I could hold nothing down, so Ma took me to the sick bay, where at last I had a wider bed and was sometimes able to sleep. I was in the sick bay for nearly three days and on the fourth I decided I had to make an effort to join the living.

How the strangest mysteries suddenly manifest themselves. At last, I gingerly moved through the ship, had supper with Ma, and started to feel almost normal. Then the maître d' made an announcement that we were all going to play bingo, or, as they called it then, housey-housey – a favourite pastime among the tourist class. I eagerly purchased my bingo sheets. After a few minutes all my numbers were coming up, and I had to shout out 'Bingo!' I had won – eureka! And then the strangest event in the world took place. The MC announced that the prize tonight would be given to the winner by a special guest and then he introduced her: 'The Hollywood movie star, Belita.' I gasped; I almost shrieked, 'How on earth is this possible?' I had just seen this beautiful woman less than a week ago.

I stood up and swiftly strode to the table where the screen goddess was sitting. She was blonde and blue-eyed and was everything you would expect a movie star to be. I immediately blurted out enthusiastically, 'Miss Belita, I have just seen you in your film *The Gangster*.' She looked at me almost in disbelief – it had only just opened in a Broadway cinema – but I pressed my case, saying, 'I liked the movie so much,' and then just took a seat opposite her. I started talking to her like I couldn't stop. It seemed to me, even if not to her, something of a miracle that I should be meeting the star of the only movie I had seen on Broadway. I asked her where she lived, since I would love to write to her, and she happily told me, 'Beverly Hills.' That was the first time I had heard those words, and I would never forget them. I asked her if I might write to her, and she took a pen and wrote down her address. I was absolutely besotted with her.

But now she told me it was time for her to go, but even then, I walked her to the dining room door. Then I had to say, in all my naivety, 'It's quite unusual to see a movie star in tourist class.' She briefly turned her head and responded quite coolly, 'We're just slumming, honey.' She gave me a fixed grin and then was swallowed up by one of the myriad corridors that bisect a great liner. And, of course, I understood only too well how stupid I had been. I kept the piece of paper on which she had written her address, but for whatever reason, she never did write back.

The next day we were due to arrive at Southampton. To make the most of my last few hours I explored the ship, and when I went to first class, I asked one of the stewards if he could inform me if any celebrities were on the ship, since I was collecting autographs. Of course, the steward could not possibly impart such hallowed information but, perhaps seeing my crestfallen face, offered me a treasured hint. 'Well, if you go to the end of this corridor, at the very end you'll find a door, and on that door, you'll see a small sign saying HENRY FORD II, but don't say I told you.'

I promised 'Of course not', followed his directions, and found what I assumed was the door. I stood in front of it for a few moments and then decided to gently knock.

Oh, how fortunate one is when a child. You are entitled to do things that are totally forbidden to you as an adult. The door opened and a fully grown man stood there and stared at me. And who else could it be but the great Henry Ford II? The great entrepreneur of Ford cars, and one of the richest men in the world, stared at me quizzically and merely said, 'Can I help you, young man?' Clutching my little autograph book, I mumbled how delighted I was to meet him, and would he be so kind as to give me an autograph?

He invited me into his first-class cabin and gestured for me to sit down. So I took a seat on the edge of the big double bed, and he started to question me, but all in a friendly way, about where I was from and why I was travelling to England. I was overjoyed to be talking to him, to the great Henry Ford II, so I chatted away freely and I felt so encouraged by him that I kept gushing and told him everything. How we'd emigrated to New York, how my dad didn't wish to stay as he missed London so much, how he'd left us in the Bronx and Ma decided that after all it was maybe better to go back to the London that she knew so well. But I also told him how much I loved America and had even gone to school, and while I was saying all these things, Mr Ford continued to pack his clothes. A woman was helping him, who I presumed was his wife. What would my mother think as she packed away our simple clothes in our third-class cabin if she knew that at the same time, I was being entertained by one of the greatest industrialists on the planet?

I didn't miss anything out, even going into detail about our simple life in the Bronx, so I didn't notice how time was flying. It turned out we had just docked in Southampton and then there was a knock on the door. This time the lady answered it, opened the door, and about half a dozen journalists tumbled in and began asking all sorts of questions. One of them, looking at me, asked Henry Ford, 'Is that your son, Mr Ford?' *Oh my God!* 'Is that your son, Mr Ford?' *Oh, oh, oh! If only, if only I was, if only he would say I am, yes, I am, if only I could be carried away from here forever.*

I looked up. Mr Ford turned to look at me and replied, 'Oh no, he's just a friend popping by. So, young man, I think you'd better get back to your cabin, your mother will be worrying about you.' I stood up and awkwardly said my goodbyes, and I imagined as I looked into his eyes that he would have enjoyed having more of my company. I quickly went to the door.

'Goodbye, Mr Ford. Thank you.'

I shut the door behind me. This had to be one of the most amazing events of my life. I couldn't wait to tell my mother everything. My imagination ran riot with *what if* – what if – *he invited me to spend a month in the Ford mansion, just for a break?* But now I was back in the cabin and looking out of the porthole and saw the most depressing sight of my life. Southampton. Grey, small, and utterly depressing. The contrast with New York could not have been greater; it was like heaven and hell.

Mum and I disembarked and suddenly Dad was there, holding Mum and fiercely kissing her. I viewed it as something slightly vulgar!

I was standing next to Ma, and it looked as if he was eating her. Surely, he could have just held her, cuddled her affectionately, or was he trying to make a point? They had been married for over twenty years! He hardly even looked at me. We entered the station and got on the crowded train to Victoria in London. We were comfortably ensconced in our seats when the ticket inspector came on and requested to see our tickets. Dad fumbled around and produced three second-class tickets, and the inspector pointedly said that we were in the wrong section of the train. Dad responded that he hadn't been able to find three seats together as the train was rather crowded. In fact, I saw quite a few spare seats, but the inspector let us pass; he probably did not wish to cause my father further embarrassment, especially in front of me. We got to Victoria and my Aunt Betty, the wife of Dad's brother Sam, was waiting for us, and we all got into a black cab and sped down to the East End of London.

I think that Dad departed soon after we arrived to go to his hotel, since there were three of us in the cab already, but I could be wrong. I had so little sense of his presence that I hardly noticed whether he was there or not. My Aunt Betty was warm to us and was going to put us up for a few days till we found a temporary flat. I remember odd sentences she said, such as 'He's already got a slight American accent.' Maybe I did, maybe I didn't, but I just went with the flow. Eventually, we drove to the city, where Aunty Betty pointed out sights of interest like the Bank of England, looking dark and majestic, and then eventually we reached a bombed-out East End.

We arrived at Aunty Betty and Uncle Sam's flat at the top of 145a Cannon Street Road. Sam and Betty made us feel really welcome. After tea and sandwiches, I was put to bed. They just showed me a narrow bed in which my cousin Barry was sleeping. His head with his shorn hair was just peeping out, and I simply got in and he moved to let me in. Nobody was bothered much about things like that in those days; we just accepted everything. I think Ma was happy to be home and to be reunited with the man who was her husband. I realised he must have left us after returning with Ma and I to the East End, since I didn't see him for a few days. I assumed he slept somewhere else.

I awoke the next morning to a winter wonderland: January 1948. Snow covered the entire East End landscape, and it was fun trudging through the snow-capped streets.

Meanwhile it was left to my mother to struggle to find ways of solving our housing problem. She was never slow in doing whatever she could to improve our situation; she was constantly vigilant and wrote to the council that provided flats for the homeless and war-torn. She wrote frequently and only ever got the same response: she was in a queue which was long but the government was building homes faster and faster, at full speed, and just be patient and they would find us a flat in a short time. And so we were.

Ma, being efficient, got me swiftly enrolled in the local school in Christian Street, the same school, apparently, as she had once attended all those decades ago. I remember the first day well enough. Ma had me wear my ultra-smart double-breasted grey suit that lovely cousin Morris had bought me. I think the other kids' eyes practically popped out of their heads. Ma booked me to take school lunches, and so at lunchtime I sat and waited for my dull luncheon. I saw no salt or pepper, which might have enhanced my sad-looking plate, so I merely stuck out my hand and said, 'Please, Miss, is it possible to have some salt?' The whole roomful of snotty-nosed kids froze.

It could have been a scene from *Oliver Twist*, but in this case the nice teacher rose from her chair, smiled as if to acknowledge that she had a right one here, said 'just a moment', then left the room and entered the teachers' area just across the hallway. She returned with a salt cellar, which I thanked her for and then calmly shook over my food. All this was watched by the entire class as if this event were a piece of theatre. Gradually, I acquired a new nickname on account of my wardrobe: 'Spiv'. This was uttered without a shade of malice; it was just a handy epithet to describe me: shady and flamboyant.

Ma meanwhile had found a room for both of us in the house opposite on the same road. We shared a large bed and kept a bucket for my nocturnal urination – the toilet was out in the yard and there was no way we were going to sludge through the snow. The next day, I was told that I had to sit exams for my scholarship, since that could determine your future life: whether you went to a grammar school for the smart kids or you failed and were sent to a secondary school.

I passed my scholarship quite easily, and my mother was then happy to be informed that I had been picked to go to the renowned Raine's Foundation Grammar School in Arbour Square just a quarter of a mile further east.

Ma was also informed that I would need to be dressed in the school uniform that could be purchased at Gardiner's Corner, just off Commercial Road. So I tried on the elegant blazer and school tie, and indeed I could not have been prouder. I was also bought a briefcase, and later that year on one fine September morning, I was taking the bus in my new school uniform, full of optimism. The only impression I had of a grammar school was, paradoxically, from American movies, where young boys and girls would return home after school with a satchel crammed with books. That's what I imagined as I sat on the bus making my way to the most dramatic event of my young life.

Once at school, all the new lads sat for a further exam to determine whether we were to be placed in an A, B, or C group. At the time, I remember thinking that the test was not too challenging; I passed honourably and was put straight away into the A group and was doubly proud. My first day at school was memorable. At the end of the day, the teacher expressed gratitude for our attention and looked forward to seeing us in the morning, but I was expecting the vital part of the ceremony of our first day in a grammar school: homework, for which I had brought my sacred satchel. I then asked Sir for homework, since of course this fulfilled my fantasy. The teacher looked up somewhat surprised and then asked the class 'if anybody else would like homework?' To my complete amazement only a few hands were raised. However, the teacher gave us some simple homework and I felt redeemed.

The next day, we were introduced to the gym in the basement, and here we really got acquainted with each other and with all its tests and trials. Once I got over just a spatter of nerves, I thoroughly enjoyed it – especially doing somersaults over the horse and mat work, as I had never done these things before. I was growing both mentally and physically stronger by the day.

Ma and I couldn't keep staying with Aunty Betty and Sam, as nice and welcoming as they were. One day Ma got thoroughly depressed, and so Dad, as a kind of treat, booked a room for her and me in the Regent Palace Hotel, where I believe he lodged from time to time. But Ma and I were alone. I don't know where on earth the man called Dad hung out. Maybe he had another room somewhere – who knows? The man was just a mystery to me.

Well, I don't know what we did or were doing there, maybe we had some lunch, but mostly we just hung about in the hotel. It was like New York again and Ma was desperately lonely, but we didn't go to the cinema this time; she just sat in the room and started crying. She cried and cried and cried and couldn't stop crying and even began howling. I didn't know what to do. What could I do? I could only keep her company. I tried talking to her, but she could not stop.

Eventually, she pulled herself together just enough to ask reception to call a doctor. She needed a husband, but a doctor would have to do. I don't know where Dad was, but after a few minutes, a doctor knocked at the door. He came in and gently asked what was troubling my mother. She tried to speak but kept sobbing, choking, wailing – I just sat there wondering about the strange and peculiar ways of the adult world. Eventually the doctor turned to me. He looked at me and said to my mother, 'You must try, really try, to control yourself in front of your son. You're only upsetting him.' I'll never forget that man or his words. He was such a very elegant and friendly doctor, but there was only so much he could do or say. What happened after this I have completely forgotten, but I do recall that Ma and I found a room just opposite Aunty Betty's.

That held us together for a few weeks, but eventually Ma found us a room with a small back kitchen which doubled as a spare bedroom in Anthony Street. It was a simple, narrow street with a beautiful cinema at the top called the Palaseum. Dad, of course, slept elsewhere, since this was only meant to be a temporary move till he found us this mythical new home, but we soon made friends with our neighbours and there were two boys my age who lived opposite. They were primitive working-class houses and the boy whose name was Connie (Cornelius) and I became firm friends and explored the bomb sites in the East End. He also introduced me to the public swimming area in the Thames by Tower Bridge. The council had imported sand to the riverbank and even included deckchairs, and so we had our own Riviera, you might say, and while the river was filthy and polluted such things weren't taken seriously in those far-off days. One just had a great swim, along with the rats and stray dogs. I went there frequently with Connie, and we always had a good time; when you are a child there is never a lack of opportunities to have adventures and enjoy yourself. I also remember going with Ma, who would sit happily in a deckchair and watch me as I swam out to the middle of the river and back.

One day I even took my mum down there and, on the way, we stopped by a street photographer, who took our picture and developed it while we waited. He had all the chemicals with him in little pots, so we waited about five minutes and then we had our photograph, which I still have today, seventy-five years later.

Sometimes during the long school summer holiday, I would go swimming almost every day at the Victoria Park lido. I spent a great deal of time by myself, but it never bothered me too much. Sometimes I would pop into the Oxford & St George's Youth Club in Berner Street, just off Commercial Road. And sometimes, if the weather wasn't too good, I'd go to the Betts Street indoor pool just round the corner, where I also went on bath days since we didn't have a bath in Anthony Street or an indoor toilet.

Once, the old gentleman who ran the pool became quite friendly to me and he told me that if I swam eighty-three lengths continuously, I would qualify for my one-mile certificate – and, of course, I did. He was about as proud as I was and when I had completed it, he put his hand in his waistcoat pocket and pulled out a two-shilling piece! Now, in those days two bob would have been a fair amount of change. I ran home and told Ma and showed her my treasure. I could not have been happier.

In the middle of summer, some of our neighbours would go hop picking in Kent. The entire family would go for a much-looked-forward-to adventure. Their trip would last about a month, and they seemed to enjoy it immensely from what they told us. It was a month in the country after the broken-down, grotty East End. The bus would pick them up on the morning of departure, and it was a tradition for all the poor East End kids to cheer them off. They were so happy to be on their way, they would throw us pennies out of the window, or even sixpences if we got lucky.

There was always something exciting to do – even at night, when I would inevitably go to the boys' club where they had classes for the kids to occupy their minds and train them. I recall one day just slopping some paint on a sheet of paper. The teacher passed by, stopped to gaze at my 'artwork', and said, 'This is really very, very good, you must go to art school.' I thought he must be joking, but it stayed in my head, since it was so rare to be praised for anything.

The only other person who praised me unreservedly was my English teacher, Mr Shivas. He was such an elegant man who always carried a spotless white handkerchief up his sleeve like an old-fashioned English gent. I simply adored him and to demonstrate my affection always came top in English. I had my report to prove it: 'Top boy – very good work indeed.' What more could I ask than this?

I kept these school reports for years, but jumping ahead just for a moment, I must relate a most bizarre event. It's about thirty years in the future and what do you know, I become a playwright, and who is my producer? A man called Mark Shivas. I thought, '*just as his father cared for me and supported me all those years ago, his son is doing precisely the same thing. What an insane coincidence.*' He was instrumental in having my play *West* produced for Channel 4. I'll talk more about that later but for now must not mix my periods up and will resume my past. I am merely excavating the memories which are so embedded in me that I cannot help but try to relive them.

There is always so much to do when you are a child, since every stick and stone creates a puzzle, every street is an adventure, and I explored my terrain. For adults, their choices are sadly more limited, especially for the women, who so often then were dependent on the men in their lives. I was free: all I had to do was jump on the number 15 bus, which would take me to the West End, and I could get off at Piccadilly and walk about. Not the wisest thing to do, because the area was a magnet for prostitution and throughout Soho one would see the most extraordinary variety of women lined up in street after street. Quite fascinating to a ten-year-old. But there was no dad to guide me or warn me, or even to go with me and show me the world.

***

I must recall my first few weeks after we returned from New York. I used to go across the road to hang out with my younger cousin, Barry. The big treat of the week was when Uncle Sam (my dad's brother but so much more like a dad to me) would take Barry and me to the West End each Saturday to visit the Cameo Cinema, just off Piccadilly, where they had cartoons running all day, and that was quite marvellous – we all thoroughly enjoyed that. It was in Windmill Street, and after the show was over, we'd walk all the way home from Piccadilly to Commercial Road, approximately four miles. Sam was an adventurer and he loved to walk. I always remember walking along the Embankment. It was such a great experience, walking along the river, and we were home in no time. I don't think that Dad ever took us to the movies, or anywhere for that matter, although I do have a distant memory of going once to the movie house with him in Stamford Hill. Maybe it was a film he was desperate to see.

Still, now we were ensconced in our tiny room in Anthony Street. The main room/bedroom was on the ground floor, and we never had any visitors, except for one: Mum's brother, Uncle Alf, whose surname was Mansfield, perhaps because as a boxer he didn't fancy having a Jewish moniker like Hyman. God knows why, since there were scores of Jewish fighters proudly using their Semitic names.

When I first met Uncle Alf, when he visited our squalid digs in Anthony Street, I was so impressed by him. He was a tragically wounded man, and his face was like one huge blemish. His nose was crushed and his lower lip permanently swollen. However, he chatted in a lively manner and told endless jokes, mainly about his blindness. It was hard for me to look at him at first, but I did get used to him and became very fond of him. He used to box as a flyweight and was quite successful in the beginning of his career. He was born in 1893, so he was ten years older than his sister Polly, and he grew up in a very tough neighbourhood and, like a lot of Jewish teenagers, learned very quickly how to defend himself. Within a few years, Jewish boxers dominated the boxing industry. It's recorded that he had 137 fights between 1910 and 1920, during which he developed a reputation as one of the best flyweights in Great Britain. He was a man of tremendous courage and even went into the ring two or three times with world flyweight champion, Welshman Jimmy Wilde, who was known as 'the Ghost with the Hammer in his Fists' because he was so thin! During an epic battle with Wilde in 1919, it was discovered that Alf was fighting blind in one eye but he had never revealed it. He had many operations but eventually lost his sight in the remaining eye when he was only 28 and spent the rest of his life totally blind. Such a tragedy, but he continued to live freely and openly.

At the end of the evening Ma would ask me to walk him to the bus stop at the top of the road and it was on these trips that he would confess to me the most outrageous stories. When I grew older, I wished that I'd taken him out and listened to more of his tales before he passed, but he did leave a lovely daughter called Paula who trained to be an actress but, unfortunately, was not successful. I remember when Alf died a few years later. Mum was crying a lot that day, so I knew he had gone. I cherish the few times we spent together.

Sometimes Ma and I got away for a long weekend to Luton, since she had some old East End friends who had also been evacuated there during the war as we were. And so it came to pass that we visited a friend of hers called Bodinetz one day and ended up staying in Luton for a blissful week. They had a lovely son called Lionel and each sunny morning he would take me to his local park and we'd play cricket. The most significant thing about this was that his cousin Shirley, who lived next door, would accompany us. She was a very pretty, lively girl with masses of long brown curly hair and blue eyes and we all had such a good time playing cricket each day.

The week passed swiftly, and soon it was time to go to the station and make our way home. I was saying goodbye to Lionel when he suddenly said to me, 'Shirley just asked if you'd like to kiss her goodbye?' I've never forgotten that. I was not yet quite brave enough; it felt too candid, too free. I became rather embarrassed and a little self-conscious. So I shyly shook my head.

Ma and I took the train back from Luton and went to our grisly home. That night I slept peacefully, thinking about how nice those last few days had been and how happy I was. Even Ma was much happier than she had been for quite a while, and that was indeed a relief to me, having seen how doleful she had been not too long ago. At least she still had some old East End friends from before the evacuation, when we were all scattered to the four corners of the country.

***

The day after we returned from our lovely sojourn in Luton, I was walking down Anthony Street, maybe returning from the Victoria Park Lido, when I saw Mum. She was in the street walking towards me. She greeted me smiling and held a letter in her hand and gleefully said, 'You've received a letter from Shirley' – the girl in Luton. I was flabbergasted. Over the moon. What a spirited young girl. The girl who had wanted to kiss me goodbye. What a bright, positive girl she was. She didn't just pine and grieve and wait for fate to let her feelings fade away. No. She wouldn't do that. She wouldn't wait. She boldly set her sights on pursuing her desires and nobody on this planet could have been happier than I was that she had written to me. I think I was immediately in love with her.

I went indoors and tore open the very sweet letter and wrote back immediately. I could not wait. Her first letter to me was quite innocent, just saying things about how she had enjoyed meeting me, hoping we would keep in touch and exchange stories about our lives. But something struck me like a thunderclap. After I wrote back, she answered swiftly and so it went on. It settled down after the first few connections were made and was less urgent, but now, both of us feeling safe in our relationship, our communication was regular and these letters continued and nothing could have made me happier. It felt so natural that I had a female friend, and my first girlfriend, at the tender age of ten. I was in love and so was she and our love seemed to give our lives a purpose that had been lacking before.

Ma and I were eventually joined by Beryl, who had remained in New York for well over a year. My father had insisted on her returning home and the peculiar thing was that Dad went all the way to New York to fetch her and bring her back. Perhaps she didn't want to come home. I didn't know, or even understand, why it was so important that Beryl returned; after all, she was having a fulfilled life there with friends and her own room at Uncle Joe's. Well, Beryl joining us resulted in Ma buying what was known as a put-you-up:

a bed that folds out into a settee after you get up in the morning. I quite liked my put-you-up and enjoyed sleeping in my own room and in my own bed after sharing a bed with my mother for well over a year. But now Beryl was here and she was obliged to sleep with our mother. It was getting a little crowded and so she quickly looked for work.

Meanwhile, I was simply enjoying my time as a grammar schoolboy at Raine's. I particularly liked the traditions that came with the school. For example, if you wished to go to the toilet, you had to put up your hand and say 'Please, Sir, may I go forth.' After a while, it even felt quite normal to be using these archaic expressions.

I did see my dad from time to time in my younger years. In those long summer months, he would take Mum and me for a week's holiday to Brighton. That was magical – the very first time I had visited the seaside. We stayed at a little bed and breakfast boarding house in one of the side streets and it was comfortable, charming, and very pleasant. Dad would show us around, since this is where he must have spent his young years. First, he took us to the famous Black Rock swimming pool at the edge of town. It was a splendid open-air pool and we went every day and nothing was as special. Sadly, the local council sorely neglected it and eventually it was so run-down they demolished this wonderful site. What a dumb thing to do. But for years I was all too happy to go for our traditional annual holiday and witness the glorious sea. True to form, Dad left after a few days but we were happy, totally happy, without him. I see now that I inherited a guilt complex from his endless grumbling about all the years he'd spent working in sweatshops, ever since he was forced to leave school at 14 despite being a brilliant maths student. He would do my algebra for me without a second thought. He wouldn't show his working, though, as he could do it all in his head – so he never received the marks!

Being back at Raine's school was great fun, except in the autumn term when we were obliged to indulge in the wretched tradition of playing the ghastly sport known as rugby. For this, we would go by underground to Hainault station and then take a long, freezing walk till we arrived at the playing field. Then, dressed in flimsy shorts, we had to run around the field in bollock-freezing weather. In the end, I just had to drop out. In contrast to our lessons in French and English and the gym, I had little interest in maths and algebra, so I just drifted aimlessly through those boring lessons and frequently chatted with my neighbours.

Now, Raine's also had a traditional manner of marking and punishing minor misdemeanours. For every minor offence, you would be given a pencil entry and after a short time it was not difficult to find that you had three pencil entries, which were then converted to one ink entry. Before long I found that I had collected three ink entries – for which you would receive a severe thrashing of three strokes of the cane! It was an experience I have never forgotten.

One afternoon, I was called to the front of the class. 'Bend over,' said the teacher. As I recall, it was the gym master who was in charge of the canings and obviously knew how to administer the strokes. There is no way on earth my darling English teacher would ever have agreed to such an act. I obediently bent over and received the first thwack; the pain shocked me and completely sucked the breath out of me. It was far beyond anything I had expected. I shot up straight in total disbelief at the severity. 'Bend over,' I was instructed once more. Thwack. The second felt even more biting than the first, and now I screamed in agony as the whole class watched silently. God knows what they were thinking – I think my screams must have gone through the entire school – but whatever it was, I'm sure it had much to do with the determination never to do anything that would warrant such a dastardly punishment. 'Bend over.' My third stroke had to be administered – now I was howling in pain the like of which I had never before experienced. I stumbled back to my desk and sat. I sat and heaved with tears, just sat and felt nothing but the burning pain. The teacher then carried on as if nothing out of the ordinary had happened, but something major had happened to me. I would never be caned again.

When I got home, I pulled my trousers down and it shocked my mother when she witnessed those three huge red welts across my buttocks. She felt utterly helpless. I think she somehow expected that this kind of primitive punishment happened at grammar schools.

It took a long time for the welts to fade, but the memory would never fade. Of course, there is a whiff of sadism about flogging a young child of about eleven or twelve. I wonder why it didn't occur to adults to try speaking to potential mischief-makers. However, I was still determined to do well in school and learn as much as I could.

My East End was now very much my playground and, as I said, I would explore it from top to bottom. Sunday was a very special day – there was nothing more exciting than diving in and out of the streets around Petticoat Lane – and on Saturday there was nothing more fascinating than a stroll along 'the Waste' – a street market opposite the great and magnificent Royal London Hospital. How I loved the Lane! One never knew what weird and wonderful items might turn up on the stalls. Old coins, medals, ancient watches, strange pieces of junk machinery that confounded me but were useful to mechanically-minded East Enders who would snap them up.

As it happens, I was strolling along the market on a Saturday morning when I came across a small but lively crowd watching a salesman demonstrating his wares with the vigour of an Old Testament prophet. He had tremendous vocal power and that, combined with humour, meant you couldn't take your eyes off him – and what was he demonstrating? The sheer marvels of the ballpoint pen. Many lay on his stall in a glittering array of colours. The salesman was tall and thin and had a huge, hooked nose and a satanic grin, but he was also typically English, so I just had to talk to him once the crowd dispersed and he had made his sales. I hovered by his stall, examining his pens, and of course we got to chatting. And once I started, I just went on and on.

After a while, he said he had to go to Joe Lyons (the famous tea shop) just opposite and close to Whitechapel tube station. He said he was going for a cup of tea and if I wouldn't mind keeping an eye on the stall! I was amazed by his apparent trust in me and eagerly stood in for the master salesman, determined to protect his goods with all the almighty strength of a twelve-year-old and ready to assume grave responsibility. I was even hoping that I might sell a pen or two; however, how could I repeat even a shadow of that electrifying performance? How did he do that? What was the secret?

Is it something you are born with? A talent that just springs out of you? What did he do? He told a story, and how; it was like he was saving the lives of his little pens. While I was standing in for him, one or two people idly fingered the pens, but I could not for the life of me do more than quote the price.

Soon the sorcerer came back. I call him a sorcerer because I was like the sorcerer's apprentice. I was still standing in the same spot as when he had left me, and I half apologised for not selling any pens during his brief absence. Now it was time for him to begin his speech. He just started shouting to no one in particular, and sure enough a small crowd began to form. He was such a weird character to look at, with a limp and yet a rather debonair manner, which perhaps added to the attraction. He would take a pen and whack it down hard on a plate to show that it was unbreakable, and all the onlookers would be so impressed.

This time at the end of his sessions, I gathered up some pens and handed them to him. It was a dramatic lesson, my God it was. If only I could achieve that. We made a deal that, if I came each Saturday as his assistant, he'd pay me the royal sum of five shillings. I was thrilled and promised to turn up the following week. This was my very first job and I stayed with the Pen King for well over a year. At the end of the day, he would head home to Holloway where he lived with two elderly sisters. Looking back now, I imagine he was gay, but it didn't occur to me then. I was always looking for a father figure and for a while he filled that role. I loved the intense atmosphere of the market, but I only wish that I could have had, or even found within me, that special magic to inspire the crowds like the Pen King did so effortlessly.

In the middle of Philpot Street there was a small post office where I began my economic life. It was where working-class people saved their money and diligently kept records in their post office book. I was very proud of my 'book' – another sign of becoming an adult. I spent two or three shillings a week and saved the rest of my weekly earnings from the Pen King. I felt modestly rich.

Ma, Beryl, and I continued to live quite contentedly in our one and a half rooms in 27 Anthony Street, although Ma continually wrote pleading letters to the London County Council telling them how desperate our living conditions were. In fact, under the Labour government, hundreds of thousands of families that were living in post-war slums were rehoused in sparkling brand-new flats, and that was to be our eventual joy after at least two years in our little domain that we shared mostly with cats, since there was an abundance of stray cats and many kittens, which I found just adorable. As a solitary child, I felt compassionate, even empathetic, towards strays. I would pick up off the street any cat that looked lost and sad and would take it home to give it milk and look after it. We had six in the flat at one point. Ma also quite liked them, and we both adored their dynamic playfulness. We would feed them and some slept in the rather grimy cupboard in the front room. Sadly, though, many of them died – they must have already been infected by living off the streets, even after all the love and care we gave them.

***

As it so happened, one day Ma did receive a letter from the London City Council offering her a brand-new council flat in Manor House, which was part of the Woodbury Down Estate in North London. It was reputed to be the largest housing estate in the whole of Europe. So one morning Ma and I got on the 653 bus. As the bus passed each gigantic block, I gasped in sheer amazement at these colossal masterworks.

Eventually, we arrived at what was called Keynsham House, about a hundred yards from Manor House tube station, which was destined to be used by its devoted voyager for the next ten years until I was 22. We took the lift to the fourth floor and walked the long gangway which linked all the other flats till we arrived at number 30. Our new home. We walked in and were nothing less than totally enchanted. A real home. A kitchen, a bathroom, and even a fridge, and three bedrooms! It meant a bedroom all for me. A living room, a fireplace, and from the windows only the view of the next mountainous block, but that was OK; we were happy with our new home for the first time since we had left Luton. We relished it and fantasised about how we would furnish it. I knew exactly what I wanted.

I almost immediately jumped on the bus to Stamford Hill, where there were several small shops, and looked at lamps. I knew I wanted a bed with a small table next to it and a lamp; that was my deepest fantasy. It took a few days to make the move to Manor House – an area that was completely foreign to me – but soon, as I discovered Stamford Hill, a fairly cosmopolitan area nearby, I felt quite at home. It was an end to travelling and felt like a sanctuary.

Of course, I would have to change schools, which was rather convenient as I had started to gather new ink entries again. Now I could virtually tell them to shove them up their arses. I had to take the number 653 trolley bus to Hackney, walk across Hackney Downs, and there I faced the mighty edifice of Grocers' School, or Hackney Downs Grammar School. It was at this stage that an event happened that would, if only momentarily, put a destructive brake on all my dreams. While in Raine's Foundation School, I had top marks in English and French and was in a grade A group, yet at Grocers', the idiot headmaster placed me immediately in a C group! I was horrified, particularly by the less-than-enlightened twerps I saw around me, and this depressed me instantly. How could the imbecile headmaster have done this? This was totally shocking to me, and I had no one to speak up for me.

On the very first day in my class, my neighbour, a boy called Tilley, wilfully started an argument with me and hit me. Of course I struck him back, but I was sickened by this, so at lunchtime I crossed the Downs in tears, determined to go home and get out of that foul school forever.

I took the bus back to Manor House and told Ma everything. She did her best to explain that it was only a way of testing me and, no doubt, I would be placed in the right class in the next term, but that was not to be. I was destined to remain in the C group – no idea why, just brutal indifference from all those stultifying teachers who cared little for the remnants of the school, which we were. I would miss, totally, that opportunity to meet the boys with whom I might just have something in common. Who knows what powerful friendships I might have made? What a loss. Just a thug for my first encounter. I put up with it and hoped for the best.

What I really hated was when Friday came. I knew I would spend the entire weekend alone, totally alone, no friends. I started to grieve as soon as Friday turned up. I've never forgotten those ghastly days. I was so isolated and lonely at Hackney Downs. At Raine's, I'd had some good mates, but here, I couldn't seem to make lasting friends. As soon as any new boy entered the class, I'd go straight for him attempting to make him my friend. I so desperately wanted a 'best friend'. But after a time, he would mix with the other boys and I would be forgotten. Looking back, I see that my obvious need for friendship and affection was my undoing: it's the kind of thing that makes schoolboys turn away from you.

There came a couple of turning points. One came when we had to go on a summer outing. These were torture – the same old isolation and bullying. But one summer when a bully attacked me, I hit back. I whacked his jaw with a power I didn't realise I had. It was a moment of truth for me and I wouldn't be bullied again.

Then, after some months of misery at Hackney Downs, somebody suggested that I go to the local Jewish Boys Youth Club on Stamford Hill, which occupied a Victorian house. At last, I had somewhere to go. I immediately met an outsider like me. He was a young boy of most eccentric tastes and behaviour called Malcolm Knight (alias Zauseman). He had been a child actor and had a small but noticeable role in an old British movie called *Passport to Pimlico*, one of those English comedy satires the Brits were rather good at. We kind of became buddies; we both loved the idea of being actors, and he already was one. For years, I had fantasised about how amazing it would be to be a film star. And I have no doubt that my delightful experiments playing Brer Rabbit in my first school sowed those seeds in me. Malcolm had the most extraordinary affected upper-class voice and yet with a face that could have come out of the Warsaw Ghetto, topped with a high quiff in his greased-back hair. But, best of all, we got on well.

After a while, I started meeting friends I had more in common with, and Malcolm and I drifted apart as I got to know slightly less bizarre chaps whose territory seemed to be Stamford Hill, and more particularly the Shtupp House – so called due to it being a pinball arcade full of the most up-to-date American machines, where it was essential to keep the metal ball in motion so it might strike the small electric sensors and build your score. In order to achieve this, it might be necessary to subtly push the machine. Well, since this was almost exclusively a Jewish area, the term used was a crude Yiddish word: *shtupp*, which means to push or shove, and even had more imaginative meanings – i.e. 'Did you *shtupp* her?'

Eventually, as I grew older, I became less vulnerable and even, I dare say, a little crude, which became a strong influence for my first steps as a playwright. Nevertheless, I still continued to write to my beloved Shirley in Luton for some years and was never at a loss for something to say and still felt as enamoured with her as ever, even though we only corresponded by mail. However, in my newly emerging growth, or new personality traits, I was ripe for corruption, for being all too easily influenced by the practised vulgarity of others. I began to hang around Stamford Hill getting to know the various types who used to cluster around the Shtupp House like exotic butterflies. I began to identify with some others whom I found totally fascinating, and there seemed to be a distinct hierarchy. Naturally a certain crude toughness determined your standing and place in that world.

The really tough one was a hard-faced brute called Harry Lee who seemed almost invincible, but he was not unattractive, although he claimed he could pound his fist through wooden doors – which he did and then walked around for several weeks with his hand in plaster. Then there was Moisha, a short Popeye-like character with a tuft of hair that flopped over his face like a tough guy in a movie. Along with them was the handsome Ronnie Mitchell, who had a peculiar yet fascinating walk like he was on a ship during a storm. All those boys were, I have to admit, brutally good-looking.

As I became familiar with Stamford Hill, I gradually got to know them but was never audacious enough to consider them my friends. There was one young man of such good looks he seemed like a movie star, but he certainly was not tough, although he pretended to be. He was a faker. They called him Ginger Paul because he had the most luxurious red hair and wore it in the fashion of the day, which was mostly led by the wonderful barnet of Tony Curtis and was given the familiar epithet of DA (duck's arse). What he did have, and that in spades, was the gift of the gab. He could have you in stitches and even invented his own language, yet I felt there was something not quite right with him.

One day, he and I, becoming fast friends, were inside the Shtupp House playing on one of those machines when a shortish but utterly fascinating man walked in. He had a broad, wolfish face and a mass of curly hair, almost ringlets. Paul looked up and said, 'This is Curly King.' I was nonplussed and looked it. 'Don't you know who Curly King is?' asked Paul.

I said, 'No – no I don't, sorry.'

Then Curly said one of those sentences that stays in your mind forever: 'He doesn't get around much, does he?'

I looked back at him again; he was like a ferocious animal – or more animal than human. He was fascinating and he was already a legend as a tearaway in the East End.

Curly then walked out of the Shtupp House and round the corner to the Milk Bar and we just followed him. Within a few minutes, there was a small crowd following him along the street as if he was the Pied Piper – yes, I could never forget who Curly King was. It was the first time I had clapped my eyes on a being who seemed legendary, and I was to see a lot more of him in the future.

Shirley and I had been writing to each other for over three years by this point. And so it happened that one day in our new flat in Manor House, I can't say exactly when, Beryl suddenly said to me, 'You know, now that you are studying at a good grammar school, you should keep your mind clear. I don't think you should keep writing to Shirley. It's not a good idea when you need to focus on your studies.'

Of course, I remember how deeply fascinated I was with that very first letter from Shirley. How I was never at a loss for what to write to her week after week, month after month, and even year after year, until my elder sister somehow used her superior age as a weapon to influence me to kill this wonderful and unique first love of mine. I never ever felt such a mindless obsession with my carnal desires. I was in love with Shirley the way I have never felt before or since. I was in love with her. It was a dream to see her once more, just once more would have been a fulfilment beyond anything I could hope for. Shirley, I truly loved you...

However, I listened to Beryl and, as if I were some kind of golem, just obeyed her blindly. I never wrote to Shirley again. I don't think that I had a mind of my own. I was emerging from the chrysalis of childhood into an early form of adulthood. I simply, for some unknown reason, felt guilty about any form of desire that I had and since I was not quite a child, not quite an adult, I could not defend my instincts. So I listened to that utter garbage as if it contained words of wisdom that I should pay heed to; after all, Beryl was a grown-up, she was clever, she *knew*; whereas, in fact, this relationship in some ways had kept my soul together. It fed me. It was noble. It was inspiring. It was safe. I was loved as I would never be loved again. It was quite unique, but now I was to see it as something not quite right, something ever so slightly illicit – even dirty. So I felt that I had to shut it off.

And from that time, the protective angels that watched over me departed. They had protected me because they had something precious to watch over. They just shrugged their wings and departed. I was no longer worth it, no longer in need of protection. They were gone. The love of my life had gone. I didn't realise it, but I was now an empty vessel. The vessel that needed to be pure, to protect and cherish this love, was now rendered useless and impotent. What need was there for it anymore? It had been corrupted. From that moment, I had nothing that I desperately needed to live for, and, even worse, I was developing nascent criminal instincts.

CHAPTER 4

Nascent Criminal Instincts

My friends weren't always the most inspiring. Although I did still have some good ones, something was missing. Perhaps love sometimes acts like a powerful antibiotic, guarding you against the unsavoury elements trying to creep in? The move to Manor House had begun the change towards adulthood, and adulthood is also about learning to live with the shames that you have to deal with as you grow older, when the rituals that should mark your years are often missing.

The first shame was the shock of being placed in the lowest grade when I moved to that abominable school in Hackney. Without mental stimulation, school became dull, and I lost my desire to study, which had once been all-consuming. We were overlooked by the teachers, who focused their attention on the supposedly more able kids. My confidence was shot. I went into a spiral. I messed around in class, I started to smoke, I skimped on my homework, and I stopped swimming except for summertime trips to the Tottenham Lido. The second shame was not being encouraged, as every young Jewish boy is, to have a bar mitzvah, especially since nearly all my Jewish friends in Stamford Hill duly had their bar mitzvahs, large or small, at thirteen, when they'd stand up in front of the family and friends and consider themselves men. When Dad was asked by a colleague of his, 'When is Steve getting bar mitzvah'd?', I heard him blithely answer, 'I'm not doing a party since I've just had Beryl's wedding.'

Beryl got married when she was 20 to a very pleasant chap called David Bentley. I was 13 at the time, and I remember all too clearly that my father had rented a large room in Green Lanes not far from where we lived in Manor House. The food was not too exciting and the feeling was that he must have strained for a bargain. Sitting at one of the tables, I felt a deep sense of shame. Even my Uncle Henry was compelled to say, 'Mr Berks has paid dearly for this.' However, when I looked up at the long table where my flushed sister was sitting, they all seemed quite happy, so I guess they must have made sure that the family table was well supplied.

Curiously enough, I got on very well with my brother-in-law and he took a great deal of interest in me. Seeing that I was a keen photographer, he actually went out and bought me an enlarger so that I might develop my own negatives and print my own photos. That was fantastic. After Morris, he was the first person in my family who ever bothered to engage my mind and teach me something. God bless David Bentley. Some years before, in Luton, Morris had given me a small box camera and I couldn't wait to buy film and use it. It just goes to show that I would act upon anything, any act of kindness, that would advance my knowledge of the world.

But I knew you didn't need a vast celebration for a bar mitzvah. A service in a synagogue with a few relatives and tea and cakes afterwards was all you needed. The shame of not being blessed with that special ritual ate into my soul. I felt less of a man. I did go to a few Hebrew classes, but nobody was encouraging me, so I stopped going.

So all these milestones that should've accompanied growing up fell by the wayside, but my body didn't fail me, it continued to grow. Sure enough I discovered the positive sides of becoming a man when I developed an intense craving for the opposite sex. I did some mild flirting at the Stamford Hill Boys Club, where girls were welcomed, and my desire was clear and uncomplicated. When I was about 14, my one good friend, Harold Harris, a very sweet and charming guy who lived in Stamford Hill and was even learning to play the saxophone, encouraged me to join him for a trip to the Royal Dance Hall in Tottenham, our local palais de danse. I am so grateful he did. This was the first dance hall I had ever been to. It was a tea dance on a Saturday afternoon and was a ritual that I would never forget!

The vast emporium seemed like a palace. There was a gigantic room with tables and chairs on both sides. The band was at the far end. I was soon able to detect that the two sides of the room were divided not only geometrically but also ethnically, since on the left side were mostly Jews from North London – Stamford Hill, Stoke Newington, Hackney – and on the right side were natives from Tottenham and further east and a smattering from East London. It was a merry ethnic mix. To simplify, you could say it was Jews on the left and gentiles on the right. As long as you kept to your side it was fairly peaceful. In all the years that I attended the Royal Dance Hall, I never once sat on the right-hand side, although I did visit it from time to time for a bit of adventure. As I got bolder, I would cross the floor to ask a young lady to dance. I was too young to feel any sense of danger and too naïve. The girls on the right were emphatically gentiles and even seemed a touch exotic.

Sometimes I did see a fight break out, usually on a Saturday night. It seemed to explode out of nowhere, lasted viciously for seconds, and then spluttered out as if it was some brief warning. Since the Kray twins also used the Royal Dance Hall as their club, they occasionally doled out some swift jaw-breakers. My colleague Ronnie Mitchell was delivered a quick thrashing one night from the Krays, which earned him two lovely black eyes that he happily paraded, given the status of where they had originated from. I, meanwhile, hovered in the comparative safety of the Landsmans (fellow natives). It was a world I had never before experienced, and I do confess that I loved every moment.

The Royal was our best local dance hall. It was our weekly chance to get up close and personal with young women. That was the highlight of the week. Of course, you'd dress up in your best and only suit, you'd wear a smart shirt and tie and, most importantly, you'd prepare your hair ever so carefully...

When I entered that magnificent ballroom, I was simply astonished at how beautiful it was. Once you'd paid, the first thing you would do, the very first thing before you penetrated into this carnival of earthly delights, was to go to the men's room and fix your hair. This was most important since your carefully created tonsure would have been somewhat muffed up during the exertions of the journey. So you had to carefully rearrange your 'barnet' (that's what it's called in Cockney slang after Barnet Fair – 'hair'). There might be a collection of elbows jutting into your face as you valiantly tried to find a portion of the mirror. Then, having combed your precious locks to your satisfaction – you always possessed a comb – you made your first steps into your 'Man World', a terrain where absolutely anything might happen. The band was playing, couples were dancing, and the odour was toxic, a strong medley of cheap but sweet perfume which hung in the great hall like a mist. Sometimes the band would play music to jive to, and this was the way you could demonstrate your skills, your technique, your sassy footwork, your elegance. This was the way to court the ladies; this was your mating dance. And I loved that. I loved it when my partner showed she could move in harmony with me; the girls that could really dance always liked it when you could handle them gracefully. When you didn't fling them around but were careful with them, very careful, but at the same time you didn't show off. Oh no, you must never do that. Even if you were inclined to show a step or two that took them a bit by surprise, that was okay, she liked that, she enjoyed that. I mean, that was why she was here.

But as the evening draws on you suddenly realise that the magic hour of 11pm is approaching! The night will soon be over, and you haven't been able to hunt down a willing lady to escort home. You haven't had the chance to chat anyone up yet. You were too busy dancing, leaping from one to another, and now it's getting late and most of the available chicks are happily hooked up or quite happy to go home with their companions and certainly don't wish to be seen as the last resort or be taken home by a stranger they have just met.

There are only a few single ladies leaning by the wall, looking, dare I say it, a mite forlorn, sad, like wilting lilies, but since it's getting late and you're facing the dire prospect of going home alone, you make a final effort to hook the best of the modest remains. You don't want to jump on the bus, alone, return to your drab council flat, take the lift to the top floor, a lift that already stinks of urine, then enter your flat and realise the week is over. Over. What you had been looking forward to all week, with mounting anticipation, is over. However, in the scrapyard of the rejects that are still possibly available, you might strike lucky. But first you've got to ask where she's from, and it might be a hell of a journey.

She might say, Hackney, Dalston, Romford, even Whitechapel. A hell of a schlepp, and of course I don't have a car, and there would be no guarantee of any satisfaction at the end of that journey. She might even say, 'I'm sorry, I have to go in, my parents always wait up for me!' Maybe the last bus has gone, so you turn on your heels and walk. You endure a very long walk which, with the prospect of an exciting frottage, would be tolerable. So, it's a gamble. You gamble your pathetic lust against the risk of nothing, yes absolutely nothing... zilch.

Yes, how sad. How very sad and even pathetic that, for whatever reason, you have reduced the wonderful, complex, beautiful piece of humanity, this unique and sensitive girl into a mere receptacle, a female crotch which you crudely use to calm your overexcited and mindless libido. How ghastly, when there was such an opportunity available to you, to ask, to know, to gently explore this world from whence this mysterious creature lives. Your malehood has turned you into an unfeeling monster.

And now, the drab and dreary walk home, to Nowheresville, after a half-hearted chat about where I can fulfil my needs, my brutal lust, my desire. Round the corner perhaps? We only need a wall, that's all, somewhere to lean a body against, to fulfil my rank purpose, while she feels she has to put up with it. The poor guy's come this far, just put up with it. Just put up with it. Tolerate it until the pathetic beast has fulfilled himself. Then escape home. At last. Thank God she can get away from this demanding dog. Yes, she's home – sanctuary! Maybe her mother is still up and waiting anxiously the way mothers do when their daughters have reached a certain age... 'Did you have a nice night? I'll make you a cuppa. Did you meet anyone nice? Oh, he took you home, that's nice. Why didn't you invite him in…? Oh, he wasn't the type. It wasn't worth it? I see, I see! Filthy dog only had one thing on his mind. Shame, such a shame, but aren't they all like that? Eh?'

Of course, she could have invited me in, but they never do. Never. Because then you'd be looked at, examined, chatted to, asked all sorts of questions. We'd exchange tiny bits of our lives, our humanity, maybe her mother would get to know me just a bit, maybe even like me, just a bit. See what sort of bloke I am. Was I suitable for her precious daughter? I could use another part of me that wasn't my dick for a while, then maybe, yes maybe, from this a seed could be sown, which may grow into something else... but nothing... the time has gone.

***

So that was a night out at the Royal, a dancehall where you might just be so lucky as to come across the most beautiful girl in the world; you might begin a romance that would alter your entire life; and you might also, if you were a tad too cheeky, get your teeth knocked down your throat, but at the end of the day, you would be guaranteed the satisfaction of a good jive! That is, as long as you knew how, and I was determined to learn, so much so that I took lessons at a small dance hall called Greys in Finsbury Park. It might have been a ballet school during the day, since there were full-length mirrors on the wall. On certain nights, a lovely elegant young man called Leslie gave lessons on the principal moves of jive and it wasn't long before I was able to spin across the floor like a demented elf. Greys was somewhat unusual as it attracted a smaller crowd and it never got violent. I remember it well. Leslie gave lessons in a corner of the room and showed you the steps, the basic steps that were easy to learn, and I learned them fast because I wanted to be skilled so that I could impress the ladies, so l became better and better. Oh, how wonderful to learn something at last, after years at a school where I learned practically nothing.

One day I discovered another small dance club. I was now scrambling further afield. It was called the 51 Club in Little Newport Street, just off Leicester Square. It was in a basement, so you walked downstairs and the music hit you. It was modern jazz and it all came from a turntable. No live group ever played there, yet it had an atmosphere, and the girls could really dance well. I liked going there on Sunday afternoon. There you had to like dancing. There was little chatting up of ladies. Nobody went there for that purpose. They went for the music and to jive. There were always quite a few black guys there who seemed to be au fait with the ladies, but I never knew anyone. I loved jiving, though, and some of the guys were really great jivers, almost, you might say, to a professional standard. That's why I always loved going there.

Sometimes I would also go on Saturday nights and I must have danced my head off. One night, I recall coming home to our council flat in Manor House and saying to my Mum: 'I think last night was the happiest day of my life.' You could say those things then. You were young, you were capable and were becoming a first-rate dancer. You didn't need to humiliate yourself in front of some young lady to be fulfilled. Thank God! Yes, I discovered there was more to life than that.

It wasn't just how you danced; you had to look right too. This was the time of the Teddy Boys, and you wore four-button suits with stiff-collared, double-cuffed shirts. I sent my collars to Collars Ltd every week for starching and laundering, and if they didn't come back stiff enough, I would go crazy! You had to look immaculate. The suit dictated how you danced: while lifting your arm, you had to keep your elbow in to your side or else the jacket would be pulled up and you'd look a mess. Retaining the right form was everything.

As I grew older, I was introduced to a palace to end all palaces: the Lyceum in the Strand. It was beyond anything I had ever seen before. A large dance hall and several balconies where you could sit, drink, and chat with your newly found leg-over. It was only several years later that I learned that it had once been a theatre. That rather amazed me, and it was several years after that that I learned the name of the man who had run a distinguished company there for several years and had a famous hit in a play called *The Bells*. One day, I stood on that very stage just for one evening, reading the role that Henry Irving had played in *The Bells*, to celebrate the 100th anniversary of Irving's death.

I was now getting into a kind of young man's London routine, which was the Tottenham Royal on Saturday night, the 51 Club on Sunday afternoon, and then the Lyceum on Sunday night as well. But the Super Cinema was the Stamford Hill Gang's choice for Sunday afternoon movies. It had become a kind of chatting-up place for young and very fertile teenagers. Before the film started, if you were bold enough, you would swiftly scan the seats hoping to spot a couple of young ladies with spare seats beside them. I don't think I was yet quite brave enough to join this search routine.

Sometimes my slightly older cousin Sidney Bennet would come all the way from the East End, since he was dating a girl from Stamford Hill called Barbara, who was besotted with him. One Sunday afternoon, Sidney and Barbara were sitting enjoying a movie but had the misfortune to be sitting just in front of Stamford Hill's most eccentric maverick, Harry Lee, who loved stirring up trouble. Sidney turned in his seat and politely asked him to quieten down, to which Harry declared quite brusquely that he would see him 'outside' after the movie was over. He was challenging him to a punch-up.

Well, they met outside and, just as Sid was taking off his jacket, Harry punched him in the face. As it was so unexpected, my beloved cousin was badly injured and had to take a taxi home. It took Sid several weeks to recover, but he was not going to let this go unanswered. Although he was barely 17, he sent a challenge to his opponent in Stamford Hill to set a date; this, I thought, was bravery to the limit, since Harry Lee was renowned as a street fighter. However, Sidney's brother Willie was a judo expert and made sure that his younger brother was well trained to defeat Harry. Yet there was no response from Stamford Hill, even after Sid was fit again, so he and Willie simply took the bus each night and waited in a shop doorway for his nemesis to turn up.

Being hyper-aware of Harry's prowess for violence, I was anxious indeed for my cousin's welfare. Yet I could not help but admire this young man's awesome courage and bold determination, to just stand on Stamford Hill each and every night, waiting. Harry had to turn up. The hill was his manor. How could he just shut off his freedom, hiding like a mouse at home? Eventually Harry sent a message. Of course, there was no alternative; as his cousin, I just had to be involved and got wind of the date and place – behind the Super Cinema in a narrow alleyway.

I was very concerned about the possible outcome and yet so daring was my beloved cousin that I could only believe that somehow he would prevail. Harry was what was known as a *Shtarker*, a tough guy. He was immensely courageous and there was a story that the Tottenham Gang had been seeking an almighty punch-up with Stamford Hill, but it was decided that as a compromise they would send out their toughest tearaway to do battle with Stamford Hill's toughest. As each one came up for battle, Harry knocked them out, one-by-one, until they realised they had no one who could beat this man. So on that night we all gathered in the appointed place. My heart had never beaten so hard. It was a small crowd. I recall Ronnie

Mitchell, Moisha, Harry's brother, Sid, Willie, and me. Then it started. Sid had been training for several weeks, yet I feared how my cousin would be able to deal with Harry's hammer-blow punches. It started slow. Sid looked confident. He had shaved his hair to a short clump, so it could not be seized. After a few seconds, Sid had thrown himself onto Harry, which caused Harry to fall to the floor, whereupon Sid mounted him and with his knees pinned his arms to the pavement. Harry struggled but could do nothing while Sid pounded him with both his fists. Eventually, Sid grabbed Harry's hair in both his fists and slammed his head onto the concrete pavement. This went on for some time. I remember it so clearly. Harry shouted out, 'Finish me off or I'll come back for you.' Sid continued banging his skull and looked as if he was determined to at least knock him unconscious.

Ronnie Mitchell stepped in as if to halt the proceedings, probably thinking that it had already gone too far. Willie cautioned, 'Don't interfere, Ronnie.' I loved Willie for that. He was afraid of no one, and they were my two beloved and adored cousins. I was so proud of them. Ronnie stepped back. Eventually Sid had had enough. Harry was still conscious. Sid stepped back and Harry was slowly helped to his feet. It was over. And as Sid and Willie turned away, Willie turned back to me and said, 'Don't let them bother you, Steve. If they do, get in touch with me.' That was awesome, that was worth half a century of paternal neglect, that was someone standing up for me. I was very touched. I have never forgotten that night behind the Super Cinema. I loved my cousin more than ever.

Sid married Barbara. I was even going to write a play about that momentous occasion. Fortunately, I visited my beloved cousin in hospital just before he died. He said to me, 'Steve, you play all these hard men on TV, but you couldn't punch your way out of a paper bag.' I almost collapsed with laughter. That was the last time I saw him.

I continued my utterly drab schooling at Grocers' Grammar School, and it felt as if I was merely passing time in the shitty C group. I felt that our teachers thought that our lessons should not be too challenging, so they gave us nothing that might even vaguely inspire us to greater heights, although History did marginally wake us up when the teacher started talking about the Renaissance. Most classes were utterly boring, though, and even my once-favourite classes, English and French, felt no better. Our very charming English teacher, Mr Brierly, who had certainly inspired Harold Pinter five years earlier, felt that it was not worth wasting time doing any creative work, so he concentrated mainly on grammar exercises to make us at least capable of 'office work'. As for French, the teacher, whose name was De La Feld, was so incredibly boring that we all learned virtually nothing. No books. No novels. No drama. In other words, zilch. He loved bullying the boys and took pleasure in rapping kids around the head with the wooden chalk eraser. I believe he was slightly mad.

Curiously, the school had a magnificent Greek-style amphitheatre, where Mr Brierly would stage quite ambitious plays. Of course, no one in C group was ever involved. I just used this magnificent amphitheatre to eat my lunch that Ma patiently prepared every day, and the only use I put the theatre to was to play Shove Ha'penny on the wonderful long surfaces. I believe I played that most lunchtimes.

What happiness when the bell went for the end of the day! Then there was a slow walk through the back alley to catch the 653 trolley bus that would take us all the way to Manor House. By now, Dad had bought us our very first 12-inch TV, so that was exciting. Once I was home, Ma had a plate of buttered half-slices of beigel, and being so hungry, I would consume most of them before she even laid down supper. I was always hungry and Ma always cooked something tasty, and yet I used to have just a tiny twinge of guilt when I thought that she had to do this each and every day, week in and week out, month after month, and year after year.

Poor Ma. I would even get into a huff if the grub wasn't quite up to my standards or was repetitive, but that was very rare. Usually, it was first-rate, and she would set my food down and often just stand there and watch me eat. Like a proud mother, she wanted to witness me enjoying my nosh. She made the most wonderful fishcakes and used a mixture of cod and haddock and fried them perfectly; they were especially delicious when served with a dollop of horseradish. Also, as an hors d'oeuvre she would make the most wonderful coleslaw that was such a delicious starter along with fat, black olives. At least once a week, she would make the most delightful chicken soup, so golden, so tasty, along with some beautiful little dumplings which were perfectly delicious and couldn't be bettered. More than once I tucked into Ma's delightful cuisine, and I used to feel a whisper of regret that there was no one there to share this feast with me. Dad was never there: he now had a tiny shop in Brixton, so would be home late. Beryl was a typist in the West End. So it was mostly just me and Ma at the kitchen table.

As Ma grew older, she just didn't seem to have the energy to go shopping or to cook, and sometimes when she put down the chicken soup, I could see that most of it had come from a packet. I'd certainly get annoyed at how my pure, genuine golden chicken soup had been adulterated, and she would apologise profusely and then I'd feel awful. Sometimes she'd cook the best barley and carrot soup on earth and other times just fry up some frankfurters and chips. That wasn't so bad. For a special treat on Sunday mornings, she always served up some toasted beigels with the softest cream cheese and delicate thin slivers of smoked salmon plus pickled cucumbers and olives on the side. That was quite heavenly. It was more than a treat – it was a celebration, a heavenly celebration.

I remember when we were still living in crumbling old Anthony Street, she would take me to a famous delicatessen called Roggs in Cannon Street Road. Roggs had just about every kind of exotic food from the far corners of Eastern Europe. There was always a queue in the shop slowly edging towards the counter, since the great treat there was the great glistening pink slabs of smoked salmon that lay on the counters like priceless treasures. When it came to our turn, Ma would only ask for a modest four ounces, since it was so very, very expensive. Many of their customers were well-to-do and could order by the pound! It actually cost a pound sterling per pound weight, which was a fortune in those days. All the salmon were freshly caught – those wretched fish farms didn't exist in the late '40s – so after Ma ordered her four ounces, we both watched like hawks as the shop owner sliced the salmon, making sure there were no funny bits added. Then he would draw his long cutting knife gently down the flesh, which came away like silk, before laying a sheet of oiled paper over that. Then he'd begin to slice another perfect pink sliver.

After about four or five slices had been cut, Ma pulled herself up to her full height, gathered all her courage, and said, 'Do you think we could have some skin, please?' This would be a vital part of the order, as the remaining skin would always have delicious shreds of salmon still left on it. She would never be refused; he just hacked off a huge slice and laid it over our newly-cut treasure. We were delighted when we saw that, and Ma would be happy and even order some other delicacies, especially new green pickled cucumbers or, the most delicious, chopped herring, the like of which one cannot possibly resist.

Thus satisfied, we would walk proudly back to our squat in Anthony Street, put the kettle on, and very slowly heat and cut our beigels, coat them with a thick smear of the softest cream cheese, very gently pull open the first precious sheet of our smoked salmon, cut just a quarter of the slice, and lay it on the cream cheese, then cut some slices of pickle and ever so carefully lay them across the half beigel. Oh heaven! Then Ma cut a small piece of the salmon skin, and I would run it across my teeth, which was scrumptious since there was always a shred of salmon left that the knife had missed. Then finally, after I had decimated every shred of salmon from the skin, I would bung the chewed skin to the cat, who would devour it with utter feline delight! We were all made happy by the delights of Roggs of Cannon Street Road.

Years later, the famous deli went seriously into decline but was still hanging in there, now run by the grandson of the original owner. He was called Barry and was invariably dressed like a hobo in an East End slum. He usually wore an old woollen pullover, which was only shed on the hottest days. After a while, the rustic glamour of the place simply became too much and, even with my love of nostalgia, I found that I just could not enter that squalid broken-down deli anymore – but it left its mark in more ways than one!

Now we were living like a version of working-class royalty, in our own flat in Manor House with the Stamford Hill Boys Club was a bus stop away, and then there was the Shtupp House on the hill itself, which was run by a most belligerent guardian of the pinball machines, and not forgetting the jukebox at the very end of the arcade. The hit number at the time was 'Jezebel', sung by Frankie Laine, who was followed by my own favourite, Johnnie Ray. For me, he was perfect and his songs were poetic tributes to misty-eyed teens – he spoke to me like no other singer. Also, I was getting to know jazz through my special friend from Stamford Hill, Harold: modern jazz, that is, played by the likes of Dave Brubeck, Gerry Mulligan, Stan Kenton, and George Shearing – perfect to jive to.

Now, as I was beginning to learn the rituals of dance, it was natural that I would continue to develop an appetite for the opposite sex. Although this was mainly satisfied by my trips to the Royal Dance Hall in Tottenham, where an occasional frottage would be the sum total of my sexual ambition, I do recall one Saturday when my dear friend Harold and I took the train to Southend-on-Sea.

It was a bright sunny day and there was a long walkway where pretty girls of all shapes and sizes perambulated. We strolled up and down, and up and down, then onto the pier, then off the pier, and all that time we couldn't attract any pair of interested ladies – we were not quite right, somehow we didn't fit, maybe we were too keen, too desperate – so eventually, after two or three hours, I said, 'Harry, I just wanna go home.' I'd had enough; our day out was turning into a nightmare. I miserably walked to the station. Nothing was working – oh why was it so important to have the company of a woman? I reached the station and, after a few minutes, Harold puffed in and said he'd chatted up a couple of girls and that they would be most happy to meet up with me! But by then I was so fed up, exhausted, and frustrated with having spent what seemed like hours walking pointlessly up and down, I just didn't have the will.

Poor Harold. I feel for him now, since he was trying so hard, but I just didn't have it in me. I wish I had. So sorry, Harold. I think I lost you that day. But I remember going all the way home then taking the bus to Manor House, and it felt so grim entering that quiet flat. Only Ma was there. Poor woman – she was in bed on a beautiful bright sunny day. She suffered horribly with stomach ulcers, so she just lay there with her pills on the side table. No sign of Dad. Maybe he was in his shop. It was just the two of us. Two desperately lonely people – why were we always lonely?

But now that I was growing mentally and physically, I found a good way to take the edge off my loneliness was simply the company of a woman; although I had male friends from time to time, it was only when I enjoyed the company of a woman that I felt more complete.

And so it came to pass that on Stamford Hill one night, I spied on what I thought of as a rather dashing redhead, whose name was Sylvia. She was a native of Hackney, and so it was just a little odd that she would hang out in this intensely Jewish area – or was it? We chatted quite casually at first and she didn't seem to have any liaison with any other chaps, so I said perhaps I could walk her home since she didn't live too far away? As I say, it was all quite calm and easy, and the chatter flowed without any tensions. I still thought of the young girl, Shirley, whom I had met in Luton and was in love with – but that was starting to fade after that brutish, warning 'advice' from my sister.

Oh, forgive me my dearest, darling Sylvia! Forgive me for all the sins committed against you. I never called you darling in all the time I knew you. When I first met you on Stamford Hill that balmy autumn evening, when everybody gathered to waffle, chatter, and flirt, I was fifteen years old. I chatted you up. I said: 'I'll take you home – if you like,' because that's what one did. You asked to take them home 'cause you only had one thing in mind: to get as close to a female as possible, since at that age, the hormones were raging through your body and tended to dominate all other thoughts. To hug, kiss, and crush this lovely female body to yours. To suck the kisses from her lips. To press your crotch against hers. It was always her hard indomitable pelvis that you frantically rubbed up against, and you'd pry her legs apart and grind up against her for all you were worth, while sucking up the kisses, as your greedy hands held her arse and you pulled her towards you, so everything – your hands, tongue, lips, crotch – were in a sublime frenzy of activity. And that was quite wonderful, it was, it was ecstatic, oh yes, it was; it was, because at the end of the week you could not be sure that this treat would be waiting for you, for the flower to be plucked. You couldn't be sure.

I believe we walked all the way to Sylvia's pre-war council flat just off a place known as the Hackney Marshes. But now we just leaned against the wall and plucked away at all the goodies on offer – and then I became ever so slightly soppy. I think too many soppy Hollywood films had infected my brain, and I actually said, 'Will you be my girl?' Maybe I thought I was being ever so slightly cute. She was attractive to me at first and had a young, virile body, and I was swiftly getting to know the mysteries of my own growing body, oh yes! And those mysteries were being discovered and explored with greater and greater frequency.

So, for a while I did have a steady date, although I had not yet left my rotten school in Hackney. Once or twice a week, we would go out, but our going out was usually no more than a stroll along Hackney Marshes until we found a nice pelt of grass. I'd take off my jacket to use as a blanket and we'd both lie there for a while – she serviced me with a delightful massage. She was so nice and obliging, but on occasion we did need just a little lubrication and Sylvia running her fingers through my Brylcreemed hair gave just the right frisson. Well, I was also determined, just as she was, to fulfil our utmost fantasy by going all the way. Yet, no matter how hard we tried, the fantasy was quelled by a hymen as strong as a bank vault, and so, in the cool evening air lit up by the distant amber lights of the local council flats and beyond that a smattering of stars, we were engaged in a desperate battle to invade the citadel.

Well, of course, one day the brave protective sheet could no longer resist the ferocious energy of teenagers and yes, it happened – but strangely enough, it didn't draw me any closer to Sylvia. It was nigh on impossible to have any sort of meaningful conversation with her; although she was immensely charming, she had no opinion on anything – never read a book – and I never even dreamed of asking her to meet my mum, let alone my dad. She was purely my sensual companion – although we did go to the movies sometimes. On the other hand, I was invited into her bleak council flat and met her mother and her somewhat delinquent brother. Her mother was a gentle woman, but we hardly spoke. She also had a very pleasant sister, and her father and I hardly exchanged a word. I don't wish to malign them for a second, but I could not wait to escape from that flat on the few rare times when the entire family would be out – maybe they actually agreed among themselves to vacate the flat so that our 'courting' might be achieved in private. After a short period of totally unprotected sex, the inevitable happened.

My main motivation in life when I started work at the age of fifteen, then, was to earn a weekly pay packet. Not studying, not learning, not improving, since I had to pay a weekly maintenance to Sylvia for the inconvenience of having made her pregnant, which was a terrible shock to my system. It was a fact that I had to live with. I badly needed advice – and recall, ironically, when my father discovered the tell-tale outline of a contraceptive in my wallet. He retrieved the 'wicked' object and confronted me with the evidence of my abject decadence, roundly abusing me for being such a disgusting tramp. Of course, he might have said 'Well done, son, oh well done and make sure you use it – never have sex without it – never!' But instead he made me feel like some filthy lout, and I was filled with shame. Henceforth, of course, I stopped trying to use it, although I always felt I should. But by then it was too late.

But nonetheless, I still felt that there was a distant beacon signalling to me through the mist, even if I had to graze myself quite badly on the endless rocks thrusting up to wound me just beneath the surface before I reached my destination. I had a modestly paid but very interesting job in the West End of London in a most beautiful shop that specialised in cashmere – but now I entered work each day with my mind grimly fixated on my problems. I just had no one to talk to. Sylvia was 17 – two years my senior – and didn't seem that bothered; she even discussed us getting a flat together, the thought of which, to me, was totally insane. Eventually, my mum found out from overhearing my heated phone conversation in the hallway and there was nothing we could do but let nature take its course.

Sylvia gave birth to a beautiful baby girl, and she was over the moon – thank God one of us was. Having a romantic streak in her for anything vaguely continental, Sylvia christened her Della. My father never got wind of this, but eventually Sylvia, quite naturally, took me to court in Stoke Newington to claim maintenance for her and the child, as I was, by then, 16. My beloved sister thought she would help by recruiting a solicitor – a friend of the family – to fight my case. I met him in the lobby of the court on the day of the hearing. We had no prior meeting, and I thought that what he suggested was nothing less than disgusting – seedy and ugly. He wanted me to suggest that Sylvia had so many boyfriends that I was only one of them. The magistrate nevertheless made a standing order against me to pay a weekly sum of a pound, which in those days was a lot. In fact, it was a third of my wages. But, of course, he did what he had to do, and Sylvia and her family were delighted with the outcome. I paid this amount for fifteen years.

Even Sylvia took some pity on me and promised to return a small portion of my weekly maintenance bill if I came to visit them once a week. It was like waving a piece of smoked salmon in front of a cat. I visited every Sunday. I am ashamed to say that, during the visit, Sylvia asked me to hold the baby, and I could barely hold her in my arms for more than a few seconds. I had not yet the slightest paternal instinct; in fact, I could not wait to hand the poor little helpless creature back to Sylvia so that I could escape.

This strange state of affairs went on until I felt I could no longer endure it and was happy to forfeit the cashback deal. I began working as hard as I could so I would not miss the money too much or cheapen myself by crawling around for it like a desperate beggar. I just could not sense any feelings of love, care, or fatherhood in me – only the reverse. Eventually, thank God, Sylvia met a builder and they got married, and I believe she had more children with him.

I should add that one day there was a knock on the door and of course I knew who it was – it was her husband, he had come to ask me to go to the Justice of the Peace. Since my name was on the birth certificate, he wished to change Della's surname to his. As soon as he entered, I could see that the man felt a great deal of loathing for me. He sat in the kitchen; I didn't wish to ask him into the living room, since for Ma this was her most precious room. We then walked to the local Justice of the Peace, and I most happily accepted the change of name. After this was done, the JP gently requested a donation from the person who desired the change – of course this was ignored. After we left, we silently went our separate ways.

Many years later, I did start to think about this poor girl – did start to have feelings for both of them. Yet, on one occasion, over a decade later, when Sylvia came to my house in Islington uninvited, I failed to act on these feelings. She simply knocked on my door and said, 'I hope you don't mind me coming. I just wanted to say hello and show you photographs of your daughter.' Beyond the expected feelings of shock and bewilderment, I also felt an overwhelming sense of embarrassment; my second wife, Shelley, was living with me at the time, and I didn't want her to know about Sylvia or the child, so I simply said, 'I can't see them now,' and turned her away.

Perhaps there was a little bitterness and grief there as well, after fifteen years of maintenance payments, but oh how I wish I'd seen her. How I wish that I had welcomed her in that afternoon. I was older then and had grown into myself a little more, but still I refused to even look at the photographs. If you are still on this planet, do please forgive me, my dearest Sylvia. I must confess that now I would love to speak to Della; my daughter would be seventy-two! It is likely that my grandchildren would be in their fifties and my great-grandchildren in their thirties.

***

Yes, I was not really fulfilling myself. Since leaving that wretched school in Hackney at 15, I had no desperate ambition except that I now would be able to take a job and actually earn money instead of begging for it each week – but what job? I had virtually no skills; I was virtually a useless blob of flesh; I had no references, no school report, even. On my first day of freedom from school, the world was my oyster, and I just picked up a newspaper and scoured the wanted ads. I saw something about an office boy wanted and so I did that for a few weeks until I was, happily, sacked – the work felt totally meaningless to me.

Then, at the end of Oxford Street, I discovered a juvenile labour exchange, so I went there and just took anything that seemed vaguely interesting. I heard about a friend of mine who was working in an advertising agency and they told me about an advertising agency in Soho which were looking for a delivery boy to pick up and deliver printing blocks and plates from the newspapers. That rather appealed to me, since I could see an illustrious future for me as a leading copywriter, so I joined and, as a messenger, I got to know my way around Fleet Street and was able to stay out most of the day. Now that I had no school to go to and no learning to do, I had little purpose but to drift around with young men who could only appeal to my criminal instincts. One such semi-hooligan enthusiastically engaged me to join him in some petty thievery – the idea appealed to me since I was poorly paid anyway, and I was also giving a third of my wages to Ma for my keep as well as the weekly maintenance for my daughter. I was sliding down a slippery path to Nowheresville. My father had virtually no interest in me whatsoever or even any desire to discuss what I might do with this extraordinary life that God had blessed me with, so I had no one to turn to.

However, my new partner in crime had a scheme: to go to Harringay Arena with some old beaten-up bike and get a parking ticket, which gave you entrance into the car park. Then, at the end of the evening, select the best bike on show, steal it, and in the rush, as everybody left quickly, flash your ticket and disappear. I did this once and was successful and sold the bike down Hackney Road Market for £5! I was moderately rich and successful in my initiation into thievery.

As I was traipsing around Fleet Street one day, I happened to see a bike parked on the kerb and, living in such innocent times, it was unlocked! How naïve we all were then. So the next day, I thought, if the bike was still there, I would ride off on it. It was, and I did. I raced off to Manor House and blithely told my ma that I had borrowed it from a friend for a day or two.

When Saturday came, I returned to the same market where I'd sold my first burgled bike. I actually felt quite good – I had been successful. I rode it to the same bike dealer, anticipating a pocket full of pound notes. After all, I had a date that night with a very pleasant young lady. I approached the dealer and maybe he recognised me from our last transaction, since he said it was a bit early in the day and he didn't have the money just yet, but to come back later when he'd packed up for the day. Better still, he said, since he only lived round the corner, why not come to his house, and he wrote down his address for me. I thought nothing of that: I wouldn't be leaving the bike, and I would return that evening. I did that very thing, and it was a night that I would never forget for the rest of my life. I dressed smartly because I was to go on and see my lady. I remember it so well.

I wore a pair of black barathea pants my dad had actually given me (since the customer who had ordered them had not picked them up), a red shirt, and a smart houndstooth jacket that was my reward for all my hard work. As I walked down the street that had been written on the slip of paper the dealer had given me, I suddenly had an intense desire to stop. Go back home. This is dangerous. The feeling was so strong – but my greed and stupidity were greater; after all, I had done this with him before. I came to the house and knocked on the door. The dealer answered. 'Oh, come on in,' he said. 'Just wait in the lounge and I'll get the cash.' Those were the last words I would hear that sounded nearly normal. From that moment, my life would change forever. I entered the lounge, sat on the sofa, and waited.

I didn't have to wait long, for two burly-looking men strode in. I knew, as they say, the game was up. They questioned me; they said that the bike had been reported stolen. 'What's your name? Where do you live? What's your phone number?' I was shaken to jelly. I begged them not to call my dad – above all. 'Please, please,' I begged, 'please, I swear I will never do this again! My father will kill me!'

But I had no choice; there was nothing I could do. I gave my number. I waited maybe half an hour, then suddenly the door was flung open. There stood my dad. He didn't speak to the cops; he just saw me and rushed in with his fists clenched and raised.

I never saw such fury in a man. The cops, of course, held him back. I'm sure he would have tried to kill me. I never saw such hate in all my life. Of course, he was ashamed of himself for how he had raised me. The cops did warn him not to lay a hand on me, but just to take me to the juvenile court in the East End in the morning. I got in the car and Dad drove me home. We didn't exchange a word. We drove in silence all the way to Manor House.

I went straight to my bedroom; the worst was over. There would never be a shock like that again, but he didn't strike me. Ma made me a cup of tea, then I slept. In the morning, Ma made me my favourite breakfast: grilled tomatoes on toast. I dressed and walked to where Dad had parked the car. He drove me to the court, which was just off Commercial Street. It was a rudimentary sitting, and I was sent to a remand home in Shepherd's Bush for two weeks, where I would be examined prior to sentencing. The usual process was to allow the courts to examine your fitness and scrutinise your behaviour before deciding whether to throw you behind bars or not. By now my fear, which was mainly to do with my father, had receded somewhat and was replaced by a curiosity about what it would be like to be a prisoner, having seen so many movies about life behind bars.

A cop drove me to the remand home. I arrived and was starving; fortunately, I arrived at tea-time and just joined in with the crowd. After tea, we all assembled in the large courtyard and mainly just hung around and gossiped. Later we were marched into a large assembly room. I would sleep well that night, but I couldn't help feeling the horror, the shame, the fear, the terrible anguish which was the very worst of my life when the cops had asked me for my telephone number. Oh, the horror of it. And I can always see the monstrous face of hatred marching into that room with clenched fists. But now all that was slowly easing off as a new adventure was taking place. God knows what conversation my parents had – it would be endless; it would never stop – but now I was entering into a new world.

The door of the dormitory swung open and a warden swept in shouting, 'Alright, up ya get, hands off cocks, get on your socks!' We rushed to dress and then we were ordered downstairs. First, we were given a pretty loathsome cup of what appeared to be coffee and then we collected our breakfast, which was no more than a sandwich we would wolf down, and at the end we were hungrier than ever. But the strangest thing was that the three lads who shared my table found the guards an endless source of amusement.

After breakfast, all we had to do was gather in the courtyard and just stand there till it was decided what duties were to be allotted to us. The days passed slowly and some days a group of us marched to Shepherd's Bush to the local swimming pool. At night, we'd all gather in the hall after supper and watch some old films; since this was only a remand home, we were not meant to be punished. Sometimes we had a visitor – Ma and my sister came once.

Then one day, I had to be examined by a psychiatrist who would make an assessment to the court regarding what kind of sentence I might get. I was summoned to a small room and sat facing him. He was a youngish man, and he started talking very informally, which I found so welcoming. He asked me how I passed my time when at home and I told him that recently I had liked to go dancing and that was one of my favourite activities; when he asked me where I went, I said that my favourite place was The Lyceum dance hall in the Strand. He was quite surprised and said, 'The Lyceum was once a great theatre; it was once a very famous theatre.' I have to admit that I found that news rather astonishing – it seemed so incongruous that a beautiful dance hall which delighted us and was host to vicious punch-ups from time to time had been, in the distant past, a theatre. I never forgot the moment he told me this; something struck a bell.

He then went on to ask me about my relationship with my family, and I told him that I had virtually no relationship at all with my father. When he questioned me further about our activities together, I confessed to him that we had none, none whatsoever, that he hardly ever spoke to me, and that I was for some unknown reason a bitter disappointment to him. I told him that Dad had never taken me out or shown me anything, apart from one time I went with Ma and him to see a movie, but that had been many years ago.

The man took notes and, at the same time, he told me that he was quite shocked at what he was hearing. He said this neglect was obviously a serious contributing factor to my present situation: having no help, no guidance, no instruction. As I spoke, he became more and more serious and concerned, until at the conclusion he said, 'There is no way that a magistrate could sentence you to confinement in a juvenile prison, since what I have heard is quite shocking; you need help. And you certainly didn't receive it. I will make all this very clear in my report. There can be no way that the magistrate can ignore this!'

'But,' I said, 'supposing he reads the report out in court – in front of my father?'

'No,' he replied, 'by law, the report is confidential and is for the magistrate's eyes only. He is not allowed to reveal reports that are given in confidence.'

I thought, '*This is my first offence, so everybody says, so it's most unlikely that I'll get anything more than probation.*'

The two weeks on remand passed uneventfully, and the day came for my case to be heard at the Juvenile Court in Aldgate. I was driven to the court by a policeman and sat in a secure side room. Eventually, my father walked in and exchanged no words with me except to say, 'Those pants I gave you. The customer now has come in for them, so I've got a pair of your old pants. So take them off.' Those were the last words he said to me that day. I took off my smart black barathea trousers and put on my old ones and gave them back to him. He said nothing, but what he did do was to examine them closely in case I'd polluted them.

We were then called into the court. I was asked to stand up. The magistrate was a man called Sir Basil Henriques, a highly respected figure in the Jewish establishment. He rambled on about my offence and that I had been remanded in Stamford House and the report was not very encouraging and then he read out a very negative comment from my charming headmaster, Mr Baulk, at my last, horrific school that had virtually corroded any future I might have had.

Then, to my utter shock, the contemptible dog started reading out the confidential psychiatrist report! How I had complained that I was denied any care from my father, etc., etc., etc. – and all this said in front of my dad sitting there! My father was as shocked as I was and stood up immediately to refute all these allegations but was swiftly shut up by this monster, Basil Henriques. My father was not allowed any response, not even a single sentence, and he was asked to sit down. The hearing was totally disgusting, and I felt totally betrayed by the magistrate, who certainly had no right to expose me so brutally in public. Those words were meant to guide him and were for his eyes only so that he should have a deeper understanding of the delinquent before him.

Then he added that he had decided to have me incarcerated in the latest young person's prison called a detention centre for three months – end of case.

CHAPTER 5

Kidlington Detention Centre for Juveniles

I was going to one of the harshest juvenile prisons that were being tried out for the first time. Called a 'short sharp shock' by the press, it was very much run in military style and was intended to shock juvenile delinquents into avoiding any future career in crime. In fact, the regime was so brutal that many 'guests' either maimed themselves or killed themselves, and eventually the authorities closed it down.

I was put with my policeman in a cab to Paddington and then on a train to Kidlington near Oxford. We then had to wait for the local line train to Kidlington, so we went to the café on the platform, and I had a sandwich and a coffee. The detective and I had a nice chat, and he asked me if I'd had enough to eat. I was still starving but didn't feel bold enough to request a second sandwich.Eventually, we arrived in Kidlington and took the five-minute walk to the detention centre. We were escorted to a room where a man was sitting behind a desk. He looked at me and asked my name. When I answered, he screamed, 'You say 'Sir' at the end of the sentence.' He shouted it like a raving maniac – so loud that I simply turned to my friendly detective as if he could rescue me from this madman. 'You are to answer 'Sir' from now on – you understand? 'Sir'!' he screamed again. The detective did give me an understanding look but then left the room.

I was instructed to change my clothes and follow an orderly to the changing room. Then I put all my belongings into a wire basket and donned my grey prison uniform, but just before this I was instructed to get into a lukewarm bath. After drying off and changing, I joined a line-up where we were instructed to run at double-time to the canteen. Four of us sat at a table after collecting our lunch and tea. We gathered that we were the most recent arrivals, noticing that there was little chatter at the other tables. As we started getting to know each other and exchanging our recent experiences, we found our stories so funny and the prison staff so ridiculous that we started giggling and couldn't really stop. I mean, there was no law against that.

Eventually, we finished our scrappy lunch, from time to time still breaking into hysterical laughter. I hadn't laughed like that for a long time; maybe it was also in relief that the worst was over, when in fact it had hardly begun. After a while, one of the prison wardens came to our table and said, 'Go on, enjoy yourself while you can; you won't be laughing by next week.' We sat and listened quietly to his admonition, and I was grateful that mind-reading hadn't yet been discovered, even in a juvenile detention centre, or he might have read something along the lines of: *You slimy shit cunt. We'll be laughing long after we leave this pigsty while you stinking piece of shit will still rot* and other such pithy thoughts.

For the first week, all newcomers spent the time in a small cell so as to acclimatise ourselves to this new way of life. So I found myself in my own cell, which was narrow yet not uncomfortable – and swiftly got used to it. The only flaw was that they didn't have room service – oh well, you can't have everything! I slept well that night, after running over and over the series of events that had brought me here. I really felt a lot of anguish for the nice lady I had been planning to meet that night; she would probably think I was such an indecent slob not to turn up. I mean, she couldn't have known of my situation; I preferred it if no one knew. I felt that it was a rather petty, juvenile crime to get sent away for. I just hoped that my few colleagues on Stamford Hill wouldn't get wind of it. I'd rather have been done for stealing a car or breaking and entering. I knew these were such pathetic, unworthy thoughts, but I had, as yet, absolutely nothing to be proud of – nothing. If I was going to be incarcerated, let it at least be for something to be proud of.

The next morning we were summoned by loud bells and then it was double-quick time to the communal showers. Then you'd sit for breakfast, which was totally unmemorable. I ate it very slowly since I was so hungry, having not eaten since last night's pathetic nibble, that I couldn't bear to see my empty plate. After breakfast, we all assembled in lines in the courtyard while we were assigned our tasks for the day. I hated that morning roll call; we could always hear the gurgling of the wastewater from the kitchen and the steam rising from the pipes while we just stood and waited.

I was assigned cleaning duties, first of all the toilets and then afterwards the dining room. At least half the boys were on outside labouring work, so I picked up my bucket and brushes and got to work. Another boy and I had about four hours to clean all the toilets and then sweep and polish the dining room, before we broke for a fairly forgettable lunch. It usually consisted of a paper-thin, scrawny slice of beef and a couple of cold potatoes. I was so very hungry after that pathetic meal that I made a deal with one of the lads on my table – once a week we could apparently purchase a chocolate bar, and so I offered half of my teatime sandwich for half of his next chocolate bar. It required incredible discipline, but I held the vision in my head of the glorious treat I had to look forward to. For the first week this worked quite well.

The day was broken up into work, break, and then we all had to report for the gym session; this was given by a slimy, toadlike creature called Mr Lees. I would never forget his reptilian face. Over in the gym, he made us do endless repetitions of squats holding large lumps of wood in front of us, and he would have us do them in dozens until we could hardly stand up. His favourite was with a small log which we held in both hands and ran around the room with our arms outstretched. Most of us collapsed after two or three minutes. The fear he instilled in us through his screaming made all of us dread the worst. Then he'd say, 'Stop!' We'd rest for one minute, and then he'd start again. He actually didn't hit the kids, but we were so weakened by the end of the session we just collapsed. After that, we went in for dinner – now I realised why all the other boys had been so quiet on our first day!

After supper, we were summoned into a large room. Our duty was to listen to the radio – particularly to the news at 6 p.m., after which the radio was turned off and each one of us would be questioned on what we'd just heard. We had to pick any segment and relate what was said. Of course, after the first few people desperately struggled to recall some scraps of the main events, there was less and less to remember. The anxiety on the faces of the remaining speakers was palpable, since if you couldn't think or remember anything, you'd be publicly humiliated. I learnt how to snatch a piece of news from the beginning and hope nobody else would use it. This was torture of a mental kind – unlike the physical kind in the gym.

I was now steadily getting used to the place and, having done my first week in my solitary cell, I was placed in the dormitory with the other 'criminals' and even began to bond with some of the lads.

After a few days in the gym with the insane Mr Lees, I happened to notice a swelling in the right side of my groin and just days later another swelling appeared on the left side. I reported this to the nurse who was in charge of any medical emergencies, and she concluded that I had a double hernia, so I was immediately taken off PT (physical training). What a blessed relief. They permanently assigned me to cleaning duties – mostly the dining room, which also required a fair amount of pushing tables and lifting, but this time I had a colleague to help me with the heavier work, so slowly my double hernia healed itself.

Other boys were not so lucky and as the weather dropped in temperature and was quite rapidly reduced to freezing, the outside work of building and digging became quite unbearable. One of the ways of getting out of it was to maim yourself by bravely smashing a brick to break a finger. I had to admire their courage and did at least feel grateful to my hernias, which got me off those murderous tasks; however, my cleaning duties were quite onerous, and I was always starving. My eating/swapping deal with another inmate had gone a little sour since it had started taking longer and longer to receive my extra bar of chocolate after I had painfully sacrificed my half-sandwich.

One day I encountered the filthy little runt in a passageway off the main area. The only way to deal with these wretched cheats was to indicate that some violence might come their way if they reneged on the deal. Well, as it happens, a nasty little warden overheard my 'threats' and gleefully pounced – it occurred to me that the wimp, fearing some response from me, had whined to one of the staff. Although that boy was a scheming little rat who didn't keep his word, the warden who 'suddenly' appeared seemed almost gratified by what he had observed, as he said, 'Ah! We have our first sweets baron!' – a juvenile version of a 'tobacco baron' in adult prisons. I was immediately whisked off before the head warden and given my punishment – one week in solitary confinement in the punishment block. This was carried out instantly and I was frogmarched to the single cells where the offenders did their time and was told, 'Just get in.' The door slammed behind me and locked. There was only a single bed in the room and a sink. Some time passed and I just sat there pondering my new future.

Hours later, the door swung open and a guard with an armful of rusty pans carried them over to the sink and told me to clean them thoroughly and handed me cleaning tools like metal wire brushes. Then he slammed the door and left me. I could only see through the one window; my room was already dark. I badly needed a piss, so I rang the bell for room service. Nobody came, so I just pissed in the sink. Sometime later, the door was opened and a tray with my supper was slid in. I was relieved that at least they acknowledged that I was still alive. The supper was miserable and nearly cold, but I ate it slowly. Later I placed my tray on the floor, where it would be collected when the door opened.

As the hours crawled by, there was simply nothing for me to do except scrape away at the rusty pots and pans. After about an hour or two of that, I got fed up with it and sat on my bed. All I could do was run through my recent life, analysing every event. I thought about my mother and what she must be thinking right now – and there was no doubt whatsoever in my mind that she was continuously thinking of me. I stood for a while and looked through the single window and, in the far distance, I could see the beams of the headlights of cars as they slowly moved. I watched them for a while. I wondered about them, wondered where they were going, what kind of life their drivers were living. I envied those drivers their ability to be able to stop, go to a shop, and buy a chocolate bar. Then I went to bed.

I barely slept and couldn't wait for the night to pass. It seemed to take forever, although I must've gotten some sleep because I was abruptly woken by my door crashing open and intense shouting: 'Get up! Get up!' I swung up and grabbed my pullover; I'd slept with my trousers on since it was so cold. 'No need for that! Get your trousers off! Everything, off! Come on, move it!' I peeled my underwear off; I was completely naked. 'Alright, double time!' I began my run, just ahead of the guard, who gave me instructions: 'Keep moving, turn right, turn left at the end of the corridor, don't stop! Turn left! Enter that room!' It was a bleak shower room. 'Right, now get in.'

I stepped into a shower cubicle. I was already shivering and he turned the showers on at full blast from the outside. Icy water rained down on me like razor shards; I howled with shock and jumped up and down just to seek some relief. I had almost fainted with the initial shock and now the strangest thing in the world happened to me – I started not to feel the cold anymore. The paradox was that it started getting warmer; my body was fighting back against the cold.

After a few minutes, he turned the tap off and then threw me a towel. I was beginning to heat up. I could not believe what was happening to me. Their stupid punishment was not working. I swiftly rubbed myself down and was told to double-time back to my cell, still naked in that freezing-cold prison, yet I felt perfectly warm! I got back to my cell, my breakfast was shoved in, I dressed. I could not get over how my body had protected me from that loathsome and sadistic act. I noticed more pans had been shoved into my sink to work on, so I'd better get on with it. I thought I'd just do it until lunch. I was afraid that if I didn't show any effort, they'd extend my stay. Nobody knew I was here – they could keep me as long as they wished. I just spent the whole morning scraping, scraping, scraping; thinking, thinking, thinking…

I'd heard in one of the rare letters from Beryl that Ma had gone to hospital for an operation on a burst appendix, so I didn't hear from her for a couple of weeks. I don't remember hearing from my sister more than once; maybe she was upset over Ma and probably blamed me for giving her so much anxiety that it nearly killed her, but after a couple of weeks I did hear from Ma again. The operation seemed to have been successful.

The days passed painfully slowly, and I waited until after supper, when I could again stare out of the windows and watch the car lights going past. The road couldn't have been more than a mile away, and again I tried to imagine the occupants. I would dream of the time when they'd let me out, when I could go into a shop and buy a bar of chocolate. Oh, what a paradise just to be free! I'd watch the car lights for an hour or so and then go to bed.

When I couldn't sleep, I thought of all those boys who had stayed on at Hackney Downs Grammar School, who had even been accepted for university. I could imagine them lying in the grass on a summer's day, chewing the ends of casually-picked stalks as they read poetry, having had Mr Brierly, the English teacher, interpret the poetry of Wordsworth, Longfellow, or Keats for them, while I was stuck scraping the rust off old pots. I thought of the uselessness of this dumb building with its stupid and sadistic punishments.

I was getting used to the freezing shower treatment and even the mindless, pointless scraping of the rust from the pots and pans. I had just decided to work on one small end of the metal tray and to work on that end until I had scraped it entirely clean, so I gave myself some motivation, and then lunch would come and I'd take forever to consume it. Then I'd work on the other end of the tray, and if I could clean that then, I'd have a nap and hopefully I'd fall asleep until supper time, but it was getting colder at night and the night was falling much faster, and I'd just stare at the passing cars again and fantasise about the people inside them.

No one in my family had visited me in the two months since my incarceration, but one afternoon and without any warning, the door of my cell opened and one of the wardens informed me that I had a visitor. Usually they screamed orders at you, but this time he spoke quite civilly. Who on earth could it be? My mother was obviously too ill to come, and it was unlikely to be my sister, since she lived too far away.

So I visited a small visitors' room. At the back stood a guard but sitting at the table was none other than my dad! I was gobsmacked. He stood up and just said, 'Hello, son.' I just stared. I had lost the power of speech. He had a bag of sweets in his hand and tried to pass them over to me, but as he did, the guard stepped between us and forbade him. I don't think the guard liked doing it and even said something like, 'Sorry, but it's the rules here.' Dad withdrew his gift and sat down again. He may have asked, 'How are you feeling, son?', but I still couldn't find my voice. I just stared at him; I couldn't believe he had come to see me.

Then I found my voice: it was a howl – a howl – and I just wept as I had never done before. I wept and wept and howled, and I could not stop. They both watched and looked helpless as I continued howling and crying as if there was nothing else in the world that I could say. The grief was insurmountable; it was as if I had a bucket of grief inside me that was desperate to escape.

After several minutes, Dad took off his trilby hat and playfully cuffed me with it, just a playful tap as if to say, 'Come on, son, I've come all this way. I love you, son, I do.' Perhaps he didn't say these exact words, but I think, maybe, he did. He couldn't help but love me once he saw me – but I couldn't stop howling. I don't know how long he stayed; it was as if I was in a storm. I had no idea what I could do to stop. I was incapable of stopping.

I was howling for all the filthy and barbaric offences that had been done to me. I was howling them out. Yes, I had done wrong, so I deserved whatever was hurled at me, but was it all necessary? Was it necessary to have me dumped in a C class in that wretched school? Was it necessary for that headmaster to defile me in the court? Was it necessary for that pompous Henriques to read out, in a contemptuous manner and in front of my dad, my private, heartfelt confession which I had so easily been able to tell a man who treated me with kindness in the remand home? Was it all necessary?

I simply had too much grief in me to stop; it had to come out. I roared, I cried, I howled, but I could not stop. Grief had taken me by the shoulders and shaken the life out of me. What a weak person I was, so pathetic. Eventually the guard decided that it was pointless to stay for the appointed time and just watch me blubber, so Dad left and I was marched back to my cell, but I did feel an enormous sense of relief. I felt emptied out. I even felt sorry for my dad; he had come all the way for nothing. But I was glad he had come and, in some way, I loved him, loved him unbearably. I always thought he was so clever, so brilliant at mathematics; he could do my maths homework so easily; he could make a whole suit from a roll of cloth. What could I do? I could do nothing.

When I returned to my cell, I felt such relief. I had unburdened myself in a way to my father like I had never done before. My tears were not just tears of self-pity – they were tears of my great love that I had suddenly found for my dad but could never express to him, and they were tears for how much I needed a dad.

A dad is a young man's solace and protector. A dad is someone you need to be proud of. Your dad is your god; your mum is your warmth and sustenance in your home, but it is your dad who created you, who fertilised the egg inside your mum and gave it its imprint – perhaps its soul. A dad does that and, as you grow up, you look to him for help, for instruction, for pride if you have done well, for love, for a trip together to the pool, just once, please, Dad, I need you, need you to acknowledge that you are the light by which I see. Just tell me good words and I'll obey them – like the time when I told you I'd sold a fellow schoolboy half my sandwich for lunch, which Mum made me each day. I told you how proud I was that I got a shilling for it, and you said, 'No, that was wrong, if he was hungry, you should have given it to him,' and so I listened, I obeyed, I learnt from you. For you were my god and I was so glad to learn from you. I needed you so much, but you weren't always there for me and when you were it was to chastise me for reasons I could never understand. But I was always there for you.

Like that time when you and your partner opened that small tailor shop in Aldgate at the beginning of Leman Street, you never even once suggested that I come down and take a look; it didn't occur to you. But that didn't matter. I took the bus all the way to Aldgate and took a look and was so pleased to see my dad's name above the shop window – what a sight, I even swelled with pride. But then I noticed something in the lettering painted on the window. It said 'mensware', but of course I knew that it had to be 'menswear'! I had to tell you and straight away leaped onto the bus to Manor House and raced home with my news.

Oh God, I was so proud when I told you. I told you that the spelling was wrong, since I was such a good speller at school, and I felt I had made a valuable contribution to your new enterprise. Did it ever occur to you that a twelve-year-old boy would go all the way, alone and, most of all, uninvited, to just look at what his father had made? You seemed quite pleased that I had gone to all that trouble and noticed it, but I thought you would be even more amazed that I had gone there uninvited. But it didn't matter to me; that's how it was.

You did invite me, just once, after I had begged for years for a suit, a proper suit. I was growing into manhood and had long grown out of those beautiful suits that my cousin Morris had bought for me in Nyack, so you said, 'OK, come on down.' And I did and it was you who suggested I try on that *schwarzer* suit with the wide knees and fingertip sleeves on the royal-blue jacket, and when I came out of the changing room, I must have looked like a clown, but I needed a suit so badly. All the other kids in Stamford Hill had smart suits made for them by proud parents, while I was still going round in 'bum freezers'. I did feel a tad ashamed. So, even if I looked ridiculous, I was determined to have it.

So you put it in a bag and threw – actually threw – it at me and said, 'Go on, fuck off.' You said that in front of your partner, Morry Bodinetz, 'Fuck off,' but I accepted the chastisement because that's how you often spoke to me – except for the time when I told you about the misspelling. So that was the only time I visited your special citadel, and after that I wore my royal-blue *schwarzer* suit. The boys looked at me quizzically, but I paid no attention.

I cried for you, Dad. For neglecting me but also to show you how very much I loved you and needed your love and love you to this day and would have done anything in this world for you.

***

On Christmas Day, I was still in my solitary cell, but it was decided that I would be released for Christmas lunch with the rest of the inmates. It felt strange mixing with my fellow inmates once more, but the food was just a mass of dull cakes and biscuits, supposedly for our Christmas treat. After the dreary lunch, everybody went back to work and I returned to my cell, but I couldn't be bothered to do any more scraping, so I just sat and waited for supper, when I hoped I would be released again.

For a while I lost track of the time. I forgot how many days had passed – four, five, or six? – but I thought it must end soon. This part of the detention centre was mainly quiet, but the previous evening another boy had been sent down there. I heard him speaking, shouting. The guard escorting him was the one with the fat, piggy face and bulging eyes. He was telling the prisoner to take his work boots off, but the young man was one of the older, tougher inmates and was shouting, 'No, I won't take my fucking boots off!' I admired him so much.

Then one day, my time in the detention centre was all over. I was told that I was leaving solitary the next day and to get ready to go to the changing room and recover my street clothes. Oh, I was jubilant. I walked this time, not on the double, and got rid of my foul detention centre uniform. I took my clothes out of the basket, and they felt soft and comfortable. Then I was sent back to my cell to wait for my departure time, which had to fit in with the train times. I waited and waited but no news. I started to have very bleak thoughts. *'Maybe they could keep me here? Did they change their minds?'* Hours passed – something was up. I was just waiting and there was no news. There was one boy whom I had made friends with, and we had decided to meet once we were both free of this wretched prison camp, but now I had regrets. *'It's better that I don't meet up with anybody from this place. I have to prove myself.'* I started to pray; I prayed that I would contact no one. I swore to it.

As if in reward, eventually I heard some steps coming my way and one of the distinctly ugly guards stood there. He had one of those faces that looked permanently scorched. He just said, 'Get ready.' I followed him out and we walked to the train station. He offered not a single word, just walked. Not even a good luck, nothing, just a dull, sorry face that had not an ounce of humanity in it. He gave me my ticket. I barely mumbled, 'Thank you' and waited for my train to Paddington. The head warden left a message for me: my father would meet me at Paddington, at the top of the escalator. I got on the train. It was almost full, but I had a reserved seat, and everything felt so light and easy; people were reading newspapers, others were chatting. It all seemed so natural, even joyful.

Then we arrived at Paddington. I didn't have much to carry: a spare sweater and a few letters which filled a small bag. I got on the escalator. I was going to meet my father, but now I felt that all the cells in my body had closed. I had closed. I had shut down; I don't know why. I'd gone through such a metamorphosis. I was numb. I got to the top of the escalator and looked for him as I turned in my ticket. He wasn't there. In some ways I was relieved. I don't know why I didn't choose to wait, not even for one minute. I looked for the tube line that would take me to King's Cross, then I'd get on the Piccadilly line to Manor House. Once in the tube, everything appeared more normal, even ordinary.

I took the short walk from Manor House to our fourth-floor council flat; I still had my house key. I got into the lift, pressed the button for the fourth floor. Everything seemed grubbier and dreary. I walked along the walkway to our flat and opened the door. The flat was cold and felt dead. Ma had not been here for nearly a month. I went into the bathroom – it was dirty and neglected. I took off my coat and jacket and started giving it a thorough clean; after all, this is what I had been doing for over three months.

Then Dad came in. He asked me why I hadn't waited. I said, 'I did wait – I thought I'd missed you.' He didn't say much, didn't even ask if I wanted to go to eat something. I guess he was cross with me for not waiting when he had gone all that way. Then he said he had to go. I carried on cleaning.

21 years old, about to embark on an acting career...

PART 2

CHAPTER 6

Metamorphosis

The tom-toms beat in Stamford Hill whenever opportunities arose or something was in the wind. Throughout Europe, North Africa, and Iceland, there were multitudes of jobs for young, unmarried men on American army bases. Gosh, what an opportunity to see the world by being a salesman on the army base in their gigantic Post Exchange (PX) stores. They were set up mainly to alleviate Yankee homesickness, and the larger menswear retailers in London were invited to open concessions. The bases were spread out across Europe like a giant octopus with tentacles reaching into the remotest outlying areas of the nations.

This information certainly beat some drums for me, to be able to escape from this fetid, drab life, and perhaps find some adventure. By now, I was an experienced menswear salesman, which was maybe half a step higher than being the local milkman. I had discovered a juvenile labour exchange at the end of Oxford Street, and from there I was sent to apply for a job as a junior salesman in a menswear shop in Upper Regent Street called Harry Fisher. He was a renowned shirt maker and had a small shop just a few doors before the Regent Street Polytechnic. Upon meeting him, I felt a definite sense that we had a bond between us. He appeared to like me and offered me the job almost immediately.

At last, my day-to-day life was not as unpleasant as it had been; I stayed there for several months, and I really had such a strong sense of empathy with Harry Fisher. The only fly in the ointment was the young manager of the shop, who was a distinct pain in the arse.

Whenever a young lady who was even vaguely attractive was being served by me, the big oaf would lean over me and start interfering with my sales pitch. Eventually, I could stand it no more and so, with great regret, I had to tearfully say farewell to Harry Fisher. I was bouncing from one job to the next and knew that at this rate I would lose my mind. I worked in an East End warehouse lugging around rolls of cloth, learning to identify fabrics and colours like Eau-de-Nil (pale green, like the waters of the Nile!). I lasted less than a week in a button shop on Commercial Road. I managed a couple of months at a Smart Weston menswear shop in Shaftesbury Avenue, where I hated the cheap clothing but honed my skills as an obsequious salesman.

I was accepted as a menswear salesman at Burberry and was sent for two weeks' training at the Ruislip branch, since that exclusive fashion house was running branches all over Europe. This seemed to me to be a bit of a scam, as the only element of Burberry true to the slogan 'the suits that were made to order' was the label! These suits were probably knocked up in some sweat shop in Leeds and sent back to the PX store, and each store had a local tailor standing by to then do the necessary alterations. But Burberry sounded nice and English to our American cousins.

I was now 18, travelling to Ruislip on the tube every day while still living at Manor House for my training period with some insufferably drab people, but I knew this was a step I must not jeopardise. When I first entered the store, a gigantic hangar, I had quite a shock when I took a deep breath and experienced a narcotic whiff of America. I loved it – that syrupy, synthetic, deodorised, pungent smell that was so familiar from my aborted trip all of eight years ago. I smelled it. It was back and, best of all, I could use their canteen for lunch – real Yankee burgers, hot dogs, tuna melts… *Oh heaven, I am back in the Bronx with Uncle Joe.*

The two weeks sped by and I learnt that I would be travelling by train to Wiesbaden in Germany via a ferry boat to Calais on the following Sunday. It felt like a dream. I was now in a constant state of excitement, anticipation, fascination, and, most of all, curiosity. I started keeping a journal, since it was far too much to take in without being able to blurt it out at some future date when I was old and crusty. I was fascinated by the stations we stopped at and the availability of hot bratwurst on the platforms ready to be served with mustard and brought straight to your window. Then the harsh German guards' voices: 'Passport, bitte!' That sound, I have to admit, did give me quite a strange sensation, like a shiver down my spine.

At last, we arrived in Wiesbaden – a large station built in the old, epic Prussian style. I had only to cross the road to find my hotel and meet my host, a Mr Collins. He didn't seem more than 23 or 24 himself. After a brief natter and a snack he gave me my schedule for the next day. I went to my bedroom, which was really strange: there were no blankets on the bed, just a large duvet and a stone water bottle, something I'd never seen before and all so foreign, so beautifully European. In the morning just after breakfast, I very gingerly explored the area and walked round the block. It was November and the snow had fallen heavily that night. Everything felt foreign and exciting. I felt it in every fibre of my body. It was a new world in every sense of the word.

Collins drove me to where I would be based: a very simple little town called Bitburg in Eifel, famous for its Bitburger beer. It was a long, pleasant drive through Germany, stopping over for the night in Luxembourg. I seem to remember that it was the time of year in Germany called *Fasching*, when the natives let their hair down and celebrate through elaborate costumes, drunken merriment, and probably some sexual freedom on the way, which would certainly have appealed to Collins.

He took me to a local bar where we sat down and within a few minutes, we were joined by two 'working' ladies who invited us to drink with them. They seemed to be more fascinated with him as he appeared to be the guv'nor. Within minutes, his lady had her hands down his crotch, and I was desperately hoping that I would also be accorded the same attention, but no such luck!

The next day, we arrived in the small, drab town of Bitburg. I was shown into the lodgings which would be my home for the next month. If I was writing or doing a thesis on German post-war life in the provinces, I could not have a chosen better place. I had a pleasant room, and my homely landlady cooked me a simple hot dinner German-style every evening and a very adequate breakfast. I was picked up and taken to meet my two cohorts in the huge PX store which contained our little Burberry concession and we got on OK. They were pleasant Jewish Londoners and seemed quite familiar with the *schmutter* business.

At long last, I was sliding onto the right path. I was learning German and each night I half-used sign language with my landlord but was picking up the jargon. Sometimes I went to a bar with my two colleagues, and we were joined by some friendly soldiers they had chummed up with, and the daily work was undemanding, so I could skive off to 'America' when I went to the canteen.

Now, as it happens, stirrings were taking place inside my head; connections were being made. The base had a very good library full of fascinating American authors, and I never failed to find a good book. I never suffered from a tinge of the same guilt as I had in that wretched school in Hackney – when, having been placed in a C group, I became desperate to educate myself by taking out books which were totally unsuitable.

In 1956, I discovered *Metamorphosis* while in the American forces' library in Bitburg. It was just by chance that, in scrutinising the shelves, I came across the strangest name: Kafka. I pulled the book out and began reading the first pages: 'As Gregor Samsa awoke one morning from uneasy dreams, he found himself transformed in his bed into a gigantic insect.' What on earth was this? I was compelled to read the whole story in the library and was utterly mesmerised, and the story even struck some bells in my head. I'd never had such a feeling of compassion as I did then for poor Gregor Samsa, the man/beetle who worked daily as a pathetic salesman, getting up early each morning to catch the train. Gradually, and likely out of sheer frustration, he turns into what he has metaphorically been all those years. Of course, the ghastliness of my own life those last few years had been a sombre reflection of his. How lucky I was. Soon after, I would be able to fulfil part of my destiny by cursing out a Nazi slob one afternoon in Bitburg.

It happened in the canteen. I had been friendly with a very charming sales lady called Hannelore and, although we had only talked together a handful of times, we were slowly growing quite fond of each other. As I was crossing the room, she just happened to cross my path, so naturally we stopped for a couple of moments to fondly chatter. As we were talking, the PX store supervisor, a short, ugly, brutish swine, approached us and began shouting at her for leaving her work post. Although it is easy to call anyone, we loathe a Nazi, this man fully earned the epithet. I turned on him in my utter shock and spat back some of the same venom that he had spewed at us. He just stared at me and, while hardly comprehending a single word I said, he certainly must have felt the deep hatred coming his way and walked off.

After my various adventures in Bitburg, I was transferred to Wiesbaden, a much nicer German town a short train ride from Frankfurt. Wiesbaden was such a wonderful contrast to the dreary town of Bitburg. It is a very beautiful ancient town with a great park running right through its centre at the end of which is a large theatre and a splendidly ornate *Spielhaus* (gambling casino) where Dostoyevsky used to dribble away his money. I found a small and cosy hotel with a most pleasant dining room downstairs and took an agreeable walk up to the base, where I met my two new colleagues. They were most congenial and showed me round the town on the first night. So far so good.

I had been in Germany for two months and was scrupulously saving my Deutschmarks. So, no matter how difficult it was at times, mainly dealing with my abject loneliness, I knew that my savings would more than make up for it. My work was undemanding and pleasant, and I once again had my familiar taste of America in the canteen. But when I ate out in town, I formed a great passion for oxtail soup in particular and *Johannisbeersaft* – a most delicious fruit juice extracted from berries. I bought myself a tortoiseshell cigarette lighter and felt most elegant.

At last, I was living in a cultured city and my activities were varied if modest. On one or two evenings, I would stroll round to the elegant *Spielhaus*, which fascinated me and was always exciting, even just to sit in. Of course, I was never going to jeopardise my hard-earned savings, so my gambling was incredibly modest. The room was quite magnificent. Very baroque, and giant candelabras hung glittering from the ceiling. When I entered this building, I always had this trembling sense of anticipation. I left my coat in the cloakroom with a porter, a rather urbane and terribly charming man in his early forties who spoke perfect English. His name was Fritz Piel. He always had a twinkle in his eye. He was eventually to become my closest friend in Wiesbaden and would become a large influence in my life within a couple of years.

I had carefully worked out a simple, if crude, system for the roulette wheels: it seemed to me by constant watching that, although red and black numbers were even bets, they did come up at most irregular times. A red may come up two, three, or even four times, very seldom five, and hardly ever six off the trot. It might be reasonably safe if you put DM5 on a red, and a black came up so then you'd double it to 10, black came up again, then 20, then 40, and even to 80 (holding your nerve), so by doubling, you spent to the max, DM155, just to secure your original bet. But if it did come up five times, it would be too risky and reckless to double any further; better to be patient and start all over again. To give yourself some insurance you waited for the red or black to come up three times, which may take a little patience sitting in your seat, and then began betting, and usually your colour would come up on the fourth or the fifth, or certainly the sixth, but you would have only been betting three times.

So this is what I did two or three times a week for the next month. Nearly always winning just modest amounts, maybe DM20 or DM30, and then leaving. But it was consistent, even if I had to wait fifteen or twenty minutes sitting quietly with my tiny pile of chips. It passed the time amiably and you could smoke at the table in those days, and sometimes I would summon the waiter for cigarettes. He would swiftly bring them over to me on a silver tray, open the packet for me, and tap a few cigarettes to bring them forward, enough for me to choose one to withdraw. Oh, so elegant. And then afterwards, I'd enjoy a pleasant stroll along Wilhelmstrasse to my seedy but charming old-fashioned hotel, maybe having supplemented my wages by at least £20 to £30.

Life was very pleasant, but a little female company wouldn't go amiss. And I did notice that there was a tea dance café along Wilhelmstrasse where I would see couples dancing or just sitting at small tables having a relaxing afternoon schnapps. How very civilised and so very elegant compared to the dance hall life I was used to in Britain. And so, plucking up just a filament of courage and wearing a smart suit and tie, I entered.

I immediately absorbed the atmosphere and then life opened up. My first dance café in Germany. I took a deep breath and smelled civilisation – yes, the sweet odour of civilisation – and for a while I just watched the comings and goings of bodies moving and smiling to the low buzz of the German language. Then I saw a very attractive lady, with her black hair pulled back tightly over her forehead and a very compelling expression. She had quite intense dark-brown eyes that, when they fixed you with a stare, made you feel quite special. She was sitting alone.

The music began and I strode over: 'Dance, bitte?' She stood up, and I slowly and rather carefully wrapped my arms around this attractive woman. Now I had a desirable lady in my arms, I had the spirit of Germany in my arms and the smell of an exotic woman in my nose. We spoke easily and fluently since her English was perfect, and we seemed most extraordinarily at ease with each other. Then we sat together, ordered coffee, and continued talking. She was married to a high-up in the American forces but loved to go tea dancing occasionally in the afternoon. Her name was Faye Wasserson. Excelsior! Suddenly I felt uplifted, transported, euphoric. How things came together! What could be better – here I was, 18 and a half, living on the European continent, a singleton staying at this charming but seedy hotel, earning a good wage, playing the casino tables two or three nights a week, and dancing with a beautiful woman in a German dance café.

How luck favours the bold. I was happy. Faye took me out a few times in her large American car. Once, she took me to a nightclub for supper, and I'd never been anywhere so exotic in my life: we were entertained by conjurers, jugglers, acrobats, trapeze artists. This was so exciting, seeing a life that I had never before witnessed and just to think that three years ago I had been scraping down rusty tins, in my cell, in my squalid Oxford jail. Could life ever change so radically? Faye was my life, my friend, my lover, and never was love so sweet. The back seat of her car was perfectly comfortable as I straddled the darling of my life. Yes, she was the love of my life. Never had I felt so deeply for any woman, not since I was a ten-year-old in Luton and so besotted with Shirley. I remember meeting Faye that day so clearly.

Something about Wiesbaden was slowly eating into me. I was

being absorbed by that strangely mystical town and I was becoming an *ersatz* German. I kept on seeing my beloved Faye and she always had somewhere fascinating to take me, either to dance or to eat. And all I had to do was fill in my time between my work and seeing her.

However, life cannot simply revolve like a record on a turntable going round and round, no matter how perfect; something has to break and so one day it did. A message came through to the PX store that our jobs were being terminated that very week. No reason was given, just a one-week notice. It didn't bother me in the least; I had fulfilled myself over the last three exciting and stimulating months, and was even speaking some conversational German, but I was getting sick to death of working at phoney Burberry. True, I would miss Faye, but there would always be another day!

On the day before our departure, I decided to have one last evening at the *Spielhaus*, just one more spin at the wheel. However, I was getting just a little bit reckless, tired of waiting for three reds or three blacks to come up before cautiously placing my tiny bet. So I took a little risk, just a small risk. I waited for just two throws and then backed the opposite on the third. However, you must stick to your system or your method, simple as it is, or you will be risking your downfall. That night, growing rather impatient with waiting, I put my money on one colour that had come up only twice, so I lost. No big deal, as I said, a colour rarely comes up five or six times. So then I doubled my money and the other colour came up six consecutive times, and I was now betting DM180. I should stop. Stop! Stop! But no, it must come up, so I put on 360. Six times it had stayed on red. Around the table everyone's eyes now fastened themselves on me; the same colour had come up seven consecutive times, a rarity, maybe once in every thousand throws. I should not bet any more, but I did, and I lost.

There were a few sympathetic groans, and I was sick to my stomach. I had spent my entire savings from these last three months, and it broke me in half. I had about DM50 left. All that work, all those pitiful hours alone in Bitburg, all those days and nights being alone, but being compensated and able to endure it knowing I had saved more money than I had in my entire life, since every week I had religiously saved over half my salary. I got up from the table with the blood drained out of my face. I picked up my coat and said goodbye to Fritz, the elegant door manager. He saw my ashen expression and smiled sympathetically.

The cold, fresh air in the park soothed me a little. I needed something and there was a small pizza house just across the road. I bought a pizza for about DM3 and ravenously wolfed it down. The next day was the last, and for the first time I didn't go into work. I turned up in the afternoon claiming I had been ill. It didn't matter, nothing mattered anymore. I had worked for three months and gained nothing. Monetarily, that is; I had in fact gained much, but the shock of the previous evening had just overwhelmed everything.

Faye appeared quite phlegmatic about my going; it had been a sweet adventure and we would stay in touch, maybe I'd come to visit or get a job at another PX store. We went to our usual café dance in Wilhelmstrasse to pass our last hours together. We enjoyed the evening, then came the time to drive to the station.

My train was an overnight service to King's Cross via Calais. We made all sorts of plans and promises to each other; the car was facing the *Bahnhof*. We both sat silent for a moment. We hugged our farewells, and then in some dark place within me I realised how very much Faye had meant to me. Knowing she was there seemed to put everything in order inside my somewhat chaotic life. Just believing in her existence and that she cared for me made sense of time, complete sense, and now there would be a huge empty hole within me. The power of her being there kept my soul alive, gave my life purpose – something that I needed so badly. So suddenly I felt that hollowness, that emptiness, my insides seemed to collapse. I howled, howled for something I had never had before, I howled for this beautiful woman. I howled for my pathetic, pointless life, I howled for throwing away the best part of it, I howled like I had never howled before. I howled like a pathetic, weak creature.

Faye was calm and in control. She didn't cry – she just watched this terrible explosion taking place. Perhaps I realised that a major event was happening, that the excitement of living in a new country and the turbulence of all the emotions rushing through me were coming to an end and, especially, that I was parting from my beloved Faye, with whom I had shared the most emotionally intense experience I had ever had with a woman.

Eventually I settled. I stepped out of the car, took my case out of the boot, waved to her, and walked towards the station. The three other co-workers were already there and grinning at me like orangutans, and as soon as I entered the station, I felt as if a heavy curtain had just descended on what was now my past. We found good seats on the train and blathered away for a few minutes, then the others brought out a deck of playing cards and we played for the duration of the trip until we reached Calais, where we boarded the Channel ferry. From then, everything went dark. I no longer remember the ferry boat, I no longer remember those two guys, everything fades; my life had no meaning. I never saw those guys again.

I was back in Manor House. Ma seemed pleased, if somewhat surprised, to see me. Within a week I received my first letter from Faye, in reply to mine. Oh, a wonderful, expressive missive so full of love, wisdom, advice, longing – so special! I've kept her two letters – that's all she wrote. Her handwriting was elegant and I loved her for missing me so much. I think, for both of us, this was a magic event in our existences. I have kept those two letters for sixty-five years; suddenly I want to hear from her, badly. Is she still alive? In one she tells me how worried she has been at not hearing from me for a while. In another, a wonderful, expressive missive so full of love, wisdom, guidance, and longing – she reflects on our times together and gives me some advice I would treasure:

> *Your letter was beautiful, and I've read it over and over again … So many times I've relived all of our moments together all over again, it all seems so very long ago, almost as though in another life. If we should never be able to recapture them again, then I shall be content with what we have known together, and reveries shall suffice for the rest of my life … My faith in you is unshakeable so please don't shatter it.*
>
> *If the day had more than twenty-four hours, I would still spend them all thinking of you and hoping you are trying to accomplish something worthwhile as I want you to do … I sincerely feel that your going to dramatic school would be to your utmost advantage. I think fate has destined you for more than just an ordinary everyday means of existence. … The road may be hard and long, but I am sure you will conquer all obstacles and one day be a success.*

Back in London, my primary feeling was my overwhelming desire to return to Germany. That was a goal, an ambition, a focus in my life. It might seem strange that a young Jewish man should be so keen to spend time there only a decade after the Holocaust. I can only say that the love of exploring a new world totally overrode any feelings I had, although I was constantly aware of the bloodbath of German recent history that hung like a miasma in the air.

Now, there was another men's store in London with multiple branches doing virtually the same as Burberry, although they did not have such an illustrious name to hide under: it was a fairly modern, crappy store called Smart and Western situated in the middle of Oxford Street next to Oxford Circus underground. I had an interview and was engaged promptly and had great hopes of returning to some other PX store in Europe, where I could reconnect with my beloved, but after two or three dreary weeks in a painfully dull shop, I was offered a job in Iceland! I did most earnestly request somewhere in Europe, but they said there was not an opening at that moment and might not be for some months.

So I decided to take a chance on their lies, save some cash, and then if nothing better turned up, just go there myself. This time I had to train it to Leeds and then fly from there to Reykjavik. I was looking forward to it – at least I was moving, something was happening. I was on the plane to the mysterious island of Iceland. I watched the sky growing lighter the further north we flew.

At last, I arrived in that strange country late in the evening and it was as light as 4 p.m. in England. I went straight to the canteen and ordered my early-morning breakfast (although the clock said close to midnight) expecting at any moment to be greeted by my hosts. I remember wearing my smart Donegal Tweed suit that Dad had made me with cloth that I had bought, together with a sweater. My hair was cut short and I probably looked more like a Yankee soldier on leave than a dreary looking 'wet' from the UK. Since the dull, balding little man sitting alone in the canteen looked like the kind of death head this firm might employ, I walked over and introduced myself, and of course he never suspected that this young man, well dressed and fit looking and enjoying his breakfast, could actually be an applicant for the death house he managed. After our inauspicious meeting he drove me to the army base and arranged to pick me up in the morning, as I had to be registered with the city council.

My room was in a typical military hut, since it was on the base this time, and close to Reykjavik, and I shared facilities with another young salesman whom I met the following morning. Early that day, I was fully registered as working for this garbage tailoring organisation and the manager did make a little effort to show me around the pleasant little town of Reykjavik. I was then driven back to the PX store, which was a rather unassuming little rat hole, more of a makeshift prefabricated shed, where I made the acquaintance of the other creatures, who, for the most obvious reasons, had all been assigned to the worst PX store on the planet.

Now, curiously enough, I always had plenty to say to the customers, many of whom were really friendly, and the Americans have never been shy at holding back. And since I might have been a tad more cosmopolitan than the three other dullards, I was happy to chat about London life. They questioned me about theatres, plays, etc., and I found I swiftly made friends with all sorts of fascinating characters and was even asked to join them for dinner on more than one occasion, something that would have been totally impossible with the others, who couldn't even make themselves understood to the customers on account of their utterly incomprehensible provincial northern accents.

As before, in Germany, the weeks passed pleasantly enough, and I spent not one minute of my leisure time off with the chaps I was obliged to work with during the day, although they were not unfriendly. One day I was invited to have lunch with one of the customers who was occupying a more academic job on the base, as a teacher. He was informing me about life in the Southern States, which I found quite fascinating, and I hadn't noticed time slipping past; I should have been back. 'Don't worry,' he said, 'I'll ask my secretary to phone your manager and say you were "in conference" with me and shall arrive shortly.' I rushed back to the crummy little place occupied by Neanderthals and former members of the orangutans, who could barely put a word together, but the manager finally spewed that if I couldn't work the hours, I was employed for, then he would most regrettably consider giving me my notice.

Since my savings were beginning to grow steadily and my main objective was held in place and on a firm footing, I decided to knuckle down.

The weeks sludged past and since I spent little time with my co-workers, even on the weekend, I would simply pass time in the forces common room playing ping-pong and thinking about my beloved Faye. I now started to keep a diary with some enthusiasm and this certainly chewed the time up most pleasantly, especially as I was relying heavily on myself for company. However, on my Sunday off, the old academic was more than happy to spend time with me and showed me round Iceland, driving me in his little car. We watched two geysers erupting and he even spent a few minutes teaching me the rudiments of driving. None of my American associates were military men but worked more in administration or in medical departments or one of the hundred other departments that exist on a military base.

After a few weeks it came to my attention that PX workers were allowed not only to use the wonderful American canteen but also to purchase goods at the liquor store, namely a maximum of two bottles of spirits per week for a ridiculously low price. But this was for American staff only. This was to prevent black market racketeering, as Iceland had a terribly expensive economy. Everything except herrings had to be imported, so in an Icelandic liquor store in 1956 a bottle of whisky cost about US$60 at least, and we paid no more than about US$10 for a maximum of two bottles. Well, this made the cells in my brain leap somewhat. Since I was still in my young years and had not acquired an instinct for alcohol, I seldom drank. This could be, for my easily corruptible mind, a golden opportunity to top up my wages. And sure enough a taxi driver asked me if I would like to sell him a bottle or two, which I gladly agreed to do. And so each Friday his cab would cruise by most casually to pick me up and I would then deliver the two bottles for about US$50, thus netting a small profit of about US$40.

As it was in such small quantities, it didn't seem to be such a monstrous crime in the wider sphere of things; to my British eyes, it was just a mild misdemeanour. But to the Icelandic government it was a gross act of treason. Of course, if found out, this rather felonious act would cause our business to be shut down forthwith. Iceland had a precarious economy, so the government was totally paranoid, since actions of such turpitude on a grand scale could certainly make cracks in the economy. The communist opposition had been complaining for some time and wanted to be rid of the US influence there as soon as possible.

Well, as it happens, the cretins I had the misfortune to be working with had obviously been in cahoots for some time to be rid of me, this noxious outsider. I had been doing my work, however, conscientiously and especially getting on well with the customers, who at least behaved like human beings, compared to my colleagues. So they didn't have any reason to fire me and were at a loss at what they could do to expel a good worker for little reason except their ire. They must have sat around their cauldron wondering what poisonous thoughts they could put into the soup.

Now, as I mentioned before, I drew great satisfaction from venting my thoughts in a diary. I had begun this habit in Germany and, as I wrote as a daily routine, I had, apart from expressing my calumnious opinions of those wretched troglodytes, been bravo-ing myself in my secret jottings. And would you or anyone believe that the grim slob who had the joining room next to mine was actually reading my diaries! What a brazen thing to do! What a filthy, despicable act to go through my private journal while I was at work. What a low, scum-sucking pig!

The following day after one of my whisky drop-offs, the mangy little manager told me I was fired and a ticket for the plane out of Iceland was given to me. Various excuses were made, since it was too hard for them to admit that they had rifled through my diary. They told me just to fly to Leeds, the head office, and get my wages and hotel expenses. They did notice that I had been taking my liquor ration of two bottles per week and suspected I might have been selling them, which could even bring about the demise of their wretched little shit house of a store. To speak the truth, I was delighted. They asked me to deliver a letter to the head office in order to claim my expenses. I pocketed the letter, swiftly packed, and after a four-hour flight found myself back in Leeds (which used to be the tailoring centre of Great Britain) after two incredibly tedious months in Iceland.

The cab took me to a hotel which had, fortunately, been booked, and after supper I was thinking about what was in the wretched letter that had been sealed with Scotch tape but, would you believe it, only at one end! Oh, cretin upon cretin! I noticed that the hotel had a tea-making kit, so I boiled water in the kettle and steamed open the other end of the letter which the idiots had not thought of sealing. The flap came away easily, and I eagerly prised out the wretched contents.

What I read shocked me to the core. Not only did they say that they had read my diaries, where I had confessed to making a 'few cool bucks', which would without question, if caught, not just endanger the rat house they called a shop but could even jeopardise the entire US base and thus undermine the Icelandic economy etc., *blah, blah, blah,* but they also said that I seemed to be, by my writings, seriously unbalanced, and since my room partner was sleeping in the other half of the apartment he was in fear of his life. I sealed the flap shut and the following day took a cab to the Leeds head office where they were waiting for me. I gave the manager the letter in order to retrieve my wages, explaining at the same time that I thought the staff quite disgusting to have read my journal, and that what they had written was mostly rubbish. The manager was quite pleasant, went out of the room, and returned with my wages and cash for my expenses to London. I thanked him and left. God, I was happy! Just regretful that I did not have a chance to say farewell to some of the interesting people I had met and spent time with. Still, I was content to think that those pathetic freaks were stuck in Iceland. I was free!

Back home in Manor House, Mum was quite happy to have me around again, and I regaled her with my stories of my adventures in Iceland, but as I lay in bed that night I felt that, although I had temporarily wandered from the path and was just criss-crossing and doubling up on myself, I was making some effort to move forward and earn enough money to do what I thought I needed to do. But this time I had saved my wages, and now I must not take too long to make my decision and stick to it. But first I had to focus. So I made my usual trip to consult The Oracle of Delphi, which means I took the 653 bus to Stamford Hill, and then I just waited to hear voices. And sure enough I did.

The latest gig on offer for school-leavers – rambling, useless, without a goal, semi-educated, and uncertain of how to pass the time – was to let time simply take you over. One voice was extolling the wonders and adventures of the merchant navy, which sounded quite exotic. Apparently, the large shipping companies had started advertising Mediterranean cruises, where passengers would be taken on delicious sun-swept trips around the Med, setting off from Southampton for Barcelona, then Cannes and Naples, and then on to Tangier, and then home. They were badly looking for staff – basically, waiters who were young, swift, alert, and charming – but you did need to have had some catering experience, preferably in hotels. Since I didn't have that I had to acquire hotel writing paper. This I did by wandering into large hotels and going into the writing room, where there was usually a small pile of headed writing paper for the guests. My sister was then commandeered to write a sterling reference.

Armed with my beautifully typed reference, I bussed down to the shipping office in Dock Street in London's East End and waited for my interview. I impressed them enough to get booked on the following week as a volunteer in the merchant navy, although really I was just a waiter. I was elated. I was given a list of requirements for my uniform, which had to be bought at Southampton and for which I was obliged to pay. I was booked on to a ship called SS *Chusan,* built for the P&O Steam Navigation Company, for trips to India, the Far East, and occasionally the Mediterranean. Ending up on the latter was rather unfortunate: the better gig was to go on long voyages, whereas the Mediterranean trip would be non-stop graft from morning till night.

I shared a cabin with four other guys, who, though they were as young as I was at 19, were seasoned old timers who knew their way round a large merchant ship and whose minds were razor-sharp in taking orders and delivering the food. Fortunately, I was in tourist class, which was a lot less demanding than first. Yet, this was the first time I had ever taken an order, and it was more than hard work – it was murderous. For breakfast, you're up, you grab a bite, then take your bucket and mop and clean around your table. It dries in minutes. You can see the faces of the passengers eagerly peering through the windows of the double door to the dining room. They had me serving, like the others, on two tables, four chairs on each, and I was positioned, since I was a new boy, next to the kitchens. At the end of my tables sat the dumb waiter, a cupboard-like piece of furniture where you kept spare napkins, silver, and condiments. I found it most useful.

On the first morning, there was a loud whistle and they, the public, came pouring in. The secret was to be relaxed, take orders swiftly and efficiently. Now, for some reason best known to the sadists who cooked up the traditions of service, you were not allowed a notebook to write down the bloody orders! No, you must keep them all in your head, so as soon as my keen and happy clients were in, I was racing around my two tables, four in each, sorting out who was for tea or coffee or juice, and that was already a nightmare. Then swiftly fly into the kitchen, just feet away, grab two pots of coffee, then back in to take orders for breakfast. And as soon as I had taken one table's order and was on to the second, I had already completely forgotten the first. I watched the other waiters, smart as whippets, carrying their trays loaded with orders while I clumsily waddled out with one plate in each hand. 'I ordered my eggs fried', 'Sorry, I did ask for poached and you didn't bring the porridge.' I dashed in and out having now to queue for the bits I'd missed, the grilled tomatoes, the toasted brown sausage, well-done porridge, slowly putting everything on the two tables, four in each, in and out, in and out. I smiled as sweat dripped down my face and onto their eggs, told them I was still a beginner, but, being Brits, they were unbelievably sympathetic with me and joined in the game. 'OK,' they said, 'don't worry, don't rush, take your time, that's better, you're getting it, oh well done.' After a while, all eight were eating happily, yet the dining room was almost empty, as everybody had already been fed and had left and my tables were still full while my customers were finishing off their breakfasts.

In fifteen minutes' time came the second sitting and the nightmare continued, but this time one of the chief stewards served one of the tables for me, thank God. I was so grateful to him, and he was not at all pissed off with me; he just said, 'It's OK, you'll get used to it.' That's what a ship is like – it's a conveyor belt – nevertheless, it was such a relief to have him on my side, as he would be for the rest of the voyage. I loved him! I just managed to get everybody served on the first table and, as before, my guests were the last to leave. Phew!

I returned to my cabin, and the other guys were lively and looking fresh and were in fact enjoying the memory task, so I showered and flopped out for a couple of hours, but then the bell went and I was up again for the lunch shift! While you are at sea, everyone loves to eat, but once in port the passengers tend to disembark after breakfast, and lunch is optional or just a running buffet, thank God. But now we were at sea and the guests had to be entertained, so I made my way back to my station and we all stood to attention as the whistle blew for the doors to be opened and in they galloped, all smiles and full of appetite and all looking at the menu.

I gave them time but now I tried to get a little ahead of the game by asking, 'Anyone fancy soup?' A few yeses peeped out, and I dashed swiftly into the kitchen, and I somewhat envied the guys working behind the counters – it seemed so much simpler than what I was doing. But now I had four soups on a tray and swiftly deposited them and was just so happy when I saw the head steward serving and chatting and smiling at my second table. This time it was fish, meat, or tossed salad, and I could remember just a bit more and I piled the mixed veg onto their spuds and the fish. I was nearly through and they were all munching away and my simply divine head steward was doing wine orders for both tables, so I was let off the hook somewhat.

It was over. I swiftly mopped up the floor, all the tablecloths were changed, and I was back standing to attention. The whistle blew. Christ! In they piled. This was certainly a test, but with one table taken care of I just about managed and prayed the head steward wouldn't leave me after today. I even had the sympathetic support of the guests, who must now have been beginning to feel somewhat sorry for me and were even perhaps finding this rather amusing.

The following day we docked in Barcelona – how wonderful! The nights were getting warm, so that night I joined the other shipmates for a nap on deck and never did stars look so gorgeously swollen and delicious. Now as dawn slowly dripped onto this beautiful city of Barcelona, the golden haze was so exotic, a colour I had never before seen. Breakfast was to be only a single sitting today, since many couldn't wait to take the tender and escape to the shore, and I was one of them. Ooh! Freedom. And I didn't have to come back for the lunch sitting, as it was buffet day. Yahoo! I strolled up the great avenue called Las Ramblas, delighting in all the smells and colours of the enchanted city. I was simply happy and I was young, what could be better?

I strolled into a shop to buy a croissant and saw a most attractive and sexy woman, who was eyeing me curiously. She was wearing one of those bum-hugging skirts that flare out into petals below the knees. She saw me gazing curiously back at her and actually smiled. Then I said, 'Hello.'

She answered me quite fluently in English, still smiling charmingly, 'Would you like to come home with me?'

I thought about it – for half a second – and replied, 'Yes, I would.' I was just being swept up by fate. You obey it, just float along the slipstream. This could never happen in London – not to me – no, you need a city like Barcelona with a great port.

So I went with her to her pleasant little flat, not far away, and I fell into a delicious, swoon-like state as we made the most heavenly love – and still I was able to repeat the act. As I did, she mockingly said, 'Ooh, naughty boy.' Then she made a cup of coffee, and I paid her the modest sum she required. Thank you, darling lady, for leaving such a sweet memory in my head.

I then walked the rest of Las Ramblas to the very top and I sat in a café and felt truly happy, as if the fates were sheltering me. And then I walked back, got on the tender back to the *Chusan*, and rejoined my mates. Such a relief to have had much of the day off and so dinner was not such a beastly chore, and I was beginning to make friends with my dumb waiter. Since most of the guests were simple, middle-class charmers from the provinces, they didn't waste a morsel and took everything on the menu. Just before they arrived I put several bowls of soup in my dumb waiter and as soon as they arrived I would chirp out, 'Soup, soup, soup,' and swiftly the soup, still reasonably hot, could be scooped out of the dumb waiter, which gave me more time to get their orders. Then I would rush into the kitchen, shouting out their desires. So, while it was still a nightmare, with the steward's help it became much more tolerable; he had been right when he said, 'It's OK, you'll get used to it.'

I was gradually able to deal with it, but now my poor stomach was on fire each night and that made everything more of a chore. I had discovered I had duodenal ulcers in London when I had an X-ray at the local hospital when I was 18 or 19, and they would flare up from time to time. I had to drink milk, which would momentarily relieve it, although word on the grapevine spoke of a miracle cure that came from some suburb, somewhere like Slough, where a chemist advertised his personally made brew, but you had to bring your own bottle. There were always queues outside his shop and when you reached him, he would ask a few questions then fill your bottle. Well, the miracle was that after a few hours of taking the substance you were completely free from pain. The medicine was of a brownish colour and slightly gritty; it felt in a funny way that if you dipped a penny into it and left it a few hours it would come out a bright bronze, but I never tried it.

I seem to remember that we were staying overnight in Barcelona and sailed at first light, and as I awakened, we were ploughing through the waves. The next stop was Cannes and again my jolly customers would stay for the day on the narrow strip of beach, so lunch was just a buffet for those who wanted to linger on deck. I served only one table, which was so much easier, but as with all holiday makers, there was always something extra that they wanted – an extra juice, a hotter tea or coffee, where is so-and-so and what are the entertainments tonight? Each night they had to be entertained, as it was advertised as a holiday cruise ship. They had no destination other than to float up and down and be amused.

After supper one night, three of us had the night off and took the tender into Cannes. What sweet relief as we walked along the seafront almost to the edge of town, where we found a cheap, friendly old café. We all ordered steak with pommes frites, which was cheap and delicious, and a couple of carafes of red. One of my companions was an older man who had quite a cultivated accent. He worked in the kitchens and was one of the many outsiders or drifters who end up in the merchant navy as an escape, and he always had a salty tale to tell. As we sat there, looking out to sea, we all glanced at the *Chusan* brilliantly lit up in the centre of the bay, and then he said something that echoed all our thoughts: 'Look how beautiful she looks, out there, glittering in the night, who would imagine that hell was in that boat?' None of us disagreed, but it was a wonderful night of freedom.

Later on the third day, we docked at Naples. Oh, what wonderful adventures to see the world like this! I had the evening off and strolled around the town, not straying too far from the port.

Suddenly, I was hungry and desperate for a pizza, so I stopped outside a fast-food café and tried to read the menu. As I was doing that, a group of kids approached me, begging, as if they were poor starving orphans, and making gestures indicating that a pizza would be welcome. I knew that this was a group of street urchins, just out to con me, but they were so audacious and charming that I let them. It was better than eating alone and the pizzas were only the price of a sandwich in London. It was so funny – the boys ordered a giant pizza with all the toppings, and I ordered a smaller one for me. We all sat at a big, round table and they wolfed it down with such glee, stuffing themselves and looking at me from time to time and laughing like they couldn't help themselves, as I was such an easy mug. I didn't mind in the least; I even liked this entertainment for the price of a pizza. The four kids were about ten to twelve years old and one of the youngest looked at me thoughtfully. He wasn't one of the laughers.

Eventually we finished, all satisfied, and walked out, and just as we entered the boulevard, I felt a tap on my shoulder. It was the smallest boy. He held in his hand a large slice of red melon and offered it to me. Even his mates seemed surprised. I took it with such great pleasure. He obviously felt a little sorry for me, feeling that they had taken advantage of me, and he wanted to make amends. I was deeply touched and strolled back to the port, happy with my night in Naples.

My stomach was getting worse as the ulcer was eating into me, but I managed to hold on till the last day when all the guests had left and all the waiters waited in great anticipation for their expected large tip. The cameraman came to all the tables, waiting to memorialise their faces for all time. I recall the exact second everybody froze, including my partner, the steward, who had made everything go well. He was a real typical Brit, tough as nails and hardened to the work of years pounding the deck. Everybody smiled. I wish I had smiled too, but I didn't wish to reveal my abject humiliation and turned my face away. I expect that all these lovely people are now sadly rotting in their graves, but I am eternally grateful to them for tolerating me.

We docked in grim Southampton, and I slipped away quietly and threw my uniform in the bin, since I would never do this work ever, ever again. My fault – if I had kept fit and not been susceptible to ulcers, I might have learned to enjoy it. I liked the customers and was even partial to acting out the role of waiter, although if only I had had a notebook to write down orders, how much easier everything would have been. But it was a hell of an adventure that I shall never forget. SS *Chusan* was sold for scrap only a few years later and that beautiful ship ended up in a scrapyard in the Far East.

CHAPTER 7

The Hooter, 1956

I was home again and seemingly further away than ever from the path that might take me to my destiny – I still wanted to return to Wiesbaden, for more than one reason. Certainly to see my beloved Faye but also to have some cosmetic surgery on my hooter! Terrible confession: I had inherited a distinct family trait and that was a slightly bulbous nose – not, thank God, nearly as prominent as my poor ma, but just enough to make me think that it stood between me and my dream to become an international movie star. A dream that had been percolating in my brain for as long as I can remember. In my last days in Germany, I had heard of a celebrated plastic surgeon and was determined to return to Wiesbaden and have my nose 'snipped' ever so slightly. Dear Mum gave me a helping hand and loaned me some of her hard-saved money.

One bright morning, I sailed on the boat to Ostend, Belgium, and felt in some way I was on a voyage of discovery. By throwing myself to the fates, how would I ever have had the chance to find that special road?

Many hours later, I booked myself into a youth hostel in Wiesbaden, but fear started to corrode my thoughts and I confessed this to a friendly young German, who replied that 'if you've come this far and you've heard that the surgeon's reputation is good, and also since you have been thinking about this for such a long a time, then why hesitate? Just go ahead and have it done. Go ahead or you will always regret it'. I went to sleep in my little bunk bed and felt so much better. So thank you, my dear young friend.

The next morning was sunny and bright. My appointment was around 11 a.m., and I took a cab to the surgery, which was in a large apartment block opposite the American Eagle Club. I had not yet called Faye – eighteen months had passed and at last I was back. I took a lift up to the floor of the surgeon, which looked most hygienic and efficient. He welcomed me effusively – a most elegant-looking, rather handsome man with silver hair, smartly tonsured. He invited me to sit down and opened a catalogue full of photographs and said I should indicate the kind of nose I should like. I said I wanted a straight, firm nose, something rather more French in style, but mainly I wanted him to remove the bulbous tip (I hoped he would at least be able to do that).

He dismissively shook his head as if to say that would be absolutely no problem. Then straight away he asked me to take off my jacket and shirt and sit in the operating chair! I was spun off my feet – I had imagined a wait and a further consultation, but no. I removed my sweater and vest and donned a starched surgical gown. I was anxious because I had my Star of David around my neck – it was only a decade since the Holocaust and he might have been a Nazi, for all I knew, but I had decided to keep it on. Ma had given it to me before I left for Germany, and I wanted to be true to my faith. I sat down and he lowered the chair back somewhat, then thrust some anaesthetic in my nose, which swiftly became numb. Then, again with no prior warning, he picked up a hammer-like instrument, and I felt a huge thump on my nose! Two heavy smashes and my nose was broken; it crunched like an ice cube breaking. I was quite stunned but felt nothing; I just heard a scraping and sawing which seemed to go on for some time – a continual scraping of my nasal bone.

After a while, and I cannot tell how long it was, I was beginning to feel something like a burning – was the anaesthetic wearing off? I raised my hand to indicate that it was hurting and he finished scraping and stitched me up. Then he put plaster over my face, and I slowly got up and walked with help to my overnight bed. It was over. I just lay there in a semi-doze for some hours, satisfied that I had done something that had been on my mind for years and at last had fulfilled this wish, then a very lovely nurse who spoke perfect English took care of me.

In the morning, I explained to her that I needed to rent a room for a few weeks. I needed at least a week before the plaster was taken off and my black eyes, the signature of everyone who has this operation, had faded away. She bought a local newspaper and there was a column for rooms to let. She found one not far away in a street called Grillparzerstrasse. Grillparzer, I later learned, was a famous German poet. The kind nurse even made the telephone call for me and booked an appointment for the following morning.

I left before midday, taking a cab to the house. I met the landlady, who was a very pleasant middle-aged woman, a rather academic type. I felt a tad self-conscious walking around with a huge plaster splint in the middle of my face and two black eyes; however, we got on well and the room was lovely, as was the house. I moved in once we had agreed the rent. I was happy and stayed there for a few days. My landlady even did some light shopping for me, so I was able to cook at home.

I couldn't wait to get rid of the plaster. I was told to return to the clinic on the fourth day, when I sat in the surgeon's chair and he slowly chipped away at the plaster and then very carefully unpeeled it from my face. The moment of truth had arrived. He then showed me my new face in the mirror… it looked perfect… just perfect… just as I had always wanted to look. However, there was only the slightest curve to it, so I had to return each morning for a week and wear a kind of brace on my nose. The surgeon put it over the bridge and turned a key which tightened around the upper part, and I had to keep this on for an hour. I was not too bothered, since my main problem had been dealt with. Miraculously, the bulb had vanished, and now I felt I had put myself on a path to glory in the movies. Though I visited the clinic every morning, I felt the slight twist in my nose was a fair exchange. And it even looked slightly dramatic and not too cosmetic.

But now it was time to see my beloved Faye. I had called her and we planned to meet up in our usual favourite sanctuary – the same tea dance café in Wilhelmstrasse. That evening I was most excited, but for some bizarre reason I did not feel in any sense the same intense love that I had felt just eighteen months ago. That now seemed vague and a tad misty.

I walked into the salon; there were some US soldiers there or maybe they were just civilian staff, as none were in uniform. I saw her almost immediately, but she seemed to be in some kind of heated argument with some Yankee scumbag who was berating her. He was swearing, she was shouting back. I should have immediately intervened but, coward that I was, I didn't interfere; I was afraid for my newly created nose! How awful I feel now, how dreadful. I had never seen her like this; maybe he was some scumbag lover and she had told him that she couldn't see him tonight… maybe! But strangely she didn't even speak to me – maybe the utter shame of me witnessing my ex-divine lover in a gross fight was more than she could bear.

I walked out. I felt nothing and it was over… just like that. But now I feel a hundred times worse. I wish I'd told the guy to cease his vile abuse, but, in the end, I did nothing. I just walked out of that period of my life.

Opposite the main central park was this quite wonderful Eagle Club for the officers and wives of the US forces. It was pleasant just to visit for a coffee or a drink. I popped in there frequently, even managing to get a part-time job as a waiter in the PX bar, since my German was now quite adequate. This I really enjoyed: it was simple and the soldiers were mainly very pleasant guys, and how they tipped on payday! But now I went to the Eagle Club and to my utter astonishment I saw the same man who had taken my coat and welcomed me in the *Spielhaus* eighteen months ago. He greeted me like a long-lost ally. He introduced himself to me this time as Fritz Pielschticker but said he preferred to be called Fritz Piel. He was a freelance salesman for the famous Rosenthal porcelain firm that produced the highest-class porcelain for upper-class bourgeois German houses. He had a small table laid out with his samples and we chatted most amiably. He seemed genuinely happy to have a chat with me.

Then suddenly he offered me a job as his assistant! During the day, he would tour around the immense military bases where they had housing estates for families and where bored American housewives would be entertained by him as he demonstrated his wares. When he drove, he loved to perform by making elaborately sweeping gestures to the peasants crossing the road. He offered to pay me expenses and a small commission on any sales. I thought this was such a golden opportunity to further involve myself in German life, and to explore living in Europe for the first time as an adult. He gave me his address, and I just had to follow him around, help him pack and unpack, and be a kind of sorcerer's apprentice. Things were beginning to wake up for me and I allowed myself to be gathered up once more by fate, like a piece of debris in a large wave to be deposited wherever it chooses. In fact, I saw myself a little bit as the character in a Thomas Mann novel called *Confessions of Felix Krull.*

The next morning, I found my way to his flat where, as was the case for so many other gay men, he lived dutifully with his mother. We sat in the basement area, and his mother made us a lovely breakfast of coffee and those special German rolls with cheese, *Käsebrötchen*. We then set off in his car with his chattels. I must confess that I have never met so charming and playful a person in my life. He was full of stories and jokes, and whenever we stopped at the lights, he would gesture to the stragglers crossing the road with a little head bow and a wonderful open arm.

Once inside the base we parked the car and carried the case of samples and knocked at the doors. Usually, a housewife would answer and then Fritz would go into his brilliant spiel, which was quite wonderful to watch. His nerve, his pizzazz, and his charm were boundless.

First, he would offer an effusive good morning and he'd claim that he was a representative of Rosenthal and by no means there to sell his goods, but merely to demonstrate his wares and to introduce this wonderful range to the great American public. He would beg just ten minutes of their time, when it would be his joy to be allowed to show his many beautiful objects. I would wait patiently and see how elegantly he laid them out while giving the ladies a brief history lesson.

Of course, once the ladies were suckered in, they would inevitably ask the price, to which he responded not only with the price, including a massive discount for US servicemen, but also saying that he was not able to sell the goods, as he was merely promoting this beautiful china service – but he would certainly be delighted to take their names and telephone numbers. By this time, and since it was costing them nothing, the ladies had become intrigued and now felt somewhat peeved that, should they wish, they could not impulsively purchase these delightful trinkets.

For his finale, he would take one of the most delicate cups and place it upside down on the carpet, and then to demonstrate its strength, he would put one foot on the cup and then raise his full body weight while just balancing on one leg. This piece of theatrical legerdemain deeply impressed the ladies; he was a full-grown man! I then would help to carefully repack the items and off we would go to knock on another door.

I was certainly impressed by Fritz and was happy to travel round with him, and after two or three demos we would always break for lunch, when we would discuss who would be the most likely candidates to purchase his precious china. Then he would regale me with tale after tale of his filthy, erotic wartime experiences. This man was a maverick and so unusual that I grew very fond of him.

Late afternoon we'd drive home, and sometimes I would cook a steak for us and he showed me how to make a good gravy. He knew that I was not remotely homosexual and it didn't matter a fig. I was just happy to walk around to his basement every morning for our coffee and rolls and set off to the bases. Once he let me go off alone for an hour or two with bunches of brochures, which I would show and ask if the lady would like to see a representative, and then he would call round the next day, having had the ground softened for him. I did so like Fritz and he felt like the brother that I never had. He never once made his sexuality an issue and, in fact, I found far more empathic civility with gays at that time of my life than with some of the hetero slobs I used to knock around with. They were sympathetic, witty, very often clever, and good company. He was always full of very useful suggestions, and I don't think I enjoyed anyone's company more than his. Naturally, I never returned to the *Spielhaus*, but I did the odd day as a waiter at the American Serviceman's Bar, since I wasn't paid too much by Fritz and my money was slowly dribbling away.

I was even getting to meet some civilised Americans. One day I had a young couple around for teatime and they invited me to go to the theatre with them. It was on the base and the cast were members of the forces. Even then I found it absolutely dire but was glad of the companionship of such an amiable couple.

However, my adventures in Germany were sadly coming to an end. I had an invitation to visit a charming French girl I had met a year earlier in the Astoria dance hall on Charing Cross Road in London, which had daily tea dances and was a most convenient place to drop in if you were unemployed, rootless, uninspired, and without focus. It filled the time and helped one to meet, or have the opportunity of meeting, lonely au pair girls from France, Italy, and Spain. I had a mild relationship with a young woman who was now working in a French resort called Ax-les-Thermes, which was in the mountains not too far from Perpignan. She said she was available to be visited during the month of July, and she had invited me to spend some days with her.

I did not wish to lose this opportunity, so one day I confessed to Fritz that I was thinking of leaving, which greatly saddened both of us. We sat in a café, and I asked him for some compensation for many of the contacts I had made when he sent me out alone. After a little bartering, he donated about DM100. I bought my ticket to Perpignan and then it was another short trip from there to Ax-les-Thermes, changing at Avignon. I did feel very sad at leaving Wiesbaden, for it had been the great love of my life. The cosmetic surgery and my best and only real pal, Fritz Piel; I will love him forever and will never forget him.

I took the train, a very long journey, to Perpignan. On the train, I happened to get into a very pleasant conversation with a charming French lady who was also going to Perpignan; we chatted most amiably and I asked her if she might know of a hotel in the town. She very sweetly offered to show me her hotel, where she was sure I would be able to rent a single room for the night! How fortunate to be floating on the wings of fate and now that fate, which had been shaping me so well and had then been rudely torn away, was beginning all over again.

When we reached Perpignan, she and I shared a cab to the hotel; I stood just behind her as she requested a room for me. The concierge shook his head. *'Ah non, tout complet,'* he responded – totally full. But then he said, and I am sure that only in France would you ever hear this, 'But madam, your room is suitable for two persons!' She turned back to me and repeated his statement. There was nothing left for it –

I would be permitted to share her room. I was more than happy and terribly grateful to her. Also, I was assuming there must be twin beds.

She went to her room; I followed behind and saw there was one large double bed in the centre. We decided to take a light supper in the dining room first. Afterwards she asked that I wait outside the door while she got ready for bed, which I patiently did. And after a few moments, she invited me in… she was already tucked into bed. I went to the other side and slid my pants off – all this done in a most decorous manner – turned off all the bedside lights and settled into the bed. I was lying naked next to an attractive young French woman and there was not a chance in hell of me falling asleep. After several moments, I found my left hand seeking out her right hand and clasping our little fingers; she didn't pull away but just said, '*Dors, dors*'. But how could I sleep when I had not felt such a heat in my loins before, never in my life? I felt I was on fire. My sex had reached its zenith; any further and I was sure it would burst.

Finally, she did permit me to kiss her goodnight and to cuddle, which we did for most of the night. It was a heavenly and unforgettable evening. After breakfast we parted, sharing a memory which I am sure will be sacred in both our hearts for the rest of our lives – how joyous is our youth when we can be led by the sheer demands of our bodies.

***

My French friend in London was a girl named Yvette. One day, perhaps I was 20, I was with a friend crossing Oxford Street at Tottenham Court Road. Being with a friend does make one just a bit bolder than usual and, as I glanced to my left, I saw a most attractive young woman crossing the road at the same time. So I just asked her how she was, and she replied in a French accent that she was very well, thank you, and so we continued the chat till we reached the pavement on the other side and bid each other farewell.

Some weeks later, I was crossing through Trafalgar Square when a young lady who had been sitting on one of the benches jumped up and ran to me very eagerly! It was the same French girl I had been chatting to on Oxford Street. Of course she recognised me, and the eagerness with which she bounded over to me like a young gazelle suggested that life for an au pair girl in London was a pretty lonely one. In fact, it was very touching. She seemed eager, very eager, to make contact with a human being. I was also pleased to see her, and this time we chatted a while longer and even went for a coffee.

Yvette Bizeau was her name and she was one of a veritable army of au pair girls working in London. I was indeed curious about this delightful elfin child of France and, for a change, sex was not uppermost in my mind. I was fascinated by her French-ness, her accent, and even took some French lessons from her.

I think we went to the movies a few times, and once I took her to a really fancy place for dinner. We gradually got to know each other, and one evening I even took her home to meet my mother. Of course, my mother simply adored her and even many years later would ask me 'How is Yvette?'

Eventually Yvette returned to Paris. She did, however, continue to write to me, and I relished her style, so French, so exotic. Even the envelopes were stylish and quite narrow, and her frequent postcards were always atmospheric photos of Paris by a famous photographer.

They gave me such a longing to visit that beautiful city. Once she sent me a beautiful diary that you could change each year, and she faithfully sent the replacements while I kept the pretty leather cover. Nobody had ever sent me such an elegant gift, especially in my household.

Eventually Yvette returned to London but never returned to her au pair job, which was only a means to an end. Instead she found work in a nursing home just off Harley Street, which also provided her with a small basement room, so I could actually visit her. How very convenient, since all I had to do was to descend the steps to the basement window and gently tap a few times. She'd then rise from her bed, open the window, and then I could easily climb in. It was quite wonderful, but alas now I was beginning to fall into my old habits. I used her as a convenient sensual plaything. After I had been out dancing at one of the many jazz clubs that now were available in the West End, I found it easy to jump on the bus to Baker Street, walk down one of those side streets adjacent to Harley Street, and a couple of minutes later I'd be tapping on the window. The curtains opened and she was always pleased to see me. There was never any time when she was not available, and she never seemed put out by my sudden and impromptu visits.

Then one day I actually took a trip to Paris. I met Yvette and took her to meet a celebrity that I had got to know in the environs of Chelsea. He was quite a distinguished black American actor called Gordon Heath, who played guitar and sang jazz and blues in his own club in the St Germain area. Indeed, I felt quite proud of myself for knowing him. The club was called L'Abbaye. It was a very sophisticated gig. When finishing his numbers, he requested the audience not to applaud in case it woke the baby!

So, we were encouraged just to snap our fingers, which we willingly did. Gordon Heath actually played Othello on BBC TV many years back, so he did have quite a reputation. I liked him enormously and he was a very cultivated man. Yvette then took me to her 'digs' which was no more than a garret on the top floor of a block of flats. It seemed that many young Parisians lived like that as they struggled in their early years.

I found it hot and rather stifling as we both tried to sleep in an awful single bed. When I could bear it no longer, I begged her to forgive me, as I couldn't stay another moment, and said I would find a cheap hotel for the night. We both descended into the street, but the mood this time had turned rather sour. Such a shame. I walked abruptly away with barely a muttered farewell. I walked round the block and in and out of the side streets of St Germain looking for a cheap hotel when, lo and behold, who do I see in front of me but Yvette! She had been walking in a completely different direction, yet by all the laws of chance or fate we ended up together again. I was happy, she was happy. We made up and I struggled once more in that Parisian garret... this time we slept!

CHAPTER 8

Drama School

After my European adventures, I was back in London after several months with Ma at our council flat in Manor House and looking for a job as usual. I loved going to the YMCA in Tottenham Court Road, since I had developed a talent for handball – a fast and furious game the conclusion of which melted away any sour feelings one may have been nurturing.

One day, I took the number 19 bus from there to the King's Road in Chelsea – I had answered a wanted ad and had been asked to come down immediately. I do believe this was my first visit to that strangely exotic thoroughfare. I met a most charming and civilised owner of a high-class menswear shop called John Michael, who immediately employed me after a brief interview. Then I happily walked back to Sloane Square in order to take the tube back to Manor House.

As I approached Sloane Square underground, I came face to face with the Royal Court Theatre, which was advertising a play called *Look Back in Anger*. The title seemed familiar; I think there had been an excerpt on TV some days earlier. This was 1956 and John Osborne's play was stirring up a great deal of attention; he had become known as the voice of the 'angry' generation. I hardly realised that this play was the beginning of an earthquake in what had been distinctly unadventurous British drama. The theatrical industry was going through a profound change, while I was going to sell shirts and ties in King's Road. Yet no matter what was changing in our society, I just wanted to be ready to at least dive into the rising tide. As a child, I had adored going to the movies; however, I was always easily shocked inside the dark womb of the cinema, my brain fizzing from the exotic images of the film. The outside world seemed so flat and ordinary, the days so empty, as the familiar red buses rolled on by. How could I ever recover after seeing *King Kong*? But in those far-off days, cinemas were closed on Sundays.

On Sunday I went to Hebrew classes nearby and the entire class was excited by the news that at last cinemas would be allowed to open on a Sunday, as the religious laws were about to change. However, our very wise and sanguine teacher said to us in a rather stern voice, 'No need to rejoice, Sunday is a Christian holy day and for many this day is revered, precious, and a day for calming reverence.' I never forgot this lovely man's words, for they touched me so deeply; even if we would be free to enjoy Sunday, we should be sympathetic to those for whom the day has deep religious meaning. I learnt much from his words.

My very first day in the movies happened when I joined the extras agency called the Film Artists Association, which actually found work for you as an extra – not as an actor, but just as a body passing by. It was amazingly easy to join the FAA, which was based in Poland Street. Once you had submitted your headshot and details, you might be called the very next day to go to Pinewood, Borehamwood, or Denham Studios, and for the first time be thrust into a film. In this way, I spent several months on film sets before I began to act in films, and it was a great preparation for my future career. At the age of 20, I was on a western spoof called *The Sheriff of Fractured Jaw* starring Jayne Mansfield and Kenneth More. I was costumed as a cowboy. The set was a smoky saloon bar. The director was something of a Hollywood legend called Raoul Walsh, working off his last years.

Nothing could have been more exciting, nothing on this earth. Here I was – 20 years old in a major movie with the stunningly gorgeous Jayne Mansfield, who was being coached through her opening song by a brilliant male choreographer gently guiding her through her movements. Then she would attempt to emulate him and actually did rather well. I was deeply impressed by the dance choreographer, who perfectly mimicked a sexy woman. Looking back, I thought I must have been transported to heaven. My position was just leaning against the bar as she was singing, and at one point she actually strolls over to the bar and, for one second, I am sharing a screen with her. Watch closely and you can see me! At the end of the day, I joined the queue to collect my £4.50 and made my way home, my head full of the most delirious memories. I couldn't wait to be called again.

Later I found myself on some exciting sets, including *The Devil's Disciple* by Bernard Shaw starring Kirk Douglas and Burt Lancaster. I only had one day on that set and sadly without the stars. However, after the shoot I was standing at the bus stop opposite the studio when whom did I see cycling back to his hotel but Burt Lancaster. It was like he had appeared out of a dream; since in my childhood, movies were like dreams to me. His hair was thick and tousled, and he looked like a Viking vision cycling along the highway, and so American. Being a somewhat naïve soul, I thrust my arm out to get his attention and the great man actually stopped. He was not in the least put out. I said, 'Mr Lancaster, I would love to be in your film, not just as an extra but as an actor.'

He looked at me, smiled, revealing his almighty teeth, and said, 'I can't help you, son, but you should contact the producer, Harold Hecht.' I thanked him profusely, and he gave me another large, toothy smile and cycled away. I had touched magic!

***

Something was beginning to change inside me as well as in our society, and that change began when a kindly voice, responding to my rather pathetic requests for acting work without a scintilla of experience, advised me, most emphatically, to gain experience and to start taking classes at the City Literary Institute in Holborn. I immediately took the advice and enrolled for the next term. This was basically an institute that catered for young men and women who had in some ways missed the boat and was very valuable. I paid my £5 and one fine September eve, after my day's work in John Michael, took the bus to Holborn.

I entered the classroom and scanned the faces. Most of them were around my age; they all seemed friendly and hopeful. I got a feeling straight away that I was home. We had a professional actor as our teacher, Murray Gilmore. Murray had had some kind of breakdown and was finding his way forward again as a teacher. He was a great influence on me: he would get quite consumed by whatever we were discussing, with his eyes bulging as he swelled with love for the art of acting. We became quite close. He taught me how to place my voice, how to understand a speech. I remember him analysing a speech from *Richard III* word by word, helping me to divine the true meaning of what I was saying and to better understand the brilliance of Olivier's performance.

My two years of part-time study at the City Lit, although it opened many doors, would be of little use in opening the ultimate door. That door required a little more pressure. An actor friend advised that I should try and enrol full-time at a drama school if I was to have any real chance of fulfilling my long-desired wish to be a professional actor. I listened most carefully to him – he added that the drama school he went to was called Webber Douglas Academy of Drama in South Kensington. He said that they might be a little more flexible by allowing me in for just a year, since they were very keen to attract more male students.

One afternoon, I took the tube to South Kensington station and then walked down Old Brompton Road, turning right at Clareville Grove. I was confronted by a small but compact building that also housed the Chanticleer Theatre. I auditioned for a rather rotund Mr Rossiter, who said he would be glad to accept me, even for the year, adding, 'if you have the necessary funds'. If not, he advised me to apply for a grant from Westminster Borough Council, which on rare occasions did offer them.

I wrote my application and they swiftly replied with a long questionnaire requesting details of all past studies, formal education, degrees, etc. Naturally this would be somewhat of a hurdle to overcome, since I was rather lacking in those requirements. What could I do? I decided that I would take a chance and be totally honest and open with them. I wrote a very candid letter briefly outlining my five years since I had left Grocers' Company Grammar School in Hackney, and I confessed that I had worked in close to one hundred jobs, none of which had been instructive to me whatsoever. I told them about my dubious friends in my teens, a time which, unfortunately, led to me suffering a four-month incarceration in a juvenile detention centre. I said I had even tried a short spell in the merchant navy, but it was only when I began studying drama that, for the first time in my life, I had felt my heart and soul being touched. I knew that I would sacrifice anything to be able to study full-time. For the first time in my twenty-one years, I felt that I saw a purpose to my life.

My days of working as a salesman in a menswear shop were about to end at last. Finally finished, over! From leaving school at 15, it had been five utterly wasted years, but I did have to reassure myself that I had learned so much about life.

There was a coffee shop a few doors down the King's Road where I would spend some time off, and the people using it were some of the most interesting characters I had ever met. It was there that I came across Gordon Heath, the actor and singer whom Yvette and I had seen perform in Paris.

One night I was sitting in the coffee shop when Gordon entered and we started chatting. What an incredibly interesting man. As we were chatting, two glasses of wine were delivered to us from across the room. I looked up and saw that the sender was a friend of Gordon Heath, an actor called Peter Wyngarde, one of England's most dynamic actors. So this was the life I was living, merely by working in King's Road, Chelsea. I believe Mr Wyngarde was about to commence rehearsals for the play *Duel of Angels* by Jean Giraudoux, in which he would star opposite Vivien Leigh, directed by Jean-Louis Barrault no less!

Within a week I received a reply to my grant application, which gave me the time to prepare for my meeting at Westminster Council, where I would be interviewed and auditioned. Two pieces were needed: one classic and one modern. So I prepared a soliloquy from Shakespeare's *Richard III* and a very comic piece from William Saroyan's *The Time of Your Life*. I felt I had acquitted myself quite well and also suspected that the council had probably never received quite such a candid grant application.

About two weeks later, their answer arrived. My wishes had been granted! They wrote that they would be pleased to support me financially – they'd pay my school fees and pay for my board and lodging if need be. They would send me a chequebook to enable me to draw on funds that would be deposited each term. I could not have been happier and speedily took the tube to Piccadilly Circus. From there, I went to the National Westminster Bank to introduce myself and receive a chequebook – my first ever – with my name printed inside it!

My first day at Webber Douglas felt completely normal – I was now, at long last, and quite unbelievably, a student. A full-time student! My shirt and tie were consigned to the dustbin. My life was about to change radically and completely. I was training to become a professional actor, and this had been the dream of my life; the gods had looked down benevolently.

The school year's three terms passed easily and swiftly. On the first day all students were given a collection of plays that we would be studying. Then we would make our way to the studio where we would be given a lecture and begin. Now I had new colleagues, some of whom would remain friends for many years, long after our creamy, waxed faces bore the brunt of time and became the mere husks of what we once were. Terence Stamp and Samantha Eggar were in my class, and I swiftly made friends with them. Stamp became a star almost as soon as he left, as did Samantha Eggar. I continued to see them from time to time. As for me, I had no such good fortune. I was just coming up to my twenty-second birthday and was now woefully undertrained by the less than adequate training at Webber Douglas, but still desperately zealous.

However, when we got to the final days, students were required to demonstrate their talents by doing auditions for invited agents in the industry who would then make comments and criticise our efforts. All the students were then given a list of the names of the agents, should they wish to contact them. I chose an agent by the name of John Penrose, an ex-actor, since he appeared to be very active in theatre and I knew that was where I had to begin. It was my ambition to learn as much as I possibly could. He was a friendly and most helpful agent, whose office was in the middle of showbiz land – i.e., Cambridge Circus. I was invited to his office, and this was the very first step of my life in the theatre. As I slowly made my way up the stairs, I felt that this was a very special occasion.

John Penrose was most affable to me and even suggested that I might like to consider playing Rodolpho in Arthur Miller's play *A View from the Bridge*. That idea somewhat scared me, as it was going to be my first professional job. Penrose's keen theatrical nose sensed my cautious response and he said, 'Why don't you consider starting as an ASM [assistant stage manager] and understudy?' I was visibly relieved, though in hindsight I might have missed the greatest opportunity I would have for some time.

Still, it was a modest beginning, but I could not have been happier. I had started and was determined. It was July 1959. I was excited to at last be paid to tread the boards.

CHAPTER 9

Actor!

In 1959, I was living at Ovington Square, Knightsbridge, in a very pleasant room that I rented from a friendly Irish chap, also an actor, Randall Kinkead. He was university-trained and was looking for a flat sharer. His last tenant, Harry Mann, was a gay South African who managed Au Père de Nico, a very trendy showbiz restaurant just off King's Road, Chelsea. So, I was suddenly thrust into the Chelsea beau monde within minutes of leaving drama school. It was a beautiful flat, but I needed to get used to the rarefied atmosphere of Knightsbridge, which was certainly a much lonelier place than I had been used to; there was hardly any of the street life or local markets with the buzz of human activity found in working-class areas. In fact, I felt that the odour of death hung about those vast citadels of money. I got on very well with Randall, and I was grateful to be introduced to many of his fascinating and cultivated friends. What a change from the simple down-and-outs I had been associating with in Stamford Hill.

I was meant to start work on the following Monday but woke that morning with a terrible head from flu. I forced myself to get up and, once I did, I just got ready and leaped onto the bus. By the time I reached the rehearsal room, located above a pub in Soho, I was completely recovered. After being introduced to the cast, a very amiable group of people, as an ASM I was immediately sent out to buy some props such as fruit. I was told to be sure to ask for a receipt, which you normally don't ask for from a market trader in Berwick Street, but I gritted my teeth and did. Then I got back and watched rehearsals. It was a start; I was now earning my first wages in the industry that I was destined to ultimately thrive in, and I was proud as punch. It was an excellent cast headed by a sexy lady, Joan Rice, who already had some movie reputation and the young me played the character of the longshoreman. I had just one line, which was me entering the stage and saying, 'Are you going bowling tonight, Eddie?'

I was at first simply terrified as I stepped out from the wings as if I was diving from a spaceship into deep space. It was the Finsbury Park Empire, one of the largest theatres in Great Britain. I waited each night in sheer terror for my cue and then walked across the stage as if I were walking a tightrope. The young actor playing the lead – Rodolpho, a young Italian immigrant – was excellent, and I watched them all eagerly. They had already been on a previous tour and were so fluent in their lines. The Finsbury Park Empire was a magnificent theatre designed by the Victorian architect Frank Matcham, who seemed to have created most of the grand theatres of England.

Apart from my walk-on, my other duties were to place the arm of the record player on the record at the appropriate time, and when I heard from my headphones the music coming up, I would increase the volume. But the music they chose was quite ambitiously *The Love for Three Oranges* by Sergei Prokofiev. There was a small chalk mark on the record, and I would turn up the volume as I heard the cue coming up, then I'd race to the opposite side already dressed in my longshoreman's costume and wait for my entrance. I tried to avoid taking a sidelong glance at the auditorium in case I fainted. It was vast, seating at least 2,000 when full. When my cue came, I could only look straight ahead to the lead actor playing Eddie Carbone as if I were hanging on to him with my eyes for dear life. The nightly walk terrified me as much as a gangplank.

Just a few years later, in April 1965, that glorious treasure of a theatre was torn down, which was a shockingly philistine thing to do by a typical philistine Labour council. I believe we toured for a couple of gigs, one gig being in a sleazy dump of a theatre in Kettering, and a second tour was lined up beginning in Bradford – again, in the grand theatre, which was also a Frank Matcham colossus. This time the cast was changed, since the others had had more than enough, and the role of Rodolpho was played by a totally miscast Scottish actor. However, the young girl was played by a very sweet Marina Martin, who I liked a lot. We became friends, and, in later years after she left the theatre, she became an esteemed agent.

My first taste of touring was most instructive and in those days the actor had to scour the notes on the stage door which listed the best digs, and then you'd phone up and hunt them down. The Australian company manager was a real dude and a lot of fun to be with. Our digs were classic actors' digs: breakfast, back for lunch, and even high tea. The show was a tad scrappy, but I was glad to have just got my toes wet.

The Amorous Prawn, 1959

While still living in Knightsbridge with my friend Randall, who was also looking for work, I now had a new agent called Vincent Shaw, who hoovered up many of the scraps and small parts that were left after the main star parts were cast. He called me with an offer of an audition for another ASM job and understudy. It was a comedy (drawing-room type) where I was to understudy three of the idiot staff of the grand country house, whose majestic owner and hostess were planning to earn some extra cash by letting rooms to American tourists, here for the salmon fishing season, while her husband, the brigadier, was away on military business for a few weeks. The play was *The Amorous Prawn* by Anthony Kimmins, something more suited to the '30s. What a golden opportunity!

Now, what made it special was that the leading lady was to be played by no less than a grand lady of the theatre, the beautiful and elegant Evelyn Laye. One of the great comedy stars of British theatre and movies, she was simply adorable and most professional. My wage was a stunning £15 per week, a huge fee, and I was feeling quite rich. I was due to rehearse at the now extinct Winter Garden Theatre in Drury Lane, which was now only used for rehearsals. Murray McDonald, a very well-known Scottish director, was at the helm, and one couldn't wish for a more charming and sophisticated man. It was all old school but very smart and dignified. Murray always wore a tailored suit to work. He stood on the edge of the stage conducting the choreography, which, for a comedy, has to be highly comical, highly sophisticated and inventive. It was a lesson to watch the play slowly being put together, and I could not do enough for Boo Laye, as she was called among her familiar coterie.

The other joy in this play was the famous and astonishingly talented comedian called Stanley Baxter, who was making his debut in London after knocking everyone out in Scotland with his brilliant impersonations and mimicry. Stanley Baxter was adorable and I much admired him. The fly in the ointment was the wretched company manager, who was always bullying or complaining about one thing or the other, but I loved the others, particularly Boo Laye and Stanley Baxter.

The smaller roles were played by East End cockney Harry Landis and Derrick Nimmo, and the two Yankee guests were played effectively by two Americans living in London and rolled out to play Yankee parts. The brigadier was played by brilliant stalwart comedy actor Walter Fitzgerald, one of the sterling British comedians. This was one of the great training lessons of my life, even if I was not acting except as an understudy. To be at the very centre of British theatrical history was such a far cry from 'tickling the floor' of the scumbag menswear dosshouses I'd been working at just a short time ago.

My immediate boss, the deputy stage manager called Chris, was pleasant, if extremely dull, and we got on well. I sat next to him at the desk writing down the moves, which entailed blocking (or writing down) all the stage directions. I think he found me a little intense, as I was determined to get all the moves right.

One morning during a break in rehearsal, the lovely Miss Laye padded over to our desk and asked for a cigarette. Chris immediately drew out his untipped packet and her response was, 'Oh, with spats, darling?' Poor Chris looked nonplussed, so I straight away offered one of my Du Mauriers, of course with 'spats' – i.e., tips. From then on, Boo and I bonded, and I would do anything in the world for her. Her husband, the actor Frank Lawton, popped in one day as he was passing by and I thought, *'Oh, what a handsome fellow.'* It further reinforced my opinion of the theatre world. Yes, we are a race apart, we are unique, to be seen only at a distance separated by a great wooden moat, the stage. Look but don't touch.

Quite curious how some buildings, either houses or theatres, carry some trace of their past, which in some infinitesimal way leaves a memory that can only be detected by a soul that was already contaminated by it. Now, just a couple of decades before I entered that building in Drury Lane, I learnt, the very first production of Franz Kafka's play version of his novel *The Trial* had played there – so out of the hundreds of venues in London and the suburbs, this was the very theatre where Jean-Louis Barrault and André Gide's version had played in translation. Kafka's seminal novel was something that had fascinated me for years and one day I was determined to do my own version of it.

But for now, I was just on the first run, supplying spats for Boo Laye. Finally, rehearsals were complete on this simple but cosy comedy, and we opened for an eight-week tour in the provinces, which plays were obliged to do in the olden days to prepare for the West End. Not only did the cast perform daily, but the author and director were nearly always on hand to keep improving, cutting or trimming. The director, Murray, was continually re-choreographing to improve the pace. Sometimes actors were given new lines in the morning and were expected to learn them and put them in that night.

The eight-week tour was a gift for me to explore Great Britain, and I realised what an amazing nation it is. We toured first to all of what they call the number-one theatres of Nottingham, Newcastle, Manchester, then the astonishing Edinburgh, ending up at the gothic silver-granite Aberdeen. Then we got to Glasgow, Stanley Baxter's hometown. The crowd roared in celebration of their home-bred boy in a West End play, and he gave a welcoming celebration party for the cast, to which I, as a humble ASM, was not invited, much to Stanley Baxter's deep annoyance, since the party was organised by the runt who was the company stage manager. It was a pretty lonely eight weeks on the road, but I tried to make use of the time by going to the main town libraries and reading those amazing books on Shakespeare called variorums – analyses of the text which I found extremely valuable.

The minutes, hours, and days just drifted away, and I nevertheless did my best to try to do something useful. And then we had two understudy rehearsals a week, which was something to fill the empty hours, but after a few weeks, that became a painfully dull chore. I was grateful for Murray choosing me, and he must have seen something in me that was lively and energetic, as he never ceased to show affection to me; although he was gay, that had nothing to do with it.

I wasn't the finest ASM in the world and often failed to replenish the coffee cups which were used to decorate the set; I received a strict bollocking when mould started to grow in them, and rightly so. Chris, my stage manager boss, should have taught me, informed me, and checked himself, but certainly he was two bob short of a quid. Also, I was weary unto death of the actors and of witnessing, apart from Boo and Stanley, their ghastly faces night after night. I think they were equally sick of each other; it is a difficult life for actors to tour, waiting all day for your evening show and trying to occupy the daytimes fruitfully or socially.

One evening, passing him in the corridor, I acknowledged one of the actors with a brief 'Hi'. He suddenly turned on me and said, 'Don't walk past me with a "Hi"; you're stage management and you say good evening, understand?' I nodded dumbly. Of course, he was quite right; I had not yet been trained in the theatre ethics properly. After that rather long and somewhat ghastly tour, I can only imagine his frustration. What I now know, and far too late, is that I should have knocked on his door and apologised profoundly for my surly behaviour: 'Dear Mr Hugh McDermott, I am sorry, please forgive me. I do so admire your performance, and I hope that one day I shall be performing onstage myself.' Too late, far too late. In fact, the man had a sterling reputation. Still too late.

After the long tour of Great Britain, we found ourselves in the final town, the crest of our tour, at the wonderful Georgian theatre, the Theatre Royal. This was considered to be the most looked-forward-to date, since Brighton has the atmosphere of oysters and champagne and it was the penultimate date before the West End. The company was excited to finally be on the edges of civilisation and near home. It was also Laurence Olivier's favourite venue and even inspired him to settle in Brighton, buying a large Georgian house in Royal Crescent on the seafront. Many of the old school of thespians set up home there in their retiring years. In Olivier's case, he even commuted daily to London when he was running The National at The Old Vic. He used the old, legendary Brighton Belle, where he ordered kippers on the train for breakfast which set him up for the day at The Old Vic.

One day, Evelyn Laye, probably feeling a tad isolated or even, I dare say, lonely, with the company when the director wasn't in, actually asked me if I might care to join her for supper after the show, and, of course, I was absolutely delighted to do so. We dined at a very elegant restaurant just opposite the Brighton theatre and we enjoyed each other's company immensely; at least, I'm assuming she did, although I might have been a tad tactless in confessing that this wasn't my favourite kind of play that the grand lady was starring in. She was lovely to be with and asked me loads of questions, so we became good friends. I believe the rest of the cast, having heard of this rendezvous, were somewhat miffed, as she had been out with none of them. Their comments were too unspeakable even for me to write down.

At last, we arrived at our final destination: The Saville Theatre at the end of Shaftesbury Avenue. I even had a smart narrow dressing room for my ASM duties, and this became my second home, as it does for all actors. On the first night, the new audience bravo-ed and, even if the critics were savage, the audiences grew and grew steadily.

The title of *The Amorous Prawn* was based on a chap who went by the nickname of 'The Prawn' and took his secret lover to his country house thinking it would be a safe place to go. One day the brigadier, who was expected to be away for at least two or three weeks, turned up in full uniform since his military requirements had been unexpectedly cut short. When the double doors opened, the audience let out a gasp, a howl, and a shriek, and it was the loudest response I have ever heard in a theatre. You could say it was a tour de force. The cast, who were impersonating country hotel staff, practically fainted on seeing the brigadier. Evelyn's character confronted him head-on when he said, 'What in God's name is going on?' Then Evelyn explained sweetly, dolefully, and charmingly that it was just an effort to try and make a little bit of cash to help the economics of the house and was so tearful and pleading that the brigadier suddenly said, 'Do you know what, that's not a bad idea.'

Now, it so happens that I had moved back to my council flat in Manor House. Telling my mother all about Evelyn Laye, I suggested that I might bring in a large jar of Mum's homemade chicken soup, which my darling Boo could have between shows on those awful matinee days. She loved it so much that we kept up the tradition for my entire stay, and I would give her each Thursday or Saturday a large jar. She then confessed to me she had never enjoyed soup so much. I still miss the lovely and very generous lady. Also, my mother could not have been prouder to make chicken soup for the grand dame of British theatre.

Eventually, I got the sack for assaulting the fatally dull stage manager during one of the endlessly painful understudy rehearsals. A prop came, of which I knew, and I was about to open it, since it had been ordered and was something quite simple, when the stage manager said I had no right to open it. When I claimed I knew what it was – in fact, I think I had even ordered it – he went on getting more and more red-faced. I then threw the prompt book at him, as he was being duller and thicker than ever. I was asked immediately to leave and so, collecting all my good-luck and Christmas cards from my dressing room, I left. Sadly, I never contacted Miss Laye again, but I know they had a long, long run, to everyone's amazement. Even Harry Landis, who was playing one of the cockney soldiers, also fled one day and never came back. For these endless runs, you do need massive endurance – aided by my mother's chicken soup. So, my first West End run came to an end.

Buxton, Derbyshire – Summer Season, 1960

Now I was a jobbing actor, happy to snatch a few days here and there between jobs washing dishes at the elegant restaurant managed by Harry Mann, who was Randall Kinkead's old partner. This was not too unpleasant and smart young actors who were successful would frequent this popular café, but at this stage of my life, I was painfully self-conscious, painfully shy, a cowardly drip, and as soon as an actor entered the restaurant whom I vaguely knew and who might even vaguely know me, I would rush downstairs to escape my humiliation and comfort myself, thrusting my hands in warm soapsuds.

One night, theatre director Anthony Page came in and got chatting to me and actually asked if I would like to join his crowd for drinks. He was about to begin his first season in Dundee Rep and asked if I was interested in joining the company. I was quite stunned but heard no more. A flash in the pan. But I read in the *Stage* newspaper that Nicol Williamson, the Scots actor, was building a big reputation up there.

Curiously enough, I did get a gig the following year in Dundee courtesy of Piers Haggard, nephew of the celebrated author Henry Rider Haggard. On my first day before rehearsals, I looked around the theatre and saw this rather surly looking man with straw-coloured hair playing the piano in the green room, and that was Nicol Williamson, who was about to leave just as we were about to start. It was only a shortish gig in Dundee of three plays, two of which were quite ambitious, being *La Mandragola* by the Italian author Machiavelli and *The Merchant of Venice*, which featured a delightful young Lynn Redgrave as Portia in her acting debut – she was quite splendid. But before long, I was hustling for work once again.

My agent, Vincent Shaw, was hearing my desperation to do some real acting and got me an audition for a gentle old couple who helped keep the provincial theatre alive by mounting summer seasons year after year in Buxton, Derbyshire. Hence, I was offered an entire season as juvenile lead. No more ASM'ing, thank God. Although I did learn a great deal from it, learning how to write down moves, blocking the play, cues, etc., which the average actor who just goes from RADA to leading actor hasn't got the faintest fucking clue about. The repertory season was for four months, sixteen plays at the rate of one show a week at the glorious weekly salary of £9. Buxton in Derbyshire is a rather charming and bucolic town in the centre of the Peak District. I settled in quite swiftly and began learning lines.

In fact, just to get ahead of the game, I'd bought the first four plays from the British Drama League in what they called French's Edition (a theatrical publishing house) – that is, plays that had been done in the West End where all the moves were zealously marked out, very useful for swift turnovers. No time to be creative in weekly rep: you come in, block the play, learn the lines, and then get on with it. In this way, the play in the French's Edition can be blocked on the first day in its entirety. The second day, assuming you have learnt the lines of the first act, you run three times. Then you go back to your digs and learn the second act. On day three, you run the second act, and if there is a third act, which was more common in ancient times, you toddle off home and hastily learn that act, so on day four, you run the third act three times. On day five, we usually ran the entire play with most of the props; Sunday was free! Then on the day of performance we had a dress rehearsal on the newly created set, which rather surprised me, since some of the sets were quite ambitious for such a small repertory company. We hoped for the best, had a break for lunch, went back to our digs for a catch-up or a nap, then the evening arrived for the first night!

Bravo, we'd got through it, and the last play that had ended its run on the prior Saturday night was now no more than a memory – leaving a swiftly decaying smudge in our brains, which was now making room for the present one to lodge itself, if only for one week. After we had celebrated the act of getting through the whole play the next morning, we were called in to block the following play, and so this went on and on and on ad infinitum.

On the opening night of the first play of the season, as the leading actors came on, the audience gave them a solid round of applause. These two well-loved and regular players – Jan Fogarty, who also directed, and Walter Wingham, the leading actor – had returned every May, year after year, for the beginning of the perennial summer season, which served as a reminder that the world had turned a complete 360 degrees. Relatives and friends had passed, wars had been fought, political leaders assassinated, and yet this summer as the audience witnessed their old friends enter the stage, stability was here, all was well. They had returned to Buxton, the world was safe – and may it always be well, for seasons to come. The audience loved us and applauded us gratefully – and then the leading actor, an Oliver Hardy lookalike, stepped forwards and made a welcome-back speech. This was a tradition, since on every first night, a member of the cast was obliged to soliloquise a friendly speech and remind the audience of the upcoming plays, most of which were either thrillers or comedies but just sometimes the producers might be bold enough to stage a 'controversial' play to the repertoire.

In this summer season, they seasoned the fare with two: *A View from the Bridge* and *Tea and Sympathy*. In the former, I was cast as the youthfully provocative immigrant, Rodolpho. I enjoyed the play, since it proves that when the writing is good, the actor grows in strength and emotional depth. For the role, I was obliged to wear a blonde wig. There was another 'beep beep' controversial play called *Hot Summer Night* by Barry Reckord, and in that play, I was playing a young Black man struggling with his new life in London, and I actually had to 'black up'! Nobody even made a comment; that was how it was then, and I should think most people in Buxton had never seen a Black person in the town, let alone in their theatre.

No rep season is quite complete without the sniff of romance to while away those wonderful work-free Sundays. Oh my God, one had to have a romance! In this, I was fortunate to have met a lovely, sweet, and charming girl called Jan Barker, and we were both enthusiastic for that kind of love that might just last out a summer season. Sadly, it all seemed to peter out just as the last play of the season was struggling to entertain the last few devoted customers. Jan has long returned to the spirit world, but I still possess her achingly wonderful letters from my first summer season.

Fortunately, the producers tried to vary the size of the parts we played – one week it might be a lead and another week a much smaller role – so you were not overstressed. Eventually, I left Buxton, rather sadly, but with fond memories of climbing those beautiful heather-filled hills of the Peak District with my darling Jan – but alas it never works once you are back in the usual routine!

Civic Theatre, Chesterfield

A few weeks after I returned to London, towards the end of 1960, I had another offer of a rep job in Chesterfield for a three-play gig at the Civic Theatre, and all quite interesting plays. Chesterfield was famous for its crooked steeple, if not too much else. I got quickly settled into my digs and started my rehearsals the next morning with a dapper young man called Anthony Cornish, a rather quixotic, feline chap who gave directions like 'If you don't get a laugh from this line, I shall want to know why.'

And, of course, I didn't get a laugh on that line. The first play, *The Great Sebastians*, was quite a bizarre piece that concerned two sham mind readers. I had little to do in it and have forgotten almost everything about it. The next play was *Antigone*, written by Jean Anouilh, the French playwright. I played Haemon, who is Antigone's lover and tries to save her life, begging his father, Creon, for mercy, but is unsuccessful. This was a bit of a stretch, but I quite enjoyed putting myself through something unfamiliar and challenging.

Back to London, then, and the inevitable waiting, hustling, begging, and even a touch of dishwashing in Au Père de Nico again, where I happened to meet a very pleasant woman called Liz Shaul. How everything has a tenuous string that connects so many events of your life that might have appeared to be pure chance! In fact, Liz was a neighbour of Harry Mann, who used to manage Au Père de Nico and thus, in neighbourly gossip, may have offered her some casual work at the eatery. Also, as mentioned earlier, Harry Mann was a prior flatmate of Randall Kinkead, whose room I now rented. When one is a floating object subject to the ebb and flow of the tide and not a single-minded entity with no pre-planned and organised journey, one is like a leaf caught in the wind, being blown whichever way, and simply floating on its moods. However, this will eventually stop.

Another repertoire interview became available, this time to meet David Giles, who was to be the artistic director of the Everyman Theatre in Cheltenham, another laidback town in the Cotswolds. This was for me the best work so far. I met David Giles in a Soho office and found him the most amiable man. He did not even require an audition and asked me if I was able to take a larger Shakespearean role: Oberon in *A Midsummer Night's Dream*.

I was coming on a little bit too fast. Oberon is quite a wonderful role, and the exotic imagery just drips off the tongue, but I was so excited I could scarcely breathe. I consulted a friend, a South African actor called Peter Zander, but since he had little advice to offer me, I made an application to find out all I could by joining the famous reading room of the British Museum. I was sure this would give me some precious clues into the playing of the role. The application had to be filled in with reasons, which I named as research into Shakespeare's comedies. I was immediately granted my membership card, which had a signature of acceptance written with a great flourish; I was very proud of that card.

I threw myself into daily rehearsals in Soho. I did know I was a bit of a neophyte, having only been employed, until now, in less ambitious rep companies. Cheltenham, at least, had ambitions a little greater than that and, while I was apprehensive, I was determined to make it work. My acting partner, Puck, was played by Tony Tanner – a shortish, mischievous, elf-like creature who could certainly move, sing, and act and was born to play the role. While I was not intimidated, I was still full of admiration for his exceptional skill. He was about five years older than me and his greater experience showed. We got on well for the short time we acted together and for me it was a fantastic learning experience.

The next play was an American play called *The Matchmaker* by Thornton Wilder, in which I was slightly better and confident of my American accent. I grew to love the idyllic town of Cheltenham. The third play was a thriller, directed by a guest director, and I was starting to grow a little more confident. Before the third performance, I actually drank a glass of barley wine in the pub opposite the theatre – I felt just a tad relaxed and the performance was still very confident, and I dropped no lines. By the fourth night, I had become emboldened and risked having two barley wines. Now, barley wine is a powerful ale and, not only did I feel confident of my lines, but I would start to embellish and play with them much more inventively, to the consternation of the poor actress who was obliged to play opposite me.

Drinking before a show is something never to be encouraged and something I would never do again, but as I walked through the town the following morning, a shopkeeper called out to me that I 'gave a hell of a performance last night, young man'. Thus, on the final night, I tried it again; I think I may have even indulged in three barley wines. I was wilder than ever and began to see why some of the old school of Harris, O'Toole and Nicholson were such imbibers. There is, in all actors, a wild and abandoned beast that has to not only be held in check but to be nursed carefully; it is a demon, a fury, that some actors just can't wait to let loose. And drink has a way of lighting the fuse.

The final play of the season was Tony Tanner's own musical version of *Thieves' Carnival* by Jean Anouilh; the music was composed by his partner, Nevil. Now I was obliged to sing, a skill I had lied about in my interview with Giles in Soho; my singing voice was dreadful. The music has wretchedly stayed in my mind all these years – it was catchy and fun but ordinary, and I was only too glad when it was over.

On the last night, on the Saturday, I decided to go back home to Liz, my fellow dishwasher from Au Père de Nico, and since it was still light, I thought I might get lucky on a hitchhike. Such a stupid thing to do as the evening draws in. I managed to obtain two small lifts taking me about twenty miles, but I had at least forty miles to go! I started walking, but it was getting dark and nobody picked up a hiker on a dark night in the countryside, so I walked for about five hours; it felt endless and I thought I'd never get over this painful journey. The night was pitch black with no moon, and I could see no more than a few metres ahead of me, with the dark world around me full of strange, looming shapes. On I went through the night, my feet growing sore and swollen, until at last I saw a sign to Oxford station. With great relief, I dragged myself there, bought a ticket on the early train, and arrived at Paddington station at 6 a.m. An act of complete madness, especially as at one point I saw some of the cast whizz past me in a car. I arrived at 6 Clifton Gardens, Warwick Avenue, W9, and went straight to bed.

The months went past with just intermittent gigs popping up from time to time, which were quite marvellous, just to keep me ticking over and reinforce the belief that, though it was crumbling and bumpy, I was on my path, albeit by a remote side route.

Since Christmas 1961 was coming, there was, as always at this time of the year, a rumbling and a stirring among much less in-demand thespians – those not strictly in the A-stream but part-timers who supplemented their incomes with a vast variety of other jobs. Many of them, curiously, seemed to sell antiquities in street markets on weekends. However, pantomime vacuums up the surplus actors and the great mob gird their loins for yet another quite ghastly Christmas season – and one wretched year I became one of them.

The theatre was the Flora Robson Playhouse in Newcastle, and the show was *Treasure Island*, where I was Pirate No. 3. I hardly recall a single soul I worked with in those dreary four weeks, except the actor playing Long John Silver, whose name, I believe, was Griffiths – a handsome middle-aged actor of the old school, with years of classical theatre experience. 'Get out of my light' was a frequent comment that would be subvocalised to an annoying pirate who may have crowded him. I made the acquaintance of a charming young lady who warmed up a few solitary days in that ghastly town, and I always remember her – her name was Paula McNamara. It was Newcastle where I became acquainted with a local beer called Newcastle Brown Ale. Paula was a tall, well-built young lady and very bright, and I was so grateful and appreciative to whatever fates had brought us together.

As for the show, it was beyond shabby. I guess somebody must have directed it, but for the life of me I haven't a single clue who. When the pirates came rushing on, they usually called over the Tannoy and would interrupt a very intense poker game played backstage for pennies. I heard the Tannoy go one night and, being a little bit keen to finish the hand, I dashed out of the room at the last minute and accidentally stabbed the nice ASM, running my sword through her leg as I rushed to get onstage. I felt utterly grief-stricken, and I could not even pause for a second to apologise lest I be late for my entrance, which is the worst crime an actor can commit. So I had to rush on shouting 'So sorry' over my shoulder to the poor young lady pouring her precious blood into the corridor. She, in fact, was the daughter of the manager of *Spotlight*, a vital trade directory where our hopeful faces stared out for something like £50 per year. I believe his name was Mr Searle. I always found him such a congenial man when I sought his advice, and I quite often had casting calls at their offices. That was my first and last panto. His daughter swiftly recovered, thankfully, since her wound was quite slight.

In those fiery and tremulous early days, one would do anything on earth to be working, and provincial theatre was still relatively healthy. I was cast for another short season at the Playhouse Theatre, Dundee. The first play of the season was *The Merchant of Venice*, where I was playing, in repertory theatre jargon, the Salads – a euphemism for the smaller roles – beginning with Salerio and Solanio, which were combined. I felt I should have played Graziano, but my agent probably favoured the other actor, who really didn't cut the mustard, the result being that I had to give him private coaching in trying to put the role together. However, Portia was played by Sir Michael Redgrave's daughter Lynn Redgrave, who was still in her pupating phase and awfully young but had a brave go at it. Shylock was played by a splendid actor who also made a great stab at the part, and one day I offered to loan him my silver Star of David that Ma had given me, for him to wear during the brief run – only two weeks, as I remember.

Curiously, I scored many laughs for my Salads, so I felt I had some feeling for the Bard. The director himself, Piers Haggard, played the Prince of Morocco as a soppy twit; however, he got the most laughs. Once Piers had woken up to the capabilities of his severely underrated young actor playing the Salads, he ambitiously staged *La Mandragola.* I played Ligurio, a rascally marriage broker, which I quite liked and which suited me, but when trying on the costume, I rather baulked at wearing such revealing tights. For the usual reason, I didn't want to expose myself so blatantly. However, I poured myself into the white tights but begged the director to let me wear something less 'demonstrative'. Then Piers took a penny piece and showed me how to wrap it into your tights round and round until the tights got tighter and tighter. But I hated it so much that I actually started bawling like a young virgin. Somehow, I got through it with my bulging tights and was reasonably successful.

It was still early days for me as an actor, and I had not yet acquired those extra layers of skin which all actors must have as a kind of protection against too much self-awareness. Piers started to take me seriously as an actor and kept me on at the Dundee Rep for another play – I was cast to play the student in the comedy *The French Mistress*. The student was a 17-year-old who was enamoured of his French mistress, and I learned that by using a very light make-up in my eye sockets, I could suddenly take years off myself, which was quite a revelation. I got through that and soon I was out of Dundee and back in London.

Now, as it happens, I went to see Arnold Wesker's play, a socialist drama called *The Kitchen* at the Royal Court Theatre, directed by one of the leading radical theatre directors, John Dexter. The production, headed by Robert Stephens, greatly impressed me. A few weeks later, to my great astonishment, my agent – a different one this time since I changed my agent more often than I changed my knickers – had me audition for the part of the pastry cook, as the actor playing the role was leaving.

I got the part and at the Royal Court no less! Having seen the amazing Robert Stephens in the lead as Peter the German chef, and thinking he was quite astounding, I felt proud to be part of it, but he was unavailable for this rerun and was replaced by Jeremy Brett, also a very handsome actor of considerable talent. Glenda Jackson was one of the team of waitresses; Edward Fox played a waiter. Rita Tushingham, another actress, went on to become a movie star.

Dexter was quite a dynamic director and very volatile, but I got on with him and, with my few lines as the pastry cook, I was asked by Dexter to mime the entire baking process from beginning to end, which I quite enjoyed. All we had to set the scene were whisks and an empty porcelain bowl. Actor Harry Landis, a well-known East End actor who, coincidentally, had played in *The Amorous Prawn*, partnered me at our little chef's table, and he was quite a handful, but very funny and we got on well. Dexter seemed to enjoy continually goading Jeremy Brett, viciously bullying him about his background and Etonian schooling, but Jeremy just smiled and took it all in good humour without ever answering back. I admired him greatly.

I was learning the banter of the theatre world, where directors would love to sarcastically abuse their actors. Of course, Jeremy went on to play one of the most famous portrayals of Sherlock Holmes on TV, but tragically in his later life he had a nervous breakdown. Later he was diagnosed with bipolar disorder. Jeremy was a highly sensitive actor and would respond to the slightest change in the atmosphere.

Glenda Jackson hardly spoke to me during the entire run, except, curiously, during a break when I bummed a cigarette from a colleague and, as she was passing by, she uttered the incomparable words never to be forgotten: 'You poncing fags again?' In fact, all the men ponced fags off each other and nobody minded in the least. I became convinced that this was a woman to avoid like the plague.

The Kitchen was quite an event in the London theatre scene at the time, and, to speak the truth, I was a tad nervous and retained the habit of drinking one barley wine before the show. It did help. I did not feel very comfortable at the Royal Court and had few allies there, but then again, I was a young neophyte and had probably little to offer. Bill Gaskill was an associate director, who was making a large reputation in Brechtian techniques, but I exchanged few words with him and found him somewhat intimidating and cold. Miriam Brickman was the casting lady, a very nice Jewish woman who seemed totally enamoured with socialist theatre, and George Devine was running the whole caboodle. I was even asked to join

John Dexter for lunch one day, which was pleasant. He asked me who my favourite playwrights were, and when I mentioned the German expressionist writer Ernst Toller, he said he'd never heard of him. We didn't speak much after that.

About this time, I auditioned for a play by an American playwright called Arthur Kopit titled *Oh Dad, Poor Dad, Mamma's Hung You in the Closet and I'm Feelin' So Sad*. A slightly soppy, pretentious trifle, with a sub-Tennessee Williams flavour and an incomprehensible plot, but highly theatrical if produced well. I was cast as one of a bunch of page boys in a hotel who always entered the stage in a choreographed style whenever needed. It was to be first tried out in the UK and starred the celebrated actress Stella Adler, doyen of the great Adler acting family, a famous New York method actress and teacher, who I believe originally hailed from Germany. The lady holding the movement auditions used to be an American dancer, famous for her performance as the tomboy in the American movie, *West Side Story*.

I was so happy to be cast in my first West End show as Bell Boy No. 4, and one Saturday afternoon, we were all summoned to the Globe Theatre in the West End for the first read-through. The distinguished silver-haired German actor, Ferdy Mayne, was to be playing the ladies' amorata. So we were all sat around a large table reading for the great New York theatre director Frank Cassaro. Stella Adler's reading was simply electrifying with that powerful American ferocity for which those old 1950s actresses were famous. It reminded me of that wonderful actress who played Dominique Francon in the film adaptation of Ayn Rand's *The Fountainhead* – Patricia Neal, whom I had the great good fortune of seeing at the Arts Theatre in the late '50s in Tennessee Williams's *Suddenly Last Summer*. To say she was phenomenal would be an understatement. I have never forgotten that astonishing monologue she delivered at the play's end under a single light bulb overhead, describing how her poet cousin was attacked by a group of poor Spanish hooligans who found him so beautiful that after killing him they chopped up his body and ate him. It was the greatest acting I'd ever seen from an actress. Sad that she married such an infamous anti-Semite as Roald Dahl.

We rehearsed the play for the usual period of four weeks, until one day we were rehearsing at the Theatre Royal Haymarket and it just wasn't going well. Suddenly Ferdy Mayne exploded onstage – to the director – which was a magnificent sight to behold. It was a thespian Vesuvius, and there are few playwrights who can tap that explosive power of a deeply frustrated actor who is at his or her peak. It is truly magnificent. Finally, we opened at Cambridge Arts Theatre and sadly for the great Stella Adler it was a bit of a disaster. She simply wasn't able to remember her lines, and these were lines that could not be acted with total confidence and power unless they were ingrained in your brain. If only she had had longer to prepare.

Arthur Kopit was a charming young man and I did like his company. As we were on the train from Liverpool Street and skirting the slums of East London, he uttered words that I would also never forget. He turned to me, smiling in his quizzical way, and said, 'Are we in Harold Pinter country?'

I replied, 'Yes, yes Arthur, we are.'

We opened at the Lyric Hammersmith Theatre, and although Stella had more of a grip on the lines, her blazing spirit, which I had seen ignited during that reading one sunny Saturday afternoon at the Globe Theatre and which I was never to forget, had diminished, and the show was brutally savaged. But I knew what Miss Adler was capable of – I had seen it.

Barrow-in-Furness and Cardiff, 1963

There was calm and a small flurry of the jobs which often manifest themselves for new actors on the scene, and one day I found myself in the godforsaken town of Barrow-in-Furness, a run-down, northern country town on the west coast of England, which had a remarkably forward-looking rep theatre. They were doing a collection of Brecht's one-act plays and the director was Derek Goldby, who I remember having fascinating verbal duets with Harry Landis at the Royal Court.

A few of the actors were staying together in the local digs and at least we were friendly. Rehearsals were fun since Derek made life easy. The plays were brilliant parables and easy to absorb; these were some of Bertolt Brecht's most cunning pieces, and I remember the music which accompanied them and can even still sing it today. One of the pleasures was meeting an actress called Hazel and she certainly made my life more bearable. We resumed seeing each other in London, but, like so many other repertory romances, it sadly fizzled out once we were thrust once more into the brutal carousel of our perennial struggles in the big smoke.

In November, I won a role in *War and Peace* at the New Theatre in Cardiff, directed by Warren Jenkins. Jenkins was a fine director and a pleasure to work with, witty and lively, except for the occasions when he fell asleep in the stalls. It was a spectacular Meyerholdian production with screen projections, music, and fire, and the Canadian actor Paul Massey playing the lead. I had a relatively small role but resolved to do all I could with it. It was while we were rehearsing the show that I heard the news of John F. Kennedy's assassination. I could not begin to understand it and was shocked, but somehow less moved than I had been three years earlier when I heard that Albert Camus had been killed in a car crash, cruelly robbing us of one of the world's greatest writers at the relatively young age of 46. Through his work, I knew Camus in a way that I could never know Kennedy, and I was deeply affected by this loss.

CHAPTER 10

Hamlet for the BBC

It was 1964, I was 27 years old, and I was sharing a flat in Drury Lane with mime artist and auteur Lindsay Kemp, mostly on account of our shared interest in the mimetic arts. I managed to get us both a job after one of my perpetual telephonic sweeps of the BBC's drama section at Shepherd's Bush, White City. The BBC was filming a full-scale production of *Hamlet* in Elsinore, Denmark, starring Christopher Plummer in the title role, Robert Shaw as Claudius, Michael Caine as Horatio, Donald Sutherland as Fortinbras, and an incredibly lovely young lady called Jo Maxwell-Muller as Ophelia. An incredible line-up and being produced by a very ambitious Canadian called Sydney Newman. I was in theatrical heaven.

I went for a meeting at the BBC in White City with the director, Philip Saville, who was looking for an actor who was skilled in mime, as he wanted the players scene to be performed entirely in mime. He cast me as the Player Queen. In those young days, I was not yet quite so confident as to tolerate being seen as a woman, so since there was another role on offer as Lucianus the poisoner, I suggested that my skilled flatmate might portray the queen, while I played the murderer Lucianus. Saville was quite happy with that suggestion, and therefore both Lindsay and I were employed for at least a month, which delighted us both.

Lindsay choreographed our scene in a dramatically stylised manner with kabuki overtones, and it was most successful, but what for me was the absolute highlight of the job was sitting in the rehearsal room watching one of the world's greatest classical actors, Christopher Plummer, at full blast. Not only thrilling, it was one of the finest acting lessons I ever had. I marvelled at his energy, his extraordinary vitality, and the immense tone he drew from his resonators and palates, a voice like a trumpet blast. In his determination to astound the audience, he would sometimes almost push an idea to breaking point – but no, it always worked. I was privileged to watch a great actor at the absolute peak of his power.

Hamlet was directed for BBC TV in partnership with Danish TV. Olivier's film of the play was coincidentally showing in London at the same time, so of course I had to drop in to make comparisons but then had to hand the laurel to Larry. However, at the next day's rehearsal, Plummer swept me away, and so I snatched the laurel back and put it on Plummer's head.

On the day of the final run-through, when all the technicians came in and watched, as is tradition in BBC television – when all the rooms are marked out with white tape, with the technicians following the action – Philip Saville gave a little speech before the run. It was to be the final run-through, lasting at least two hours. He addressed the cast quite solemnly and asked us to be still and utterly quiet during the run, and when we were offstage, sitting. The doors to the outside were closed, no one would be allowed in or out, or to go to the toilets after we began. Robert Shaw was not too impressed by TV rules or lectures and rather pooh-poohed this degree of theatrical intensity.

But the show had to be done, the timing had to be immaculate, as this was to be the first and only dry run, and we all did what we had to do and took our seats. We would start when the bell struck 'action'. I sat frozen with Lindsay until our scene, and I had never until that time witnessed anything like this. This was simply an extraordinary performance, and my bones, viscera, and heart observed every cell of it. Our scene was coming up and our beating hearts accompanied it, and it went as well as could be expected, thanks to Lindsay's assured and original choreography. Needless to say, Plummer was awesome. This was a run-through like no other as well as a lesson in acting I would never forget.

Denmark

The following day, we flew to Denmark, since *Hamlet* was being filmed at the actual castle of Elsinore. Our hotel was excellent and on the first night of freedom we explored Copenhagen and delighted ourselves with the Danish hot dogs, which were served from super-hygienic hot dog stands, where ladies in crisply starched white aprons would serve you the most delicious frankfurters, accompanied by finely chopped onions. After the filthy hot dog stands in London purveying a soggy, stinky excuse for sausages with their melting, rotting onions, this was indeed civilisation to us.

Filming, though, was slow and held up by storms, so alas, for the BBC, we went into overtime! At night, after a hard day's filming, Plummer entertained us in the bar on the piano, thus shaming us even more with the man's limitless talent as well as his capacities for drink. Fair to say he had played the role before in Canada, directed by Tyrone Guthrie. In the make-up room in the morning, gazing at Plummer's exquisite profile, I was strongly reminded of photos of Henry Irving – that same classical demeanour, that same slightly Roman curvature.

As a slight diversion, my young lady from costumes was totally irresistible and did help to make the occasion more than memorable, and we became firm friends. A theatre company, on location or on tour, tends to meld into a family and as such reveals more of themselves than they normally would. Robert Shaw would reveal a rather opinionated character at times, although he was an excellent Claudius. Michael Caine was, and still is, the funniest cockney raconteur I have ever heard and had us all on the floor gasping for breath! Such confidence in telling a mixed group of artists his wonderful stories, while Plummer, in his cups, tore strips off the British theatre directors he had worked with, which gave immense fuel to us minor thespians gasping for more hideous revelations about those nasty directors who always turned us down – stories which Plummer enjoyed giving as much as we enjoyed gulping them down.

The production was beset with many problems – sometimes the weather, sometimes technical – but all in all it was a tremendous production of *Hamlet*, mainly through Plummer's extraordinary dramatic gifts, let alone his thrilling vocal cords. Everybody's wages were greatly inflated by overtime, particularly Plummer's, who actually bought a house from the proceeds!

A few years later, Peter O'Toole was to give his *Hamlet* at The Old Vic under the direction of Laurence Olivier. Having spent so much time with Plummer, I'm afraid that O'Toole, although quite a brilliant actor, seemed by contrast totally out of his depth; he had not the classic skills that Plummer had in spades. I did eventually see O'Toole's quite brilliant performance in Bernard Shaw's *Man and Superman*. Of course, I can never forget his astonishing performance as Bamforth in *The Long and the Short and the Tall* – a part that I played at the Liverpool Playhouse in 1966.

Perth, Scotland, 1964

Now I was offered a summer season in a charming theatre in Perth. The company commenced with Oscar Wilde's satirical comedy *The Importance of Being Earnest* with myself as Algernon. The other play scheduled was an Italian play, adapted by the celebrated author E. M. Forster, in which I was down to play the Italian lead. This was to be followed by *A Streetcar Named Desire*. So, with much enthusiasm, I joined the company, found my digs, and eagerly began rehearsals.

I shared a dressing room with a very pleasant young fellow who was playing Jack. We both had a touch of nerves before the off and so, sharing a dressing room, we each had a glass of wine before going onstage. Something I would never even dream of today, especially after my alcoholic indulgence at the Everyman Theatre, Cheltenham, but it seemed to help us.

We had a genial, if biscuity, female director named Joan Knight who hardly ever exchanged a word with me but was efficient and got the job done. And so we opened and I was indeed under the illusion that I was more than satisfactory. However, the review in the local paper was not overtly favourable – but I soldiered on, boldly improving night by night and gradually getting less and less nervous.

I was waiting to see the cast list for our next rehearsal for the play adapted by E. M. Forster, where, I was convinced, I would be cast as the excitable Italian. Sure enough, the cast list went up and, to my absolute horror, I discovered that I was to be cast in a minor role while my acting partner was to play the role eminently suited for me! I must say I felt rather cheated and had not reached that age of maturity where actors learn to put up with a few minor disappointments, and thus, exhaling a jet stream, I tore into the old folk's office and told them that this was simply not tolerable. I then threw in my notice for the end of the run of *The Importance*, which was to be the following week. They both looked absolutely shocked – this was an intolerable situation for them – and warned me that I had an Equity contract to 'play as cast'. I then added that I might indeed walk now, before the end of the run. There were no limits to my pathetic temperamental effusions. My last days were miserable indeed, but I got through them and fled Perth forever, never to see that miserable theatre again. Later, I came to see this moment as the turning point of my career. As painful as it was, my decision directed me towards a new life, and a new way of looking after myself: I would not allow myself to be so hurt again.

Influences – Jacques Lecoq

Now, as it happens, I would stop at nothing to improve my art, and so I went to dance classes at the Dance Centre in London's Covent Garden, where I took fairly strenuous lessons with a brilliant black teacher whom I remember as Ray. Even his warm-ups were utterly exhausting, before you actually got to the dance routine, which I quite painstakingly tried to learn each week but never quite managed.

My favourite classes were my academic introduction to the world of mime, taught by an ex-student of the French maestro Jacques Lecoq. I had been fascinated by the mysteries of mime ever since watching Marcel Marceau on one of his frequent visits to London. I found that he completely dominated the art of the performer and showed us actors what miracles can be performed by a body and the imagination. The name of my teacher was Claude Chagrin and her teaching was exemplary, and slowly I learned to embrace mimetic techniques during our two or three classes per week.

And what classes – so brilliantly and technically detailed! Claude had studied full-time with Jacques Lecoq for three years and was a gifted teacher. She was no less of an inspiring choreographer and was used by director John Dexter for the brilliant physical effect in *The Royal Hunt of the Sun* at The Old Vic – also *Equus*. A group of young actors, including Edward Petherbridge, would meet in the morning and hungrily gulp down this new and exotic art. We were probably, for the first time, defining our bodies and the magic that we could achieve with full knowledge of them. For the first few weeks, we studied the mime of illusion and trained our limbs to be both flexible and inventive.

Our first exercise was, since she always spoke the names of the exercises in French, *marche sur place*, when we would walk while appearing to remain in one place. This was not just fascinating but also so instructive, since we learned many forms, such as walking to the side and, using the same technique, mounting stairs. Suddenly, we were feeling as if our legs and arms were developing magical abilities as we used our limbs and muscles not just to get from A to B but to express the inexpressible. It was as if we were rediscovering our own bodies and amazing ourselves at the wonders we could achieve. The *marche sur place* gradually became the signature of every street performer on the planet, eventually reaching across the ocean to Michael Jackson, who, cunningly, not only learned it but reversed it to create the astonishing moon walk.

Then we experimented with *pressures* and *pulls* as we would flatten ourselves against an object and push the object by leaving our hands firmly on it while our bodies withdrew. Then our bodies would dive into the object, leaving our hands there, which defined where the object was, and again withdraw. Consequently, it was by withdrawing, or 'reacting', that you established the scene. There were no limits to the possibilities. Mounting the stairs is quite a beautiful action, since the outstretched arm is virtually the banister and the illusion of movement is when you withdraw your arm backwards as you would when mounting a real staircase – but your leg has taken a step upwards as your arm retreats.

So, basically, these early mime exercises concentrated on the mechanics of mime. What is beautiful about the art is the act of 'giving' to create the magic of the illusion. A ball is thrown and you catch it, but you don't just open your hand to grab it; you receive the ball by a swift, almost involuntary, gesture of withdrawing your hand just as you are about to receive it, so you 'give' to make the gesture pure. The simpler, domestic details are important; for example, you do not take a hat and ram it onto your head – you 'introduce' your head into it. The same with a glove or a coat, so the act is implicit. Lecoq created some exercises where all the movements of thrust and withdrawal can be visualised; for example, he created an exercise called the punt which, when performed well, is quite beautiful and is reminiscent of a Japanese etching.

Figuration mime is a stage further and higher and takes it to a completely new level. Figuration means to use another body as your material or clay, and that also can be mesmerising. There are no limits to what you can express with the body. The only limit is your imagination. One of the body's most expressive movements is undulation, where you can perfectly imitate the serpentine writhing of the snake or even the waves in the sea. You start the movement on the floor. You push your knees into the floor, which raises your hips, then you push your hips back to raise your stomach, and as you push your stomach back, it raises your chest and finally your head. You're now in the start position lying flat. You push your knees back into the floor and repeat. Our spines are the most wonderful tools of our bodies. But with figuration, the excitement is in the discovery of the unlimited possibility of creating with another human.

When Claude Chagrin demonstrated this technique, there were no defined movements as there were for the physical exercises such as walking, running, climbing, pressure, etc. It's up to you and, most of all, the audience, who have to 'read' it; also, they must read it swiftly since the art of the illusion is swift and ephemeral. A man becomes a staircase while the second man is climbing the staircase and before you have assimilated the picture it has changed, as the second man, who was the climber, reaches the end of the first man's body, has now replaced him and become the stairs. The sheer efficiency of creating the actual environment of the set is not only inspirational to watch but, most of all, the method of interpreting a complex play, particularly a Shakespeare.

I have witnessed far too many heavy, set-loaded Shakespearean productions where fortunes have been spent to create the reality of the setting. Peter Brook put his discovery of the empty space to brilliant use in *King Lear* – a production I recall to this day. On the rare occasions I have been asked to direct Shakespeare, any qualms I have had have been totally assuaged by my belief in Lecoq's methods, and inspired teaching will come to my aid almost automatically.

When later directing *Coriolanus* in New York for Joe Papp's Shakespeare Festival Theatre, I came to a pivotal scene where Coriolanus and his men ram a huge city gate open, and in every production, I have ever seen, the gate has been the main feature. The cost must have been humungous. But what does the gate mean? It is merely a force that must be overcome. When our actors performed this scene, they acted the gate. Eight able-bodied men rushed the invisible gate, arms outstretched until their outstretched hands hit the invisible wall now made visible by sixteen outstretched palms. Holding the palms in what is called a fixed point, they then withdrew their bodies, arms still outstretched; they then heaved their shoulders into the 'gate', which slowly gave way. Coriolanus simply says, '*The gates are open*', a simple and effective solution. The death of Coriolanus usually follows an elaborate sword battle, taking weeks of valuable rehearsal time that is often beset with unfortunate injuries. That said, children will love it.

In our production, Christopher Walken played Coriolanus and was quite concerned about the death scene, since he had naturally heard of Olivier's famous depiction – as had the world. But we used no weapons, we acted them – after all, we were actors – and the result was quite successful, ending in a coup de grâce when Coriolanus is pinned to the floor as Aufidius thrusts a sword through his prone body. Impaled, the dying warrior still attempts to move and eventually, with superhuman effort using both hands, painfully withdraws the sword from his body. Fuelled by the audience's imaginations, it was as dramatic as it could possibly get. No weapons were used, only the human body plus imagination, the most powerful tool of all. And when Aufidius hunches his powerful body to deliver the final horrific thrust, no audience member could have the slightest doubt as to what he was doing. But what we did avoid were endless hours of meaningless stress.

***

There is something about the theatre that connects you with the world. In film or TV, you mostly connect with your colleagues on set. In theatre, however, one is exposed and, in being so, is daring to reveal what you believe are your insights, or talents, or even your opinion of the world we live in and the world that has passed. You accomplish this by several different techniques; either through language, performance in acting, or even through gesture and movement. How thrilling this can be once you have decided what it is that you want to do, and to apply yourself wholeheartedly to it! There is something that ticks away in your heart, and then beats faster and ever faster until you feel that you will never get any peace until you have plunged into your obsession and dealt with it.

I experienced this in that moment I mentioned earlier when, as a child, I saw our landlady's piano for the first time, in the front room of the house in Luton where I was evacuated during the war. From that moment, hardly a day passed when I didn't plead with my mother to allow me to have piano lessons, but alas it was not to be. No matter how many times I asked, there were always the same excuses... 'After the war is over' or 'We're going to America one day'. Well, the war ended and we went to America, but I never did see a piano. When I was 17 and already going to work, she did actually allow me to rent a piano and even paid for a weekly piano lesson. But I knew that it was too late if I was going to fulfil my dream of being a concert pianist. I practised every day and after three months I could just about play Mozart's concerto in C… but then I could bear it no more and gave it up. I would find some other route to releasing those secret demons that lay deep within me.

So, I was determined to become an actor! But not just an ordinary actor, I would have to go far beyond those limits. I would explore that art to the very core, but first of all I would have to learn the simple basics of learning lines and then learning the hardest part of all, which is to actually get on stage, in front of an audience, and deal with the terror that grips you in its claws until you feel that there is nowhere you'd rather be. And even when you have scraped together the few shreds of courage that enables you to get on that stage, there may come a moment when the most precious element in your brain, your memory, suddenly blanks out...

Even as you are achieving what you think will pass as acting, there comes a moment when you fear that your precious lines will just desert you. For some actors this is beyond torture, and even as they are saying those precious words, another part of them is seriously considering just walking off the stage... escaping into the free and open air. Ahh, that feeling is the very worst. But, but... you concentrate and turn that loathsome anxiety into power. Yes, it is possible. But it takes time and constant repetition until one day you find that you enter that stage fearless. Yes, utterly fearless and confront that anonymous audience as if they were no more than a mass of strangers who demand to be not only entertained but astounded, thrilled, excited, won over, enthralled, inspired, moved, frightened, even horrified. Yes, your live audience carry all those nebulous desires within them, and you must satisfy them. Yet it's hard to let go when you are working with other players and must at least try to conform to what you have rehearsed. But the play must allow you to actually combust, to act scenes of explosive power... but this is rare. Even so, you should also be so inspired by the playwright, so enamoured by what they have written, that you only wish to serve the writer.

So there comes a moment when you become so inspired that you begin to lose who you are and actually become the character you are playing. You are transformed. There even comes a moment when you feel transcendental... touched by a force so much larger than yourself. An artist – whether they be a musician, painter, singer, or actor – will, if they can touch that luminous spark within them, feel as if they are guided by a greater force than their mere selves. Perhaps it is at this moment that one can say that they have been touched by God. When I watch the hands of a classical pianist race across the keys, giving life to thousands of notes, in perfect order, at astonishing speed, I am in awe of what the human being can achieve. It's beyond belief. It defies the imagination. Probably that is why I yearned to play the piano.

When I witness just what a human brain can achieve, I bathe in the glory of what humanity is capable of. How is such a thing possible? So I never fulfilled that aching desire to be a concert pianist. Oh, what a loss was there, but could I at least try to achieve that in the art of acting? I could never be an Arthur Rubenstein, but I could try to at least emulate an Olivier, a Scofield, an Alec McCowen, a Jean-Louis Barrault. This French actor became my hero when I saw him perform brilliant mime in the film *Les Enfants du Paradis*. The film was directed by Marcel Carne and shows life in 19th century Paris. Barrault plays a mime in a theatre that does not allow the spoken word. Only the so-called legitimate theatre was allowed to do that. We see him languidly sitting in a marketplace watching the crowd. He observes a sneak thief robbing a fellow spectator of his pocket watch. The victim howls that someone has stolen his watch and presumes it to be the attractive lady by his side. He screams for the police. The *gendarme* appears and the rather pompous man demands that the lady be arrested. Meanwhile Barrault, who has been watching all this, signals that he knows who the thief is and tells the whole story in the most exquisite mime that I have ever seen. Of course, he is helped in the film by music which greatly enriches his mime. But I did think at the time that mime was a skill I would dearly love to have.

Maestro Barrault was not only an actor, but a man who explored all the elements of the theatre. He wanted to expand and explore all the possibilities of the actor. He trained under another mime artist called Etienne Decroux who became a famous teacher of mime and was himself featured in the film *Les Enfant du Paradis* as the theatre manager.

In 1965, a couple of years after doing the City Lit mime class with Claude Chagrin, I headed to Paris to take the summer course with Jacques Lecoq himself and actually had the great fortune also to do a class with Decroux. He held his class in a large studio attached to his house. I arrived early for the class. Eventually, Decroux appeared. His thick silver hair hung low beneath his neck and he was wearing a dressing gown. He then started to speak and gave his instructions for the class today. I gathered what he required and it was something to do with 'preparation'. Several students volunteered to go up onto the small stage.

I thought what they did was utterly breathtaking. My heart was pounding. I had never felt anything like it in my life. No words could ever begin to have the same effect. They must be his regular students. After several more students had appeared, I decided that I must make some effort to get up. I had some sense of what was required and, judging from the two earlier and brilliant students, the style of the movement.

I went on stage and began. I wanted it to be *perfect*. I froze like a statue at first then began to tell my story. The class was frozen silent. When I finished Decroux faced the class and said that what we all saw was a perfect example of how the body can be more profound than speech. I was very proud. I left his studio and once more poured into the Parisian life. I would never forget Etienne Decroux.

Playing Lucianus (The Player) in *Hamlet* for the BBC, 1964

CHAPTER 11

Naked and Shameless

Through the actor's grapevine, I heard that the Theatre Royal Stratford East was looking for a youngish actor for a play called *The Zoo Story* written by American playwright Edward Albee. At the time, I was house-sitting for a charming young American actress who was trying to make an impression on the London stage and was returning home for a few weeks. The grapevine is such an important part of actors' networking, and we all so much rely on each other to spread any bits of news, all of which is gathered up eagerly like squirrels feverishly gathering nuts. They were looking for an actor to play the part of Gerry, who is a loner, an outsider, neurotic, and even psychotic, and I felt that this sounded like a strong fit for me.

Theatre Royal Stratford East was a celebrated theatre made famous by the brilliant Joan Littlewood. Her remarkably dynamic shows never failed to excite me, and her public was always massive and adoring. Who could ever forget *The Quare Fellow* by Brendan Behan, *A Taste of Honey* by Shelagh Delaney, and *Oh! What a Lovely War?* Alas, she gave up the theatre at the end of her last season, and now the theatre was run by two worthy, if not overly inspired, chaps.

Of course, it was a very difficult position to be in, to follow in the footsteps of the great Joan Littlewood. A forty-minute curtain-raiser for the main show (which was Molière's *George Dandin*), *The Zoo Story* starred Ewan Hooper, a talented comedian who was to play opposite Gerry. Having looked at the size of *The Zoo Story*,

I found it far too intimidating to take on two roles at once, so I was allowed to opt out of the second play, which, obviously, did provide a nice role for an ex-colleague of mine who had been in the Cheltenham Rep at the same time as me, Peter Brett. The key element in *The Zoo Story* is a fifteen-minute monologue about the anti-hero's relationship with the landlady's pathetic dog. The speech is a brutal stinger and five pages long.

I rang the theatre, as many actors are often obliged to do, and fortuitously an appointment was made for me to go down to Stratford East to audition. I happily took the tube to Stratford and read for the director David Thompson. When I read it, in my American accent, which I felt was fairly faultless at that time, it felt as if the play was indeed a good fit for me. The director seemed to be quite impressed with my reading and he asked me to read again and make it a bit more excitable, even with the book in my hand; he then told me that it was a good reading and that I would have the part if I wished it.

One of the coincidences, or chance happenings, of the theatre is that you have to be in the right place at the right time and for the right role, as well as a whole list of other circumstances. First of all, the part of Gerry was originally to be played by another quite well-known actor, but he was in Spain filming a massive Shakespearean epic called *Chimes at Midnight* directed by Orson Welles. It was common knowledge that if you happen to be employed by Orson Welles, it would be folly to plan future engagements for the next few years, and true to form this actor was held up and could not leave the film with the great master. In consequence, the part of Gerry was suddenly free and avaialble and floating around the ether of the London theatre world, eventually reaching my severely underused ear.

I took the tube back to Victoria and headed home to Ovington Square as happy as Larry, but I still had my night understudying job at the Vaudeville Theatre. So I swiftly gave two weeks' notice as required and, to my surprise, this was not taken too happily, but by then I couldn't care less. Each night I returned to my dressing room, but this time I was learning the moves and words of Gerry in *The Zoo Story*. I felt the words sinking in, and slowly I felt such a sympathy for him that I was almost beginning to feel as though I was turning into him.

But then, as expected, a bout of nerves wrapped itself around me like electric cables. In those ancient days, the opening night of a play was the critics' night; there were no such things as previews. You opened cold and I was gradually feeling these cables tightening themselves around me. It was unimaginable to think of the first night with a huge West End crowd.

As fate would have it, whom did I bump into one day on the Strand but Jo Maxwell-Muller, the charming young woman who had played Ophelia in the BBC's *Hamlet*. Naturally I told her what I was doing, and about the pre-first-night collywobbles that I was feeling, and lo and behold, she had an answer – Librium, a tranquiliser that preceded Valium. She said, 'This won't interfere with your memory but will take the edge off your nerves.' She added, 'Many musicians take it.'

I was utterly grateful to this smart and lovely young lady, who is tragically no longer with us, so I was determined to try it. I had a prescription from my nice East European doctor and began each morning's rehearsal with one tablet and after a week increased it to two. I actually started to relax and had no side effects either. Oh, Jo Maxwell-Muller saved me – good night, darling lady.

Although I was just in the curtain-raiser, it felt to me that it was provocative enough to be an exciting partner to the main show, and also it had rarely been performed. I felt totally bound up in it, like a chrysalis in its pod, ready to burst open at the appropriate time, and assisted by my green and black magical helpers, oh thank God!

The big day was getting closer and closer, and I was rehearsing each morning onstage, and the most curious element of this story is that it was Christopher Plummer's dynamic acting in *Hamlet* which I had absorbed like a sponge – his daring, his acute inventiveness, his lyrical movement. He had invaded my mind; he had stirred my imagination and rattled my soul. David Thompson, the director, seemed totally happy with what I was doing and rarely gave me a note. I was beginning to be an actor and do work that was highly challenging and that I could be proud of.

Now for the dress rehersal. The day was finally upon us, and the set was merely to be a park bench upon which Ewan Hooper as Pete, that hapless Mr Everyman, would be found sitting, waiting to have his bourgeois world ripped apart by Gerry, the outsider. Yet the icy fingers of terror were beginning to clutch at my heart. I was hoping to have the entire cast of the Molière in the auditorium to come and see me at the dress rehearsal so that I might get a little used to having an audience in front of me and to take the nervous edge off.

The penultimate day came, and the Molière started first. I waited and waited, but *George Dandin* had 'set problems' and demanded many adjustments. The stage manager knocked on my dressing room door, where I had been waiting for a few hours, and sent profound apologies from David that he was so much delayed with his Molière and would I come in tomorrow a little earlier, which was the day of my opening night! So all the nerves in my system, the army of demons that congregate inside your head ready to explode, had nowhere to go except out.

I raced downstairs to the stalls, where the whole company were assembled still in rehearsal, and discharged the demons at full throttle. Howling, shouting, screaming, all to do with the fact that I was being denied the opportunity to at least put a protective seal on my performance before the next night. I was naked and shameless and a cry rose from the pit of my stomach that shocked everyone sitting there – it was the outburst of a hysterical, insecure actor. All actors have at least one of these touches or tumours or raging hysterias growing inside them until finally they discharge them during moments of great tension. I have witnessed one or two of them. It is a sight, and sometimes it is thrilling to behold, not that I am claiming mine was.

I returned to my dressing room and David Thompson was close on my heels. He told me that he was so sorry, but he had too many problems with the Molière, and he tried to reassure me that I had absolutely nothing to worry about and that the company would most certainly watch it tomorrow morning. Also, he had asked my colleague from the Cheltenham Rep, Peter Brett, to come back with me, to keep me company, and to console me as best he could.

Peter was in fact the man I am grateful to for introducing me to Antonin Artaud by giving me Artaud's celebrated book, *The Theatre and Its Double*, which I devoured like it was the Holy Writ. Artaud articulated everything I felt about what the theatre could be: how explosive it could be, how it might reproduce our dreams and imagination rather than naturalistic 'reality'. The book became a bible for me. Reading Artaud took me back to when I first read Kafka in Germany; its effects were similarly profound.

The next day I came in – I'd taken my usual dose of Librium, perhaps three 10 mg pills – I came onstage for the run-through, and the cast sat, it seemed to me, a trifle coldly but politely, and I, awkwardly, got through it. There was little to no response from the cast. At least I had done it, and I returned to the dressing room.

There were several hours to go, so I tried to nod off. I took a couple more Librium pills and half-dozed off. Time was now speeding up. I felt rather calm, but just to be on the safe side I would risk one more. It was now six! I just sat in my chair and feebly responded to the stage manager's call of 'half an hour, please,' then 'the quarter', then 'the five', and finally 'beginners onstage, please.' I walked drowsily downstairs and took my place onstage; Ewan Hooper was already there on the bench. The curtain was down, and I could hear the rumble of the audience. My nerves were still playing around but were somehow kept under control by the onslaught from the pharmacy. The curtain rose like a giant eyelid; the lights went out on the assembled audience, then came on and fell upon the stage.

I stood there, frozen. This was the biggest challenge of my life. It began. Gerry turns to the man on the bench and says, 'I've been to the zoo.' Forty-five minutes later, it was over and there was a positive applause; I had not dropped a single line nor a word. It was over. I went to my dressing room and changed for the Molière, since I had been persuaded to do a small walk-on, which I gladly accepted.

When it was all over, I sat in my dressing room alone, since I rarely invite anyone to a first night in case the worst thing happens, but David Thompson knocked on my door and said, 'Very well done.' I am so grateful to him as I am thinking about this, fifty-eight years later. After this, there was another knock on my door and it was

Lisette, a part-time Swedish girlfriend I had met at mime classes at the City Literary Institute. It was a surprise, and what a splendid surprise – I was so happy to see her. She told me that she had been so nervous for me that she'd had to heave up in the ladies' loo. I was terribly touched by that, then we took the underground to Knightsbridge and went to a beautiful Russian restaurant, now sadly gone, called Luba's Bistro, which was still open since the play went up early. So, it all worked out as well as it could.

We then stayed at my flat in Ovington Square and we were happy together. We both woke early and she returned to her home. About half an hour later, my phone went, and it was Lisette. 'Steven,' she said, 'the reviews for *The Zoo Story* are great, all of them.' I could not have been happier.

Now, a couple of weeks after *The Zoo Story* was playing, I had a call from *The Sunday Times Magazine*, as they had chosen me along with five male actors to promote as up-and-coming performers of 1965. Journalist and writer Kathleen Tynan, the wife of celebrated literary critic Kenneth Tynan, had been commissioned to write a piece about the 'new guys on the block', and none other than Antony Armstrong-Jones, the husband of Princess Margaret, was to be the photographer. *Good God!* And all this for the astonishing reviews I had received. And yet something inside me felt that this was just a little too much.

However, I went to the *Sunday Times* building in Gray's Inn Road and met the celebrated Lord. He was most friendly, outgoing, demonstrative, funny, and elegant, while I felt like a complete nerd. He shot away while I kept my Lennon cap on, since I didn't much like how my hair was just beginning to desert me. After this short-ish shoot and chat, he had completed the task. The other actors chosen for the article were Terence Stamp, whom I went to drama school with, Ian McKellen, who now lives on the same street as me in Limehouse, Nicol Williamson, whom I followed into Dundee, and Peter McEnery. I thought, '*What am I doing here?*' But for the commentary, Kathleen Tynan interviewed me and, for whatever reason in the world, neither of us were able to reach a satisfactory editorial, so when it came out, I was totally embarrassed by the gross banality of my comments. But now I had calls from the leading repertory companies across Great Britain. This was a great step up the ladder.

I had left Ovington Square, since Randall wished to have my room back to accommodate his resurgent love life, and I was now, in between Ma always being there for her peripatetic son, somehow criss-crossing London, as is an itinerant actor's habit, to rooms as they became available.

It just so happens that Lindsay Kemp, with whom I had once briefly shared a flat in Drury Lane, had seen me in *The Zoo Story* at Stratford East. He had come with the lady from whom he was renting a room in Islington, N1, and one evening he invited me and Wesley Murphy, an Irish actor whom I had befriended in Lincoln, to have dinner with him and his landlady, Alison Minto. As I remember, it was a very pleasant evening, and we all enjoyed Lindsay's repertoire of comic antics and impersonations. Alison cooked a most delicious stew, and I was quite fascinated by her. When it was time to go, true to form, I slipped downstairs to wish Alison goodnight and rather overstayed my welcome... until the next morning. I remember it so clearly and we'd made love so sweetly. As I left in the morning, I felt no more about it, and headed back to Ma, my usual safe haven in between jobs and digs.

A few weeks later, Alison phoned me and actually suggested that I move in with her since Lindsay was moving out. I was quite flabbergasted to be asked to share a flat with a woman whom I had only met once! Some women are very bold. It wasn't long before I became ensconced in Islington with her. I found Islington far more friendly and stimulating than Chelsea. Alison quite happily gave Lindsay his notice, since he was not too passionate about paying his rent!

At first, we got on very well though when not working, as is the case for most actors, I went through periods of intense boredom. Although I liked Alison, I was still determined to attain the ultimate goal of having a flat of my own. I had left my name with an estate agent in Upper Street in Islington and one day received a brief letter from them suggesting that I should look at a flat for rent in Devonia Road just off Upper Street. I felt that I simply had to take it. I recall stepping inside and being completely overwhelmed by the beautiful double room on the ground floor in that typical Victorian style with double doors linking the two rooms. It was quite wonderful, so I had to take it. So that's what I did.

I remained there for nineteen long and fruitful years. I accepted the flat for £6.50 a week. I possessed the basement and ground floor and let one floor to a tenant to help pay the rent. I was happy! So happy. I had never been so happy in my entire life. Alison remained my dear friend and sometimes she would visit and sometimes I would visit her. I suppose it would be called an open relationship, although we were married for a short time.

Camden Passage, an ancient street and antique market, was just round the corner and Chapel Street food market was just by Angel tube station. Not only was I happier than I had ever been in my life, but I was also free. A few years later in 1970, I bought the house for £3,500 – no one else wanted it because the top two floors of the house were let to controlled tenants, ancient pensioners who were rather batty. I soon had to get used to 'Meals on Wheels' banging on the door daily at midday with their lunch. One of them was an old lady who kept saying to herself, over and over again, 'I don't care because I can't care!' It became something of a mantra for me in later life. Sometimes she would switch on her gas hob, cover it with a saucepan while she wandered off to the lounge to look for matches, then forget what she was looking for and settle down to something else, while the house filled with gas. I told her welfare worker that she was at risk of blowing us all up, but they always assumed that I was just trying to get rid of the tenants.

However, I had arrived at a momentous point in my life and was quite proud of myself. I even started to build shelves in my room with the advice of Alison's smart network of friends. Peter Stobbart, another architect, sketched out a staggered shelving system for me which I carefully built. I also made myself a large bed out of pinewood. I was alive, I had purpose, and I was happy; I had my very first home.

Now, at least I was master of my own destiny, and through Alison I gradually began to improve my social life. My dear friend Alistair actually built a most beautiful desk for me. It was long and had thick wooden drawers and shelves built in. It was a masterpiece. It was the most beautiful gift I ever had and I wrote at least a dozen plays on it and so bless you Alistair. Recently you passed on, and of course I miss you dearly, even though we didn't see each other for many years. He moved to the south of France and actually became a part-time busker since music became his modus vivendi in life.

As Gerry in *The Zoo Story*, Stratford East, 1965

In *The Tell-Tale Heart*, the first part of *One Man*, 1981

PART 3

CHAPTER 12

Upgrade

No more second-rate repertory companies. The first upgrade was Glasgow's Citizens Theatre, under the direction of Michael Blakemore. The Citizens, as it was known, carried a great reputation as one of the most adventurous theatres in the country and attracted some of the country's best talent.

So, in 1966 I became a member of that illustrious theatre, but yet I run before my horse to market, since just before Glasgow I was invited to the Liverpool Playhouse, where the talented and passionate David Scase was the artistic director. I was employed for a short season, starting with a naff play called *Seidman and Son*. It was largely a piece of sentimental schmutter and a vehicle for Jewish comedian David Kossoff, and also where the famous West End producer Duncan Weldon began his theatrical career. He was mainly Kossoff's minder and assistant, and at that time was mostly interested in photography, as I was, and so we became quite friendly. My 'digs' consisted of a large dumpy room in Hope Street opposite Liverpool's great modern cathedral.

I loved being in Liverpool, especially as I became quite friendly with the talented actress Lynda La Plante. I managed to get through the awful *Seidman and Son* without too much agony and then was cast in a miserable, dull Australian play of sublime awfulness. My memory of it has mostly been erased, but I do recall that as an actor, I went through a kind of Pauline conversion and simply started the lines with as much sincerity as I could muster, and it transformed my whole being.

And now for the big one. In the beautiful city of Florence, Italy, they had been staging an anti-war festival for a number of years and companies from all over the world were invited to submit an anti-war play. David Scase won an invitation to the festival for the play *The Long and the Short and the Tall* by Willis Hall, which originally premiered at the Royal Court Theatre in 1959 starring Robert Shaw and Peter O'Toole. I had, fortunately, seen it in the West End, so I did have a feel for it. O'Toole, of course, was quite amazing in it as Bamforth, the strutting cockney private. I could never forget him, and I saw him with his original nose!

So, we rehearsed, and in Liverpool, 1966, I played Bamforth, who is the rebellious clown in the piece, and I think I got the hang of it – I felt it was my best performance since *The Zoo Story*. I got on quite well with the lads and was happy every morning. I would get up very early, walk down to the theatre, eat breakfast at the little café opposite, and be onstage and running my lines at least one or two hours before the others trotted in. I learned the text speedily and felt quite good.

We all got on the plane to Florence and found that a pleasant hotel had been booked for us, then we went straight to the theatre called Teatro della Pergola, a truly magnificent theatre, mainly used for opera. To my astonishment, the Italians had built a complete replica of our set in Liverpool. It was perfect. We rehearsed by running the entire play, had a break for notes, and then the following night we were on. The play started well and we all enunciated our words with just that bit of extra clarity. Interval – cheerful applause. I was happy – there was much laughter from the audience, and it seemed to be going well – but the interval went on and on. I thought, *'For God's sake, when shall we continue?'* But this is the Italian theatre style. The interval stretched out for a whole hour! Almost as if it were an opera.

Eventually, we did finish the play to the biggest ovation we had ever received. As it died down and we exited the stage, this seemed to be an excuse to start the applause up again. It was a thrilling night, and I thank David Scase for such a great opportunity. We were all beaming and the next day's press was nothing less than ecstatic, especially for my physical work and clowning with the Japanese prisoner.

Duncan Weldon had driven David Scase to Florence, but now David wanted to fly back to Liverpool, so asked if I could go with Duncan Weldon, which he permitted. We drove all the way back to Paris from Florence, from where I flew back to Liverpool. It was quite an adventure. I finished the last week of *The Long and the Short and the Tall* in Liverpool and said farewell to that charming city and to David Scase, whom I loved like a dad. But at least I did keep in touch with him until he died.

I had certainly been promoted in the public domain and was now asked if I would be interested in playing opposite Vivien Leigh in *Sweet Bird of Youth* to be performed at the Citizens, but regrettably that never came to fruition. I was asked up anyway to do a short season of plays and another double bill of *The Zoo Story*, but this time with the sharp and clever actor Edgar Wreford, to accompany Strindberg's one-act drama *The Creditors*, in which I was to play the artist. I was not too brilliant in the role and hated playing it.

Next, I was cast as the lead love interest in Doris Lessing's rather wet *Play With a Tiger*, in which I had far more success. Michael Blakemore directed and he was a real actor's director because he had started his career as an actor and was familiar with all the petty foibles that can creep surreptitiously into your head. And as an actor, he had a brilliant way of batting the damn things away and continually encouraged me. One day Doris Lessing came up to Glasgow to see her play. The cast, all happy to meet her before the show (big mistake), gathered in the green room and took tea with her. I may be a dumb actor but not so dumb as to meet the author before going on, and for the first time. So I stayed out of their wretched little conflab and went onstage that night fighting fit, while all the others fell apart with their self-consciousness. I met her after the show, as was normal, and she said she was 'happier with my performance than the actor who played it in the West End'. I was mightily chuffed.

I loved Glasgow, and the small studio theatre we played in was called The Close; apparently that was the name given to the filthy narrow alleys between the slums that existed in Glasgow mainly in the last century. Ours was no longer a slum but a small theatre seating about eighty people – very intimate and a wonderful place to practise your art. Sometimes I'd get there in the late afternoon and go to the local butcher's shop for what was a popular Glaswegian dish called Popeseye steak – a small, well-marbled piece of meat the butchers tend to keep for themselves and a rare treat. I'd cook it up on the club stove and then hang around before the performance. There was an old caretaker whom I liked chatting to and he liked teaching me old working-class folk songs from the Gorbals, which I have never forgotten.

Fortunately, I did have some female company, a very charming actress called Eliza Ward, so I didn't suffer too much loneliness. When she returned to London, I used to visit her from time to time in her very homely flat she had in Hackney. She got a job in rep and asked if I would like to take care of her kitten, which I gladly did, and when Eliza returned, I said the cat was now so used to its new home that it would be unkind to take it away. Anyway, I had become extremely fond of the cat, and I went on to keep her for the next eighteen years, plus assorted kittens! I loved Pottle dearly; she was a tortoiseshell and so affectionate.

Then I was once more back in London in my wonderful ramshackle Victorian house in Islington in Devonia Road. I lived in the lower part of the house – the ground floor and basement – and could not have been happier, despite the sitting tenants on the top two floors. They had been placed there so as to empty their old house, which was then fodder for the property market. Eventually the sitting tenants were moved to care homes since they were incapable of looking after themselves. The day they left, I have to admit I was not only mightily relieved, but jubilant. I walked upstairs and bathed in all that space and decided to make it as beautiful as possible.

In 1967, I found myself back at Webber Douglas, but this time as a teacher. I had been out of work and needed money. Ralph Jago, the principal, encouraged me to teach and I accepted. What started as a necessity became the most profound and productive experience I could imagine, for I learned more as a tutor at Webber D. than at any other time in my career. The classroom was like a laboratory full of specimens willing to be experimented on, and our discoveries taught them how to act and taught me how to teach. I asked myself how I could use all I had learnt from Claude Chagrin and Jacques Lecoq and found a way to do it that ensured all in the room were equal participants in the mime. I created a way of teaching that used the energies of every student in the room, not just those who had the most lines, and this approach informed my teaching and directing from then onwards.

The Resistible Rise of Arturo Ui, 1968

Michael Blakemore, the director of the Citizens Theatre in Glasgow where I had worked so happily three years earlier, did not forget me and offered me a job in Bertolt Brecht's *The Resistible Rise of Arturo Ui*. This production had been invited to the Edinburgh Festival in 1968, and I was offered the role of Givola, whom Brecht loosely based on Hitler's evil propaganda minister, Goebbels. It was not a huge role, but it was a pleasant diversion, since the cast was so good. Leonard Rossiter played the gangster Arturo Ui with panache and vicious humour.

Now, for some reason I did not feel too comfortable in the role and even suffered nerves, but I persevered and managed to get through it. Part of the reason, I think, is that I was both on and off-stage, which is never the best way to get acclimatised. Michael Blakemore actually flew to Berlin to see how the Berliner Ensemble did it – quite a sensible idea, especially for handling the mass crowd scenes, which at that time was not a particular skill of British directors. Del Henney, a wonderful Liverpudlian actor, played Roma, and Bruce Myles, an Australian actor, played a variety of character roles. But the main thing was that all the actors were exceedingly jolly, friendly guys. They all became good friends, as did Leonard Rossiter, and we even remained friends for many years after, spending endless hours playing poker at Bruce's home after the show on Saturday nights, since Arturo had transferred to the Saville Theatre in the West End.

I, of course, turned down the invitation to transfer with the show to the West End, since I had my own production which I produced, directed, wrote, and starred in at the Roundhouse. I didn't need a flipping walk-on role in *Arturo Ui!* I believe that Laurence Olivier came up to Edinburgh to see it, since Michael Blakemore was offered a directorship at the National Theatre no less. He then went on to successfully direct plays in the West End and on Broadway for many decades to come, and bravo to him. He was a very decent bloke. He was from Australia – a land I was soon to visit.

Metamorphosis, 1969

Time passed and women came and went, since I always loved to spend time with them as companions and not always to merely open my flies... And so yes, I was improving and started to value the sheer wit, company, and understanding of the female sex.

Like many young men, I collected plenty of names and numbers in my black address book, and so when feeling a bit lonely, I'd call one after another until I found someone, anyone, who was free. How appalling is that? Basically, I think I really wanted to be part of a society of friends. Of allies. Of work colleagues. But for whatever reason, I seemed to have few good friends during that time. All that changed when I began directing my own productions. Now I began to feel connected to the world. I was totally discovering myself. Then I was happy. Then I made friends, many, many friends. Then I was able to discover the world. Most of all, discover what I could do, what I was capable of …

My very first production was to be the most extraordinary short story I had ever read and, of course, it was by Franz Kafka. I was planning to adapt his brilliant and bizarre *Metamorphosis*, and the thinking of the time was that an evening in the theatre had to be of a certain length, so I thought *In the Penal Colony* would make up the time perfectly. Also, it had a hell of a central role which I felt suited me: the insane commanding officer.

My wonderful new friend Alistair Merry built by hand the 'execution' machine for the play. As I have mentioned, I met him through Alison; and it was also through Alison that I met Martin Beaton, an architect who not only helped me design the set for *Metamorphosis* but also shared with me the investment costs. Thank you dear Alison, and God bless you. Now I had friends I was proud of and could work with.

The years in Devonia Road were probably the most creative years of my young life. I had the whole house to myself, I was totally free, and it was here that I adapted Kafka's *The Trial* and *Metamorphosis*, since I had been thinking about the latter for years. Only when I had seen a student production in Oxford did I realise how dumb I had been by not showing the beetle onstage in my original adaptation, as the brilliant young student director did – simply showed the beetle hidden behind a small box which only revealed his top half with his arms criss-crossed. This immediately galvanised me into doing a full production, which I tried out at the London Academy of Music & Dramatic Art (LAMDA) with a scaffolding steel set in early 1969. I got the idea when, during my frequent visits to the YMCA, I noticed huge scaffolding in the centre of the gym. From this, several athletes were performing the most daring twists and turns. The effect was compelling and I knew at once that this had to be the basis of my set for *Metamorphosis*.

During the production there came a time when I felt, as a beetle, I ought to try hanging upside down from the ceiling. I had not yet practised this, so when the scaffolding set was erected at the LAMDA studio, I crawled out onto the scaffolding and very slowly let myself hang from my legs, crooked over the steel bar, with the stage manager and others standing underneath just in case I landed on my skull. I gripped the steel bar with the backs of my knees with such force it was as if I would melt the steel, but gradually I got used to it.

It was a little crazy to have put the show into two parts, *In the Penal Colony* as the warm-up and then my one-hour adaptation of *Metamorphosis*, but we did it and the shows went on. I had originally tried out *In the Penal Colony* in the Arts Laboratory in Drury Lane, a quite wonderful, almost magical environment run by a curious American maverick, Jim Haynes, who started up the Traverse Theatre in Edinburgh.

Alastair's execution machine was quite extraordinary. The base was made of wood, which acted as a kind of bed, but then, following the story faithfully, he added the top piece, which was folded down and encapsulated the 'victim'. In the upper half were row upon row of needles that worked on a pneumatic system slowly puncturing the victim's back until the victim realised that a 'sentence' was being scrawled upon him. The crowd watching this execution was waiting for that eureka moment when the prisoner suddenly realised what the words were spelling out to him! They were spelling out his crime, and the moment the prisoner read the words with his pain was the main purpose of the machine, of course, until the prisoner's eventual demise.

Halfway through the dress rehearsal, George Hoskins, the CEO of the Roundhouse, called me into his office to tell me that the critics were showing reluctance to come. It had already been on (as a try-out) at the LAMDA theatre. He begged me to call all the offices of the arts editors and explain it to them, which I did and then got on with the dress rehearsal. We opened successfully, the cast were splendid, and reviews the next day were better than we could have hoped for. The theatre began to fill up most nights. *The Sunday Times* review would not be in for the first week, but hopefully the second week, and we were only booked for three weeks! But when Harold Hobson's review came out the following Sunday, it was nothing less than legendary, and we played the final week to a packed house.

I'll never forget that feeling I had as I lay on my back with my arms stretched out and my fists gripping the steel bars of the set. I was proud to be working with steel and not the flimsy ephemera of the 'well-made' play. I was utterly exhausted, having finished the final Saturday doing two double bills, matinee and evening – i.e., four shows. However, I felt utterly triumphant – just nine years in the business, starting with Buxton in 1960 and now at the Roundhouse in 1969. It was the happiest day of my life – by far! And I was 31. I was most certainly on the path.

Now I had confidence and even a teeny bit of fame, but hardly any offers or sparks of interest from the dull establishment.

***

July '69. The Rolls-Royce was waiting outside for me: a beautiful, shiny black Rolls parked already in the forecourt of London's celebrated theatre. I was determined to celebrate the final night of my greatest achievement so far. I was so proud and even prouder to share my illustrious chariot with my cast, who were all over the moon.

The Roundhouse in Chalk Farm, once a railway turning shed, was now a magnificent theatre created by the acclaimed Jewish socialist playwright Arnold Wesker, who saw its incredible potential. Now this theatre was mine, all mine, for at least three weeks. Three glorious, magnificent weeks, since I had hired it to put on this production of *Metamorphosis*, written by me, directed by me, and performed by me, aided by my good ally Martin Beaton, who co-designed the set and put up half the money for our first big adventure in London. At the end of the show, the lights faded and the audience exploded into bravos… I felt on top of the world.

After the final performance, I washed and dressed and piled into the Rolls with Alistair Merry, Christopher Muncke (my assistant director), and my girlfriend at the time, Janet Chappel, an actress at the RSC. We headed down to Kettners, a beautiful restaurant in Soho. I had pre-booked a table and all was in order. We took our seats and sucked up the attention like hungry wolves while the Roller dutifully waited outside in Romilly Street.

I recognised one of the waiters from the YMCA, where I used to go almost daily when I was an unemployed actor. In the YMCA, all men are regarded as equal but now in Kettners he was my subordinate, ready to attend to my every need, and I noticed that he avoided my eyes to save me any embarrassment or acknowledgement since our positions were now unequal, but I called out to him, eager to confirm our friendship.

We all ate and drank simply and happily. I felt that I had crossed the border between life and death, between enslavement and freedom, between pointlessness and inspiration. Up to now, I had been crossing and recrossing, but now I saw the road ahead. It was in the far distance, but it was getting nearer. That Saturday night I was exhausted, ecstatic, and euphoric; I was firmly on the first step and no one had shown me the route, which made the journey all the more severe but all the more rewarding. I had to crawl through the woods myself and more than once I wanted to give up on it, but I didn't, even if I had to drag myself along a flinty road.

But my lovely and devoted Alison (God rest her soul), and Martin Beaton, Alistair, and Chris Muncke were always there to help me, let alone the late George Little, a splendid actor of the old school who didn't always agree with me but whose expertise, in the end, I much appreciated. And, of course, Jeanie James as Mrs Samson and Petra Markham as my sister, Greta; altogether a splendid cast – God bless you all.

I received some very gratifying reviews, including the one from Harold Hobson in *The Sunday Times*, who spoke of the moment in the play when I crawl out of my room as the gigantic beetle, which he felt was so dramatic that he compared me, rather hyperbolically I thought, to what the great Victorian actor Henry Irving might have achieved in the play *The Bells* at The Lyceum! I was receiving signals near and far.

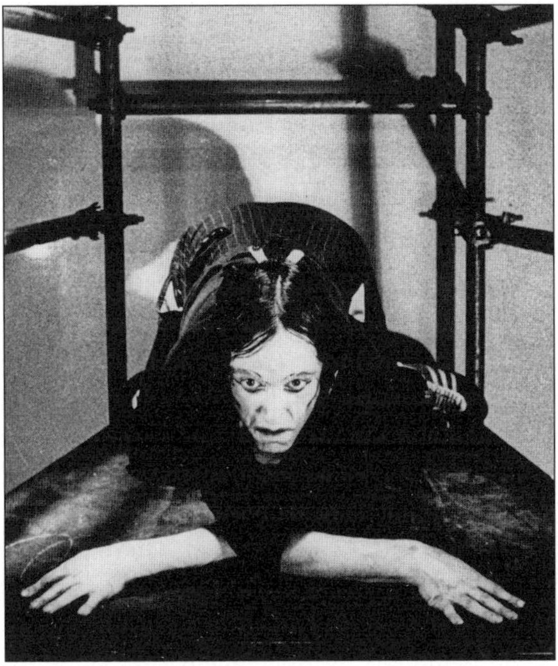

As Gregor in *Metamorphosis*, 1969

CHAPTER 13

First Trip To Israel

After I had staged *Metamorphosis* at the Roundhouse in 1969, I made my first journey to the extraordinary nation of Israel. The writer Wolf Mankowitz invited me to join the film production he was shooting there. The film was called *Bloomfield*, a feeble story of a footballer in Tel Aviv who befriends a small fan. To call it the very worst gauche, slushy, sentimental film ever made would be an understatement. Wolf Mankowitz had seen *Metamorphosis* and believed that I was the up-and-coming wunderkind, and that I would be useful to help with Israeli casting, shooting a video about the production, and coaching the child, etc. However, nothing seemed to work. And gradually our relationship, which had been so promising, became corroded by all the petty arguments that Mankowitz was having with the Israeli producers, and most of all with the talented Israeli director Uri Zohar, who was a sensational comedian-turned-filmmaker and had a strange habit – familiar, it seems, to many Israelis – of shouting his head off whenever he greeted an ally in the street. It was, apparently, a sign of extreme machismo.

Richard Harris was, bizarrely cast as an Israeli Jew, which would stretch even the most vivid of imaginations. We had all been waiting for his arrival with anticipation, and I was slowly getting used to Israel and the torrid heat in Tel Aviv. Two years earlier, the Six-Day War had left Israel in a triumphant mood and the whole population seemed to be happy, when not shouting.

By the strangest coincidence, at the very first party I was invited to, I met the daughter of Max Brod's personal assistant. Max Brod was the great ally and editor of Franz Kafka's work and was largely responsible for saving much of it. I felt this was extraordinary, having just performed *Metamorphosis* at the Roundhouse, that the very first person I met in Israel was so connected with Kafka's work. She was a charming lady and introduced me to her young architect friend who was seeking to rent out a spare room in her flat, which I took after later being booted out of this bizarre film!

I was growing sicker and sicker of this appalling movie and Richard Harris seemed to take a peculiar dislike to me; I felt as intensely about him, though I did not show it as much. Wolf Mankowitz was finding just about everything in Israel overwhelming to deal with and also took up the habit of shouting, but he did have a very sweet assistant who had a soothing effect on me.

Finally, the film managed to begin and I continued dribbling around as assistant, desperately trying to make myself useful. Initially, Wolf Mankowitz thought that the filming might inspire a documentary to be made at the same time, which I agreed to enthusiastically. However, the chaos that always seems to arise while shooting films in a foreign country was doubly increased in Israel. I arrived there with the goodwill to make myself as useful as possible; I took part in searching for actors, arranging auditions, and even coaching the miserably miscast young boy. But when Richard Harris became belligerent after I tried to give the young boy some notes, suddenly shouting out 'don't interfere!', I thought, *'What the hell am I doing in this dump?'* However, I went on to take photographs of the city of Tel Aviv, including the exotic food market, and visited Jerusalem on my days off. I found, through my new architect landlady, a room where I could develop and print my own pictures.

So, I helped the casting lady, coached the young boy, but nothing seemed to impress the production team. Richard Harris seemed to excite the director, mainly on account of his huge frame; he also impressed me, since he was forever singing to himself when he wasn't on set. Apparently, he had just recorded a hit song and felt that he had to demonstrate his loose, free Irish demeanour at every minute. I was feeling less and less secure on this wretched set and just put up with his shenanigans. Eventually, even the director was fired. Yes! This shocked me, and I think it was a shock to him that was so intense that he turned overnight into a Hasidic Jew – this is a person who is utterly devoted to a rigorous study of Hebrew religious texts. A bizarre metamorphosis for one of Israel's greatest comedic heroes.

Now Richard Harris decided that, after all, he should direct the film, but he needed an actor to stand in to run his scenes while he looked through the camera's lens. I was to be suggested, among all my other tasks as the actor's stand-in, which intrigued me somewhat, as I wondered how I would deal with the love scenes with the beautiful Romy Schneider, the German movie star who was playing the female lead. Just as I was contemplating the situation, the overworked and undertalented production manager informed me that they didn't need me anymore! I was offered one week's wages as compensation. This was a typically trashy offer but, truthfully, I was only too glad to escape from that madhouse.

I had a room to live in with a very nice Israeli lady and now decided to explore Israel. After a few days, I took off for Eilat in Southern Israel, taking the bus from Jerusalem, which is only an hour's cab ride from Tel Aviv. In Israel, you can all share a cab. The cabs are called sheroots, like the cigar. There were three people in the back and one sitting next to the driver in the front. It's a wonderful and cheap way of travelling. Now, the best thing you can do when hiring a sheroot is to make sure you get there early so you sit in the front; otherwise, you might be crushed in the back. On this occasion, I waited till I was at the head of the queue and got into the front seat.

However, a Hasidic Rabbi had a problem sitting in the back since there were two women sitting in the other two seats. For this poor, devoted Israelite, this was far too dangerous and so one of the young ladies, before we set off, tapped me on the shoulder and said, 'Excuse me, would you mind changing seats with this man because he is a very religious man and cannot sit so close to a female?'

I was not in the mood, so I said, 'Well, that's too bad, let him get used to it. Females are made in the image of God as are males, so he should attempt to get used to it.'

She then said to me so gently and sweetly, like I was a gentile from some village in Bavaria, 'You see, he's a religious man and it is very

Me, my sister Beryl (left), and her friend at Blackrock Pool, Brighton, 1946

Left: Blind Uncle Alf (centre);
Right: Uncle Sam and Aunty Betty, 1941

Right: Me in 1954, aged 17, wearing my royal-blue *schwarzer* suit;
Left: Me and Yvette Bizeau in London, c.1957

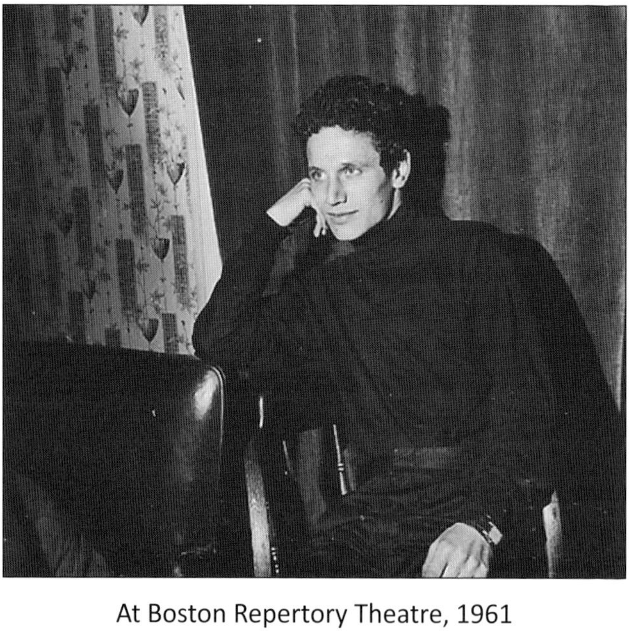

At Boston Repertory Theatre, 1961

In *The Long and the Short and the Tall,* 1966

In *Metamorphosis*, c.1972

As Detective Constable Tom in *A Clockwork Orange* (1971).
Warner Bros. Pictures

Left: As Mike (left) in *East*, 1975. Photo: Roger Morton;
Right above: Alison Minto, my first wife;
Right below: Shelley Lee, my second wife

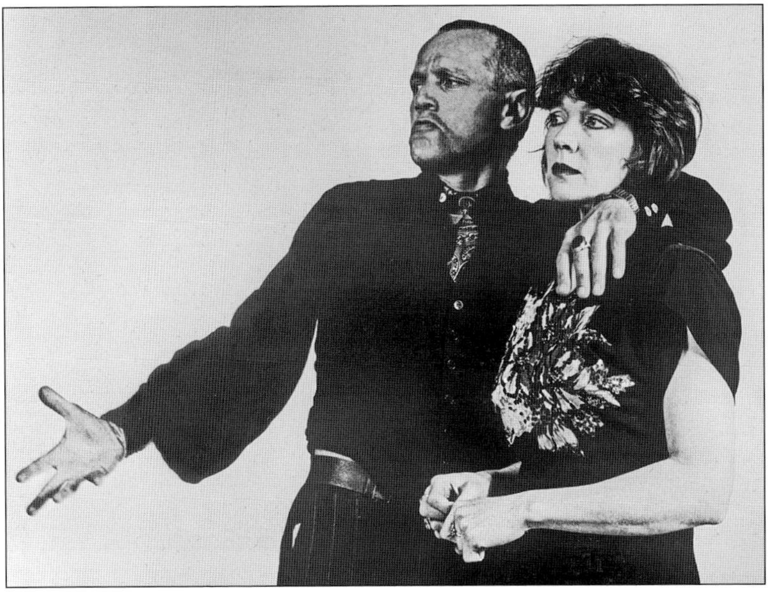

As Hamlet with Linda Marlowe as Gertrude, c.1980.
Photo: Roger Morton

My first office in Devonia Road, Islington, c.1982

Left: As General Orlov in *Octopussy* (1983). Eon Productions;
Right: As Victor Maitland in *Beverly Hills Cop* (1984).
Paramount Pictures.

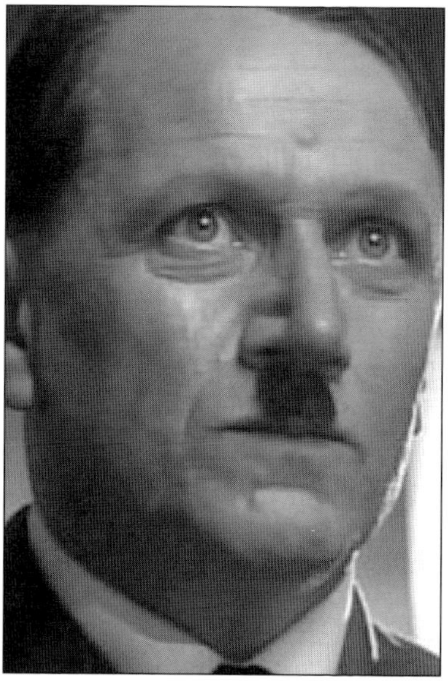

Above: As Lt. Colonel Sergei T. Podovsky in *Rambo: First Blood Part II* (1984). TriStar Pictures; Right: As Adolf Hitler in *War and Remembrance* (1988). Warner Bros. Television

As George Cornell in *The Krays* (1990). Fugitive Features

As Steve with Joan Collins as Helen
in *Decadence* (1994). DeLux Productions

As Reginald Shaw with Angelina Jolie as Elise Clifton-Ward in *The Tourist* (2010). GK Films

Left: As The Shakri in *Doctor Who* (2012). BBC Studios;
Right: As King Olaf the Stout in *The Vikings* (2019–2020).
MGM Televsion

difficult for him,' so I said, 'He'll get over it,' and snuck myself into the front seat quite contentedly.

Once on the bus from Jerusalem, I finally saw the beautiful land of Israel unfold before me. We drove down to the Dead Sea until we arrived in Eilat – about a four-hour drive. I was now breathing the wonderful fresh air of ancient Israel, liberated from that ghastly production. Once in Eilat, I explored the small streets of this slowly emerging city and scanned the wanted ads pinned up in one of the small stores offering accommodation, except it was necessary to share a room with four others; Eilat was now a booming new tourist destination since the Six-Day War. Nevertheless, I quite liked my quarter share of the room – I felt I was part and parcel of this new and exciting world – I neatly set out my possessions, lay on my single mattress, and felt completely at home.

The other chaps were friendly young men from Germany, Sweden, and France, and were happy to show me the ropes and the work opportunities that were available. I was beginning to feel like a sabra (a bittersweet fruit that metaphorically describes a native-born Israeli). I was invited to join them for an early-morning coffee no later than 6 a.m. This would be when the trucks would draw up, wanting labourers for the day. It was not easy work and you had to be young and tough. You were employed to either carry large rocks or drill new roads (a first for me), and some days hoist hundredweight sacks of cement on your back. The work was murderously hard, but you could take water breaks whenever you wanted.

The day ended early since it was way too hot to work in the blistering heat. Then we would collect our wages, which were excellent, since labour was short and young men were a valuable asset – except, I wasn't that young, around 33, and I looked enviously at these lean, muscled Swedes who threw these rocks around like they were candy bars. Then we'd sleep in the truck and head out to the beach at Eilat and throw ourselves into the sea with tremendous relief. This was work like I had never known it and I enjoyed the friendly young company.

Every morning, I clambered out of bed, rushed down to the coffee shop, and waited. Some of the guys knew what the work entailed and avoided certain trucks. They were smart. However, I took everything that was offered and one day I was humping cement bags for hours and at the end of the day leaped into the sea when our work was done. But as soon as my back hit the salt water, I screamed in agony: the cement from the bags had obviously eaten its way into the surface of my back and, in that sweaty 30 degree Celsius heat, the sea salt was like a punishment in the wound. I suddenly decided I'd had enough and that being a pioneer for Israel was not quite for me, so I bussed back to Tel Aviv.

I was happy to be back in my flat with my lovely architect lady. I did manage to make an appointment with a leading Israeli theatre company and show them the rather fantastic reviews I had won at the Roundhouse in July before I became a labourer in Israel. Unfortunately, the director didn't seem to be interested, to my utter astonishment, so I eventually returned to London. The film that had brought me to Israel was shown at the Berlin Film Festival, where Rex Reed, the festival's leading critic, gave it a review describing it as the biggest piece of garbage he'd ever seen. That's schadenfreude with a dash of salt. A reasonably accurate description, I think. But my relationship with Israel was not quite over yet, although several years would pass before I heard from them again.

The Trial, 1971 – The Rope

The breakthrough moment of my life came in 1971 when Raph Jago suggested that I direct a play. From now there was no turning back and my purpose in life was beginning to take shape. I chose for my first project something wildly ambitious, but I believed in it far more than merely choosing a play. We decided to adapt the seminal Franz Kafka novel *The Trial* as I also believed that the use of mime would enable the production to take shape. The student actors threw themselves into it with great relish and excitement and eventually the production took shape.

For many years Kafka's novel had fascinated me, and I knew that one day, once I had been able to absorb Lecoq's technique, this would be a work that would be brilliant to adapt. As I have mentioned, mime figuration – where you would work using other bodies – is the most enthralling to watch as well as being a most apposite metaphor. I was inspired when thinking about the set for *The Trial* to create twelve free-standing screens which would be a multipurpose set. I felt a sense of mystery as I stepped through the twelve wooden frames, as did the rest of the cast. Figuration is probably the most profound of Lecoq's techniques, one might almost call it metaphysical.

An empty room. Two guards enter the room of Joseph K and inform him that he is under arrest. Following their usual procedure, they search not only his room but his very being: his wardrobe, his chest of drawers, his personal possessions, even taking it to the most absurd lengths. Using figuration, you are so free, temptation is irresistible. For example, Miss Grubach, the landlady, is about to bring Joseph K his breakfast as she usually does each morning, though this morning she was about to abandon doing so. In the scene where the guards beckon her in, we turned Joseph K into a table, quite simply: as K complains about his treatment, one of the guards strikes a blow to K's midriff, which doubles him over and suddenly he is an effective tabletop. Miss Grubach swiftly puts the tray on the 'table' and the two guards feast on K's breakfast, which has conveniently been placed on his back. While the guards feast, K, even in this position, is quite able to discuss openly his predicament, holding a conversation with the audience. It worked perfectly for me, since in searching the room, you are virtually ransacking the person who occupies the room. K becomes a set of drawers and also a wardrobe containing his suits. As I said, in some way, what you possess is also metaphysically part of you. By using K's body as a set of drawers, you are violating him. You are what you possess.

Not only could we see the extraordinary pliability of the human body, but we could also use certain objects that are flexible and allow themselves to be almost willing adherents. In the later scenes in *The Trial*, K has an assignment to meet a 'client' in the local cathedral. It is a beautifully written scene, and I chose to narrate the passage in plainsong. It was quite beautiful and the poignancy of the music created an atmosphere that hinted at a less than happy finale. Once inside the church, and having been sermonised by the priest, K is guided out by two men. For this, we used a singularly simple plain white rope. The guards each hold one end, which suddenly becomes K's journey. As K reaches the end of the rope, one of the guards merely turns, thus creating an immediate right angle to which K travels. When K has come to the end of the right angle, the second guard lifts the end of his rope, thus creating a staircase. After K traverses the staircase, the rope has become a straight line once more. The two guards, now in unison, swiftly criss-cross each other. The wall has now become a trap, and as the guards continue to criss-cross each other, each one effectively strangles poor Joseph K as he announces his own death. I always found the rope scene extremely exciting. Without knowledge of Jacques Lecoq's techniques and ideology, one could not have even begun to attempt such a production.

***

When I felt ready to try my hand at staging student productions professionally, I began by advertising in a theatre trade magazine for actors. They poured in and I began my first attempts in directing theatre, as well as acting and even producing.

One of the actors who walked in that day was called Pip Donaghy. I immediately felt that he would be a good ally to have and he was. Also, he brought in other actors from where he had trained at the Drama Centre in North London which put great emphasis on movement. Soon we had a team of about eight first-rate actors. It was amazing, and I now had my own company, all of whom were willing to work for no wages... purely in the belief that we were going to create innovative theatre, the likes of which had seldom been seen. But it was also intimidating. Especially so on the first day. It was a Sunday, and I had found a perfect rehearsal space in a church hall just opposite to where I lived. I felt mightily insecure as they all gathered in the hall and waited for me to begin the proceedings. I was not only directing but also playing Macbeth. So how was I to start? Now I was acutely aware that modern theatre groups used quite vigorous workshops which were marvellous and effective methods of discovering unique ways to create the production.

I had been wildly influenced by a stream of American productions that had come to London and made explosions in the ho-hum British theatre. I saw the La MaMa theatre group and the Living Theatre, particularly their incredible production of *The Brig*, which I saw at the Mermaid Theatre, and thought it to be one of the most astounding pieces of theatre that I had ever seen. At the small

Mercury Theatre in Notting Hill, I was also amazed to see a spellbinding production of *Futz*.

So, after a brief welcome, we started on some theatrical exercises. It was a beginning, sometimes successfully and sometimes awkwardly, but I had to be bold, be purposeful, and, most of all, be confident. Of course, I somewhat overdid the workshop and after an hour we would make an attempt to start the play. That was an awkward change from play and improvisation to focus. This is where I realised that I badly needed an ally, a partner. How to begin? Well, most of all it had to be an ensemble. Pip was becoming a very positive ally, and I was grateful for his presence. I made the decision to begin the play with the witches, leading into the battle. I created a vertical line for the battle where the actors stood one behind the other, some of whom then moved from side to side, and some up and down.

From the group, the witches appeared. It actually began to look stunning. It was a start and from here it started to grow. But I was not thinking clearly yet. We certainly should have read the bloody play first. I had not even placed myself into the production.

The actors were all enthusiastic and they all came to Islington and began to feel enthusiasm for the way we were working; inevitably, some did find paying work and had to leave. I got in touch with LAMDA drama school to see if they could suggest actors who were willing to do experimental work with me. So one day I turned up to have an interview with the artistic director. I was asked to wait a few minutes in the office. Sitting behind the desk was a receptionist. When I described to her what I was looking for, she promised to keep me informed of actors who were keen to work with me. She was unusually pretty with large brown eyes and very long straight hair. I informed her that I was working on a production of *Macbeth*, and she said again that she would certainly stay in touch. I told her that I would keep in touch with her. Her name was Annie Cheatle, and she reminded me of a Renaissance painting, or a character from Peter Pan painted by Rossetti.

She did, in fact, suggest several actors, but in the end I chose to stay with the actors Pip Donaghy had recommended to me from the Drama Centre. We worked together for at least six weeks, and the production was growing daily while we rehearsed in the evening from 5 p.m. to about 10 p.m. Then at the YMCA, I broke my ankle while attempting to do a somersault. Even so, my hardy group actually lifted me across the road to the rehearsal room, and I just directed while not being in it. The delay meant that I had to lose my most brilliant friend and ally, Pip Donaghy, since he had to earn some wages, but we remained friends. In the end, we performed it at the theatre belonging to the London School of Contemporary Dance.

The show was exciting and adventurously unique. Critics were invited but few came. One Sunday paper that did come was the *Sunday Telegraph*. I eagerly sped down to Leicester Square to catch the paper as soon as it came out. I was full of anticipation. I felt that we had created a bold, new interpretation. Just after midnight, the papers came out, and I tore it open eagerly. What a slimy, uninformed, and stupid review.

The idiot wrote that there should be a moratorium for theatre groups that stand in circles. Nasty dog! We only used that particular formation once when we all lay down to sleep and it was quite beautiful. All our feet met in the centre. Slowly out of it, as if in a dream, a hand rose into the air clutching a dagger! Macbeth awakes and sees it, then declares: 'Is this a dagger that I see before me?' As he attempts to seize the dagger, the hands transfer it from one to another. It was such a special piece of staging, and I was very proud of it. *Never mind!* I had to get used to these moronic critics and we soldiered on. We were now even beginning to get dates from other theatres around the country. We had certainly begun, and most of all, I was now in proud possession of an Arts Council grant!

Of course, once one is dealing with the Arts Council, or any government body, one must be prepared to get royally entangled in masses of paperwork. After all, you are receiving cash from the state, and every penny had to be justified. First of all, you must give all details of your forthcoming productions, estimated income from them, and where they are. And so, you're in a position of foreseeing the future. Plus, costs of all the actors you may or may not use, plus sets and costume etc. This meant of course that I had to hire an administrator to deal with all this. And a good administrator is worth their weight in gold. I did eventually find one. Now I was in a position where I had to keep planning ahead and not plan a production as the mood took me. It was a struggle, but I soon got used to it.

Meanwhile, a regular visitor to Islington was the lovely lady whom I met in the office at LAMDA. Annie was a rather sweet and appealing pre-Raphaelite, and we got on very well and made a habit of spending weekends together, like a practice run for cohabitation. In fact, now that I had my own home, I was becoming more humanised and less desperate, less hungry for the body of a woman to vent my lust as if that was the sole purpose of my existence. I no longer felt I had to almost justify my existence through the adventures in the flesh. By then my home in Devonia Road, the first real home that I had ever possessed, was for me the ultimate and utter freedom.

Now that I was in receipt of an Arts Council grant, I was able to pay actors and form what was to be the makings of a semi-permanent theatre company. So, in order to loosen the strings of the grant, I repeated *Metamorphosis* at the little Hampstead Theatre Club, a prefabricated squat in Swiss Cottage. This time we were helped by having a brilliant Scottish actress called Maggie Jordan. Although not the easiest person to work with, she was a luminary on stage and I was surprised that she was never chosen to be a major star. Our Hampstead season was very successful.

Greece, 1971

It was summer 1971, and Annie and I decided to take a month off in Greece, touring round the Greek islands. I fortunately was able to cash in my return ticket from the ghastly film I had worked on in Israel, *Bloomfield*. Consequently, we were able to travel first class all the way to Athens by train and what a splendid adventure that was. Once we eventually arrived, we found a hotel near Syntagma Square. The next day, we went to the port of Piraeus and took the ferry to the magical isle of Skyros, the southernmost island in the Sporades, where the poet Rupert Brooke was buried. Also, incidentally, Skyros was where Achilles sequestered himself to avoid being cajoled into joining the Trojan War. When I was lining up for tickets, I was in absolute torment trying to make up my mind which island to choose. There were so many and they all looked quite wonderful in the brochure. As I was standing in the queue, I heard a young lady in front of me ask for a ticket to Skyros. I looked at her, and she looked like a seasoned traveller with her knapsack and weathered face. I then took a chance and said: 'Two tickets for Skyros, please!'

It was a longish but wonderful overnight journey, and we arrived the following evening in Skyros. It was beyond wonderful; it was a piece of heaven, and we could not have been happier. From the port, we took the bus that was waiting for passengers to the village high up on the Plaka. Our long journey had finally come to an end. We got off the bus and were surrounded by a small gathering of Greek ladies who cried out to us in Greek: '*Dormatheria, dormatheria, dormatheria*' ('sleep, sleep, sleep'). I was then drawn to a typical, smiling face of a Greek middle-aged woman and she signalled to follow her, which of course we did. After a few minutes, we stopped at a small, whitewashed stone house. We climbed just one flight of stairs and there was our room, our home to be for the foreseeable future. It was a spotlessly clean, bare room with two single beds, one at each end of the room, and we thought it heavenly; we were in paradise. We were, yes indeed, and we both slept right through the night and woke at dawn. What woke us was the sound of bells – bells that tinkled in our ears and were hung round the necks of goats. Apparently, each bell had a slightly different tone, so a well-attuned farmer would be able to keep an ear on his flocks and even detect when one went missing.

Our month in Greece was nothing less than magical, and we even became more adventurous, hopping from island to island: Skopelos, Alonnisos, and then further south to Milos, and all were quite wonderful. We even repeated the experience the following year, and it was an experience we would never forget. It was 1971. It was a world I'd never seen before and we both felt utterly transformed, and now the curious thing is that we were in Greece for almost a month and sex seemed to be the very last thing on our minds... it felt that we were supremely content just to be together enjoying our shared passions: walking, talking, exploring, eating Greek food, taking photographs.

The frenzy of the flesh seemed more activated by the frenzied activity of the mind that one felt in London. Each day, we'd take a long walk after breakfast to one of the many beaches, which was a sheer delight, as were some long winding walks where we would pass endless fig trees with well-ripened fruit longing to be picked. We also found a small fisherman's cottage that served food on their large veranda and so, after our glorious swim in the clear glittering and warm water of the bay, the owner would prepare a sumptuous lunch for us, which was mainly a delicious Greek salad, boasting a large slice of feta cheese surrounded by large, blush-red tomatoes and olives... ah, to call it heavenly would be an understatement. And as evening came, we'd take the most enchanting walk back to the village on the hill. Then we'd always dine at a local café and passed the time as though we had been transported to paradise. On one island, we released a sparrow we found in a cage, but its wings were weak since it had been caged for so long. I saw a cat preparing to pounce on it and began to curse myself – but then the little bird found new strength and flew away until it became a dot in the piney hills. I could relate to that bird: newfound freedom can be strange for a while, but then you take flight.

Fortunately, I had my Pentax camera with me and so we memorialised our trip in hundreds of photos which I still have today. We took the ferry to other islands in the Aegean and each almost surpassed the other... then of course the time came when we were scheduled to go home. We stayed a few more days in Athens and then reluctantly boarded a plane, this time to Heathrow. When we arrived and took a taxi to Kensington where I was to drop Annie off, we both couldn't bear to end our great journey, and so we stopped off at the Hard Rock Café and slowly munched our burgers. But then alas, it was over. She went to her house and I went to mine.

I began work on my adaptation of Aeschylus's *Agamemnon* which I had directed at RADA several years ago. The journal that I religiously kept in Skyros was certainly a source of inspiration. The version I directed at RADA was so dry and academic that I thought I would write my own version and attempt to make it passionate and profound. In fact, I became quite inspired during the writing process, and I love this early work of mine even to this day. However, my relationship with Annie slowly weakened since I was still married to Alison and it was monstrously unfair to both of them. Alison was still my best friend. I was still visiting Mum each Sunday with Alison for lunch and then going back home where Annie would be patiently waiting. I always had lodgers at Devonia Road and one of them was a Polish chap. I didn't think much about it until one day, after we'd been together four years, Annie took off with him. I was heartbroken – until I realised that it was for the best.

Meeting Joe Papp in NYC

After doing short seasons with three plays at the newly opened Cottesloe Theatre at London's National Theatre, I felt emboldened enough to ask Peter Hall to give me an introduction to Joe Papp (whom up till now I had only known by reputation) at his New York Festival Theatre, a three-theatre complex in Lafayette Street, Lower Manhattan. Perhaps Joe, having received the request from Peter Hall, was enamoured with the British establishment theatre.

I arrived in New York in 1974, and the response was immediate, forthright, and enthusiastic. 'Come in tomorrow, midday!' Such a contrast to the response of our 'overworked' directors in London, who are always 'in rehearsal' or 'too busy' to provide a meeting within a month, often two or three months. I arrived in New York and very swiftly found a cheap hotel on West 8th Street, quite a funky area. I quickly acclimatised to my new environment, which I found to be nothing less than totally fascinating. The very next morning, I walked to the Shakespeare Festival Theatre. It is a large building that houses three separate spaces and had been bought for the Joe Papp organisation a few years back. I took a lift and was directed to Joe's office, which was large and festooned with dozens of posters advertising the myriad productions plus their stars which had played there. This served as a backdrop to Joe as he sat at his desk. The man was instantly likeable, utterly charming, and listened to my theatrical history with great interest. Even my Edwardian dress coat fascinated him, which I had bought in a junk shop in London's Islington.

After a while, I told him about a recent production of *Hamlet* that I had been touring through Europe earlier that year. This seemed to really engage his interest. He added that they had recently had a production at their theatre but was quick to say that such a play deserves a production every year. He then asked whom I'd like to see playing Hamlet in New York, and while I was trying to think of American actors, he swiftly jumped over my meandering thoughts: 'What about Dustin Hoffman?' But before I could express any opinion, he was already on the phone telling his secretary to put a call in to him. 'Not answering,' he said, 'but I'll send him a message.' He concluded our meeting with a firm handshake and a promise to contact me as soon as he had some news.

Agamemnon / The Fall of the House of Usher, 1973

Through my friend, the actor Bruce Meyers, I discovered a dancer who wished to work with me in *Agamemnon*. She was actually giving Bruce movement classes at the London School of Contemporary Dance. Her name was Shelley Lee and she was a dancer-choreographer. Shelley was a most elegant mover and I did believe that she would help the production. I gradually got to know her and it so happened that one day she asked if she could rent a room from me since I now had a spare room in my house. At this stage, I had no romantic feeling whatsoever for Shelley but with enough proximity these feelings do tend to grow. Shelley played in *Agamemnon* at the Roundhouse, but when *The Trial* began our working together ceased. However, she continued to rent a room in my home in Devonia Road. We did become much closer and eventually one day she told me that her permit to live in the UK would be expiring shortly. She could only stay on, which she desperate wished to do, if she got married. She said she would be willing to marry anyone in a kind of 'arrangement', and since I was now divorced from Alison, I meekly offered my services. I was always ready to do someone I was fond of a favour, even if I was not wholehearted. We were married at the same registry office where I had married Alison. But this time and for the first time, we were living together and we were a married couple, and even best of all we were able to work and create together. And so, we did.

For several good reasons, I felt that having adapted Franz Kafka, a writer of extraordinary imaginative powers that were almost surreal, it was necessary for me to adapt another writer who explored those strange territories. I had long wanted to make a stage show out of the bizarre short story by Edgar Allan Poe, *The Fall of the House of Usher*. At this time, conventional plays did not excite me nearly as much, especially what seemed to be the vogue of the working-class – whinge plays – so it was natural that I should gravitate to Poe. Shelley was equally enthusiastic and we started to rehearse the text in our rehearsal room in Marylebone. As a dancer, she had brilliant physical coordination and was perfect for the role of Roderick's febrile sister, Madeleine Usher. We created the chamber piece for three actors and one musician. I felt that we needed a harpist who would capture the strangeness and brittleness of the tale. Of course, as per usual, my partner did find a talented harpist at the School of Contemporary Dance. His name was David Ellis, and he was the grandson of harpist maestro Ossia Ellis. Once I heard his sensitive and skilled fingers on the harp, I knew that we were safe and we had a marvellous rehearsal period.

I read that Antonin Artaud, the brilliant French analyst of theatre, had an obsession about the role of Roderick Usher, the protagonist in this strange and somewhat horrific tale. Roderick is described as the last of a decayed family who lives in the ancient family house which is itself decaying, and thus you have the tale as Roderick reflects and symbolises his environment. He is hypersensitive to an alarming degree which also makes him acutely aware of everything around him. He is almost painful to be around, as if he were a creature with no outer skin. Artaud wrote that no one in the theatre world could play the role like himself. No one was as raw, as stripped down to his nerves, as himself. But I would tend to disagree. There was someone else and that person – I felt deeply – was me. I felt that no one could inhabit the character as I could. I too was utterly suited to interpret this bizarre story, since about this time, my nervous system reacted to anything that seemed to infect my unconscious and I would unravel spools of totally puerile indecisions.

So, aided by my bright new partner Shelley, we went to work. I decided to express Usher as much as I possibly could through the variations of his voice. In his madness, he could be an entire orchestra of sound. Again, being the fortunate partner of a clever woman, I was able to tap into her resources and she was always able to help find solutions. This time she brought in a voice maestro called Vladimir Rodzianko who had been giving vocal lessons to dancers at the London Contemporary Dance School. Vladimir specialised in breaking down your voice until your whole being felt free, and hence you unblocked yourself of all tensions until you could produce sounds that were intensely expressive. He came to rehearsals one day, and after his sessions, I felt I was walking on air for at least two days. He was a most charming man who also had a touch of the Svengali about him. Never had I felt that I had learned so much about the human body or voice before this.

We had classes with him for several weeks and I felt myself grow vocally much stronger. Soon we began rehearsals. I have to admit that some of my ideas came from just watching Shelley rehearse with the other male actor, a very clever South American actor called Alfredo Michelson. Shelley's movements, having studied dance, were so fluid that I was totally drawn to emulating them.

I had never worked with a woman who was also my partner in life – I felt I would be far too self-conscious – but, to my great surprise and satisfaction, it seemed to work. We started very slowly in the rehearsal room, just off the Marylebone Road. These were some of the most rewarding rehearsals I ever had. We were all really very happy and the music from the harp wove itself round us like a magic web. Sometimes, I watched Alfredo and Shelley work on the opening scene together. They moved so beautifully and carefully that I was able to see the way in which the play should develop, and gradually I evolved the idea that Roderick actually embodies the house itself.

Now, with my voice stretched out and strengthened by my brilliant Russian voice teacher, I was somehow able to evoke the old, senile, decaying mansion. We rehearsed each day in this beautiful old church, now mostly used as a gym. I knew that this could only be accomplished by some imaginative musical accompaniment – hence the inclusion of harpist David Ellis. When his delicate long fingers plucked the strings, I felt as if he were plucking the chords of my heart. I felt so connected to the music – as did my movement and my voice – and it was exactly the instrument I wished to accompany the action. And now, with Alfredo Michelson as the friend who comes to visit, we had the perfect team. I felt that Usher himself was a crumbling relic of the ancient family that Poe describes so brilliantly in his short story.

Shelley's voice was a bit too modern American – but she was a quick learner and improved rapidly. We were happy as we very carefully put the play together, piece by piece, as if it were a tapestry. I knew that the opening had to set the mood, so I would boldly stand centre stage and begin as if I were about to introduce myself while describing the house:

'The House of Usher
My walls are bleak walls
Ancient eye like windows
Set amidst a few rank sedges
White trunks of decayed trees
I have stood here for years
Minute strands of fungi overhang my whole exterior
Like a fine tangled webwork from the eaves…'

Now my voice, after some intense vocal warm-ups, expressed a very curious mood or feeling. Perhaps Usher was getting through to me, as small events would seem momentous. As I stepped onto the stage to begin, I always saw Shelley ready to go on in the corner near the wings. Suddenly, she seemed so powerful, so awesome; her presence affected me so much that I felt forced to look away, but once she was onstage, she seemed to return to normal and I swiftly recovered.

Onstage as Usher and waiting for my friend to arrive, I pull an invisible bell for my servant to come. A light comes up on him, far upstage, as he hears the bell. He turns and makes his journey to his master, which involves him walking endlessly towards us, descending endless stairs, opening doors, closing them, thus clearly describing the structure of the old mansion. At last, he mimed appropriately the large double doors to our room where my sister and I wait. He opens the doors with a flourish and says, 'You rang?' The audience would laugh and I enjoyed that mad humour.

Now I ask for news of our much-anticipated guest. He dramatically thrusts his hands on the make-believe handles of the double doors and opens them. Suddenly, a huge gust of wind and rain pours into the house, the curtains billowing. We mime our bodies yielding to its force by bending backwards as we struggle against its power.

Eventually, the servant manages to close the two great windows together, and he says, as if in answer to my previous question, 'The weather is more inclement today, sire, and there is a terrible wind coming in from the west.' I reply, 'Thank you, Oswald, I don't require a weather forecast.' He retreats.

We now see the friend as if in the distance slowly riding in on horseback while describing what he sees as he approaches the house. Since the same actor was playing the servant, Oswald, and the friend, Edgar, Madeleine and I move upstage to welcome him by opening the giant doors of the entrance. Both my sister and I are attempting to animate the very walls of the house. Edgar greets us and walks through the house as he intones the highly descriptive words of the text. As our guest speaks, Madeleine and I enact the walls and passageways by extending two long poles from our hands to create the walls and doors, and they even become the banisters of the staircase.

At last, we climb to the top of the stairs, where I lower the poles which then become the doors to the main room. These are then opened to a vast room which our guest now steps into with much aplomb. Cue for dramatic music. We have now entered the room but, just before this, I greet him profusely. Greetings have so many varieties, and so I greet him in three different ways, returning to our original positions after each one. Quite why I did this, I can't really say, but there is something about greetings that is quite ritualistic and it seemed to work.

We have now placed ourselves at an imaginary table. My guest is at the upstage end, while my sister and I face each other left and right of the stage. There are, of course, limitless varieties of behaviours at the dinner table, especially in such a case as ours where not only have Usher and his sister not entertained human beings in years, but they are also hopelessly eremitic (or totally reclusive). Words come haltingly while I try to keep a watchful eye on Madeleine sitting directly opposite me, who is shyly attempting to communicate, while my dear guest Edgar also attempts to keep a desperate gaiety going.

So far, the great master of movement, Jacques Lecoq, had served us perfectly and not only served us but given us the keys to stimulate our imaginations so we could interpret the play effectively using figuration mime. We drove ourselves to the play's purpose, which is the apparent death of Roderick's beloved sister, Madeleine. Actually, in Poe's story, she has suffered a catatonic fit which closely resembles death. When this happens in the play, my guest, believing her to be dead, helps me to convey her to the family vault.

Now, Roderick Usher's purpose of conveying his sister to the vault is not only that she should be near him, but that he should, perversely, be able to hear her. Finding herself locked in a coffin, she desperately tears at her appalling confinement. Through his hyper-sensitive hearing, Roderick is the only person aware of every struggle from the deep vaults beneath. Edgar is truly sympathetic and tries so hard to comfort me in what he obviously believes is my sister's sad demise. From time to time, we can see Madeleine as she hopelessly claws at the wooden coffin, as we had hung a long black cloth centre stage at the back. This simple device, when lit from behind and high up, reveals Madeleine in her death spasms as she drags her torn and bloody nails down the coffin lid.

Our talented musician, David Ellis, brilliantly captured a musical equivalent of this on the harp. Eventually, Madeleine escapes from her dungeon and makes her way to me. I know because I can hear her, slowly and painfully, crawling up the stairs. This was the trickiest part, since she has escaped and makes her way to the room and eventually takes revenge on her brother while the friend escapes. As he does so the decayed house, so much symbolising its possessor, sinks into the marshy swamp of the tarn, thus putting an end to the House of Usher.

These last few scenes I found the most difficult, since so much happens in the story of a house crumbling and sinking and being consumed by fire at the same time. A more stylised approach might have worked. I absolutely loved working in a totally non-realistic way, since I felt that we would convey the drama of the story and its bizarre locale on a stage only by using the techniques of Jacques Lecoq that we had learnt, but also by working the vocal sounds of that extraordinary voice maestro Vladimir Rodzianko, who, as I have mentioned, taught us to bear our souls by opening our throats.

We secured a tour of Holland, since the book was on the school syllabus, and we had the great pleasure of touring the entire country, visiting twenty cities. Most of our young audiences paid great attention to our work, but in the more industrial towns the kids were utterly awful, and we slowly lost faith in our beautiful production and couldn't wait for the end to come.

Apart from that, we enjoyed the Edinburgh Festival and then played at an experimental theatre in Munich. Finally, in London, we were invited to take it to the National's Cottesloe Theatre, where it was most successful. And I felt so proud that I could actually work with my female partner. Shelley, too, was happy in her very first acting role.

Me and Alan Perrin in *The Trial* in 1991, twenty years after its first production. Photo: Alastair Muir

CHAPTER 14

East

I wrote my play *East* several years before directing and performing it for the Edinburgh Festival in 1975. The reviews were so positive that this led to an invitation to the Cottesloe Theatre. Sir Peter Hall had been appointed artistic director of the National, taking over from Olivier, who was priming himself for the job, but it was not to be. Sir Peter now had to find programmes for all the three theatres, and it was apparently decided that the Cottesloe should be for playwrights, actors, and directors hailing from all parts of Britain. A very sensible idea. I was fortunate in being one of the many who were contacted with a view to perform there, and of course I was doubly chuffed.

I had, over the past few years, decided to adapt what I felt to be the most exciting and stimulating works that were then still in the short story form. I had adapted, up to then, *In the Penal Colony* by Kafka as my first piece, *Metamorphosis* as my second piece, *Agamemnon* as my third, *The Trial* as my fourth, and lastly *The Fall of the House of Usher*, but I had never felt it was in me to write an original play. I was more excited to adapt other writers' works and create a different kind of drama from what existed on the British stage till then. These dramas were rarely, if ever, adapted to theatre. The chief reason being that the scope of a novel goes way beyond the limitations of theatre, which was largely several actors shouting at each other. Yet, it was these very limitations that were most challenging to me. Of course, these adaptations were made possible by the techniques of mime, where nothing is prohibited from being expressed onstage. Mime is the most beautiful tool to unlock the problems of drama.

One day, my acting ally, John Joyce, suggested I write an original piece, but I countered that I had nothing to say that was original compared to the phenomenal works that already existed and which were ripe for plucking. However, John's words did strike a few chords in my brain and I began by investigating my juvenile past. In my decision to be original, at least, I wrote a play that totally expressed the language of the rampant, sex-starved, sex-mad juveniles in the East End of London. I called the play *East*.

As I started writing, I found it seemed to flow from some deep well inside me. It just poured out. There was no real theme, except it was based on a family who graphically described the most exciting and profound moments of their lives, the things that moved, thrilled, and affected them that they carried within them forever. I tried to find, for each of the characters, something that made a profound impact on them. Once I had found what seemed to me to be the keynote of their lives, it became much easier to write. It still didn't have a real theme to it, but somehow, we managed to link the scenes. Having finished, I gave it to my friend at the time, actor Hilton McRea, who had been in one or two of my productions. He said he knew a few actors, and they would do a private reading of it to get a feel for it.

After a week or two, he called me and said he had read the play with some young actors, including two women, and they found it 'quite fascinating to read, and almost impossible to either learn or perform'. It was a step too far. I took the play back and then – eureka! – I had a sudden idea, even a revelation. I would use what I had written, trim out the more salacious and totally unnecessary language, and rewrite it in verse. Now, as I started to write in verse, the play developed a stylised sharpness and became even more intense, and I found that it also became far more distinct from hearing what was, after all, East End louts communicating to each other in verse. From loutish, it became elegant. For example:

'MIKE: Bung us a snout Les.
LES: OK Mike, I'll donate to thee a snout.
BOTH: Now you know our names.
MIKE: Mike's OK after the holy Saint. Mike with a hard 'K' like a kick swift. Not mad about Les.

LES: It's soft, it's gooey, but choose it I did not, in my Mother's hot womb, did she curse this name on me, it's my handle, and under the soft it's spiky, under the pillow it's sharp, concealed instrument offensive weapon, lies waiting.

MIKE: Oh he doth bestride Commercial Road like a colossus ... that's my manor ... where we two first set our minces on each other. He's my mucker, China or mate.

LES: And he mine ever since those days at least twelve moons ago when sailing out the *Black Raven* Pub in Whitechapel the self-same street where blessed Jack did rip and tear in cold, thick nights, so long ago. Those muffled screams and slicing flesh no more than sweetest memories of him that went so humble about his nightly graft. Tell how it chanced that we sworn mates, was once the deadly poison of each other's eye.

MIKE: He clocked the bird I happen to be fiancé to, my darling Sylv (of legendary knockers) and I doth take it double strong that this long git in suede and rubber, pimples sprouting forth like buttercups on summer days from off his greasy boat, that he should dare to lay upon her svelte and tidy form his horror leering jellies, so I said to him 'Fuck off thou discharge from thy mother's womb, afore with honed and sweetened razor I do trouble to remove thy balls from thee.'

***

One day, I was invited to have lunch with Sir Peter Hall in his office with stunning views over the Thames at the National Theatre and discuss when I would open with *East* at the Cottesloe. I was very excited and almost flattered to be sitting with the famous maestro. I remember lunch was pink roast beef and salad, which I enjoyed immensely. And then he very charmingly showed me round the Cottesloe Theatre with all its tricks and niceties. I opened my Cottesloe season with *East* a month later, in 1976. It was very successful. I think, though I'm not sure, that Peter Hall did actually come to see it, being a very busy director. Several days after we finished our short run of *East*, a man called Michael Halifax, who was the general manager, introduced himself to me and said they would be very happy to have me back, just to fill in a few dark nights, and did I have anything else in the cupboard? So I suggested, since we had recently performed it, that I could revise *Metamorphosis* for a few nights, which I did with Terence McGinity playing the beetle, and very well too. I was exceedingly proud to have a talented group of actors in my company, which I couldn't help thinking I would never have achieved if I had been working as a hired hand. It was fated that I had to do it myself.

A week or two later, Michael Halifax got in touch with me again and asked me to come in. He took out his large diary, and said, 'Oh, we do have another space the following week.' I was both intrigued and mightily proud that I should be asked to continue to support the National Theatre's Cottesloe with what would seem to be an endless variety of work. We had now done three quite innovative and unusual shows (the last being *The Fall of the House of Usher*) in the last month, which came to the attention of journalist Sheridan Morley, to whom I gladly gave an interview for a cover article in *The Sunday Times Magazine*. After that very successful and also quite demanding short season, I felt at last I was on the right road, and I was now, if not part of the establishment, then at least courteously received by them. But I never heard from Sir Peter Hall again!

A Clockwork Orange, 1974

By the early '70s, I was now a proper actor, with no more extras work, and one day my agent called me to put myself on tape for Stanley Kubrick, who was casting *A Clockwork Orange*. This is how Kubrick worked – unusual then, but it is now commonplace. No need to interview actors in person, unless they are stars. I read for a British cop – only Kubrick could have possibly cast me as a British bobby – but he did and in the most controversial movie of the decade! We were shooting at Brunel University, a suitably dystopic and grim building. I turned up confident and expectant and met the great man.

First, he shot the scene where our hero, Alex, is being chased by his probation officer, a fairly comic scene. But the older actor playing the probation officer kept fluffing his lines. Kubrick said, 'You should have learned your lines before we started.' In response the actor said, rather pathetically I thought, 'Oh, Mr Kubrick, I prefer to learn them as we block the scene.'

Kubrick responded, 'You're an actor, that's your job… you learn the lines and then we block it!' It came to my scene and, of course, I hadn't just learned my lines – I had them practically tattooed into my skull. We did about twelve takes, each one perfect, never dropping a word. I think Kubrick rather appreciated this.

While we were setting up the lights for the reverse shot, I had an opportunity to have a chat with the great master. I asked him how he had achieved certain visual effects in *2001: A Space Odyssey*, such as the stewardess in the spaceship turning a full circle, appearing weightless. He was only too glad to explain how – as she walked, they simply turned the camera. I found him so congenial that eventually I did feel a close affinity with him. I finished the day feeling I had made a new friend.

My production of *Metamorphosis* was being reshown a few weeks later at the small Hampstead Theatre Club in Swiss Cottage, and I left a message for Kubrick to see it, since I believed that he might find it compelling and miles away from the 'ho-hum' theatre that he avoided like the plague. The Hampstead Theatre Club had a reputation for supporting original works, even if the place itself was a bit run-down. Many of these smaller fringe theatres have a compulsion to put out the begging bowl, and this theatre was no exception. Displayed on the wall, as you walked up the steps to the auditorium, was a box with a sign printed in bold letters: **PLEASE DONATE TO OUR FUND FOR AIR CONDITIONING.**

Kubrick confirmed that he would attend the show during the last week, and each night after the performance, I sped to the lady in the box office: 'Has he been in?' Every night she said, 'I'm afraid not tonight.'

This went on for a whole week, and on the last Saturday, I felt that he must come in. He was a reliable man, and I was sure that he wouldn't give his word and not fulfil his promise. But the box office lady looked at me rather pityingly and shook her head. Of course, I was very disappointed and waited until Monday before I decided to call him. 'Stanley,' I said, 'I'm so sorry you couldn't make it last week.'

'But,' said Stanley, 'I did make it on Saturday night.'

'Oh really? I must tell you that I really don't mind.'

'But I did see it and I really enjoyed it.'

Now, taking some advantage of my newly-found relationship, I decided to risk it. 'OK, Stan, then what do you especially remember?'

'Alright,' he said, 'as you go up the stairs to the auditorium there is a box attached to the wall – please contribute to the theatre air-conditioning fund!'

The Luck of Barry Lyndon, 1975

My last association with Kubrick was when I was called by his assistant to ask if I could put myself on tape again, which I gladly did. I failed to win the larger role, which went to Hardy Krüger, the svelte German actor, and I was given the role of the aristocratic Lord Ludd in Stanley's adaptation of Thackeray's 1844 novel, *The Luck of Barry Lyndon*. This is a fascinating book and yet such an odd choice for Kubrick. It was bold, very brave, and beautifully directed, and yet a small and rather cynical part of me felt that there were other pressures at work: a sense of wanting to be seen as a highly cultivated human being on Kubrick's part.

But I was glad to get the role and, as usual, aided Stanley in the choice of casting. When he was looking for unusual Nordic aristocratic types, I suggested the German actor Wolf Kahler, whom I had worked with in my theatre company for several years, to play one of the aristocrats. He did this superbly and it was one of the highlights of the film. I was togged out in a magnificent costume for a rather indulgent playboy aristo.

My first visit to the set, in one of Dublin's great government houses, was on a day of furious storms. As I entered the building, I could not help but notice the gigantic lights, called brutes, being supported by two strong Irish labourers on each. They were set on the balcony, shining into the room. The two Irishmen were wrapped in oilcloth and holding on for dear life – like ships riding a gale.

I walked up the staircase to the magnificent room where all, by contrast, was quiet, the howling storm outside barely making an impact. But what struck me, however, was the sight of Hardy Krüger and Stanley in deep and earnest conversation. Hardy had the script open on the small table where they sat, and he seemed a bit agitated about a sentence which didn't make perfect sense to him. Kubrick listened attentively and attempted to assuage his fears. I watched at a slight distance, with half an eye on the windows, where through the gauze I saw these stalwart Irishmen gripping the arc lights for all they were worth; the bitingly cold rain sprayed their faces like icy bullets. Meanwhile Hardy Krüger kept waffling on.

I went to the wardrobe. I knew that in a short time I was to have a fencing scene with Ryan O'Neal, who was playing Barry Lyndon, but he never seemed to make time for rehearsals. He was in nearly every scene, but to keep myself on form, I checked out another fencing master in Dublin, even at my own expense.

At last, Kubrick was shooting the gambling scene where Patrick Magee cons his willing clients. The set was beautifully dressed; hundreds of candles lit the scene. The opening shot was on Magee, who had a few problems: he couldn't pronounce the perfect French he needed for the opening request to the players, *'Faites vos jeux, m'dames et m'sieurs.'* He would always say *'Faites vos yeux'*, which meant 'make your eyes' not 'make your bets'. Stanley was very patient and kept reminding Patrick of the correct pronunciation, but after twenty-five takes decided to call it a day. The cards that were meant to fly from his fingers got sticky with sweat and so Stanley decided to go for a reverse – that is, onto me. I have to say I felt supremely confident, having watched the poor Irishmen near collapse. I made a vow to myself that the camera would break down before I would. I would do any number of takes, and after about twenty, Stanley called for a new scene. 'Already, Stanley?' I replied, half mockingly, 'I was just getting into it!' The camera operator had a rather nasty red indentation around his eyes where the lens had bitten into him. But the next day, Stanley's assistant rushed up to me and declared that the scene was as good as they had hoped. It had all the flair, joy, and decadence they needed. I was happy.

Then suddenly, we all flew from Ireland, since it was said that Stanley had been threatened by the IRA. I loved Ireland and couldn't wait to visit the Gate Theatre in Dublin where Orson Welles had found sanctuary in the '40s. However, I still had to complete my work on the duel with Ryan O'Neal, to make amends for my character's alleged cheating. We got to work, but unfortunately Ryan was unable to remember the moves, since we had not rehearsed them sufficiently. Kubrick then said, 'Well, just improvise.' That's what we did, with a handheld camera, and it seemed quite successful. But, as I say, one day we were all notified that we were upping sticks and returning to the UK. Since the film was insured, we were able to shift the entire, rather massive, production, with its thousands of costumes, to Salisbury. So I continued the fencing match with Ryan there, and then my work came to an end.

I didn't hear from Kubrick for some years, until he started shooting *The Shining*, when he called me out of the blue. He asked me if any of my actors could be extras in a special dream sequence in the film where time has changed and gone back to the '20s, and Stanley would much prefer to use actors rather than extras. I relayed this to the actors in my company and they were all very excited to be in a Kubrick film, even as background, but when I asked Kubrick what the fee would be for the week, I was shocked at how low it was. It was so low that no matter how keen the actors were, they felt like they were being exploited and turned the offer down. I went back to Kubrick and pleaded with him to increase the offer, even by a small amount, but to my great surprise he would not raise it a penny. Did he think that actors were out to exploit him? Such a shame, and then I didn't hear from him again for some time, which is not unusual since it takes him years to make up his mind about a project.

The Passenger, 1975

In the meantime, I did have another offer in 1975 from the great Italian film director Michelangelo Antonioni. He was directing a movie with Jack Nicholson and Maria Schneider called *The Passenger*, and I was asked to see him in Limehouse, where he was shooting the British element of the film; so strange that I was destined to move to this very area just ten years later. Antonioni was very charming and we discussed how to shoot the scene; he seemed keen on my suggestion of Jenny Runacre in the role of Rachel, the cheating wife of Nicholson's character, David Locke. He thought I might be a man toying with his huge train set, which I felt was a tad ordinary. I then suggested using my tortoiseshell cat, which had only one ear, since the other had sadly shrivelled after an operation on a swelling. Antonioni rather liked that idea, so he said, 'Very well, bring the cat.' I left feeling rather pleased with myself. However, the next morning as I got ready to leave with my beautiful and devoted cat, he was too reluctant to get into his box and I didn't have the heart to force him into it. The last time I'd put him in his box had been to go to the vet, the results of which were most unhappy for him, and he had a very bad feeling about the box. I turned up and of course Antonioni had been thinking about how to shoot the scene with the cat. I had to explain to him that Pottle just would not cooperate.

Jenny Runacre, an attractive actress, was to do the scene with me, but he decided that we should both be totally besotted with each other and be locked in an endless clinch, chewing each other's faces! It wasn't unpleasant, since Jenny and I got on quite well, and so this seemed to go on for most of the shoot day, until at the end we were both, quite frankly, worn out. I left at the end of the day and never returned to the area until I had bought my own flat in Limehouse. I walked down the street until I came to the house where we had shot the scene and peered through the front window; it was just as I had left it. I actually didn't see the movie for some years, but when I did, I found it a trifle confusing. But our little canoodling scene, I thought, was quite effective – at least I wasn't embarrassed by it.

The Trial in Düsseldorf, 1976

Günther Beelitz, the producer of the Düsseldorfer Schauspielhaus, visited London where we met courtesy of Estella Schmidt, who I believe had been at university with him. The theatre was a huge post-modern building and in its early days was under the directorship of Gustaf Gründgens, who'd had a contract with the Nazi government, though not a Nazi himself. He was a huge celebrity in German theatre and played in the brilliant movie *Mephisto*, directed by István Szabó and starring Klaus Maria Brandauer.

For me, working at the Schauspielhaus in Düsseldorf was quite an adventure, and I directed my version of Kafka's epic novel *The Trial*, in German, of course, but first I had to cast the ensemble, since the principal roles had already been cast. I spent two or three enjoyable months there and had been booked into a most charming small hotel near the theatre where, just as in Kafka's novel, breakfast was served promptly at 7 a.m. each day. It was absolutely delicious, accompanied by exquisite German coffee and cream.

It was the autumn season and the sun still poured down lavishly as we sat for our breaks in the gardens outside the theatre. Once I started production, the company really took to it most seriously. The actor playing Joseph K, the principal character, was quite brilliant, as was the actor playing Huld, the hopeless and rather insane lawyer. And this cast really seemed to enjoy working physically. I even used three extra women, since they complained to me that they were severely underemployed, although paid by the theatre as part of the company. I could not resist their plea to be used and decided to make an alternative female chorus – they were delighted.

I worked hard to make it as unique as possible, but since I had created a version which I had also done at the Roundhouse in London, I felt I was treading water and needed something more demanding to test my brain. I felt that I was not creating – I was just copying an earlier work, something I had never felt before. Each morning before rehearsal, after my breakfast I would practise on the piano for an hour, which was a good mental warm-up. For some reason, this seemed to make me more alert during rehearsals and also helped to assuage my guilty feelings that I was not creating something new. The weeks flew past and I had a very capable bilingual assistant who would bring me tea (laced with brandy) during rehearsals, which helped me to relax. I was perhaps going through some early middle-age period of guilt.

At last, *The Trial* opened and it was immensely successful. Shelley Lee had come over, and I was proud to have her in the audience. After I had seen it in, watched it, and refined it for a few days, it was time to leave, and I decided to have a short break in Amsterdam, where I suddenly felt very lonely; I was glad to get home. I had probably what is called post-production blues, perhaps not unlike postpartum depression. *The Trial* ran in Düsseldorf for a considerable time since it was so successful. Beelitz asked me back to direct another Kafka, and, of course, this was my version of *Metamorphosis*. I had a first-class company of actors for the play, except for the poor father, who was miscast. Throughout my many revivals of this production, I had always found the men had much less vivacity or style than the women. However, the production did have a simply brilliant Gregor, and I could not have asked for more.

Australian Tour

In March 1977, a major Australian producer called Eric Dare came to see *East* at the Cottesloe Theatre, since he was always looking for shows to wake up the Australian audiences. He had hitherto invited Lindsay Kemp with his production of *Flowers* for a long tour of Australia, which was highly successful, and was seeing if he could pluck out another of the new companies that were making their marks on the London stage, and preferably with something a little naughty. He invited us to perform *East* on a sixteen-week tour of Australia and the company was thrilled. However, our beautiful leading lady, Anna Nye, just could not bear to return to the land she had escaped from several years earlier and dropped out of the company, so we replaced her with a very lively young girl called Sarah Mason. Just before voyaging to Australia, I managed to rent the New London, a beautiful theatre on Drury Lane, for three weeks. It was dark and afforded me a great opportunity to retune *East* with our new lady and, while I was at it, I revived *The Fall of the House of Usher.*

One day in late 1977 I received a letter from the novelist Philip Roth at the stage door.

Dear Mr. Berkoff,

I tremendously admired East, *and wondered if you were familiar with my novel,* Portnoy's Complaint. *I'm enclosing a copy in case you don't know it. Watching you in* East *and in* Metamorphosis, *I thought you could do a one-man show with this book, a dramatic monologue, playing all the roles, etc.*

It was done that way in a Belgrade theater a year or so ago, and though I didn't see it, friends there tell me it was pretty good.

I am in London until June and, whether Portnoy's Complaint *interests you or not, I'd like to meet you. I can be reached at the above address or by phone at 352-2371, though it's probably easier to make contact by writing, since I'm off in a studio without a phone most of the day.*

I hope I'll hear from you.

Sincerely,
Philip Roth.

Of course, we met for lunch. I was so proud that I had recently joined a smart new club called The Zanzibar just off Drury Lane, and I took him there. I was inordinately gratified that I could take my illustrious guest to a place I deemed a worthy venue. We chatted away merrily; he was much enamoured with my production and we discussed his suggestion that I would adapt his novel for the stage! I was in the mood for being utterly frank with him and told him I didn't really think it was a right fit for me, as much as I had enjoyed reading it (I didn't – it was just a bit too gross!). I was mightily honoured, though, that on seeing *East* he saw me as having the abilities or talent to adapt his work. *East* was, I admit, awash with genital frivolity, but mimed so playfully, and the biggest applause of the night was when I mimed a gigantic vagina into which I crawled. It took me, however, weeks to build up to that point, if not months, but by getting just a little bit bolder each night I managed to accomplish it. It was simply monstrous, but redeemed by being hilarious, especially when I mimed getting trapped inside.

On the final night, Philip Roth came a second time, this time with his wife Claire Bloom and her daughter by Rod Steiger. This was the first time I had met the charming lady and I could not have been more delighted. Philip Roth and I stayed friends for a while and he sent me his latest oeuvre, *The Breast*, which was highly inventive and surreal. Roth sadly passed away in 2018.

But now we were off to Australia and the whole company got on the plane to Dubai, where we had a three-hour break and where Sarah Mason encouraged me to buy myself a silk jillaba. I liked the jillaba very much – it made me feel like a prince, but I would have settled for something much simpler, since I was always far too modest to treat myself to anything that I really wanted. But Sarah said, 'Go on, Steven, it suits you.' So, encouraged by her simple enthusiasm – she broke down my petty doubts – I bought it and wore it in my hotel rooms all over Oz and was grateful to her for helping to liberate my spirit and encouraging me not to be too mean to myself.

We tumbled out of the plane in Sydney and then took a domestic flight to Adelaide, where we were opening at the famous Adelaide Theatre Festival. However, we were so utterly exhausted after the twenty-four-hour journey that we all took the famous old tram to

Glenelg Beach and gratefully threw our exhausted and sweaty bodies into the refreshing Aussie sea. Even though this was 1978, I can recall every moment of it! Even my bed/sitting room, which looked like it had been part of a deserted shopping arcade, thrilled me. It was cosy, and I loved it and loved the wonderfully quixotic Aussie breakfast and sandwiches which were always stuffed with beetroot. To top it all, we were sold out in advance for the entire three-week run.

This was in no small way caused by a furore in the Aussie press about how disgustingly scatological my play was. It came hard on the heels of my old colleague Lindsay Kemp's ball-baring production of *Flowers*, loosely based on the book of Jean Genet, the homosexual French writer. Since there was a sizeable gay population in Aussieland, Lindsay's presence was like the emergence of the gay messiah and he had set a precedent for the Christian extreme right group in the South Australian parliament. Discussing *East*, an MP stood up and forecast that doom was coming from the UK in the shape of sexual depravity. The MP held the paperback script in between two fingers like it was something putrid and alarmed the entire country with the news that 'the female pudenda was crudely mentioned something like twenty-five times! And on one page!'

The box office meanwhile gurgled while it chomped down on scrumptious Aussie dollars, and I opened a bank account, saving my money religiously week after week. In spite of its scurrilous reputation, *East* received highly respectable reviews. We all enjoyed Adelaide, made a few friends, and I even bathed once on a nudist beach, which I did actually find highly liberating. I also found a curvy Oz lady called Jan whom I became quite fond of – but like some fine wines, the relationship didn't travel well, and so when she visited me in Sydney, we found we were drifting apart.

The whole company simply adored Sydney. It was a thriving, thrusting, dynamic new city with a magnificent opera house on the harbour. Even so, it did have some strange areas curling at the edges, particularly Kings Cross, where some less than wholesome hookers plied their wares from morning till night, and massage parlours satisfied a bulging population. We had a splendid opening night at a wonderfully seedy theatre aptly called The Valhalla, where *Flowers* had played some time before. This became our home for the next eight weeks and we loved every moment of it. I felt redeemed by our wonderful new Aussie friends, who showed such enthusiasm for what we were doing. Even the Sydney Dance Company came en masse to see what the fuss was about and its sensitive and highly original leader, Graeme Murphy, had rented a yacht as a treat for his company one Sunday and invited us all to join them, which we gladly accepted. I met some winsome young dancers there.

On our opening night, producer Eric Dare took us all out to celebrate at an utterly astonishing diner that had been converted from a cinema and had a gigantic screen with a projection of Manhattan as a backdrop. I'd never been in such a place in my life, and that is where I met the glorious Australian star Kate Fitzpatrick, who spoke the English language like an aristocrat. Sadly, this once great and unique restaurant has long since vanished; it was probably just too ahead of its time. Meanwhile, compared to Adelaide, the box office in Sydney was strangely quiet; it was thought that the public imagined wrongly that it was for the 'raincoat brigade', since it followed hard on Lindsay Kemp's outrageously camp *Flowers*.

I have to confess I was impressed by Lindsay Kemp's energy. He made a reputation for himself by teaching classes in every city he toured in Australia, and of course I just had to follow suit. I advertised and taught two classes in mime and movement per week. There were some very interesting Aussie actors who regularly came and many of them became friends, especially an actor called Ralph Cotterill, whom I later chose to play the beetle in my first Australian production of *Metamorphosis* at the Nimrod Theatre in Sydney. This I did when the *East* tour ended in Tasmania.

Barry Philips and Matthew Scurfield, my two main actors, whom I had worked with for years and who really were a massive creative help in nearly all our productions, were so enamoured by their newly discovered country that they both applied for work permits to stay, but unfortunately both were denied. They already had an abundance of actors! However, they were less reluctant to employ a British director/author, so I was blessed, and I extended my sojourn for six months.

Those months were some of the most meaningful of my life. *Metamorphosis* opened to excellent reviews, which gladdened all our hearts and ensured a few repeat visits to Australia. Ralph Cotterill even introduced me to his yoga class in Bondi, which I began on my 40th birthday, as if to celebrate a new beginning to my life. It was there I met Beryl, a very charming young lady who lived with a bunch of New Agers in a large house in Centennial Park. She introduced me to her housemates and although I was always a bit of a recluse, I felt I was finally bonding with like-minded friends. I loved it. Somehow Australia was a new world for me! But it was now time to leave after an unforgettable six months in that magnificent country.

Return to Israel

Straight from Australia, I headed back to Israel, as I had always wanted to work in the Israeli theatre. I was all too keen to learn about the tribe I had come from and all the exotic mysteries of their expressionist theatre seen at the Habima in Moscow, led by such pioneers as Vsevolod Meyerhold. But this brave and brilliant man was executed by that thick moron called Joseph Stalin.

When I first went to Israel in 1969, I visited a theatre showing a successful play called *The Lion in Winter* by James Goldman. What I saw was old and stale and had nothing whatsoever to do with the ancient Jewish theatre in Moscow, where Israel's Habima Theatre had its origin. That form of theatre was dynamic and surrealistic, but now Israeli theatre was catering to a form of Broadway shtick, and so I became all the more convinced of my desire to bring back the old Yiddish theatre.

The following year *Agamemnon* was to be staged. Of course, there is no problem for Westernised and European Jews seeing a well-written naturalist play translated into Hebrew – it restores their faith in a world that is familiar to them and is comforting – but I had a strong image of the early Jewish theatre of Russia, which created such mystical works as *The Dybbuk* and *The Golem* where Kabbalistic magic was a strong element of Jewish life. I had read of theatre directors like Vakhtangov and film directors like Eisenstein who created masterpieces of the imagination. I had no time for American shlock. But it did take some time before I was able to persuade the Israelis to take me on.

My return in 1978 came after an actress with the Haifa Municipal Theatre had highly recommended my production of *Metamorphosis*, which she had seen in London, to the theatre director Amnon Meskin. He straightaway contacted me with an offer to direct the production in Israel at the great and celebrated Haifa Municipal Theater. I was ensconced in a very pleasant flat in Haifa up on Mount Carmel in this beautiful town in Northern Israel.

The next day, I met the cast, which included a young actor, Asher Tzarfati, whom I had taught at the Webber Douglas Academy in London and who subsequently worked with me in my very first production of Kafka's horrific story *In the Penal Colony*. Asher was now ten years older, had toughened up, and was a leading actor in Israeli theatre. He had married and had a beautiful little daughter whom he doted on. The musician who was chosen was an Iraqi Jew called Zohar Levy, now living in Israel, who created a first-class score and became a friend.

Rehearsals proceeded smoothly and yet not without the usual problems, where actors simply have not taken the trouble to study movement or mime and are woefully inadequate in those areas. However, Asher was brilliant and used his body as an instrument; he was expressive and so inventive and was to be the best of the many Gregors I had worked with. He was simply so passionate about playing the young man/beetle, and we worked together successfully and had an excellent first night. The show was an instant success and toured every town in Israel – even the most remote kibbutzim had a good working theatre. Asher was now a nationally proclaimed actor, but I have since heard that my dear friend developed dementia and has now sadly passed. God bless you, Asher.

Amnon Meskin made a promise to me that, after my initial let-down and disappointing response from my previous application to work in Israel, he would employ me forever. So, for my second show, I chose my version of *Agamemnon* by the Greek playwright Aeschylus, which I had performed also at the Roundhouse in London, but it never really took off. However, I used mime and ensemble work and a heightened language. I tried to create, for example, the impression of horses racing home as Agamemnon returns triumphantly with his troops after the ten-year battle with Troy. We staged descriptions in slow motion of the battle scenes, which were utterly extraordinary, simply using the mime techniques I had learned from Jacques Lecoq, including the feat as the herald races to Argos to dramatically tell his story. It was run on the spot and was quite breathtaking. It was a work I was immensely proud of, but it took a while for the Israeli company to absorb it. Clytemnestra was played by a brilliant American Israeli actress called Joanna Peled, who was totally in the style of the play, and Agamemnon was played by my now stage star and friend Asher Tzarfati. I had always had a fascination with the highly stylised costume of American football players, with the enlarged padding giving the impression of a super-muscled athlete, so I commissioned the costume makers to dress our chorus of actors in that style, and I have to admit that they looked quite magnificent. The effect heightened their ensemble work. Sadly, Joanna Peled passed away in the USA in August 2009, but I have never forgotten this remarkable and beautiful lady.

I used a technique that may also have come from the brilliantly experimental Living Theatre Company directed by Julian Beck. One of the many techniques that they used involved a group of actors crossing the stage along a straight line, the restriction of which stimulates the imagination of the actors. The actors can only move along the straight line to reach the other side, even if it means crawling, climbing, or clambering over each other. The effect was inventive and quite beautiful, resembling a slow-moving piece of sculpture as figures crawled over, under, and around in order to avoid slipping over the line. I think the Israeli audience had some problems with it, though, since they were still not used to experimental or dramatic theatre.

In spite of Amnon Meskin's commitment to my longevity in Israel, it was a long time before I was offered further work at the Haifa Municipal Theatre. It was 1991 when I directed a radical production of *Hamlet* there. That was based on the *Hamlet* I performed in the UK in 1980, and which toured Israel very successfully, especially to the kibbutzim. Of course, that time it was a British company that came, headed by me as a slightly ageing Hamlet.

For the Israeli production, I had a splendid, intelligent Hamlet and a first-class translation by a brilliant academic. The production was very successful and was even invited to Rome in 1999, which was a tremendous adventure for the company. We played at the magnificent 1,000-seat Teatro Valle, where, on the first night, I did my one-man show *Shakespeare's Villains*, and *Hamlet* opened the following night. One of the last productions I ever did in Israel was to direct my adaptation of Kafka's novel, *The Trial*, which I did at the Habima Theatre, Israel's national theatre. However, we did not have a particularly committed cast, and I have mainly forgotten all about it. One of the producers explained to me that the lack of audience was due to the fact that many wondered where the set was! I used multiple metal frames to show a self-creating set, which was, unfortunately, far too radical for the Neil Simon crowd.

Greek – Its Origins, 1979

I knew that there was something in my psyche that needed expression from time to time, and yes, I really had a form or shape that would just go fossicking around the debris in my unconscious. Just throwing down words, sometimes, would be enough, as if I was dropping the bait into a deep-flowing river of my mind. Just a sentence might begin a small explosion and shoals of multi-coloured fish would rise to the surface and happily I would haul them in.

When I began to work on *Greek*, I had no idea, until two or three pages in, that I was writing my version of Sophocles' *Oedipus*; it just slowly wove its way inside those peculiar pathways in the brain and became an experiment in recreating *Oedipus* in modern times. I had merely started with one line: 'So I was spawned in Tufnell Park – that was no more than a stone's throw from the Angel, a monkey's fart from Tottenham or a bolt of phlegm from Stamford Hill.' I created a mock dystopian, working-class culture, gleefully describing what I saw as a depressing image of low-class suburban life. Slowly, an unending potpourri of London was streaming out of me, my disgust was endless... I could not stop.

But only when I was describing my decrepit family did the plot gradually evolve. Dad suddenly says, 'Sit down, son, I wanna talk to ya,' and then he relates an old story of going to a funfair and, just for a laugh, consulting a fortune teller, who then tells his mum and dad a most shocking story, that he sees an image of his son murdering his father and then bedding his mother! Well, now the plot exploded in my face. Dad says, 'You don't fancy your old mum do you, son?' From then on, the curse on Thebes in the original play by Sophocles was transferred to London, and it fitted beautifully. I was never once at a loss for material for a plague-ridden London.

The finished work was probably one of the best plays I had ever written. It culminated in Eddie totally rejecting the Oedipal curse and dramatically running on the spot, going back to his mum. Eddie says:

> 'Yeah, I wanna climb back inside my mum. What's wrong with that? It's better than sticking a stick of dynamite up someone's arse and getting a medal for it. So, I run back. I run and run and pulse hard and feet pound, it's love I feel, it's love, what matter what form it takes, it's love I feel, for your breast, for your nipple twice sucked, for your belly twice known, for your hands twice caressed, for your breath twice smelt, for your thighs, for your cunt twice known, once head first, once cock first, loving cunt, holy mother wife, loving source of your being, exit from paradise, entrance to heaven.'
>
> BLACKOUT.

CHAPTER 15

How *Hamlet* Began

And now for the big one… I had been thinking about this for years! I had the desire to create a highly skilled, physically dextrous company who were willing and able to take on any task and who, most of all, were imaginative and used to thinking off the grid. I was going to play Hamlet and direct as well as produce, while I still had the invaluable assistance of the Arts Council of Great Britain. We would start slowly with my three principal actors and build up carefully and methodically once we had created a blueprint, then we would bring in the other players. This is what we did, with Matthew Scurfield, Barry Philips, and I sketching out most of the other roles and finding the most inventive way of playing them. This was one of the standout creative rehearsal periods I have had.

The seed of the production began in Edinburgh in 1976. I was living there with my second wife, Shelley, in a thick-walled granite flat in a charming old working-class tenement which we truly loved, and which I had bought on a whim for only £6,000, having just been rewarded with a healthy fee from the Düsseldorfer Schauspielhaus. I had been directing my adaptation of *The Trial* and did truly feel that it was one of my best works. Shelley wrote to me that this flat, which we had been renting during the previous Edinburgh Festival season, was now up for sale, and so, without much hesitation, I bought it. I stripped the old slum down to the floorboards and revealed a beautiful small flat.

One day, I was feeling desperately frustrated and seriously underused. I was getting no offers of work and had no plans and therefore saw no future after my wonderfully exciting tour of Australia. I even went with Shelley to her dance classes, joining her at the bar where she would be doing the steps in front of me and I could meekly copy her. I envied her daily ritual at the dance school, while I had nothing to do. I was dreaming of doing *Hamlet* one day, but somehow I did not feel confident enough to begin without an ally or some help.

Like many actors, I coveted within my heart those special roles that we hope one day to explore but seldom get the chance, unless you have achieved some degree of notoriety or fame. Despite years of dedication to hustling whoever was the head honcho of the various companies, I always received the same stale and deadly response, even when I had forged something of a reputation. So, the only solution that remains, of course, is to do it your bloody self.

After one miserable and lachrymose morning, Shelley said, 'Go to my rehearsal room in the church, just up the road, and begin by yourself.' So I did. I walked there and unlocked the front door of this modest Scottish church that Shelley was using for her dance rehearsals. I began, just me, alone with Hamlet. I thought I would start with a monologue, and I imagined King Claudius in front of me in the scene where he is praying for redemption for having killed his brother. I placed a wooden chair where I imagined his body reclining in solemn despair. Hamlet has come across him by chance as he is trying to exculpate his sins. I slowly and secretly approached. Now was my opportunity to slaughter the beast. I imagined a knife or a sword in my hand, and I began the first lines, which are the first lines which I would rehearse in this production:

'Now I might do it pat, now 'a is a-praying;
And now I'll do't – and so 'a goes to heaven,
And so am I reveng'd. *(pause)* that would be scann'd: *(pause)*
A villain kills my father; and for that,
I, his sole son, do this same villain send
To heaven.
Why, this is hire and salary, not revenge…
No!
Up, sword, and know thou a more horrid hent.

When he is drunk asleep or in his rage;
Or in th' incestuous pleasure of his bed;
At game, a-swearing about some act
That has no relish or salvation in't –
Then trip him, that his heels may kick at heaven
And that his soul may be as damn'd as black
As hell, whereto it goes…'

I went over my speech many times and it felt so right. I felt the electricity of the lines begin to ignite me, and I was definitely drinking from the cup of Hamlet and nothing felt so reviving. I loved doing it in that large, cool church room. Thank God I was slowly coming to life. After running it a few times, I felt as if I had awakened the slumbering spirit inside me, and I was happy again! Thank you, Shelley. This felt like, at last, I was in my omphalos of creativity, merely by learning Shakespeare's lines, and then I was debouched into the open air.

I then corralled some of my brilliant team of actors to come and do the workshops and slowly but surely it came together, and it looked quite stunning. After a couple of weeks, we brought in Linda Marlowe for Gertrude, and then we booked the Meyer twins, Tony and David, for Rosencrantz and Guildenstern. Of course, the fact of them being twins brought in many benefits, since Hamlet is always mixing them up. We worked for several days with our enlarged troupe, then we brought in Ophelia, played by Chloe Saloman, and now we were blocking the whole play. For Horatio, I asked my old chum Gary Whelan, who was my understudy in the West End when we performed *East*. He was always highly dependable. Finally, David Auker played Polonius, and he could not have been more different from the usual geriatric Polonius we see wobbling on the stage. Auker was a heavily-built robust Polonius, even dangerous, and was quite brilliant. But, unbelievably, in years to come, he would give up the acting game.

I decided to stage it as if we were a small orchestra. And the cast would be in dress suits, except for Hamlet who wore a modest lounge suit. The group simply looked quite startling. We sat on a dozen chairs in a perfect line and played when our cue came. I had always felt that the actors in a classical play should be able to perform as virtuoso musicians in a concert, with no need to dress in elaborate costumes to fulfil the characters – our words and actions should be enough. So we staged it in a rectangle, with ten chairs on each side where the actors/musicians would sit.

We started rehearsing in a church in Holborn. The room had markings on it like those of a basketball court. I found the marks quite fascinating, so much so that we used it as our setting. The white lines we treated as if they were an architectural layout for the walls and the rooms. So there was a blueprint, so to speak, of a castle, which we obeyed assiduously. We opened the production at the Edinburgh Festival for three weeks, where it was a resounding success. And like our rehearsal room in Holborn, we put white tape on the floor to demarcate the structure of our castle. The performance space we had in Edinburgh had no facilities for any ambitious lighting except for one overhanging grid, so for the first time, we used just one stark lighting state. That was quite startling, as it made us totally exposed to the audience with no possibility of hiding in the shadows. Since that time, I have used only one lighting state for all the tours of our show, which does save us a hell of a lot of time. Furthermore, since the audience was fully lit, it made the performance all the more intense, as they were forced to keep their full attention on the actors.

During one soliloquy, I not only noticed but was virtually assaulted by the actions of a member of the audience in the front row. He took out his large camera, holding it directly in front of me, and began to click away. The only way to handle this, I thought, was to demonstrate my extreme displeasure by shouting my lines directly to him as aggressively as I could. I felt that he would get the message and put his camera away, but he merely continued clicking as if I was performing it just for him! The audience were now totally fascinated by this event. There was no way out, since not only was he annoying me but also he was distracting the entire audience. I stepped forward, seized his camera, and hurled it to the ground. After this, I merely stepped back and continued with the scene as if nothing had happened. I was due to do Hamlet's scene when the ghost appears the second time and says, 'This visitation is but to wet thy almost blunted purpose.'

The production brought us a major European tour plus a tour of Israel. This was under the guidance of European producer Jan de Blik. Our European tour ended up in Paris at a theatre called Théâtre du Rond-Point that was under the artistic direction of Jean-Louis Barrault, France's leading theatrical genius, and I had the great pleasure of meeting the maestro whom I have admired for as long as I can remember. It was a hot summer, and we were not playing in the main theatre but in the smaller studio and so were all sweating like pigs.

Paris was unforgettable and on our last night we had some of the most prestigious creatives of France in our audience, including Polish film director Andre Wadya, who came to my dressing room with his two small children and told me that our production was the best *Hamlet* he had seen in his life. I think this was for the simple reason that we made the play live by a combination of movement with the language, so nothing was left out, not even the horses that inspire Hamlet to make his monologue beginning, 'Witness this army of such mass and charge'.

Jean-Louis Barrault waited till the very last night to see us. This was terrible for my nerves, since each performance I had to play as if he was in the audience. On the final night, the master came backstage to wish us well during the interval and begged forgiveness for having to leave after the first act, since his wife, Madeleine Renaud, was suffering from a heavy flu and he had to be back to take care of her. So I had just one short act with total freedom.

The Roundhouse, London

The box office advance for *Hamlet* in London was quite healthy, and I was anticipating a good season; anyway, we were only there for a five-week run. The outside of the curved building of the Roundhouse is perfect for advertising what is to come, since it's such a dramatic building and captures the eye as you drive in either direction. Unfortunately, the people who put the posters up were not available, so for the three weeks of advance booking, the outside of this magnificent building was still showing the crappy old musical that had failed in it so lamentably and had closed weeks ago. This was so different to the glorious poster that had adorned the building ten years ago for *Metamorphosis*, but different people were now running the Roundhouse.

Another production of *Hamlet*, directed by Richard Eyre, was our only real competition and had opened at the Royal Court some weeks earlier, headed by the brilliant young Welsh actor Jonathan Pryce, whom, coincidentally, I had directed at RADA in *Agamemnon*, where he gave a stunning interpretation of the role of Agamemnon. I could see, even then, that with his powerful Welsh voice he was destined for great things. Although the production was conventional, what was unique in his performance was his ability to absorb the role of his father's ghost to the extent that the ghost spoke through him as if it were in possession of him. This made Pryce create a terrifying voice as he emulated the dead king. I caught an excerpt on the TV and was mightily impressed. I didn't fear the competition, for, as radical as Pryce's interpretation was, the rest of the production was quite unchallenging, while our whole production was radical. As is often the case with the first night, the devil comes to torment you. I wasn't then the youngest Hamlet in the world. I was already 42 and so was vain enough to go to a local hairdresser and ask them if they could darken down my few emerging grey hairs. Unfortunately, it came out with an orange tint! Ah well.

As I drove on my Honda motorbike to the Camden Roundhouse with my new punk haircut, some blithering idiot opened his car door on the driver's side and, although I swiftly braked, I keeled over and grazed my hand. After some useless chat with the moronic driver, I continued to the theatre considerably shaken up as my hand really hurt and was bleeding, while my hair seemed to be growing more ginger by the minute. But once inside that beautiful building, I suddenly felt calmer and my spirits were restored, particularly by the actors who consoled me for my unfortunate adventures and even added that the hairstyle was rather good since it brought out the punk in Hamlet, which would at least give the critics something to hang their notices on.

Alas, the wonderful and supportive George Hoskins, who had been the general manager for my previous productions at the Roundhouse, was no longer there, and the present regime was, frankly, appalling, and so they shall remain nameless. I dressed in my elegant Twenties pinstripe suit, while the rest of the cast dressed in their black tie and tails and did look quite stunning. As I said, I felt that actors were not unlike classical musicians in an orchestra and were perfectly capable of expressing the play without the gallimaufry of elaborate costumes. As before, our set was the rectangle of light and about forty or so black cane chairs. The cast remained on set throughout, watching the proceedings and sometimes, where necessary, being part of and supporting them. Our only set, apart from the chairs, was a big roll of white tape.

We all came onstage and took our places. A fierce drumbeat struck and the stage was immediately bathed in an intense white light. Then the two guards (Marcellus and Barnardo) slowly rose and walked diagonally from opposite areas on the stage. Both miming holding spears, they met in the centre when their paths merged and began with 'Halt who's there?'

Having the theatre in the round is an exciting way of performing since the actors must be aware continuously that eyes are boring into them from all directions and try not to become 'fixed' as if they were on a proscenium stage. We opened as well as we could and everybody was on form that night. Matthew Scurfield was a splendid and dangerous Claudius, Terry McGinity a formidable Laertes, and Linda Marlowe a suitably lascivious Gertrude. Wolf Kahler, a tall German actor whom I had first seen with Nancy Meckler's Freehold Theatre Company, was the ghost, and Chloe Salamon was perfect as Ophelia.

On our European tour Sally Bentley, an ex-ballet dancer, took over the role. She gave Ophelia a delicate and vulnerable quality which only a classical ballet dancer could, and David Auker, our Polonius, was like no other, a heavy, blunt, and menacing ally of the king. John Prior was our musician. The music was close to perfect.

When we toured Israel, we took with us our photographer, Roger Morton, whom I had known for many years, so we do have a wonderful gallery of many of the productions we staged. While we had a first-class team of actors, our stage management wasn't quite up to scratch. I found I had only one shirt and after the first act, it was wringing wet; I happened to glance into the costume room and witnessed my dear ally Roger, unasked, actually ironing the shirt for me, thus helping to have it almost dry for Act Two.

While on tour, we had the now celebrated theatre director, Deborah Warner, as company manager, whose calm exterior soothed many problems, the worst being when actor Gary Whelan, our Horatio, was hit by a car when crossing a dimly-lit road and was incapacitated with a damaged leg for several days. My immediate solution to the problem was that Deborah Warner would step in! She was a perfect substitute for Horatio, although slightly light in voice. She was no actor, but her performance did make a big impression on our foreign audience. And, most of all, I liked working with her. In Hamlet's death scene, as she said, 'Good night sweet Prince and flights of angels sing thee to thy rest,' she put her hand over my eyes and gently drew it down to close them. It was such a surprise because up until that time I had got used to Gary Whelan's heavy male hand and the contrast was astounding. Deborah went on to form her own youthful company.

Now, there happened to be a very pleasant bar at the back of the theatre that opened pre-show, during the interval, and at the end. Since our reviews rather reduced the patrons, the management decided in their wisdom that it wasn't worth keeping the bar open after the curtain came down. So we had nowhere to entertain our friends in the audience unless we swiftly dashed across the road to the grotty pub to have a swift post-production drink, if we were lucky enough to be served.

One of those reviews that stuck with me was by Nicholas de Jongh in the *Guardian*, which called me 'fatally miscast'. I came across said critic in a Covent Garden nightspot called The Zanzibar. I strolled across to him and made a totally silly threat to kill him, just to frighten him; I never dreamed he would take it seriously but obviously he did and called the police. The police never even got in touch with me since they obviously thought it was a spat between two precious luvvies. However, since that time we have become good friends!

***

One night Dustin Hoffman came to see us, and I immediately saw him in the audience as I began my big scene, the closet scene, when I reprimand Gertrude. Catching his face, I suddenly went into overdrive and put all my energy into the scene. It was early in the run and the reviews had not yet decimated our audience, due to the healthy advance. I returned to my dressing room quite happy, as I always was after the show, and there was a knock on my door. Of course, I guessed who it might be, and I was right: it was Dustin Hoffman, the great Hollywood movie star. He came in and was exceedingly fulsome and complimentary. I said that I'd swiftly change into my civvies and meet him in the bar downstairs, where at least we could chat and I could introduce him proudly to the rest of the company. As it happens, the theatre was keen to lock up, so we were shunted outside. I felt so ashamed of our pathetic nation, where one of the world's most celebrated actors couldn't enjoy a drink with us. We chatted miserably in the cold night, while all I could think of was how nice it might have been standing in the bar exchanging stories. Hoffman told me he was amazed that British actors drink so much. Here they spend their free time in the pub, he said, whereas in the US they spend it in the gym. But this works well for the theatre companies – it's one thing dealing with a drinker, quite another dealing with an actor with a head full of ideas!

However, Dustin was impressed enough to turn up yet again with a companion the following week. Again, almost at the same time as I began my scene, I saw him in the audience and this time I felt ashamed that our audience had been so decimated by the wretched, ignorant press. Because of this, during the final week the audience were no longer sitting in the round, since there would be too few of them, so the 'clever' management decided to place them on one bank of seats. I went again into overdrive, doing my best to fill the thinly populated theatre with as much energy as I could summon. The lights came down to an enthusiastic applause from our small but devoted audience. I went back to my dressing room but this time there was no knock on the door, alas!

In actors' lives, there seems to come a time when, for whatever reason, a peculiar 'bug' penetrates their unconscious as if to disrupt the perfect clarity of their lives and seek to create some ancient disturbance, perhaps from some old and distant wound. The bug is something you just have to live with, and it can grow rather nasty and comes in so many different forms. Perhaps in some bizarre way it's there to protect you from the bigger fears – fears of drying up, of forgetting your lines, the actor's worst fear of all. Even Olivier was struck by monstrous and irrational fears. On some occasions, I had an actor in the company to whom I could confess my tribulations. He had become an old friend: John Joyce, whom I just knew as JJ. He always had an answer, a remedy, a solution, and enabled me to continue. Some of these insane quirks are almost too appalling to put into words or to confess, but sometimes I solved it by simply accepting the bug.

During rehearsals of *Hamlet*, I was preparing myself for a final dress rehearsal at the Almeida Theatre in Islington, which I had borrowed for one day. In those far-off days, there would be few places left open to eat when we finished our dress rehearsal at 10 p.m. or thereabouts, so I had asked two of the actors round to my house, conveniently in Islington, after the show. Preparing the evening supper, I bought the mince, cooked it in onions and tomato sauce, half-boiled the spaghetti, and laid out the salad. Then I walked to the theatre.

Now, once we started the run-through, the strangest thing happened: I felt as if I was reciting the lines out of my own head, as if they were conversations. I had never felt so at ease with *Hamlet*; in fact, I thought I ought to be a little more casual, trip up a bit, test myself, but no matter what I could not distract myself. I was Hamlet. The second dress rehearsal, after an hour's break, felt equally confident; I came to the conclusion that by preparing for the rehearsal, by shopping for and preparing the post-show supper, I had placed my mind into a sense of order. I think I had learned something that day, and it was that if you put your mind into an ordered place, everything else would be affected by that rhythm.

This production of *Hamlet*, for me, joined *Metamorphosis* and *The Trial* as the apex of my career.

***

I never really got too close to my dad since my early memories of him were too fraught with tension, fear, and a nagging anxiety that, God forbid, he should discover some trivial fault and blow it out of all proportion. My relationship with him had remained distant. He never once came to see me perform in any of my shows. I just could not understand the man. However, as I grew older, I began to sympathise with him and even grew sorry for him when he could work no more as a tailor. He had to hang about the house or else go to a Jewish men's club on Stamford Hill, and when his sight was good enough, he'd still play bridge. Apparently, he was a skilled bridge player and even ended up earning a living from it. That was a mystery to me, as it was to all of us back home. Of course, the other mystery was where he spent his nights off when he didn't come home... he always claimed that he spent the night at the baths, the Turkish Baths in Russell Square. In fact, I went there myself a few times in my late teens, sometimes all night after dancing myself silly at the Flamingo jazz club. I even wrote a short rather shocking story about it which was published in my first book, titled *Gross Intrusion*. It was published in 1979 by Calder and Boyars, a radical and daring publisher who also published William Burroughs. Of course, I never once showed my dad anything that I'd written.

When Dad was working, he worked really hard, and he had the guts to open a small tailor shop in Brixton, where he catered almost exclusively to the West Indian population. Before long, he had gained a good reputation amongst the locals and started to take more and more orders for his zoot suit style. At the end of the week, Ma always loved to tell me how many orders he had taken – sometimes as many as ten, fifteen, and so he did quite well for a few years in Brixton but when his sight failed him he had to sadly pack it in. I think I went there just once out of curiosity and, while he welcomed me, he never asked me back. Naturally, he was quite proud when he did well – and he wasn't spending the takings in the betting shop upstairs, as he had done when he'd had a shop in Aldgate with Morry Bodinetz.

But now he was growing old, and what was really sad was that I seldom went back home to visit him. I always visited mum on Sundays. I never forgot to do that. Mum always had her most special chicken soup and bagels and smoked salmon ready to serve up, and I always enjoyed that and sometimes brought Alison, and later Shelley. She really loved Shelley.

One day, Shelley decided to introduce her parents to my mum. That was a very special day. Her parents lived in a very pleasant house in Wisconsin and her dad was a successful metallurgist. My dad couldn't be there since it was a weekday, and he couldn't shut up the shop. Mum rushed around and made the living room as pretty as possible and decorated each surface with flowers. Oh, how curious Shelley's parents must have been to visit their son-in-law's family, albeit only one member of them. I wasn't there, but I was anxious all the same and hoped the local kids hadn't pissed in the lift. Apparently, they got on very well. They were absolutely enchanted with Ma and loved the food, and so it went well, thank God. I was very happy about that and began to feel like a normal human being. And Shelley was proud too since she really loved my mother and they got on so well. Ma even went to see Shelley's dance company at the Roundhouse when she was performing a short season there. Oh, how very proud my mother was and she never forgot it. And to speak the truth I was as proud as punch that my mother could see that I was married to a woman of some substance, a far cry from the days when she had to go to the magistrates' court in Stoke Newington to pay my arrears for child maintenance. Mind you, those were the bad old days when I was still growing up and hadn't yet found the right road.

As poor Dad got older, one day got very depressed about losing his sight and his health and decided that it was best for him to get out of this situation. His brother, my Uncle Sam, had lost his sight too – they had all worked in tailoring for many years and when you cut the cloth, all the dust comes up into your eyes. So Dad spoke to his beloved wife and they apparently discussed what they should do. He had accumulated a lot of sleeping pills and he asked Ma to go out and buy a bottle of whisky. All was planned coldly and so it was carried out. It sounded like a terrible old Jewish tragedy set in the council flat. It certainly knocked him out, but Dad survived and Ma called the hospital, and an ambulance picked him up and took him in.

I even went to see him in Tottenham. By this time, I was in the clouds over my new relationship with a charming lady from New Zealand called Helen Henderson, but I found it too difficult to contemplate splitting up with Shelley. There was Dad, lying in bed having recovered from a suicide attempt, and there I was moaning to him about my love life. He even offered me some advice which was practical. For the first time in years, I was really talking to him. A few weeks later, once he was out of hospital and my sister Beryl took him into her home in Devon. That's when he reached out for the very first time in my life. He rang me practically begging me for help. The doctors had told Beryl that he couldn't just lie in bed all day and that she should get him out, even for a short walk, or he would soon deteriorate. He couldn't take this and then they told him that they would have to put him in an NHS care home, a prospect which he hated – and that was when he called me.

I told him that I wouldn't let them do that, and I would carefully watch over him. I suddenly felt such an overpowering love for my dad, for maybe the first time in years. I even felt somewhat proud that, since I now possessed my own house, I could even have him looked after there. Wow, what a turnabout that would be... However, a few weeks later, on 24 May 1980, Dad passed away, and so I could never fulfil the promise that I made to myself, but I often think about it, even today.

***

The European tour of *Hamlet* was triumphant for the company. We were also booked to show the production in Israel, touring to the kibbutzes, which couldn't have been more exciting, and ending up in Jerusalem. It was on the Friday of that week when my sister phoned me to say that my mother had died. This was on 11 April 1980, after Dad's attempt at suicide, only six weeks before my father died. Mum had been ill for a while – she had little quality of life, and I had been concerned for her for so long that the news was almost a relief. But this feeling transformed into grief within moments of putting the phone down. I found that I had no idea what to do – tell the cast of *Hamlet*, break down in tears, try to carry on? Beryl suggested it was serendipitous that I was in Jerusalem – I think she saw it as God's HQ – and that I should take advantage of this and do something that might speed Mum's flight to the next world. So I went to the Western Wall, also known as the Wailing Wall, and approached a rabbi with a group of Hasidic Jews in an area to the left of the wall that led into a sepulchral underground vault. Old prayer books lay on tables, and the atmosphere was eerie but serene. I confessed to them my anguish. They were most sympathetic and said that they would form a *minyan* (a quorum) and pray for her. I was utterly relieved and told them the name of my mother. The group quickly assembled to read the *kaddish*, the Jewish prayer for the dead. I heard my mother's name woven into several of their chants and then it was over. It had only lasted a few minutes. I was disappointed. I had expected to be moved but I felt nothing during their rushed incantation.

I said: 'That's it?'

'That's it,' said the rabbi. 'That is the prayer for the dead and please give generously.'

I pulled out a ten-dollar bill and offered it to him. He looked at the bill and then looked at me somewhat critically, but I said that was enough since it had only been a few minutes. I went into the open air and was dizzy and confused after being in the dark enclosure. I made my own prayer to mother by the wall. Then I wept and then I felt somewhat purged of my grief.

As I was rather aimlessly standing in the great open square, a man approached me, probably having seen my bloodshot eyes. He looked like a tourist and was wearing a smart trilby hat. He spoke very gently to me and I was happy just to tell him why I was there. I told him what had just taken place, and I also asked what I could do for my mother.

He replied simply by saying: 'First of all you must keep the Sabbath. You must start with that!' He even asked me if I had anyone to pass the Sabbath evening with. I told him that I was an actor and wasn't working tonight since it was the Sabbath. He then replied that he knew some people whom I could celebrate the Sabbath with and wrote down the telephone number for me. I felt that he might have been an angel looking for lost souls. But I didn't phone them. I wish I had, but I just couldn't bring myself to call people whom I didn't know. Instead, I wandered around the old city which I always found absolutely fascinating. I sat in an old Arab café, ordered a mint tea, and wrote out my funeral oration to my mother.

I was at peace.

CHAPTER 16

And Now, *Decadence*

In 1981, *Greek* was touring odd dates in Britain, and I thought it was time to write a piece that absolutely fulfilled my own needs. A piece for two actors with a zonking great role for me, since, as I had spent considerable time directing other actors and being happily obliged to deal with all their needs and problems, my thespian spirit felt a little neglected.

My acting team in *Greek* were tailor-made for the roles and were receiving accolades wherever they played. We had opened at the Half Moon Theatre, Alie Street in Whitechapel, just around the corner from Dad's tailor shop in Leman Street, although that was fifty years earlier and was no longer there. Walking those streets again took me back there. I remembered Dad's shop, a little hole in the wall that was full of West Indian customers every Saturday buying 'zoot suits'. The jackets were always single-breasted and single-buttoned with a narrow lapel that stretched to the hips. They wanted the jacket sleeves to reach their fingertips and the trousers to swell out at the knee. He reversed the pleats and dropped the loops so the belt wouldn't ride over the waist. The lining had to be satin. The black community knew that no one in London made a zoot suit like my dad, and he was famed around the city for this. I was so proud of him. He never seemed to want me around the shop, though; I always felt I was getting in his way. Upstairs was the betting shop where he frittered away his profits on the horses and the dogs.

I loved the dirty, mice-infested old synagogue that my director chum, Robert Walker, had now brought to life as a theatre. Since *Greek* was based on *Oedipus*, I felt that the cast might be more enlivened by the influence of Greek sculpture and decided they should perform in white mask-like faces. I thought the effect was quite powerful. Barry Philips played Eddie (Oedipus), Matthew Scurfield played Dad, Linda Marlowe played Oedipus' rediscovered mum, and newcomer Deirdre Morris played the Sphinx. All of them were quite wonderful.

Greek did its four weeks at the Half Moon Theatre to, on the whole, very positive reviews, except for one or two less than insightful critics. And then I found that the Arts Theatre off Leicester Square was becoming free, and so I transferred *Greek* there, where it ran for a further six weeks.

But while business was slowly growing by word-of-mouth, unfortunately it wasn't quite making its money back. I felt it was a terrible shame that, now we had accomplished the difficult task of having our own theatre building, we should abandon it so easily. So one day I approached the actors and told them that if they would take a small cut in their wages, as I would, say 30%, then we could break even and maybe have the theatre for as long as we wished. Yet to my astonishment, these actors, although well connected to their roles, did not possess the commitment that I had or the foresight to possess our own theatre. They didn't wish to take a pay cut. I couldn't quite believe it, but then again, I was the author/director and had more at stake. Nevertheless, this would certainly not be the end of *Greek*. It was just the beginning.

While writing *Greek*, I felt the play just flowed out of me, but then I came to the tricky part at the end, where our ill-fated hero chooses to blind himself as a form of self-punishment for being blinded to the truth. At the time, I was in a close relationship with Helen and she read out a section of a book she was reading, which I believe was called *The Seven Arrows*. I found it so inspiring and moving that I completely changed the ending of *Greek*, so that Oedipus renounces his fate and refuses to tear his eyes out. This became the most powerful part of the play. I was everlastingly grateful to Helen for bringing it to my attention.

Later, when touring *The Fall of the House of Usher* in Australia, the phone rang. It was Susan Loewenberg, a fringe theatre producer in Los Angeles who was actually rehearsing *Greek* there and asked if I'd be willing to fly out and cast an eye over it. *Wow!* By an amazing coincidence, Helen was at that time living in a rented room off Venice Beach, LA – just a short five-minute drive from Susan Loewenberg's office! So, after *The Fall of the House of Usher* was over, I swiftly rushed over to LA and plonked myself down in Venice Beach. This was the first time I had ever been to the exotic West Coast, and I will never forget my introduction to the area. Helen took a cab from the airport and asked us to be dropped off at Rose Avenue – how those beautiful words stuck in my mind, it felt so American.

I was so grateful to Helen for opening up the mysteries of America to me, starting with the extraordinary funky areas of Venice Beach. I had quite frankly never seen anything like it in my entire life. I was happy being there with Helen, and enjoyed living in California. I bought a beautiful second-hand Goldwing motorbike and sometimes I gave her lifts to the gigs where she would be singing. On weekends, I liked to drive with her out to Palm Springs.

Soon after my arrival, Susan Loewenberg picked me up and drove me to the small Matrix Theatre on Melrose Avenue, LA where they were rehearsing my play *Greek*. Here, I was introduced to the British actors, many of whom were just hanging out in LA, hoping that they might, with some luck, obtain some movie work. In the meantime, they were happy to accept what was known as equity waiver work, where they might just be given a tiny portion of the receipts, often not much more than what was known as a car fare. But they were more than happy to do this since at least they would be seen!

I stepped into the small but charming bijou theatre, and the actors began to show me what they had achieved so far with their current director, who was standing by. I watched what they had fumbled with for half an hour and could not really stomach any more of it, although I could not blame the director for not having a clue, since the play used my own particular, evolved style. So I simply said, 'Let's start again.' I gathered the four actors around the table and just asked them to be stone still. From that stillness, Eddie spoke first, and the other three, like waxwork dummies, reacted at certain parts when it related strongly to them. Suddenly, I felt the theatre energy once more.

The actors weren't bad at all, considering they were doing this on equity waiver. I only had ten days free before returning to London, where I was putting together my production of *Hamlet* for a large European tour. I managed to block the play in the ten days. The current director was gently let go and was swiftly forgotten about, and the show had the best reviews it could have possibly hoped for, winning every fringe award for best play, best ensemble, best production, etc., and so I had made my first notch on my LA king post. Everybody was exceedingly happy. (Except, I imagine, the current director.)

***

Helen was heavily into meditation and gurus, and each guru seemed to attract their little band of faithful acolytes. They also provided somewhat of a social haven with much interconnection. Helen had her own flat facing the Pacific Ocean. In my early days in LA, I'd swiftly jump out of bed in the morning and jog to the Santa Monica Pier, which was a perfect length to jog, being just over a mile, and then the sun would be up and warming my back. At the end of the pier, there was a small diner, and I used to sit outside and drink my coffee accompanied by the most delicious tuna melt – a totally divine West Coast sandwich – and nothing in the world tasted better. Then I would write for an hour before taking the walk back.

Yet it was on the weekend that the pier really came to life and never had I seen such a phenomenal display of street theatre. The mime, breakdance, roller blades, comedy, acrobatics, there was no limit and I wandered through the crowds that gathered like metal filings around the performers. I saw more sheer skill in these young performers than in a decade of West End shows. Such daring, such invention – I felt that this was a new world, and I was completely captivated.

***

We opened at The Matrix on Melrose Avenue. Vidal Sassoon came to see it, brought along by his old East End chum, the great musical and dramatic actress Georgia Brown. I think the show touched their early memories of East End life. Now, based on its success in LA, the producer took a gamble and decided to raise enough money to transfer the play to a New York theatre, but this time in an off-Broadway theatre called the Actors' Playhouse. Georgia Brown, who'd seen the play in LA, took over the roles of Mum and the Sphinx. The actors and producer were all excited with this great opportunity and we could not help feeling, based on the rave reviews in the LA papers, that we would take the New York critics by storm. Quite unfortunately, this was not to be, and the play was shot down in flames by some of the most ignorant, idiotic, and ill-written reviews I had ever received. Nevertheless, our few backers were so passionate for the play to keep running that they were willing to risk their entire investment, but sadly Susan Loewenberg, being rather more practical, decided to pull it off almost immediately. It was a sad two weeks.

Nevertheless, I promised Georgia Brown that when we revived it yet again in London, she would see what the British would think of it. And so, lo and behold, I revived it once more in London at the beautiful Garrick Theatre on Charing Cross Road. Georgia was quite wonderful, the reviews were excellent, and thus, having given my word that she would see a completely different response, I was vindicated and the play ran in the West End at the Wyndham's Theatre for eight weeks in 1987. I played the part of Dad with the spirited help of Georgia playing Mum as well as the Sphinx. She was utterly sensational and I loved playing onstage with that most wonderful and generous lady.

At this time, I had a new producer called Christopher Malcolm, so at last I had an ally. As so often happens, if the part you've taken on is not absolutely the best fit for all those frustrated thespian demons writhing around your soul, the little buggers may take it out on you and manifest themselves in all sorts of absolutely absurd problems and irrational bugs.

I felt it was even a form of madness, but I *did* manage to get through the short ten-week run. While I had no problem with the role of Dad, or his lines, which I had written, I suddenly felt that I would have expressed myself like a demon as Eddie and been free. However, playing the role of Dad, I managed to find all sorts of bizarre problems which I had to overcome. And so, I really was relieved when the production came to an end.

It was during this time that I received a call from Joe Papp who ran the Shakespeare Festival Theatre in New York, in which he asked me simply if I'd like to direct *Coriolanus* in New York, to which I said, 'Of course, that would be fantastic, I'd love to.' And then I sat down at home every afternoon trying to read this formidable play which was so complicated that I could rarely get to the end of the page. Yet it was something I was determined to do. So each night, as I went on stage to play the dad in *Greek*, I worried not only about whether my waistcoat should be open or shut, about whether my shirt sleeves should be rolled up or down, but also about how I was going to start *Coriolanus* in New York.

McVicar by Himself, 1980

Tom Clegg was directing a movie about the amazing prison escape of notorious criminal and hardman John McVicar, who was tagged 'public enemy number one' by Scotland Yard. But after serving an eight-year stretch, he decided that his criminal activities weren't paying off and to take a postgraduate degree at the University of Leicester. He wrote a terrific book called *McVicar by Himself.*

Roger Daltrey is a dynamic performer, as seen in *Tommy*, a film based on a Pete Townshend musical, and he was cast to play McVicar. When I went for my interview with director, Tom Clegg, I was reading for the role based on Charlie Richardson, a South London gangster who also, paradoxically, did a postgraduate course. Daltrey was at the interview and knew I had written an East End punk play about young tearaways. Suddenly, after we had been chatting a while, Roger lay back in his chair, looked me in the eye, and said, 'Give us some verbals, Steve.' I was ready and my play *East* was still in my head, so I did. In fact I shot out some early parts of that play:

'Oh, he doth bestride Commercial Road like a colossus
That's my manor, where we two first set our mincers on each other
And those Irish yobs walk under our huge legs
And peep about for dishonourable bother,
He's my mucker, china or mate.'

I got the part straight away and felt most comfortable with Roger. We shot the first half of the film in the prison where Roger, as McVicar, makes his daring escape. It was quite a well-constructed movie, detailing the meticulous planning of the escape, but I felt the prison riot scenes were awkward and British in the worst sense of the word. I did the best I could and had a very strong scene with Roger Daltrey. Adam Faith played his partner, Wally Probyn, a famous prison escape artist. The title of 'public enemy number one' was pronounced by the media when McVicar escaped from Durham prison, but poor Wally Probyn broke his leg scaling the wall, so that was his bad luck. But the film was, on the whole, fun to make, even if it hardly advanced my film career.

Decadence, 1981

Decadence just exploded out of me once I had decided on the social background of my protagonists. My production of *Greek* was on a short British tour, and I was watching it in some provincial town, maybe Leeds, and dealing with some of the perennial problems that arise when touring that are par for the course. Barry Phillips, a splendid actor I had worked with for over ten years, was playing the hero, Eddie (Oedipus), and intoning all the lines that were close to my heart, but, though I admired his performance, as I did Linda Marlowe's as Eddie's mum and Matthew Scurfield's as his dad, I bitterly regretted that I had not taken the bit between my teeth and played the role myself, since I felt it was me down to my very bootstraps. But I also felt it was so much of a personal confession that it might be much wiser to stand outside it, so I did.

One bright summer afternoon, I decided to write a new play with a great whacking role for me, since I still had a deep, unsatisfied hunger for performing. I recall reading an article on Vladimir Nabokov's writing methods: he would always use plain white index cards, which rather intrigued me. That very afternoon, having bought a pack of these postcard-sized cards, I sat on the terrace of a coffee house and began. The shape and form of those pristine white cards also naturally affected how I wrote; it had to be formal, clear, and precise. Since two of my characters were drawn from the upper classes, I felt I should start with a very articulate couple who are having an affair. Very simple. I felt the writing should express, very wittily, their complex attitudes and petty frustrations. I gave the female lead the name of Helen, based on my inamorata at the time, and I called the male protagonist Steve, of course! Why not? But secretly this gave me the opportunity to fire off a few choice barbs, which I hoped might go unnoticed. The play commences with Helen sitting on a beautiful white leather sofa, and Steve, in dress suit, enters the scene:

> 'HELEN: How sweet of you to come on time. Bastard, sweet darling, you do look divine. I've been so bored, have a drink, what? Oh, a Drambuie with soda and a dash of Cinzano with masses of ice. I've been so bored tearing round to find what would enchant you to eat me for breakfast… [raising her skirt a few inches]. *Charmant, n'est-ce pas?* Does it get you a little on heat…?
>
> STEVE: So bleeding dextrous, wouldn't you know, too much bloody ice, love, tastes like a crow, you asked me the cause for my glum face, wait till you hear what I have to say, unzip your ears and let me flood them with verbs and make your mind a jangle of nerves.'

Writing in this loose verse style stimulates the mind to wonderful invention. Fulfilling the rhythm, the scan, the rhyming words inspires you to reach further in your quest to be creative, and so I never once felt at a loss for words. The secret was knowing these wretched upper-class characters, and sometimes their confessions were quite sad, as when Steve confesses his 'horrid public school life'. There was never any shortage of material, since we had all been saturated for years with lurid tales of upper-class depravity, but what fun to play. It could have been a parody of *The Seven Deadly Sins*. My speech celebrated endless margaritas leading to absurd drunkenness or fox hunting, in which I played the horse; all part of the fun and games in the secret lounges of the beau monde, gourmandising to the limit, and all the courses taken in mime, which gave me ever greater pleasure.

Well, this is the life of Steve and Helen. The two other characters are called Les and Sylv, two utterly British working-class characters. The difference is that Steve is married to Sylv, the daughter of a wealthy builder, and is having a secret affair with Helen, who obviously is more his crème de menthe. Sylv has hired a private dick, Les, to spy on Steve, since she swiftly discovers 'he is emptying his teapot in somebody else's kitchen sink'.

Now, the beauty of this is that two actors play all four parts, and as soon as one scene is complete, there is a swift lighting change, since that is all that it needed, and Steve and Helen now become, with all the skill that the actors possess in body language and voice, Les and Sylv. Fortunately, I was partnered by Linda Marlowe, who carried it off to a tee, and for me it felt that I was taking a short break as I went from one character to the other. Rehearsals started quite well, although I had just a sliver of anxiety and did in fact hint to Linda that it might be better to cast another actor, leaving me free to just direct it. I just had one of those flights of nerves which many actors are all too familiar with. But she wouldn't hear a word of it, and once I nailed my first sentence, I felt my wings begin to grow and then I just glided through it.

We opened at the little New End Theatre in Hampstead, which once was a morgue and then was beautifully turned into a small theatre. We played a very comfortable six weeks and never missed one performance, even when my lady Helen and I booked a hotel room overlooking the Strand so that we could enjoy the sight of Prince Charles and Lady Diana making their way to St Paul's Cathedral to celebrate their marriage. We enjoyed it thoroughly until I had to leave for my evening show.

Then we were invited to the Edinburgh Fringe Festival, but since availability was very tight, we were quite happy to perform in the cloakroom area of the great Caledonian Hotel. We opened for the whole three weeks of the festival, which was most enjoyable, and I was really developing the role and received rave reviews from the local Scottish press. One day I received a very warm-hearted card from actor Paul Scofield, which pleased me enormously:

Dear Steven

Joy and I saw "Decadence" in Edinburgh and thought it quite superb. Hope you'll have a wonderful and successful time in London and many congratulations to you both.

Yours with admiration,
Paul

I had even decided to produce the show using my own money at the beautifully restored Arts Theatre just off Leicester Square, where we played to almost full houses for a further eight weeks, before we were obliged to stop to fulfil our European tour of my production of *Hamlet*.

After our great tour of *Hamlet*, hearing that it was available again, I booked the Arts Theatre forthwith for a fifteen-week gig of *Decadence* this time and I was never so proud. Since it was just the two of us, namely Linda Marlowe and I, should no guests turn up after the show, we would just stroll down the Strand to Joe Allen's Americanised London restaurant, and we were always happy to eat there. There was, frankly, no restaurant quite like it; it was pure showbiz. One night Joe Papp came by and the Arts Theatre had a bar/restaurant upstairs, so everything was easy. He was regarded as the number-one impresario in the United States. At last, we finished our fifteen-week gig and, since I was the producer and investor, I came out with a reasonable profit.

That year Susan Loewenberg, for whom I had directed *Greek* in LA, invited us to return to do *Decadence*, so, full of excitement, off we flew. Helen still had her apartment right on Venice Beach, but by then we had drifted apart, so I chose to stay at the Marina Pacific Hotel, which was perfect. I was living the Californian dream. I went in for my American driving licence and eventually bought an old second-hand car, having relied on my trusty Goldwing motorbike up until then.

***

One day during our six-week run in Hampstead, Linda Marlowe invited me to a late lunch at the house of a friend who went by the name of Bambi. Naturally, I replied, 'okay', since we could go on to the theatre straight after the meal, about five or six. Perfect. So, I arrived in the early afternoon, and we three proceeded to have a very pleasant lunch together. Then, towards the end of the afternoon, a third woman suddenly opened the door and crossed the room without a word. Bambi, noticing my confusion, said, offhandedly:

'Oh, this is Clara. She's my tenant.'

'Oh, hello,' I replied.

'She's a pianist.'

'Oh, very nice.'

And I thought nothing more of it; my afternoon with Bambi and Linda continued without further interruption.

Loneliness, though, was slowly creeping into my life. So one day after a performance, in one of my occasional lower moments where I would usually pick up the phone to one of my female friends, I rang up Bambi for a little company, but she didn't answer the phone. Instead, the phone was picked up by the pianist who lived there. So I asked, 'Is Bambi there now?'

'I'm afraid she's not here at the moment.'

A pause.

Then I asked, 'What are you doing right now?'

'I'm just sitting quietly practising.'

'Oh well, shall I come around and hear you practise? I can also read you some of my poems?'

The pact was made and around I went; Clara played Beethoven delightfully on the piano while I read my soppy, yet charming poems. She liked the poems. We turned them into songs, and she played as I read, and then we discovered we wanted a bite to eat, and then *Boom!* Just like that, we were away! Romance had blossomed, and all the mess that comes with it.

A couple of weeks later, I got a call from a New York producer saying he had seen *Greek* in LA and had liked it, so he offered me the chance to direct it at an off-Broadway theatre. Marvellous, I thought. Yet there was one small hiccup: my cat Kitty. I would need someone to look after her while in America. So, having grown quite close to Clara by this point, I decided to call her up and ask if she could perhaps look after Kitty for a few weeks. She said, 'Sure' and promptly moved into my apartment – piano and all!

Well, off I flew to New York, the show was performed, and five weeks later I returned, ready to relieve Clara of her cat-sitting duties. Yet when I returned and saw how much better my precious cat looked, I simply had to ask her to stay for a while longer. Quite a lot longer as it turned out...

We've now been together for over forty years. The cat has passed on, but we are still mysteriously, happily, and even amazingly in a partnership which seems to be going the distance...

Octopussy and General Orlov, 1983

It was a welcome relief, after restaging *Greek* in LA and New York, and then a European tour of *Hamlet*, to be offered the role of a Russian general in a Bond movie. I had a very pleasant meeting with producer Barbara Broccoli, who had taken over from her father, Cubby Broccoli, who had recently died. Now, by chance Barbara Broccoli had seen my play *Greek* in LA at a fringe theatre. She told me how much she had liked it and, partly on the strength of that, I was offered a leading villain role. It didn't seem to matter a wit that writing a successful play didn't necessarily make me a good actor but, in her eyes, after the meeting, she felt that it did. I was mightily chuffed, for now I was getting, if not silly money, as Hollywood wages are sometimes called, then at least a decent fee and a good role. John Glen, a Bond stalwart, was directing and was a real gent.

So, costumed and shaven-headed, I turned up for work on my first day's shoot. The set was quite fantastic: a huge circular monster that was built on a giant revolve. As the set revolves, a giant screen reveals a map of Europe, detailing all the cities that the mad General Orlov is determined to unleash his nuclear missiles on. (Does this remind you of anyone you know of?) I step up from my chair, grab hold of a long cane, and approach the massive screen, illustrating, with the use of my cane, the prime targets of my insane nuclear desire. It was quite a dramatic scene and sometimes it helps an actor to have an image of a character in one's head, and all I could think of was the brilliant performance of American actor George C. Scott in the war room in Kubrick's masterpiece *Dr. Strangelove*, which has to be one of the greatest anti-war films of all time. I have to admit that I leaned on Mr Scott somewhat in that scene, and it did seem to help.

My final scene is when I make my big confession to Roger Moore as Bond about how all my plans are in place for a massive attack on Europe, after which Russia will dominate the world. For some reason, the lines didn't stick in my brain, and I sat in my dressing room anticipating, in my mind, a large scene with the principal actor, growing more and more anxious. It was to be the last scene of the day, and I had to dominate it as a psychopathic lunatic. But as the saying goes, 'Sometimes there is a God'. There was a knock on the door ... 'Excuse me, Steven, the director regrets that we don't have time for your scene today... We are running late... so you are free and we will do it first thing tomorrow.'

'Yaaaaaaaaaaay!' I couldn't have been happier.

I slept well, and the following morning I came at the scene with all guns blazing. Now, for whatever reason, Roger couldn't hold the words; they kept slipping away like wet fish... He couldn't do the scene, and they had to shoot it one line at a time. In previous scenes, he had remembered them all, so I started to wonder if he felt uncomfortable with me. I didn't feel at all comfortable on that set so perhaps I made him feel ill-at-ease. We were such different characters. Still, we managed it almost one sentence at a time, and eventually it was all in the can. The film was successful and forty years later it is still airing frequently.

Beverly Hills Cop, 1984

Having read reviews that I was in LA, a casting agency called my new agent, Martin Gage, who made an appointment for me to meet movie director Martin Brest at Paramount Studios. This was my very first Hollywood interview! Martin Brest was a friendly, charming young Jewish director. We got on very well and he even came to see me live in Santa Monica Boulevard, playing a raving Brit in my play *Decadence*. I got the job, playing Victor Maitland, a sophisticated British art dealer, in *Beverly Hills Cop*.

Now it was time to be interviewed by the star, as he was at the time – Sylvester Stallone. I was led into a large office and sat in a chair facing a longish desk behind which sat the movie team. Stallone was seated dead centre, and his acolytes were spread on either side: the casting agent and assistants, producers, costume, make-up, DP, etc. Sly was charming and friendly and I felt at ease with him. I just had to tell him how, when I saw his first triumphant movie, *Rocky*, in New York, there had been an exciting moment when the whole audience roared their approval as he raced up the steps in Philadelphia after his fantastic preparation. Then we ping-ponged compliments and when he declared how much he loved the clarity and vocal power of the British actor, I had to answer that since the pubs in England close at the ridiculous time of 11 p.m., our hard-working theatre thespians make a swift dash to the pub, screaming out 'A PINT OF LAGER PLEASE!'

Stallone responded with, 'Now you've destroyed my illusion.' Cue laughter from the table. I was booked. I got the job on my first meeting – a dream had come true.

I finished off the last night of *Decadence* way up Santa Monica Boulevard, and my new partner, Clara, was there. Since the last-night-party treats had been scoffed by the time I took my make-up off, Clara and I went to The Dome, a super-smart showbiz eatery on Sunset Boulevard.

No sooner had I been booked for *Beverly Hills Cop* than I learned that Stallone had walked off the film because he had some problems with the producers. However, it didn't affect the film, since the role was swiftly filled by Eddie Murphy! And to add to my American phantasmagoria, Stallone made me an offer to play the Russian military hard guy out to get him in his follow-up to *Beverly Hills Cop – Rambo: First Blood Part II.*

So, two major movies in one fell swoop! This was an astonishing stroke of fate on my side, which happened not only through hard work and ambition to explore the world of film, but also by making personal sacrifices, no matter how difficult or painful. Energy seems to attract energy, and my theatre work was definitely the fuel that kept all my spirits on highest alert; it was the work I was most proud of, which was, in my mind, original and dramatic, and that fulfilled me from my toes to my skull.

I loved the filming work, loved being on a set, loved all the gallimaufry that goes on there, loved being in Hollywood, but I especially loved the extra freedom it gave me to finance, on occasion, my own work, when it had been turned down by almost everyone. That did not stop me. And I loved the way film sometimes acts as a magic carpet that transports you to the four corners of the world.

But when I watched a movie I had worked on, as much as I valued, and at times even needed, the work, I was never quite so touched as when I used up every tiny filament of my being in the theatre. In other words, I felt I was fulfilling the reason God put breath in me.

Rambo: First Blood Part II, 1985

The next year I was back in LA, working as usual for the Odyssey Theatre, trying out a play called *Acapulco* which was based on my diary kept when filming the sequel to Stallone's movie *Rambo*. Now, with his creation of *Rambo*, Stallone mined a very lucrative territory loosely based on the Vietnam War. The idea for the plot was of our anti-establishment hero discovering that the government had tried to cover up America's POWs that were still kept as hostages – an interesting plot line.

We shot all the Vietnam scenes in and around Acapulco in Mexico, in the jungle just outside the city, which doubles very well as Vietnam. The film didn't start too well; I was flown out to Mexico, but then a huge storm broke and washed the entire set away. My military assistant in the film, a huge hunk called Voyo, and I, were told to make ourselves ready to go by helicopter, flown by the film's stunt pilots, who could just avoid the storm's second surge, but we would have to fly through the eye of the storm, which we did. There were sandwiches and coffee on the chopper, which were welcome since we had been pulled out before breakfast.

Eventually, we landed in Acapulco in a waterlogged field and slushily made our way to the Acapulco Plaza Hotel. At last, peace and sanctuary. There was no shooting for a few days, since the jungle set was being rebuilt. Mind you, I was content in the beautiful resort hotel with a wonderful view over the sea. I connected more with the actors playing POWs, whom Rambo was determined to find and rescue. These were rough-and-ready small-part actors, some of whom scratched a living in Mexico, though God knows how. My lieutenant, Voyo, a powerfully built Serbian, was delighted and each day asked me, 'How long left, Berkoff?'

Since the storm had increased everybody's wages, there were many smiling actors. The room where Rambo is interrogated was on set, but the atmosphere had to resemble that of a jungle, so no air con. Stallone's body had been whittled down to pure muscle and did in fact bear a slight resemblance to a Renaissance torso, and since he carried not an ounce of fat and would be susceptible to catching a cold, the room temperature was pretty high and everybody was dropping pints of sweat. The director, George Cosmatos, kept almost obsessively staring at Stallone's body, as if he were bidding for it at an auction!

I first glimpsed the magnificent nude body as he was being suspended in a mud bath decorously covered in leeches. I, his Russian nemesis, descend from the chopper, and this is a big moment in the film. I step down, desperately trying to look macho and hoping not to trip over, and descend the hilly slope through the mud pool, past all the tough stunt guys who were lined up viewing me with just the merest whiff of contempt. The splendid first assistant now trundled up the hill spraying his sweat on everyone as he passed, to give me the director's notes.

'Steve, would you look a little bit more military.'

I think he meant macho, and I now regretted that nobody thought fit to put me in a gym for a few weeks. I walked down the slope, again self-consciously, putting some stiffness in my spine. That was better, and I was now acting with the great man, who was sunk up to his neck in this wretched mud. I take out a huge, serrated knife and delicately slice off one of the fake rubber leeches. As it dropped off his chest, I saw that in my keenness I had, with my razor-sharp knife, taken off some flesh and left behind a bloodied patch! I stared at the wound in horror before I realised that it was skilfully applied make-up. Stallone as Rambo is giving me a hard stare; we broke for lunch.

Next, we are inside a primitive Vietcong hut where their communications centre is installed. Sly Stallone is revealed in yet another pin-up pose, this time strapped down to the metal springs of a broken-down bed, wires attached to his flesh so that he will reveal his contacts upon receiving a massive electric shock. But, unlike the leeches, the electric current was real! As he remains silent on each successive electric charge that goes through him, I increase the voltage – this has the effect of inducing his stomach muscles to writhe like excited snakes. Sly got rapidly used to the voltage and kept asking me to increase it, which I was glad to do. But then he had had enough and we called it a day.

Now, Voyo was a most naïve dude and loved nothing more than sounding off at night with the rest of the POWs at supper, across the road in a funky Mexican café. First up, it was all the girls he'd chatted up and then bedded – 'Prick like a horse,' he used to brag –

his conversation was rather limited. And then, after exhausting his tales of wooing, he would talk about his up-and-coming fight scene with Stallone in the chopper: 'How can he ever beat me? I'm so much stronger than him – the audience won't believe it.'

He somehow failed to understand that it was a movie, where you can invent anything. However, word got back as it always does on a movie set; you can't hide anything and stars are incredibly touchy. One early morning, the phone rang in my hotel room; it usually was the second assistant telling you to stand by for an hour or two since someone had just got fired. There was a lot of sacking on that movie. Not a good sign. Stallone was most particular when he saw the 'rushes'. First the DP was sacked, then the assistant director, so there was always an odd day off until they had been replaced and we were ready to go again.

This time, when I jokingly asked the second assistant director, 'Am I sacked today?', he replied, 'No, it's Voyo, your partner… he's been shouting his mouth off.' I knew Voyo couldn't help it; he was a simple-minded clown, but, on the other hand, so far he had been excellent in the film. Oh dear!

I got dressed and dashed to Sly's trailer. I fear that that indomitable British 'fair play' spirit that the English can't help expressing overwhelmed me, and I knocked on the door. Eyes were following me with great curiosity. Sly opened the door and looked at me rather quizzically. 'Come in.'

I said, 'Look, Sly, I hear that you want to let Voyo go?'

Sly replied, more or less, with what I had heard from the second assistant director: 'He's got a big mouth, and he can spread bad feelings on the set.'

'I understand,' I said, 'he does have a big mouth, and I will do my best to get him to shut it, but please don't fire him, Sly. He looks so good in the film.' Then I added, 'Let me take care of it.' I subconsciously flexed my abdominal muscles.

Sly looked at me and said, 'Sure… like *Mice and Men*' – a great Steinbeck story when the big, stupid brute is protected by his minder.

I said, 'Yes, exactly.'

'OK,' Sly responded, 'you take care of it.'

'Sure I will.'

I knew that Mr Stallone had a secret respect for the British savoir-faire. I stepped down from the trailer feeling as if a weight had dropped from my shoulders. I walked back to the hotel and had a second breakfast. I saw Voyo, but I never once told him what I had done – I'd saved his job and his massive salary. It would have shattered him to have been removed, but I merely told him to button up his comments as they were going round. He got the message and luckily, he did shut up.

After we finished, we all returned to LA. God, I couldn't wait to get off that film, and I wrote a play about it called *Acapulco*. I cast a group of actors as close to the originals as possible and put the play on at the charming Odyssey Theatre about a year later.

As the first night came, I invited the original actors who had played the POWs in the film, who were living in LA, to come and see it. They absolutely loved it, but Voyo turned up with his girlfriend, and I simply had to include a few of his juicier comments, since there wasn't much else to say about him. Voyo said, 'That's Berkoff, he makes it up, he's a playwright, they all make it up.'

Enough said! Voyo Goric, a.k.a. Sergeant Yushin, did well. The irony is that Stallone eventually employed him as his bodyguard.

Decadence, 1981, with Linda Marlowe. Photo: Roger Morton

Shakespeare's Villains, 1998

PART 4

CHAPTER 17

OCD

In his book *The Naked Ape*, the zoologist and writer Desmond Morris examines humans as a species, and what is so dangerous is that the ideas in his book are so persuasive. My journey into OCD (Obsessive-Compulsive Disorder) began in theatre when I had to learn plays, and when I did, I felt satisfied, as the language became easily part of me.

Desmond Morris's central theme seemed to be quite straightforward if not simple. If bees, wasps, and other stinging insects don't wish to lose their sting, they evolve a system of decorating themselves with coloured bands to warn off the predator. The human race, in some way, emulates the status symbol. A relatively insecure person, viewing his neighbour's expensive watch (for example), would be inclined, like his insect relative, to project all sorts of images of confidence, power, and success onto that watch and even feel somewhat threatened.

Now, it just so happens that my eyes fell upon the sight, in a second-hand jewellery shop, of an old red-gold Rolex wristwatch and for some curious reason I was drawn to it. I have never ever craved human booty in my entire life, and so why on earth did I find this undesirable surge of desire welling up inside of me? It made no sense, none whatsoever. But the urge still wasn't strong enough to compel me to part with the sizeable wedge of cash.

However, Clara having heard me drone on about it, decided to purchase it for me for my birthday. So now it was a fait accompli, and I had joined the mob of status symbol wearers! But it came with a few caveats. I couldn't possibly wear it when I was working as an actor, director, or interviewee. It would render me somewhat jaded or weak. I identified my work as a gift from the gods, and I must be raw, naked, and ready to face the world with no need for petty baubles. But the thing that affected me was a two-faced beast. It chose to move in any direction so as to threaten me whichever way I faced.

I now started to hold those who possessed such things in some high regard, since they seemed totally unaffected by their baubles. In other words, they felt that they deserved them. They earned the right. They were manly. Something within me suggested that I had not earned that right. There remained in me something of the boy who wanted to please his father and could never succeed. At times I was convinced of my status in my chosen field, at others I never felt quite good enough; I certainly didn't feel accepted by much of the theatrical world. Perhaps even the steady rejection of childhood desires had worked its way maliciously into my psyche. Either way, the end result was that the only time the watch had the desired effect on me was when I was at a social gathering and had nothing to prove. I had earned it; it had not been given. My wrist carried its weight, nobly.

As time passed, I began even to avoid these bolder, braver, men and women who wore these treasures easily, without effort. Even when I had the bloody thing at home, tucked away in a drawer, I was not free from its effects. As I grew older, I found myself craving the purchase of paintings. When I did, it gave me no guilt whatsoever and I started to feel proud of my paintings. After all, they were art. They had skill and came from years of study and were even imbued with compassion and soul.

No, here, I had no guilt. My choice of painter was the Scottish realist Peter Howson. His work touched me profoundly and I even identified with him. Some of his paintings reminded me of my own work – the hyper-stylised rendering of hard-working men. I also loved the human body as an art form when choreographing my productions.

I continued to work, even with this bug occasionally attempting to throw me off balance. Mostly I won the battle – but not always easily. I continued creating productions that were as dynamic as I could and tried not to be deterred. I had to work out ways and strategies to evade the beast.

Once, I was setting out for my first night of my own West End show, my one-man show that had successfully premiered at the Edinburgh Festival earlier that year, and I was caught in a dilemma. After the show, I wanted to possess my treasured 'timepiece', as they are now stupidly called, but dare I? Dare I take it with me? *No! I shall go in raw and naked as usual. I don't need such a thing – no!* So instead of thinking only about my work and the demanding night ahead, I was cogitating furiously on what I should wear on my fucking wrist.

'But that is what protects you,' uttered Clara.

And she was right. I took a cab to the Garrick Theatre in Charing Cross Road. The show was highly successful and the reviews were excellent. Once I had got over my first-night bugs, I virtually flew through my eight-week run and was happier than I had been for a long time. The show was called *One Man* and I was proud; I was standing alone on a West End stage in a show I had directed, written, and performed in.

One Man – the Garrick Theatre, Australia, and NYC

Oh, the horror, the horror of reading in my morning newspaper a dreadful story about how a pit bulldog recently imported from the USA had in a moment of frenzy seized a young child and savagely mauled the poor creature. Tragically the child died and the reaction from the public was immediate and intense – 'Get rid of them – put them down – ban these wretched, violent beasts.'

My first reaction was how on earth could the government have ever allowed such savage demonic beasts to be imported into our benign and gentle nation. Such madness. These dogs were originally bred from bulldogs and terriers. They were bred to be fighting dogs. Yet paradoxically, some owners say that with loving care they make great family pets. Like humans, the more socialised they are, and the more love and friendship they receive, the more loyal they will be and loving in return. So treat them with respect and you will be rewarded for your effort – keep them entertained and you will have a great family pet – but neglect them and they can become bored and destructive. Sounds pretty familiar if compared with juvenile delinquents.

I have to admit that I did become fascinated with this creature and saw in it a possible outlet for a controversial theatre piece, and so I began writing a one-act play detailing the daily life of a pitbull whose simple working class owner adored him, almost like a son – however, the play's energy that the dog naturally expresses did get out of hand one day. Nevertheless, as I started scribbling away, my actor's instinct came into play and as I wrote out my pitbull's thoughts and words I started to totally empathise with the beast. I even relished and identified with his moods and desires. In the same way that an actor takes on the character of the person he is supposed to represent, so I started to immerse myself into the soul of the beast – into almost becoming the unpredictable, dangerous creature. But I was also its owner – its simple instinctive working class bloke whose love for his animal knows no bounds – so I played both characters, leaping from one to another and enjoying both. Then one day I decided to take my 'dog', called Roy, for a bit of a romp. I opened the show, entitled *Dog*, at the Edinburgh Festival – it was the third of three pieces collectively performed in *One Man* – the first being *The Tell-Tale Heart*, the second called *Actor*, and then a swift change into my yobbo uniform of Union Jack t-shirt and Doc Marten boots and I was away!

The public response was unanimous. The play grew steadily with nightly repetitions. The other two pieces never expanded with such relish as *One Man* – at first, it was utterly exhausting pulling against my imaginary lead, but I rapidly became accustomed to it. By the time I had finished my three-week run in Edinburgh I was ready for the West End. I opened at The Garrick Theatre for a limited run of ten weeks. I had pushed myself deeper into a character than I had ever been before – while on the stage I became Roy, fully and deeply – but I never took him off the stage. I left him in the dressing room along with my sweat-drenched t-shirt and stinking boots.

***

In 1982, I believe, we were invited to go to Australia again for a twelve-week tour, and, again, I was obliged to do two performances per night. The first was *The Tell-Tale Heart*, but by this point Roy was growing just a mite tired. He still had the energy for an eight-week run in New York, the best run of all, but Roy had had enough and I had to sadly let him go into retirement – like me.

Therefore, for the second performance after the interval, I painted up for *The Fall of the House of Usher*. It was there that the mental strain of those two performances started to form cracks in my psyche. Shelley could not do the tour of Australia and it had been taken over by Annie Stainer, a very talented performance artist, and Terry McGinity playing Edgar, the friend. We began our tour in Melbourne but before all this took place, I was feeling strangely exhausted. While we were scheduled to begin in late January 1983, and since Christmas was crawling towards us with basilisk eyes and foaming teeth, I thought I would escape before the monster had his grip around my throat and I booked a flight to Sydney on Christmas Day itself, thinking, *'Oh, that is a wonderful idea, then I don't have to think of anything except being waited on in a cosy, comfortable plane!'* That would knock Christmas Day on the head, and I was sure that there might even be some celebration on the flight, which was due to take off about 8 p.m. I still had the day to get through.

I always detested the lockdown which always happens around Christmas and in the past, I'd found a solution with Shelley – we had escaped from the lunacy of that time to lease a place on the idyllic island of Tenerife in the Canary Islands, which was a dream, a perfect relief. We found ourselves on the south coast, with its reputation of everlasting sunshine, in a village called Adeje, whose charms I have never forgotten. We found it when a cabbie took us to a small café on the main street which let rooms, and there Shelley and I were ensconced and simply could not be any happier.

We awoke in paradise and went downstairs to the bar for breakfast: beautiful, crunchy, freshly baked rolls, homemade jam, and ham and eggs. A lone parrot chirped away in the backyard… Later, we walked to the coast, and the quickest way was through the gigantic banana plantation at the end of the village, and we felt we were so much part of nature as we walked through these giant yellow hands. Eventually, we reached the shore, where a fisherman was landing tuna and I took a photo of Shelley, who placed her hands sympathetically on the shiny metallic skin of the dead fish. In the evening, we ate in the village, sitting outside and simply relishing the night, and what we especially loved was the way the locals made tomato soup with crushed nuts and herbs – just delicious. From then on, at home Shelley always made all those savoury dishes of Europe. That was a time we would never forget.

Now, whenever I happened to be alone on Christmas Day, it felt horrible, as if I was trapped in a no man's land where the world was gathered in a multitude of familiar groups – families, children, grandparents, school chums, lovers – and at the same time there were the outsiders – the divorced, the misfits, the alienated.

Anyway, that year on Christmas Day, I slowly packed my suitcase and suddenly, like Roderick Usher, was possessed by a bizarre attack of angst. Like a tiny cell, it worked its way into my mind.

On my first trip to Oz, when we were doing my play *East*, on the plane I was sitting next to Sarah Mason, our gutsy actress playing Sylv. I happened to notice she was carrying in her bag a cassette deck. Nothing unusual in that, but my first reaction was utter amazement that one would carry such a thing when you could hear music everywhere and anywhere. Why on earth would you need to carry such a machine thousands of miles? I would never have a need of such a gadget. But this perverse concept must have lodged itself in my mind. Like the proverbial splinter, this incident had crept slowly into my brain like an incubus, and it wouldn't go away.

That afternoon I packed my suitcase for my Australian trip to perform *The Fall of the House of Usher* and *The Tell-Tale Heart*. And for some reason, I carefully placed my cassette player within the case, protectively surrounded by my clothes. This was the first time I had ever toured with such a thing. So what? Maybe it would come in handy, I thought. What if I entertained or had some mates round for drinks?

But then it seemed to attach all sorts of crazy bugs to me: *I'm pure, I don't need these superfluous and trivial toys like that needy actress!*

That Christmas Day passed quite horribly, and they were the loneliest hours of my life. Eventually, I opened my case, pulled the cassette player out like a terrible tumour, and left it at home – so far so good. It was now time to go to the airport. Yes! At least I was on the way. The rest of the cast were to join me in a couple of weeks, since I would be spending New Year with Helen in her home in New Zealand.

At the airport, I hovered around the duty-free electronics department and my eye alighted on a small cassette player.

Yes! Why not? I have to have it!

So I bought it and placed it in my hand luggage, boarded the plane, and placed my newly acquired toy in the overhead locker. I sat on the aisle of a three-seater.

There were no celebrations on the plane, not even a mention of that dreaded word. The food was utterly ordinary, while my poor brain festered as if it was haunted by the beast in the locker. I read and I drank and was very grateful for the break when the plane touched down in Dubai. It was here where, just a few years ago, Sarah Mason had encouraged me to buy the silk jillaba. I did go back to find that very same store but, alas, it was no longer there.

I boarded the plane for the second leg of the flight and time passed a little more easily; eventually I arrived in Sydney and taxied straight to my favourite hotel, the Florida Motor Inn in Potts Point, just off Kings Cross. With its sublime view over Sydney Harbour and the Opera House, it was heaven. I unpacked, took out my precious machine, and plugged it into the power socket, but I couldn't insert it – wrong plug! All I needed was an adaptor, that's all, but I had suffered too effing much. I had had enough; I was furious with this beastly little demon and was determined to kill it, and so I did. I stamped on the thing as if the evil incubus was lodged inside. I stamped and stamped and smashed it to death.

When I had done that monstrous act, a feeling of great relief swept over me.

Oh God! I was free! Now I could enjoy the world once more. I phoned my Aussie producer to tell them I had arrived and strolled into the early-morning sun-drenched street, actually lighter and happier! So that was dealt with.

The following day, I flew to New Zealand to spend the New Year with Helen in the South Island in a strange little town called Invercargill. The whole family waited for me at the airport and thank God, no more planes, no more packing, no more kvetching; just peace. Helen's family were utterly charming to me and the week passed pleasantly enough. The town they lived in was right at the base of New Zealand and was not too exciting, but at least I did have company, and the bitter acid of loneliness slowly leaked out of my bones.

In consequence, I was in a much better mood when I flew back to Sydney and I got there in good time to return to my hotel. Just up the road, there was my favourite second-hand store, and I found a perfect second-hand cassette deck for AUS$40. I carried it out of the shop and actually kissed the bloody thing. No bugs, no kvetches, this felt right. I plugged it in as soon as I entered my room and it sounded just perfect. Ahhhh thank God, at last!

Terry McGinity flew into Sydney, as did Annie Stainer, and we lay around the hotel pool quite contentedly: everything was falling into place. We then flew to Melbourne for the opening night. The theatre was massive and called the National Theatre. I opened with my one-man show of *The Tell-Tale Heart*, and then we got into *The Fall of the House of Usher*, which felt a little lost in a theatre of that size, although *The Tell-Tale Heart* had received one of the greatest reviews I ever had. I was feeling positive, alive, and energetic.

It was to be a twelve-week tour, and our next stop was Sydney at the beautiful Seymour Centre, a far more congenially-sized theatre. The newcomers, like Terry and Annie, all fitted in perfectly. John Prior replaced David Ellis and was a much less temperamental musician. John did not play the harp but made up for it with his skills on piano and drums. Progress was easier. Sydney was successful and our houses were almost full nightly. I was happy and, most of all, unimpeded by the devils that love to worm their way into the skulls of all performers. I was earning a good wage, since I was simultaneously adaptor and actor and director.

After three weeks of blissful contentment and blazing reviews, we headed far west to Perth, on the lower left flank of the huge continent. Our touring manager, Paula DeBurgh, a very smart lady, helped to keep me on an even keel, but then I made a dreadful mistake. Not so dreadful if one has a more normal disposition – but in mine anything can trigger an earthquake.

I hadn't learnt my lesson well enough. I was using a massive amount of energy doing the two pieces nightly, and I did give in to the demon that loves to prey on me. I felt quite simply that I needed a little reward for my efforts. Here, I was banking my wages every week; surely, I deserved a little treat! Glancing into a smart high-tech radio and TV shop, I felt that now my most efficient second-hand cassette deck, which I truly adored, was a little too modest for such a star as I thought I was, so along with Paula I bought a sleek, shiny, slim new cassette deck. Oh, how joyful I felt when I left the store, but I didn't kiss it. I took it back to my hotel room, carefully unwrapped it, and plugged it in, and now I had two cassette players.

Now a most peculiar thing happened – it awoke the nasty incubus inside me that had been dormant for so long. I played my cheap second-hand cassette, then played my beautiful new one, believing that my new treasure would sound absolutely incredible by contrast, but in fact there was very little difference. After a couple more test runs, I found that I was actually turning into the insane Roderick Usher, let alone the murderous psychopath I play in the curtain-raiser, *The Tell-Tale Heart*. I was becoming possessed. My joy of acting and touring the world had vanished; I had to solve this dilemma. *Fuck it!*

So I spoke at some length and depth with Paula, and she did agree that perhaps the best idea would be to sell it, even at half price, if that would rid me of this demon. Once that was decided on, my mind could rest and the joy of performance returned to me. At the beginning of each night's performance, I felt relieved that I was shortly to be rid of this silly little gadget, and my performance was top dog, but when the morning came, it would start nagging in my brain again. Of course, I could not feel free until I had once more made this nightly pact:

'Paula, please sell it. I need freedom.'

Paula agreed, and once again I entered the stage feeling liberated. Paula came backstage and said, 'The performance was as good as ever.' So now, feeling somewhat transcendental, I said, 'OK, no need to sell the blasted thing.'

The next day broke, and I felt OK until the afternoon, when the madness would start to creep back into me like a slow-release poison. I had to convince myself to sell it before each and every performance; I was surely going insane. The production, however, was successful, since in my mind I was going to be free, but I could not enjoy my days off. In the end, I was reduced to consulting a doctor but he confessed total bewilderment and could not help me. It was a three-week season in Perth, a beautiful town, and I prayed for the end. Eventually, Paula told me one afternoon she had sold the damn thing, and I felt a similar relief as when I had stamped up and down on the one, I had bought in duty-free. But though now able to work and perform again, I was not completely back to my old self – but tons better.

After Perth, we flew to Tasmania, where we had played *East* six years earlier with much success. Meeting people and happily socialising, I felt free. Tasmania was lovely and it was only a week. We took beautiful day trips with the company. I was slowly healing, thank God. Then we returned to Melbourne for a further week. Now we knew it a little more and relished the convivial street life near the theatre with its gorgeous Italian coffee houses.

On one fine day, we were walking down the main boulevard looking into all the bookshops, when I just happened to notice in one of the shop windows a large poster advertising and selling the books of world-famous psychiatrist Thomas Szasz. I just thought, almost subconsciously, '*Strange name*'. That evening after the show, there was a knock on my dressing room door; I opened it to find a young man standing there with an older man in the background. He entered, saying, 'Good evening, Dr Thomas Szasz would like to meet you.' You could have blown me over with a feather – are such things possible?

'Oh, do please come in,' I cried, then gushed, 'I saw your books on display only this afternoon and I am so pleased to meet you.'

He looked me straight in the eye and said, 'Excuse me, but what I witnessed on your stage is the most profound description of schizophrenia I have ever seen.'

I said, 'Oh, thank you, thank you,' but before I could continue, he asked to meet the actress playing my sister, Annie Stainer. I took him a short way down the corridor and introduced him. 'This is Terry McGinity and Annie Stainer.' They had, most fortunately, been with me in the bookshop, where I had commented on his unusual name. They were sharing the dressing room for company. He more or less repeated his compliments to the actors and then fled, since we three 'disturbed actors' were probably more than he could take. But, of course, we were all thrilled to have met him and ever so slightly amazed, having only just seen his works displayed in the bookshop that very afternoon.

We never saw him again and seldom, if ever, mentioned him; it's only now, writing these words in 2025, some forty-three years later and in the age of the internet, that I have looked him up and discovered that sadly he died in 2016 and was regarded as an intellectual giant of the twentieth century. I am proud all over again. I wonder if he could have helped me with my little problem, but then I realise that the very malaise it created in me may have provided insights that enabled me to create something that could so impress a man like Thomas Szasz.

At last, it was over. I flew back to Sydney, stayed for a few days, and then flew back to London. It was 1984. Such a relief to be back in London!

I suppose it is almost natural for actors to suffer the malaise of something like OCD, since we rely on the masses of nervous energy that stimulate us and provide fuel and ideas both for the performance and for our wish to release ourselves from the normality of our day-to-day lives. On the 'boxing ring' of the stage, we can express ourselves in ways that would be totally impossible during our daylight hours. We are surely Jekyll and Hyde. That sense of abandonment can be totally intoxicating… You have metamorphosed into another being. Of course, it's acting, and as you create the dynamic monster onstage, there is still a tiny watchman up there in your frontal lobes that is keeping a shrewd eye on the proceedings, lest you lose yourself and the character takes over.

But as you are excavating those ancient vaults, you might also find yourself exposing some old wounds, which by now have developed into obsessions. These nascent obsessions generally make no real impact on you during your quotidian activities. But acting seems to make a deal with you: if you want the nirvana of total freedom, then you must be pure, ascetic even, or you will not be permitted to reach those heights. Or it can feel like you are making a pact with Mephistopheles.

When Laurence Olivier bravely confessed his mental agony to his entire cast at the National Theatre, it must have taken a huge act of courage. He gathered them all together onstage before the performance and made a bizarre request. He asked them not to look him in the eye during his scenes. What terrible pain he must have felt, but he feared he could not continue if they did. Some actors will feel that the energy has in some way depleted and is no longer protecting them. Thankfully, over a period of time, he managed to recover, but by then he was reaching the end of his acting career.

I was acting quite a demanding role some years ago and found that there was one member of the cast I just could not bear to look at. He was not an especially impressive actor, but I feared looking at him and catching his eye, lest I lose my lines, so I had to avoid glancing at him and my lines flowed easily and fluidly. Why? Why did I fear this very ordinary being? I sensed he was antipathetic and didn't even like me. Perhaps one's energy depletes as one ages, and one has to know when it is time to hang up the gloves.

Onstage that is.

***

I somehow managed to avoid the bug's worst effects and even did try on occasion to interpret it as a positive 'snarl', for it stopped me thinking about the most ghastly traumas that a stage can bring, such as worrying about 'drying' – to be in the middle of a scene and worrying about what words will come next. The terror of that uncertainty is among the worst emotions an actor can feel. So, in some curious convoluted way, my bug even protects me. But the bug doesn't like to be defeated and will attempt to inveigle itself into my life in whatever way it can. Unfortunately, it has never really vanished, so, as old as I am, I have lived with the bugger for some years.

Yet it is curious that even the most profound malaise can almost secretly make itself the source of inspiration as it did with my play, *Kvetch*.

Kvetch, 1986

For many actors, there comes a time when the after-effects of our trade begin to manifest themselves. I am sure it is no different for singers, directors, writers, comedians, etc. What could be the reason? Possibly our brains are put into a position of full alert, since performers, once exposed to the outside world, are in a life-or-death situation. A mini death occurs should one suddenly lose the thread of the structure that is keeping their character alive – i.e., losing their lines, the actor's worst nightmare! Though this is rare; the actor's brain concentrates with such intensity to imprint those words, moves, and gestures that they must trust their wonderful brain to guide them through.

Also, in compensation, you have that most extraordinary of medicine: adrenaline. This is so potent a drug that it has the power to transcend all other problems and distractions, but this most precious psychic substance is elusive. Yet, if you trust it, it will protect you, and then release you with its power until you are entirely within its grip. Eureka, or something called *duende*, describes a state of being that all performers strive to experience at least once or twice during a run. It is a sensation of such heightened perception that it is akin to a trance, utter freedom… Nothing can possibly go wrong. A godly spirit has entered your soul.

Fear is a vicious sensation that traps you in a gigantic spider-web and, being trapped, you respond to each and every gust of wind, each tiny tremor. And yet this fear is also a formidable source of energy that, paradoxically, can be of immense power. When your mind is on high alert onstage and there are a thousand human eyes boring into you, you feel you are never more exposed as you trap every petty, trivial thought that has bugged you.

One day, I gathered all these tiny and not so tiny bugbears and exposed them all in a play: *Kvetch*. Once I started writing the play, there was no stopping me.

Oh, the agony of every negative experience poured out like a lava flow of neurosis. But the paradox was that the worse – or even more painful – the confession, the more the audience laughed their heads off. It even won the *Evening Standard* Comedy of the Year Award; I was very proud of that. I was also thrilled by the letter I received from Harold Pinter, who had become a good friend by this time:

Dear Steven

Thanks for Kvetch. I think it's a terrific piece of work and really bloody funny. Nice of you to ask me to play Hal. What with one thing and another, I'm afraid I can't – but I'd love to be out front on the first night.

Good luck.

Yours
Harold

I had a first-class cast, and for the wife, Donna, I was so fortunate to have the services of Anita Dobson. For Hal, the visitor, I cast Henry Goodman, whom I had taught twenty years earlier at RADA, where I put together my very challenging production of *Agamemnon*. It was the small but funky Odyssey Theatre in Los Angeles that gave me the opportunity to try out *Kvetch*. I was blessed with a superb cast led by Kurt Fuller, who was a superb comedian. Unfortunately, the play was shot down in flames by the New York critics. However, this did not hinder the health of the play, which I then opened in London.

We produced *Kvetch* at the charismatically grotty King's Head Theatre in Upper Street, Islington, which American maverick Dan Crawford opened in the '60s with that most wonderful play *Kennedy's Children*. We then took it to the Edinburgh Festival, where we were equally successful, and then Dan Crawford was able to get us into the Garrick Theatre in London's West End, where we all had a great time for our brief two-month run. The beauty of playing in the West End is that it is just like an exclusive club; you become an honoured member and the world might just get to know you are there. I remember the great actor/manager Sam Wanamaker coming in. We met and got on very well. He insisted that once the

Globe was up and running, I must definitely be part of it, but after the great man died, I never heard from the Globe Theatre again.

Never mind! There are always a few hiccups! We theatre folks ought to support each other just a little bit more. When I have been supported, even if it's only by a charming old smelly fringe theatre like the King's Head, it has still meant so much to me, and I loved Dan Crawford.

Poster for *Kvetch*, 1986.

CHAPTER 18

Prince, Spielberg, and Polanski

In 1986, I happened to be in Nice doing a film called *Under the Cherry Moon*, which was eventually directed by the world-famous music star Prince. How it started was painfully simple. I had been sitting quietly at home in Limehouse, deciding what to do next, when the phone rang. It was my agent, Martin Gage, from LA. 'Terence Stamp has walked away from a film and they want you to replace him as the father.' I thought, *Wow, that's great news!* He told me to get on the next plane from City Airport to Nice, which of course I immediately agreed to, since I wasn't doing anything more than cogitating.

Terence, whom I had known and even studied with in drama school, had apparently walked off after a cast reading in the hotel in which they were staying. Before the reading, Prince and his whole entourage had got fitted up and measured in beautiful suits, then when he saw Prince's mates fooling around at the reading, Terence just up and left. He could be a bit sensitive like that.

I think readings can be very dangerous in film, since you might be sitting around for hours waiting for your few lines to turn up. Meanwhile all the principals are having a great deal of fun, laughing and giggling together while you just sit there glumly waiting your turn. Fortunately, I was spared this, so I happily flew to one of my favourite cities in the south of France. I enjoyed Nice immensely. The role of my daughter was played by Kristin Scott Thomas, who was at the beginning of her career. And hasn't she done well!

When I joined the cast, Mary Lambert, a quite charming woman, was directing the film, however she later left the project after Prince didn't like the rushes. So instead he said he was going to direct it. Fine. Yet, he had one odd directorial quirk: he didn't like being in the room while we were shooting.

Kirsten and I would be acting together in a scene while Prince was watching it on a monitor in another room. Then the scene would end, there'd be a brief pause, and then I'd hear the 'click, clack, click' of his high-heel boots as he approached from down the corridor. Then he would say something like, 'Oh Steve, when you say that line, "She's on her way back", it should be "She *is* on her way" instead.'

'Right … I'll do that,' I'd reply.

Then he'd turn on his heels and click-clack-click away back to his monitor, and we'd do the scene again. It was like that for weeks – he was an eccentric character. The film went on to be one of the flops of the century, although in recent years people have given it a little more credit than it perhaps deserves.

War and Remembrance, 1987

It was during my stay in Nice that one of the actors happened to mention that he was helping producer Dan Curtis cast his mega TV series *War and Remembrance* and they were looking for good actors to play the Nazis – Hitler in particular. When I heard the name 'Hitler', my ears pricked up, since the role of the Nazi beast was one part that I had a good chance of nailing. It was summer and I asked my smart new agent, Simon Asdair at ICM, to request, most emphatically, an audition for me. I felt the part was suited to me since I too had an army, which was my actors, and we invaded countries, but we won them over with words not bullets. Simple as that seems, that sufficed for me.

The day of my audition was set up in London, but first Dan Curtis wanted to video me in full costume and wig. I was sent to Wig Creations to be fitted with wig, moustache, and uniform. The wigmaker actually made one to fit, even though it was just for an audition. The wig was carefully placed over my skull with the famous parting on Hitler's right side and the smear of black hair flapping over his forehead. I stared at the mirror almost willing the beast to appear, but I still looked too much like me with a funny wig on. The hairdresser said, 'Let's try on the moustache.' He took the little rectangle of hair out of its tiny box, added some glue for the gauze, and attached it beneath my nose… *Shazam!* He appeared, suddenly, out of thin air, or rather that smudge of hair – that little tache definitely pulled everything together. So eerie! I stared at myself and was ecstatic. At least I had the look.

On the day of my meeting with Dan Curtis, we were joined by his lovely assistant Barbara Steele, an ex-actress. I took my costume – my little box with wig and tache – and taxied over to Dan's office at the Hyde Park Hotel. I took the lift to his room. He opened the door, and I entered smiling. I felt overconfident that the part was mine. I had rehearsed alone the previous day and was determined to give it full welly.

As I entered the hotel room, I said, quite lightly, 'Here is your Hitler.'

He looked at me briefly. I looked healthy, had a light tan, and couldn't look less like the monster. He responded with some slight fatigue in his voice.

'OK, let's hope so.'

I think he must have seen a few too many Hitlers that day. I entered the bathroom, changed into my costume, then donned the wig but was not yet convinced of the magic in the little box. Perhaps it was wishful thinking. I took the little smudge of black out of the box, added a smidgeon of spirit gum, and attached it to my upper lip. I walked out of the bathroom.

Dan looked up; it was immediately clear to me that he was somewhat disturbed. For most actors, putting on the accoutrements of such a famous Nazi could only reveal the actor all the more, but I felt that in my case, for some reason, my features seemed to eagerly reshape themselves. I knew that Dan and even Barbara Steele were somewhat shocked, and they were silent. It was as if Hitler himself had stepped into the room. Dan just said, 'OK, Steve, let's do it,' and I started.

I tore into the script as if to the manner born. They said nothing. Barbara Steele looked intensely at Dan, and eventually Dan said, 'OK, there's another character I'd like you to read.' At this Barbara Steele looked at him with a shocked expression; obviously Dan Curtis didn't wish to show his true feelings for whatever reason. Soon after, I left. I knew I had it. I had no doubt about it.

The next morning, Simon Asdair confirmed it with a very healthy fee. It was mine. My star was beginning to twinkle... thank you, God. Herman Wouk wrote the book and sometimes came on the set. It was an incredible shoot with an amazing cast, including the famous German film actor Hardy Krüger as Rommel – the 'good Nazi' – with whom I had had the pleasure of working in *Barry Lyndon* in 1975.

The shoot was going well, and Dan Curtis and Barbara Steele never failed to express their happiness with my performance, but one morning before shooting a critical scene with Hardy Krüger, Hardy gently took me to one side and gave me some advice about playing Hitler. He felt that there was always the temptation to play him as a raving maniac and that this had become something of a cliché. 'Don't forget,' he said, 'that, at the beginning of his leadership, he helped to create an economically sound Germany, brought about full employment, and rescued Germany from the terrible slump it had been in. He could not possibly have done all these things if he was a half-mad demigod.'

I listened carefully to his comments, which were made with goodwill. I mentioned this to Dan Curtis, who replied, 'We are shooting the period after 1943 when Hitler was certifiable and when he was beginning to lose the war. Play him that way.' So, when I did the scene, I let rip, and Dan was most satisfied. I finished the shoot.

War and Remembrance was first shown in the USA and the reviews were excellent. Sometime later I received a call from Steven Spielberg's office asking me to come to a reading for a film he was about to direct called *Schindler's List*. He did add that he thought my interpretation of Hitler was the best he had ever seen on film. I looked forward to meeting him and duly turned up at his immaculate office, where a long table had been set up with coffee and bagels for before we began. I had received the script in advance and around the table were the usual group of high-ranking British actors. I sat next to Charles Dance, and Ralph Fiennes sat opposite, and we began the read-through. I gave a toned-down Nazi reading but Steven asked me to tone it down even more, which I did, and we read it once more. However, it was Ralph Fiennes whom he chose for the role. It was fascinating to have met the great man, and I was not at all disappointed.

Paris, 1988

Metamorphosis stayed with me for a very long time. I did productions in Australia, LA, Düsseldorf, Tel Aviv, and then I revived it for myself at The Mermaid Theatre in London in 1986. The Mermaid was an exceptionally friendly theatre. Its audience sat on one level, like in an amphitheatre, and so on that vast stage you felt much closer to them than on an old-fashioned proscenium stage. With my new producer, Christopher Malcolm, I felt emboldened, since I now had an ally as well as a friend.

Christopher and I went to The Mermaid Theatre to make a deal with the management and opened the production a few weeks later, but, of course, we had to find a compelling actor to play the beetle. It was when I saw Tim Roth in a contemporary television drama that I thought we had the man; I thought he was absolutely dynamic, and he was as keen as I was to be in the production. The reviews were excellent and we had a great cast that included Saskia Reeves as Greta, the daughter, Linda Marlowe as the mother, Mrs Samsa, and me as the father, Mr Samsa. Now, it just so happens that the production excited or caught the interest of the French actor, director and producer Roman Polanski, and he sent his manager, Georges Baum, to cast an eye on it. Monsieur Baum obviously felt that this would be a positive move for Roman Polanski. As a result, I was asked to direct *Metamorphosis* in French in Paris, which excited me greatly.

I flew to Paris to meet Roman Polanski to discuss what was a most exciting project for us both. At the age of 50, he would play the sad outsider Gregor Samsa. It was a brave decision to make and I could see from the beginning that Roman was a man not lacking in courage. We all met in a swish Parisian hotel and I took a pew in the ultra-soft armchair. When he walked in, I found I could hardly extricate myself from the armchair; I felt like a beached whale. He shrewdly perched, just like a lively jackal, on the arm of the chair while I was sucked into its nether regions. Polanski was accompanied by Georges; he made some fairly simple chatter as I sank even deeper into the abyss of foam and leather.

The following day, we met in the Théâtre du Gymnase for a reading, and this was where we were supposed to iron out any problems. Roman had brought his lovely wife along, since he had already decided that she was to play the Samsa family's young daughter, Greta. I think that is how they work in Paris. The decisions are made by the powers that be while the simple hired hand, the director, is obliged to merely go along with it.

But, regrettably, they found the wrong guy in me. For while I was sinking helplessly into the overstuffed armchair, I still took my work very seriously. I think I had made *Metamorphosis* a work of art as much as I could, while still serving the author. All elements flowed into each other: text, movement, and music. And the actors should, and usually did, flawlessly play to the rules as I and previous actors had conceived them. I spoke about the style continuously and how very important it was to conceive the family through the body of the actors just as much as through the text. Roman liked the idea; after all, he was not going to expose himself in a simple-minded production and I am sure that Georges Baum would have advocated quite seriously on my behalf. Hopefully.

I was, of course, more than delighted to be directing Kafka with the one person who fully related to such a paranoiac theme and probably identified with Gregor Samsa as much as I did. Roman came to rehearsals the first morning, rosy-cheeked from the wintry chill and a scarf wrapped round his neck like a cheeky schoolboy full of optimism, as I was, for the first day of term. And I was not insensible to this man's enormous talent as an actor and film auteur. He even echoed my thoughts by saying, 'This feels like the first day of school.'

We read through the first half in French and then had a swift lunch break. Since he had brought his wife, I decided that she should at least demonstrate a little of what is expected of her character, but her reading was only a little less than listless. So I gently showed the company what was expected of them. I carefully and slowly demonstrated to them how we conceived the style. You see, the family, being a petty bourgeois family, are ruled by time – always being concerned about wasting time and how late it is, and worrying that their Gregor will not be on time. Their bodies reflect the time and soon Gregor's insect state loses all fluidity and moves more mechanically like a large black insect. It is an effect which immediately grips the audience's attention. This is how I conceived it all those years ago, when I worked with a metronome. I doubt I should do that today, although why not? They move, eat, sleep – the intent is to intensify the action.

We slowly moved through the first scene. Most of the actors seemed to cope quite well with this strange technique, but the young lady had problems, as I knew she would. However, it was more than necessary to show how the technique we used, when done well, can not only intensify the story but look quite compelling. Alas, the poor thing had a cold and was continually snuffling and pulling out tissues. She was not an actress for the theatre, although I learned that it had been a dream of Roman's to act with his wife. What a shame for him. By the day's end, regrettably, she resigned. Shame – but in a way, good.

As Polanski drove away, I just managed to catch him to offer up my sincere solicitude and say that theatre is a different world from the movies. To which he surprisingly replied, '*Non*, there is no difference.' Of course, any first-year student knows that there most certainly is. And with that he drove off. I was very sad that our relationship was somewhat soured at this early stage but privately very glad to be rid of this charming but somewhat inexperienced female performer.

We continued working for the next five weeks on and off, since he was still editing his latest film, *Frantic*. I was disappointed not to have at least bonded with him or sat with him in a local café for a coffee and a chat, since we really had so much to talk about. But apart from the first night in Paris, when he took me to La Coupole and we had a very enjoyable chat, in the entire period of rehearsal we never shared even a carafe of wine or a cup of coffee, and I was never invited to his home – not surprisingly, I suppose. I was persona non grata.

Eventually, after many breaks for his editing work and then for his Christmas skiing holiday, we did manage to open and, fortunately, we found an excellent actress for Greta. The cast was a little wonky since the father was having difficulty, which is a huge understatement. What is it about actors who play fathers? But he struggled on bravely and managed not to embarrass us too much.

On the opening night, the cast received a standing ovation and everyone was happy. Roman came to centre stage, put his hand over his heart, gazed out at the cheering crowd, and gratefully bowed like an ancient actor-manager of the nineteenth century. Watching this display, I was very happy for him and kept my bile way down in my throat. Of course, Roman and his friends all went to the trendy nightclub Le Bain Douche, while I went with the producers to a beautiful Parisian restaurant. Thank God it was over. The reviews were, on the whole, excellent. Roman wrote me a letter once the run was under way:

Dear Steven,

As you certainly gather, we're still doing strong, packed every night. However, I had bronchitis and we had to stop for a week.

We started again last night, and it went extremely well, but I do believe that your short visit for a couple of rehearsals would be very useful. As with every show, it degenerates gradually and it needs tightening up. We still have some eighty performances to go.

My movie has opened in the United States to some excellent reviews, some bad ones as well, but the business is sensational as they say in Hollywood. We've been at the top of the list.

Best wishes,
Roman Polanski

By then I had escaped to Dublin, to the Gate Theatre to direct *Salomé* by Oscar Wilde. It had all started when I had a two-week gig at the Gate Theatre with my production of *Decadence*, which I performed with Linda Marlowe. The theatre had a legendary reputation and is where the young Orson Welles began his theatrical career after touring Ireland on a donkey. The director, Michael Colgan, was planning a revival of a 1928 season when the then director, Hilton Edwards, decided to direct *Salomé* – a very brave choice at the time.

I eagerly accepted the Gate's offer, since it just so happened that *Salomé* had enchanted me inexorably. I had recently read a biography of Oscar Wilde that had moved me so much that I was determined to create a production which not only was unforgettable but also honoured his memory. I was going to make sure that the actors were highly skilled and able to move and speak almost as if they were enacting a séance. I was determined to do it in slow motion, as if the language was so fragile and delicate, like faded pieces of papyri, and the actors never failed me. But the driving passion I had to one day direct *Salomé* was largely driven by the extraordinary role of Herod, which I felt was mine to play. The language was as exotic as anything Wilde had written in drama. It was seductive and sexually exciting and contained an image of a man hideously dominated by his passions until he became a crawling, cringing beggar. I was most tempted, as I was used to begging.

After four weeks, I heard from Paris that Roman was getting better and better; however, I returned, as he requested in his letter, so we could do some fine-tuning and try to do something with the father, who seemed to possess three legs. By this time, Roman seemed to have thawed somewhat and took me to lunch, which was most pleasant. I saw the matinee, and it was indeed all over the place. The two women were excellent, and it was such a relief that we had found the perfect Greta. Madame Cohendy as the mother was simply splendid. Strangely enough, the men simply didn't have the grace or lyricism that the women possessed so effortlessly. I have found the same problem in almost every city throughout the world where I have directed the play, except perhaps New York City where I was blessed with Mikhail Baryshnikov as the beetle and the late René Auberjonois as the father.

In fact, I came to be doing the play in New York because Mikhail Baryshnikov had been to see the production in Paris and quite fancied the idea of doing a drama, since, as a dancer, he knew that a dancer's world is far more limited than an actor's, and I'm sure he could see that this role was certainly a halfway house between dance and drama. Perfect! He obviously knew Polanski; superstars always seem to know each other. And it may have been Roman who suggested it to Mikhail, for which I am duly grateful to Roman.

When I was told that the leading actor was to be Mikhail Baryshnikov, I leaped with joy! I was going to rehearse with one of the greatest performers in the world. It was 1988 and rehearsals in New York were going very well, since this time I had done the casting and they were an impressive group of actors. I wanted desperately to show Mikhail that actors could be as skilled as great dancers and not the slobs we see all too often. Mikhail was not disappointed and the cast were so very patient as Mikhail continued to ask to rerun scenes again and again and yet again.

Roman and I ended up on good terms. I have another letter from him, sent from Paris in November 1989, by which time he was experiencing difficulties with getting his next movie made:

Dear Steven,

This may come like mustard after dinner as it is over two months since you wrote to me. But I had a dinner with Misha Baryshnikov last night, we talked about the play and about you, of course, and I realized I never answered your letter.

Well, all I can say is, next time you cross the Channel, please call. We'll have a French meal or English drink and will reminisce. Meanwhile, I hope your 'Profile' came out brilliant. I'd love to see it one day. I gather you're no more an 'Off Broadway' director having a success at the National. Great! As for myself, I don't have any immediate theatrical plans, just trying to put a movie together – which is becoming more and more pain in the ass as the industry changes into some sort of fast food business.

With my best wishes,
Roman Polanski

CHAPTER 19

Coriolanus

When Joe Papp called during *Greek's* [1988] run at the Wyndham's Theatre to ask if I would like to direct *Coriolanus* at The Public Theater, it brought to life a dream I had nursed for decades: at last, I would be working in New York. Joe wanted to stage it in what he called 'the Shakespeare marathon', where over a number of years, he intended to produce the entire canon.

I began reading *Coriolanus*. I had only seen it once in a Peter Hall production with Ian McKellen, so I had no clear impression of it. I kept reading it, but no style or shape surfaced in my mind. The only idea I had was to create within the ensemble a disgruntled crowd of East Side lowlifes, which felt dead right, and the crowd would be used first as Coriolanus' soldiers and then, with the use of the simple trick of costume, would magically transform into the army of Aufidius. I slipped easily into a healthy NYC routine, living in the Gramercy Park Hotel and taking a jog around the square every morning before breakfast at a diner on Third Avenue and 21st Street. I would walk down to The Public Theater on Lafayette Street in Greenwich Village, passing all the homeless and unemployed who tried to subsist on selling junk outside the theatre. I was both terrified and excited by the prospect of directing a play I had no experience of, and every day I took a deep breath as I entered the theatre and prepared to devote everything I had to creating a production that would honour the play, do myself justice, and repay Joe's faith in me.

Papp had cast all the principals, since he knew American actors far better than I ever could; alongside Christopher Walken and Irene

Worth, we had a quite wonderful Black actor named Keith David to play Aufidius. I cast the ensemble, which became the backbone of the play. When casting, I chose the ones that the casting director, Rosemarie Tichler, vetoed as being either too flashy or not classical enough, which showed how totally different our ideas were. One actor wrote to me begging for a chance to audition since he had been turned down for some unearthly reason. His name was Patrick Page, and he is now one of New York's finest and most famous actors and has been a friend ever since.

Coriolanus had a sticky start, since most American actors had little idea of ensemble work, but gradually they not only adjusted to it but positively embraced it. It gave them so much more to do and to invent than our British spear carriers. Chris Walken ambitiously learnt the whole role before starting, so it was impossible to give him any cuts and expect him to remember them, but he did have a powerful voice when he chose to use it and worked well with the actress playing his mother, Irene Worth. She was totally delightful at first and continually complimented me on the initial staging, but when I took exception to her overdone costume, which was far too elaborate for the movement, she suddenly completely lost all interest in me and stopped talking to me! It didn't help that I had had to have words with her and Chris for discussing the scenes together as if no one else were in the room.

I felt for the poor young woman playing the wife, who was having to hang around while the 'stars' talked among themselves. I recognised this behaviour as a product of that absurd system where one or two actors are the 'stars', and the director fawns over them, while the rest of the cast sit meekly in their dressing rooms waiting to be summoned. That's not how I work. Equality across the cast is of vital importance. Miss Worth was not accustomed to this; she was a fine actress but something of a grande dame and expected a bit more reverence. Still, the approach I took paid off: the production achieved the best reviews of the marathon. *Hooray!* And my relationship with Papp strengthened and I felt I had a great ally in this wonderful man.

***

"Superb Berkoff proves he is perfect match for Coriolanus"

To watch his crisp, stripped-down *Coriolanus* kick off Steven Berkoff's residency at the long-under-used Mermaid Theatre is to witness a triumph of theatrical matchmaking, Simply put, Berkoff and *Coriolanus* were made for each other.

Shakespeare's play has a muscular poetry which is echoed in Berkoff's own works. The titular Roman soldier has all the arrogance and ferocity that characterise Berkoff's performances.

Coriolanus is a vital force in Roman society, shunned because of his intemperate opinions and his obstinate refusal to kowtow – which is rather like Berkoff's position in British theatre.

All that said, age and familiarity with the play – he first conceived this production nine years ago in America, playing the lead last year in Leeds – seem thankfully to have mellowed Berkoff. There are only sporadic traces here of the self-indulgent actor-director who goes over the top with all the suicidal verve of the British infantry in the Somme.

Using atmospheric music and mime instead of a set and props, he stages this story of combat and compromise with a clarity that puts most recent shows by the RSC to shame. The investment demanded by its threehours-plus running time is amply repaid.

The production's minimalist expressionism includes the 'design concept', for which Berkoff receives yet another programme credit. Coriolanus's Rome is suggested by a row of imposing pillars and black chairs, while the monochrome costumes mix totalitarian chic, businesswear and a dash of fetishism.

The ruling patricians act sometimes like Nazis, sometimes like mafia dons, but always with distaste for the ragged commoners. In this uneasy situation, Berkoff's sneering, abrasive Coriolanus is like a lighted match held to a petrol can. Stocky and with a thickening midriff thrusting at the buttons of a double-breasted suit tucked into jackboots, Berkoff controls the stage with his fierce presence. At 59, he could easily pass for 40, such is his pugnacious vigour. He mimes Coriolanus's bloody victories over the Volscians, led by Colin McFarlane's stentorian Aufidius, with chilling conviction.

Back home in Rome, his fixedly grinning forays among the unwashed suggest the disgust of a noble man of action confronted with the sleazy role-playing of politics. On a personal level, he plays down the Oedipal dimension of Coriolanus's relationship with his mother, Volumnia. His scenes with her (a suitably imperious Faith Brook) and Coriolanus's wife Virgilia (Sara Griffiths) are surprisingly tender. Of course, the old, excessive Berkoff sometimes rears his wilful, shaven head. The evocative choreographed movement sometimes teeters on the brink of absurdity, as when a troop of horseless riders bob up and down to the strains of Wagner's *Ride of the Valkyries.*

The tribunes who incite the mob to banish Coriolanus are presented as obviously dodgy spivs – one Glaswegian (Tam Dean Burn, adequate), one cockney (Michael Jenn, awful). And there's a certain campness in the sway of Berkoff's hips and his sensuous pouts.

Such quibbles vanish, though, at the hideously effective finale. It remains to be seen whether Berkoff's tenancy can revive the flagging fortunes of the Mermaid. But his opening production and his restrained, magnetic performance are more intelligent, exciting and promising than anything seen at this venue for many a year.

– Nick Curtis, *Evening Standard,* 13 June 1993

***

The theatre had some very strange customs, like doing two shows on Saturday and two on Sunday so they could have Monday off! Such a regime would kill most actors; paradoxically, however, the stage manager would call a break every two hours, even in the middle of a scene, in case the actors were overworked! Dumb Equity rules.

I firmly bonded with the ensemble part of the cast; the reason being that they were called upon to be creative and inventive at all times – perhaps closer to the dynamics of a dance company. Meanwhile, the principal actors, with one or two exceptions, nearly always had a problem and could seldom remember their moves, so we had to rehearse them over and over again. I can't blame them entirely, since that is how they had been directed by lazy plodding directors, and if I emphasised the importance of remembering their movements, they would tend to get impatient or even angry. Chris Walken became really upset when I insisted that we had to work out his climactic death scene. He wanted something special and quoted to me something he had read about Laurence Olivier's famous death when he played it at Stratford-upon-Avon. I confidently replied, since the rehearsals up to this time had been going quite well, that 'we will do something that will top even Olivier's sensational death.'

'OK,' he said, 'what do you have in mind?'

In front of the ensemble, since they were all part of it, I briefly demonstrated to him the principles and asked him to have a go at it, to get used to it, but to my surprise, he didn't want to rehearse it with Aufidius, whom it concerns more than anyone.

'Please, Chris,' I begged, 'why can't we just slowly plot it?'

'We'll do it later,' he responded, 'no problem.'

I had to insist, which I had done very little of so far, that we do it *now*.

'I'm a dancer,' he replied, 'it's no problem.'

I repeated that it was important for the whole cast. He stared at me coldly for a few seconds, made a comment which didn't make too much sense, and walked out of the production! Joe Papp was summoned and had to deal with him. Chris Walken, of course, came back, and to his credit he did do it, albeit in his own style, and it worked out well… in a way.

Joe was happy and asked me if I'd like to take on directing *Othello*, again with Chris Walken, this time as Iago, and with dynamic Puerto Rican actor Raul Julia as Othello, but to tell you the truth, I had had a much better offer from Germany to do *Coriolanus* in German and decided I'd had enough of The Public for the time being; much as I loved it, the wages were minuscule. Joe died before I could be summoned back to New York.

Coriolanus in Germany, 1988

Bumping into Günther Beelitz (for whom I had happily worked in Düsseldorf when directing *The Trial* and *Metamorphosis*) reminded him that I was still alive and that I had just directed *Coriolanus* in New York. Günther Beelitz was now the producer of the Residenztheater in Munich. He paid a proper salary for a director, so I was quite happy to return to do *Coriolanus* once again in German.

When we were flying over Munich, the steward had made an announcement over the plane's speakers about a place of natural curiosity as if he was describing a part of the bucolic countryside: 'We are now flying over Dachau.' He might have added 'the notorious Dachau concentration camp'. Naturally I made a mental note to visit.

As it was a state theatre working with a long contract, there was good camaraderie among the actors. After meeting them on the first day of rehearsals, I explained the form of the production, and we got to work swiftly plotting the play. The role of Coriolanus had been cast by Günther Beelitz and was a tall, leonine actor called Rufus Beck, and, while he felt he didn't have quite the appropriate build for the temperamental general, he spoke the lines with energy and dynamism. He was not always easy to work with – at the outset, he complained that the text was a bad translation, wooden, and too rhythmic. It was actually written by the 19th-century German Romantic poet Johann Ludwig Tieck, whose works Roderick Usher reads in *The Fall of the House of Usher*. Until then I had imagined he was a fictional character created by Edgar Allan Poe!

In trying to get the feeling of a highly drilled Roman army, I attempted to create a physical and highly volatile team of players. This was developing day-by-day and was beginning to look impressive. But to my astonishment, a couple of actors started complaining about the work or the style – I knew not which! One of them was particularly belligerent and he was playing one of the tribunes, rather well I thought, and the curious thing was that I thought the scenes he was in were exciting and successful; however, I kept glancing at him whispering in corners and desperately attempting to disrupt the proceedings.

A few days later, Günther Beelitz was coming to watch rehearsals one morning, which is a usual practice for the intendant to do. Just as we were about to run Act One, with Günther sitting waiting eagerly to see it, what do I notice but, yet again, this pest bent over the producer's ear, hissing his complaints! I, frankly, had had enough of him, and I could even see how his poisonous barbs had affected some of the company. One of the actors actually said to me, 'Do you really need professional actors for this kind of work? I mean, anyone off the street could do this.'

Then a second actor actually had the temerity to say to me, 'Do you come to Germany just for the money?' It was no secret that Germany paid high salaries to its directors.

I thought the comment was beyond disgusting but had no doubt of the identity of the scumbag who had peddled this filth. What was even more mysterious was the fact that this production was going very well. So, when I saw the twisted features of this actor's face as he doled out his lying spew, I marched over and told him that he did nothing but complain and this was poisoning the production and it might be better if he left. He then burbled and mumbled something, but now my patience was wearing thin, and I just thrust out my arm and said, 'OUT!'

And he did that very thing. He slunk out like a rat. I glanced at the entire team of actors. No one spoke up for him, even when he actually turned to the entire room and pleaded, 'Will no one speak up for me?'

No, mister! No one spoke up for you… A grand, majestic silence.

When we continued the rehearsal, it had never gone more smoothly and he was easily replaced. I was quite surprised that no one in that room would give him even an ounce of support. After I'd sacked him, he confirmed I was correct in my assessment of his character by running to the press. The Munich newspaper he bleated to didn't even bother to contact me for my version of events – they just printed his lies, spouting nonsense such as the claim that I didn't discuss his character with him, whereas of course I did: together we had also worked on the character's body language, which enthused the other actors too.

Munich is a lovely city and after rehearsals and to relax, I loved walking through what they call the English Garden and stopping at one of those brilliant old-world beer houses and even indulging in a bratwurst or two... What could be nicer? And such a contrast to touring the drab lands of the English provinces. There is a never-ending wonder of living on the continent of Europe.

We were soon arriving for our first night and desperately trying to get the most inept costumes beefed up and to put just a little more fizz into the principals. However, Rufus Beck went from strength to strength, especially when his mother, Volumnia, who had been walking through the war-ravaged lands with his wife and child, pleads for mercy and begs him not to take revenge on Rome. This was the best it had ever been with the amazing Sona MacDonald as his wife, who slithers between his legs like a devoted dog as his mother is making her impassioned plea.

There was a slight hiccup at the curtain call. When the lights went down, there was an eruption of applause littered with cries of 'Bravo!' I was invited to join the company onstage to take a bow, as is quite usual in European theatres, when a booing broke out from a section of the audience, no doubt from the sour coevals of the filthy wretch I had been obliged to get rid of. I turned towards the sound and merely smiled and punched the air triumphantly with my fist. This was the first time this event had happened to me and so ironic it should happen to a Jew in Munich of all places.

But few events are as exciting as first night, especially to your partner or wife, who has joined you, and you wait with keen anticipation to show them what you have been fiddling about with all these weeks you have been here. Hopefully, now, you have made new friends and they will be friends for all time. I have noticed, since writing, that Rufus Beck has now become one of the biggest stars in Germany.

Metamorphosis, 1989

Mikhail Baryshnikov played Gregor Samsa the beetle in 1989 at the Barrymore Theatre on Broadway for a short but intense season, when it was shot down by the most malevolent critical response it has been my misfortune to experience. He worked so very hard and was very pissed off at the disgusting review in *The New York Times*, but not half so much as I was. But the show still attracted the warmest response from Sir Isaac Stern, David Bowie, and Martha Graham, plus Nancy Reagan on the first night.

When I was ten and in New York and living in the Bronx, I took the subway for an adventure, taking great care that I learned the way back on these trains. I went into the city from 174th Street East to Broadway no less and sat in a diner right opposite the Barrymore Theatre. The play showing at this time was *A Streetcar Named Desire* by Tennessee Williams and starring Marlon Brando. It was one of the greatest theatrical hits in New York. I sat in the same diner right opposite the theatre and watched through the window, the crowds swirling and gathering like moths around a bright light, the limos slowly pulling in and pulling out and people discharging fur coats.

And now, forty years later, *Metamorphosis* was at the same theatre, in my adaptation, direction, and design concept. I waited for a while and decided to go in and give my good wishes to the cast. René Auberjonois, a considerable New York stage actor, played the father, Susan Esterman played the mother, the daughter was played by Madeleine Potter, and the lodger by funny man T.J. Meyers. I made my rounds and then sat in the stalls with Clara. I waved to David Bowie sitting a few rows behind. Martha Graham was sitting in the front and the president's wife, Nancy Reagan, sat in a box.

We had just tried out this play at Duke University in North Carolina. It went very well and gave Baryshnikov some warm-up time to get used to speaking in English before an English audience for the first time in his life. Our producer, Lars Schmidt, who was Swedish and was once the husband of Ingrid Bergman, had booked a table for the heads of production at the Carlisle Hotel after the show. It must have been terrifying for them to all go on in front of that hard-bitten New York audience, let alone the critics who were salivating to get their teeth into it. Clara, with whom I was living in London, flew out for the first night.

The show went extremely well, and the cast gave their best performances so far. The standing ovation at the curtain was one of the most striking and explosive that I had heard in my theatrical career. After the curtain call, I rushed backstage to pass on my congratulations to my fine team, whose nerves were well under control, especially Mikhail. My LA agent, Martin Gage, also came rushing backstage. Mikhail, of course, had the star dressing room, which had an anteroom in which the magnificent Martha Graham sat on the sofa. Then we all sauntered across the road to the famous first-night restaurant Sardis for drinks, and Sir Isaac Stern, the virtuoso violinist, congratulated me fulsomely without a trace of effort to be nice. Coming from a great genius like him, this was something I was very proud of.

Then we beetled to the Carlisle, while the producers waited for the 'exam' results! All of us sat in an elegant private room upstairs waiting. The food was good, and after a couple of hours, our charming, sophisticated Swedish producer stepped out to pick up the first edition of *The New York Times*, upon whose critical opinion the whole world waits with bated breath: producers, backers, actors, directors, costume designers, theatre owners, it was so unequal to the event. We sat digesting our supper totally unconcerned since the audience response had been electric. How could any critic gainsay what they heard and saw, let alone deny the achievement of adapting for this theatre one of the most powerful and moving novels of the twentieth century? However, Lars came back thirty minutes later with a long face that was almost scraping the floor, a copy of *The New York Times* under his arm. It wasn't even a negative review; it was one of the most repellent reviews I have ever experienced. The critic Frank Rich did his best to destroy the production:

> 'It's hard to guess who will suffer most at Steven Berkoff's theatrical version of "Metamorphosis": devotees of Franz Kafka, whose story is distorted into Marxist kitsch by this adaptation, or fans of Mikhail Baryshnikov, whose stage debut as a dramatic actor, however dignified, amounts to little more than a sideshow to the loud circus surrounding

> him. But at least one constituency, albeit a smaller one, should be happy – the Berkoff cult. The director doesn't even have to appear in the flesh to upstage Kafka and Mr. Baryshnikov throughout this piece's interminable (and intermissionless) 100 minutes.'

The piece went on for nearly a thousand words…

I wanted to laugh and almost did; that these grown, powerful men, these astute and even legendary producers, went weak-kneed over the contemptible comments of the scumbag critic who had decided to vomit up his hatred for me. Ridiculous, since London, with its high-quality papers including *The Guardian*, *The Times*, *The Telegraph*, the *Daily Mail*, the *Financial Times*, and the four great Sundays, gave the most controversial work a chance to escape the claws of the savages.

What a sad, culturally moribund city, but it was sad for them, and so we slinked back to the seedy Gramercy Park Hotel. That was, of course, before it was totally refurbished (and ruined). *The New York Post*, however, was good, as were all the radio stations, but it is the readers of *The New York Times* who go to the theatre. *The New York Times* is the bible and the dumbass had just about killed all our hopes for a dynamic new theatre production on Broadway. Alas, the New Yorkers seemed content with the opinions of one or two major critics, and they were the papers that counted.

The Krays, 1989

In 1989, Peter Medak, a very charming Hungarian film director (who fled to London after the Russian invasion of Hungary in 1956), decided to direct a movie based on Britain's most well-known and attention-seeking gangsters: the Kray twins. Kray is an evocative name and everything about those notorious villains was so bizarre that the subject cried out to be filmed. Medak approached me to play a tough East Ender called George Cornell, who was shot dead in broad daylight in *The Blind Beggar* Pub in Whitechapel Road.

The interesting thing about the Krays is that they were well known to all of us teenagers in North London, particularly Stamford Hill. Known as frightening tearaways, their legend grew year by year.

They had to be the cynosure, almost immortals, who feared no one but made sure that everybody feared them. Curly King, the terrifying *shtarker* I mentioned earlier, was merely a minder for the Krays and I found him not only a frightening beast but somewhat of a mythic being: short, devilish, with piercing dark-brown eyes. So the Krays were the background noise of our young North London lives and nobody was more admired or even adored by the East End fraternity.

Once they were imprisoned for murder, it became a passion of every film director to immortalise them on film. Again, the Brit gangster film is so lacking in danger, power, terror, and sadly shrinks before its American counterpart. In those days, we hadn't even got the right kind of tough actor to play them, so we resorted to casting the Kemp brothers from pop group Spandau Ballet as the two most dangerous criminals. I must say, they really had a brave go, and Peter Medak made a very bold attempt.

On my first shoot day, I had stupidly learnt the wrong scene. I apologised profusely to Medak and said I'd 'wing it', which I did with some nifty improvisation, and it worked. I almost danced my way through it. I've called it overcoat acting, since at that time I had become famous throughout the entire black taxicab industry – for some reason most black cab drivers are Londoners and nothing relating to London passes them by.

''Ere, weren't ya in that Kray film?'

Slightly sullenly, I answered, 'Yes, yes, I do believe I was.'

'Yeah, that was triffic, triffic. Who was that geezer you played? What's 'is name, yeah that geezer… He shot ya.'

'George Cornell.'

'That's it, that's it, triffic.'

A second Kray film was made with the remarkable Tom Hardy playing both the twins. Although Tom Hardy is a dynamic actor, the film was severely criticised.

Richard II, 1993

Several years passed and the next producer I heard from was George Woolfe, who had recently become the Artistic Director of The Public Theater. I was delighted to have heard from The Public again, and I was asked if I would be interested in directing *Richard II*. Although, it was the Shakespeare play least known to me, but I decided to have a go. At least I was being invited to direct Shakespeare in New York again – something that would be virtually impossible in the UK.

As before, the principals had already been cast and I chose the ensemble. This time the lead, Richard, was to be played by Michael Stuhlbarg, a young, classically trained actor, and we got on famously. It's wonderful to get on with your principal actors without raves and rants. I once again chose Patrick Page and also, to my great pleasure, a Black actor called Earle Hyman who played John of Gaunt, the father of Bolingbroke. I couldn't wait to inform this stately, elderly man that I had had the great pleasure of seeing him when I was a student in London and had been invited to a dress rehearsal of that famous American play *A Raisin in the Sun* by Lorraine Hansberry. I will never forget his entrance onto the stage; he seemed to explode onto it! I'd never seen an entrance quite like it. I found Earle to be utterly flexible and charming. Since he was, mainly, in the early part of the play, I suggested he should go after his rehearsal was over, but he asked me if I wouldn't mind if he stayed as he so enjoyed watching how the play was coming together. I was so touched by that, having seen how some of the others couldn't wait to rush off, on the stroke. Sadly, Earle is no longer with us, but I was proud to have directed him.

Richard II received a rave review from the *New York Post*, from the English critic Clive Barnes; it was a review that you could almost sing. I had a good cast and an excellent musician in Larry Spivak. I had only to hint that a certain scene called for a sound without being able to define it, and he would understand immediately and instinctively create the most brilliant score. I became good friends with Michael Stuhlbarg and had not even a whisper of some of the problems I had had on *Coriolanus*. I remain friends with many of the cast even to this day.

Decadence – the Movie, 1994

The time had definitely come to direct my own movie; otherwise, I might wait forever. I managed to find a couple of Aussie businessmen who decided to come on board. One was Lance Reynolds, who was totally encouraging, but there were always problems with the money coming in, although we still managed to get the thing moving by hook or by crook. He decided, with his partner, that the best way to achieve financial security was a convoluted method where you shoot the film in several countries, then claim foreign film funds set up to encourage filmmakers to film in their countries.

We sent the screenplay to a few female stars, as they couldn't raise the cash without a real headline name. Much to the chagrin of Linda Marlowe, who had played in *Decadence* onstage with me from the very first day, Joan Collins came back with a positive response.

I had worked with Joan before on a bizarre TV series called *Sins* and we got on very well. The character of Helen – a fancy, elegant, witty, sexy, arrogant lady – might have been written for her and I could not have been happier; she was, after all, a world-famous star.

Since she was also playing her nemesis, Sybil, a tough working-class bitch, there may have been some problems. However, there was an actress, Denise Evans, who had played it quite brilliantly onstage in a fringe theatre which I saw at the Edinburgh Festival, where she played opposite George Dillon, a young, highly inventive actor. I swiftly made her an offer to coach Joan line-by-line and Joan came up trumps in both roles. Her speaking voice was already very clear and succinct with that idiosyncratic high-pitched upper-class lilt, and her switch to Sybil was effortless.

Joan has many friendships she cultivates, and these include actors like Christopher Biggins and Edward Duke and the late director Michael Winner. Joan was cosseted with her ever-loving chums and we began. I even managed to persuade Stuart Copeland, of Sting's band The Police, to compose the music! Celebrated French cinematographer Denis Lenoir was responsible for lights and camera, and the design was by the lovely artist Yolanda Sonnabend.

For the extravagant dinner scenes at the end of the film, I asked if we could borrow the services of Pina Bausch's dance company to play waiters, virtually dancing and twisting through the restaurant. I believe we got her students, but they were quite brilliant. I was determined to make the film as visually exciting as possible, to somehow negate the cliché that you can't film stage plays. My personal challenge was to convert the production from the stage, where the movement was exquisitely mimed, to the realism of film.

Some scenes, like the fox hunting, had to be done as if we were simply upper-class twits playing on the carpet – and it looked stunning, since we used slow-motion cameras and I played the horse. It was great fun, and Joan sailing through the air as I rear up in slow motion was really quite wonderful to behold. On the first day I was nervous but determined to be as bold as possible.

We started in Luxembourg in a hotel. I had quite a long scene with my chums in the lounge, but now I had spread Joan's lines between all of them. Of course, knowing my lines backwards was a huge help. Joan's buddies weren't quite so comfortable, but we managed to get through it, and they all looked good in the end. Denise was incredibly helpful and Joan absorbed her readings perfectly. At last, the first day was over; we had broken the ice, and the film was beginning to grow. The set looked quite beautiful, and Joan looked ravishing in her white gown. The days were flowing and I was full of energy and excited at this, a completely radical adventure for me. I was aided by a most capable assistant, Dominic Berger, nephew of the famous writer and essayist John Berger.

Decadence is a compilation of scenes of hedonistic upper-class life contrasting with its opposite: a foul, brutish, revengeful lower class. Since our actors are playing both characters, it is meant to suggest that, but for the accident of birth, there is nothing much between us except conditioning. Joan made a brave attempt at the lower-class Sybil. I did suggest to her that, in her scenes with me when I am playing Les, the cockney detective, she should wear no make-up. This may have been the first time she had ever filmed without it. There could be no compromise or halfway house. But the most amazing thing was, just seeing her naked, raw face was compelling. She looked quite wonderful.

There is something special about directing your own movies, since you feel you are tapping every tiny cell of your creative spirit and you are on the very edge of your abilities. And yet I could not utter the word 'action'; it felt too weird and old Hollywoodish. I left that to the first assistant by merely nodding to him. I wanted to be truly creative and do what had never been seen on film before but sadly was let down by our hard-working production team – never enough money, again!

But we did get through it. Yolanda Sonnabend, the designer, said she was saving our budget for the last mad feast at the finale of the film. Of course, onstage I mimed the entire dinner scene, but that would not work well on film, though we found an incredible catering master from Holland, who set up a banquet table which was utterly spectacular. This time I had to do what I had so joyfully mimed onstage, like tossing a mushroom high in the air and catching it in my mouth, which was easy if you were miming it… but for real? I explained the problem to Denis Lenoir, our DP, and he just said, being typically French, 'Try it.' So I did. I sat back on the banquet chair and tossed a real mushroom high in the air and… yes, I caught it – but then the camera was too slow, so we did it six more times until they got it.

Finally, we managed to capture on film, everything that had been mimed. Where it had been a two-hander onstage, on film we had a room fitted out with at least fifty tables, and with our dancing waiters it was quite wonderful, almost like a military drill. The best of all is when Steve, this indulgent, drunken sybarite, stuffed full to bursting, almost explodes in a series of almighty farts. The anal explosion had me whizzing round the room. I imagined myself as a steel ball on a pinball table bouncing from table to table spinning around till my eventual collapse. Joan took it all very well. I think she thought I was a tad experimental, but I know, since I heard her say it, that this was her favourite role in film.

Fair Game, 1995

Some years ago, I performed my one-man show at the theatre in UCLA, LA, comprising *The Tell-Tale Heart* followed by *Actor* and then *Dog*. The *Los Angeles Times* gave it a very positive review and the following day my agent received a call from a prominent Hollywood producer and, lo and behold, I was invited in for a chat with leading producer Joel Silver, who is mainly known for movies with much boom and blast. This was to be no different. It was called *Fair Game*, and it was meant to be a bit of a vehicle for curvaceous model Cindy Crawford and tough guy William Baldwin, one of the talented Baldwin brothers. Of course, I was to be cast as a very cunning and wicked Russian. The director was a neophyte called Andy Sipes, for whom this was to be his first film. The script was not quite so abysmal as many I had read and a decent fee made it all worthwhile.

After I had been costumed up for it, it appeared that my work visa had expired, so I had to leave the country in order to return and be validated for a new visa. I was sent to the Bahamas for a few days. Back on the set, Andy Sipes and I had a man-to-man and decided that, while the dialogue was exceedingly rancid, between us we'd be able to do something with it. This was most encouraging, since it stirred my creative juices. Happily, I let my improvisational skills flow, but after a few days, Mr Silver dropped a hint for me to cut out my verbal curlicues. Such a shame, since this was an opportunity to create something out of this mess. However, I sullenly obeyed and looked forward only to the end.

The next order was to play down my Russian accent. After a while, the continuous assault on my efforts to be just a mite creative did lead to somewhat of a breakdown of communication. This culminated in an unholy row. Onstage, a fire was to break out on the ship which my character is desperately attempting to rob. I requested a stunt double, since the heat was intolerable and special effects guys were putting oil on my face as protection against burning, which got me a bit worried. My request was denied. However, after much drama on the set we got through it and then I packed up swiftly to get out of that madhouse. Then word got back that Mr Silver was not too impressed by the fire and wanted something more dramatic. Next, I was told that a huge tank of water was to descend on me from a great height. Now, with all the electrics and cables on set, I felt sure that this was to be my end! I raised concerns about my safety, which caused Silver to come screaming onto the set. The whole crew gathered round for the bloodletting. Joel Silver then shrieked out, 'CLEAR THE SET! CLEAR THE SET!' This was something that had never happened to me before in my entire life. I felt like I was in a movie!

Once the set was cleared, he miraculously calmed down. He actually said to me, 'Look, I love my actors. Would I do anything to hurt you?' In response to my natural concern about all the exposed wires and plugs mixing with the water, he said, 'Look, I'll sit on the set with you, just off camera.' I couldn't turn that offer down. Action started and this great bath of water came crushing down on me while I was desperately trying to purloin, via the computer, my ill-gotten gains. We finished the scene. I could not have been happier, and I was transported back to London.

After a few days, I received a call from my agent saying that Joel Silver had put on a showing of the film where the public were encouraged to write their enlightened views on a form that was handed out. Some of them suggested that, among other things, Russian villains were now a bit of a cliché, therefore, I was asked to return and dub my whole role into a British accent! I got on the phone to Joel Silver. I told him quite reasonably that my body language in the film didn't agree with a British accent. I was playing Russian and expressing that physically. After much swearing and him threatening to sue me for my home, plus a threat to have me banned from ever working in Hollywood again, I conceded. It was annoying to do the post-synching but in the end, he said, 'If you don't do it, I'll get another actor to voice your role.'

This meant nothing to me, so I said, 'Go ahead, I'll be delighted.'

Months later the film was released and utterly slaughtered by the entire national press. Paradoxically, I scored good reviews for my stripped-down 'bizarre reading', but the lovely Cindy Crawford didn't fare so well. Of course, I never heard from that company again, but I have to say that working for Joel Silver was an unforgettable experience.

CHAPTER 20

Shakespeare's Villains

Shakespeare's Villains evolved through improvisation in a way I had never worked before, and it was somehow drawn out of me like a web from a spider. Over a period of years, it developed into a clear and defined analysis of villainy in Shakespeare. It grew and grew until I had enough material for two or even three shows. I never once sat down and wrote it out, since that was not the way it had started. It began purely as an acting exercise simply because I wanted to get up on a stage and act and, in a way, give a demo on Shakespeare. Ian McKellen had done it, and well, as had John Gielgud, fifty years earlier, which of course I remember seeing. It was called *Ages of Man* and was superb.

Mine was simpler. It was a decision to concentrate solely on the villains, since this would give the piece a theme, and I would try to detect some of the villains' psychic DNA, which I felt I did, over a period of time. There's something about the repetition of dialogue, the playing it over and over again, the painstaking learning that allows you to notice certain kinks, certain patterns in the text that keep repeating and that a reading would never, or almost never, reveal. It's in the heating up of the text through constant retelling that the ideas are squeezed out of it. So I started learning and getting my touring manager, Jan Ryan, to start looking for dates.

I had my show together and Jan found my first date in Utrecht, Holland. So off I went with Nick Mattingly, my lighting man, and my stage manager, whom we called Botch, though his name was Botcher. They were a fine pair of mates, and we settled into our hotel, swam around the lake nearby, and everything had a calm, relaxed feel.

The first performance went well. It was simple and direct with only a brief introduction to each character. I was, at first, anxious as to how I would begin the piece, and I ran through it in front of Botch just to get the feel of the thing and to have a kind of intro for the first character, Iago – much as I might have done in the old days when I would do my endless auditions for rep companies. After a few performances, I started to add just the smallest amount of information about the character as I relaxed into it.

By the end of the week, I sensed something growing slowly, like a tissue of impressions, that was weaving its way between the joins. A play was actually starting to grow. The next gig I had was in Liverpool at the Everyman Theatre, a small semi-experimental theatre which complemented the more commercial Liverpool Playhouse, where I had worked in the mid-60s under the brilliant direction of David Scase. He was the only director I had ever trusted and truly liked, apart from Michael Blakemore, with whom I later worked in Glasgow at the Citz Theatre, as it was commonly known.

By now I was growing a little more confident and allowing all sorts of random thoughts, impressions, and movements to grow into the piece, although I still wrote little of it down but let this thing just drip, ooze, and seep out of me. When there was laughter, I knew I had tapped into something ironic that made an impression or an inroad to the audiences' unconscious minds, and so I would pursue that line. I was now being bolder in my impressions and these inventions would only come during performance, as if in the release of adrenalin, I was also releasing curious insights, observations, and even wild fantasies.

I had worked like this before, where familiarity with the text inspired some kind of counter-text, some imp that wished to reflect on it, satirise it, and sometimes present a cartoon of it. It could even become intoxicating as I followed the path down which the imp wished to take me. Some of it would be based on reading or interpretations by academics, and some history to put it into perspective. At other times, my training in mime would have me invent, visually, an object or being that would define my thought processes even more. It was growing but I didn't want to twist the text around too much, lest it became deformed and over-comic.

In Liverpool, one day the head of the Theatre Royal Haymarket, Arnold Crook, came up to see it; he was scouting for someone to take over Barry Humphries' season at the theatre, which had all but collapsed. It was quite a good night, and he had driven all the way to Liverpool, a good four-hour journey, and then driven back after the show. That's what I call dedication. The upshot of all this was that the next day he sent a message inviting me to come down to London and open at the great, renowned, and majestic Theatre Royal Haymarket, one of the most illustrious theatres in London!

To put it mildly, I was in a state of shock, since this was just a show I had evolved as a workout, mentally and physically, with a bit of a wage at the end of it. I had never ever dreamed of taking it into town. That was beyond my original remit. However, I couldn't turn it down, in spite of my fears of thrusting myself into a West End theatre after such a brief run, since fate has a way of directing you so that once you take the initial steps, the wheels of fate will start to turn almost of their own accord. I now concentrated very hard, since I had just two weeks to go and advertising would have to start almost immediately. I had one more gig in Cyprus, where I would attempt to fill in any more gaps. On most visits abroad, one is feted, wined and dined, celebrated, cosseted, and, most of all, socialised and fraternised. This opportunity to meet your fellow cohorts is, of course, not only valuable but educational and stimulating, and builds bridges. One meets other actors, writers, and directors, and sometimes one forms friendships that can continue for many years.

In Britain, however, the theatres that invite us don't even think it might be of value to inform other acting groups or writers or even any other member of the arts to get a bit of cross-fertilisation going. You do the show and are maybe offered a beer in the bar with the theatre manager and that will be your post-performance treat. In all the years that I have toured Britain I must have played in at least fifty theatres and there was not one that made any effort to take advantage of the fact that we were there for the first time and maybe the last time. We met no one but ourselves, and after our quick complementary drink, we'd slope off sullenly to the nearest curry house and there we would be greeted with far more enthusiasm than the host of the theatre had shown. Sometimes one doesn't even meet the host. You just go in, do your work, and get out. This happened in Belfast, where the festival director had to see another show that night. I heard from him neither by phone nor in person. However, the less said about these sad creatures the better.

But in Cyprus, my small team and I were treated like kings and stuffed ourselves silly and enjoyed each other's company and tales, and it was more than social; we were able to learn about each other's culture. I did the two shows and crammed in as much new material as I could risk, since the next stop would be the great Theatre Royal Haymarket. I was nervous in a way I had seldom been before, but the audience's response in Cyprus had encouraged me somewhat with standing ovations at both shows. The piece was growing by leaps and bounds.

The characters in *Shakespeare's Villains* were initially Iago, Richard III, and Macbeth; later, I added Lady Macbeth and Shylock; later still, I added Antonio, then, perversely, Hamlet, Coriolanus, and Oberon. I had directed *Hamlet* in 1980, and after a successful tour of Europe, it was severely trounced in London, but since I knew the role, I chose to see Hamlet as a late villain who, because of the task that was imposed on him by his ghost father, gradually becomes immune to the pain he causes, and even sounds like quite a cool killer after dispatching Polonius. In fact, swiftly after skewering him, he gets highly involved in a sex lecture to his mother, begging her not to touch his stepfather.

Shortly afterwards, he indulges in gallows humour about the body to the king in front of the slain man's daughter – so, I slipped him into the 'villains' category. Equally with Oberon, since I wished to find unusual villains, and Oberon's drugging of his queen, Titania, so she will, or would, leap on any live thing after the effects of the drug, had him down as a bit of a villain. It was a fairly eclectic choice, and my main purpose was to be both entertaining and informative, if not a tad irreverent!

I was now ready for the Theatre Royal Haymarket and was shitting the proverbial bricks that actors are famous for. A young producer, Julius Green, was called in, and his partner was Donald Sinden's son, Mark Sinden, who helped direct the play and gave me some valuable hints and a novel way to start. I always had a problem with what I was going to say first and sometimes left it to chance, since I firmly believed that something would just pop out. The brain would not let you die onstage.

I got to the theatre, and Nick Mattingly was now both my lighting man and stage manager. I walked in through the stage door and was offered my choice of dressing room! How proud I felt, how bold and daring to be acting Shakespeare in one of the country's great theatres. Arnold Crook also proudly guided me through his palace, offering me the grand double room upstairs, where guests can wait in a kind of anteroom, or the splendid large room just as you enter the stage door and to the right. I chose that.

Oh glory, oh sweated, painful glory, as I sat in front of the mirror where all actors sit and contemplate their mortality. What had brought me to this place where I sat and stared at myself as if I could work out some intractable problem and pray for the best? How did fate, within a few weeks and from a small venue in Utrecht, suddenly bring me here to this testing ground? In fact, fate is your alter ego. It's what you naturally want, what you desire most of all but haven't the courage to admit to, so you make the first small step and that sets up a blueprint in your head for the best possible outcome and fate goes naturally to where it should, ignoring all your little fears and anxieties. It's always that first step. You wanted it all along.

My black silk shirt and black pants were on the hangers, and my black elastic-sided shoes were polished. Nick calmed me down for the few previews and he called 'Beginners!', meaning I had five minutes to get onstage, which was just a moment away. An actor is two people: on the stage and off the stage. The one before the stage is concerned, sometimes even frightened, sometimes wishing for a calamity to take place – anything to prevent what must take place at a certain time when there is nothing you can do to prevent it. But once you are on, a door opens in your brain and a strange beast leaps out, or it may even just sniff around first and then slowly come out, but whatever happens the beast is there and waiting and will only come out when the bait is there and ready – and you are the bait. Outside the stage, your flesh and blood are worthless and tasteless, but once on, it is a different matter.

You never know before you go on, no matter how many times you have done it, that your beast is there and intact; but something in you simply trusts. Sometimes, as it happens, in one of my one-man pieces where I have given myself free rein, in the middle of a tornado of emotions when I am acting the complete and utter clown, I stare at myself with wonder and think, *'Look at me, so wild, so free, so abandoned in the luxurious madness of the moment and doing all this in front of five hundred people'*, when really I am such a bashful soul. I expect that's why we do what we do, to release our inner beast, which we might otherwise pacify and anaesthetise with booze, drugs, and overeating.

So now I was standing in front of the great curtain at the Theatre Royal Haymarket and waiting for it to expose me, to reveal me standing in a spot and ready to begin. The audience were in and seated and the house lights went out and then… swish… the curtain rose, and I was in the 'go' mode and could think of nothing else but my first line. After a few strange starts I settled on Iago's first lines:

'And what's he then that says I play the villain?
When this advice is free, I give and honest,
Probal to thinking and indeed the course
To win the moor again…'

I stopped, full lights came on, and my villainous tone became calm and the audience friendly, and I said, 'What is a villain? A person who is motivated purely by their own lust, desire and greed, irrespective of the pain it may cause you… [small smile] or even, inspired by the pain it may cause you…'

This is how I began, and the audience usually immediately responded, since no one has been entirely untouched by villainy, and so I went on with what was now a reasonably hefty introduction to an actor's analysis of villainy. Laughter came swiftly, since I had long pursued this vein, picked up the scent, and hunted it down to whatever was the source.

Other ideas slithered into my peregrination class, such as exploring Iago's jealousy and not Othello's. My own frustration, of course, fuelled the debate: the bitterness of seeing second-raters promoted to jobs beyond their skills merely because they were part of the Oxbridge mafia. Part of me has some of the poison that infects Iago. Then politics seep in, political correctness, race prejudice – there is much sneaky giggling as I lampoon Othello as a grinning ape. The audience is slightly shocked at this, or maybe they are merely laughing at Iago's slovenly audacity.

After the intro, I step back into Iago's persona and continue the speech. The looser I feel, the more playful, the better it is. Iago is alone with his thoughts, smug, always happiest when he has tripped someone up, when he has spat into the clear waters where some poor victim will drink. Which then leads me into Richard III.

When I begin my spiel, I introduce myself as a kind of lecturer categorising villains to make them more accessible to you, the audience. Iago, in my mind, is a mediocre villain. He's one of those mediocrities that feel threatened by anything or anyone who might cast a slightly larger shadow over his own petty achievements, and this touches me again. Do I detect this in people who for years have always seemed to put up a polite barrier to my pursuance of my work? Don't I see mediocrities everywhere as if it is becoming an obsession? Slaving away at their mediocre talents, trying to squeeze out of the nearly juiceless fruit some little drop of watery substance. Yes, I see these mediocrities everywhere and their behaviour is not too dissimilar to Iago's – evasive, always seeming to be honest, always hugging their fellow mediocrities with enthusiasm while fearful of even touching those who just might see things with a different eye.

However, we all have that gene of inadequacy within us where we might just shrivel a little at being faced with the icy blast of another's fearsome talent. We just have to accept it and, the best-case scenario, even embrace it. 'Aye, there's the rub.' Most of us go on and do the best we can with our limited abilities and just keep the door shut on the poor beggars. But Iago cannot do this. He has to kill, not because Desdemona makes him feel mediocre – he is already that – but because she has the love that no one will ever give him, not in a thousand years. No one will ever love a mediocrity, except possibly their mother.

So, I did the show, one and a half hours in one big gulp, and no one could be happier than I, no one – for I had stood before that audience, a West End audience, and proved my worth and entertained them and even had a few bravos at the end! God, I was happy, for there is no emotion more powerful than that sense of relief when you have managed to get through something that you not only feared facing, which all actors do, but that you knew was a river you must cross or face a spiritual death. But I didn't die; in fact, I thrived. For what doesn't kill you, must, as the old cliché goes, strengthen you.

We had a few previews and, slowly but surely, I was getting into the swing of it, since doing seven shows a week was good for me, and I developed a rhythm, even if I did feel slightly sick each night standing before that blasted curtain. At last, the critics came in, but they were in the mood to chastise me for my impudence in bringing this strange, satiric – albeit Shakespearean – show to the hallowed columns of the Theatre Royal Haymarket. While some were a tad less cruel and did see some virtue in my actorish delivery, which put them in mind of the old actor-managers, others were determined to annihilate me in no uncertain terms.

Well, we actors have to get used to a certain amount of punishment and my skin has been lashed so often it has rather toughened up. Nevertheless, the wounds were deep enough to deter me from stepping onto a West End stage for many years. True, not all the reviews were negative, by no means, and some were even favourable, hinting that even in my worst indulgences, there was still something worth watching, despite all my flaws, banalities, and grossness! And some shared the opinion that it might have been better if I had been born a century earlier, as if I were one of those Victorian narcissists who stood centre stage and delivered. But most agreed that I had a mobile and expressive face and a plastic and versatile body, and I made do with that. One or two were a little too infused with some deeper distaste, verging almost on disgust, which in turn filled me with the greatest abhorrence for their lack of self-control – for surely it is possible to criticise, and boldly too, without being insulting? But who cares, for soon, hopefully, they will be consigned to history and to yellowing scrapbooks.

But I was happy, oh so happy, for did I not have a show in town and a show of my own invention? And nobody can take any credit for it but me and a few allies who supported me and gave advice, like Mark Sinden and, of course and above all, the intrepid fox, Arnold Crook, who drove all the way to Liverpool, on a hunch, and brought me into the West End – and so, bravo to him. But the play grew, night by night, as I grew braver and bolder and found that those little imps of perversity poured out of me shamelessly – and so my invention was growing more daring.

Now, as it happens, just when you are climbing out of adversity, when you are crawling out of the dug-out, trusting that no more missiles are coming your way, some wretch has just got to hurl one more grenade your way and for no good reason. While I was on my pre-West End tour in Cyprus, I had one of those press junkets where you try to inform the public what you are doing and to impress upon them your love for the city or country you are in. I was asked about the British audience and, in a flippant and unthinking manner, since, after all, I was in Cyprus and could vent a little, I said that they could be really simple and unaware and on occasion even a little bit dim. I was thinking of all those playwrights whose works I found totally moribund and conventional in the extreme being patronised by audiences who really didn't know better since this was the kind of material that they had been conditioned to. The kind of plays that were foisted on them with the same names going round and round. So I, in my jealous, Iago-like manner, decided to vent my bile and happily spewed out my opinions of this little island.

Lo and behold, one of those snarling journalists, whose brief it is to crawl up behind you and give you a savage bite, was sent my little squib from the *Cyprus Times* and decided to give it prominence in the centre pages of *The Standard*, where I was portrayed contemptuously as some kind of maverick who doesn't even like the audience who pay to come and see me! Which wasn't the point I was making at all, not even in the slightest. But who cares about that? No one. With a show struggling to find its audience and just getting over some savage mauling, and word-of-mouth bringing in the patrons, I get struck down by this! How horrible. The paradox was that this man had been an ally of mine, a supporter and champion of my work. What on earth could have turned him into such a snarling pitbull, lusting to take a bite out of my throat? No one will ever know. Something I did or said must have irked him mightily. Critics can at times share some of the traits of villains in that they will poison us worthy citizens merely doing their time-honoured duty, but really, they are using their power to fulfil their own poisonous agendas.

The season continued with thin to fair audiences, and one or two good ones, and the work was growing in confidence and assurance. Saturday matinees were ideal times for 'rehearsing' and allowing some kind of free flow. I felt that a daytime audience was more relaxed and I could just let myself free associate, and some of the most curious ideas came out of this. Sometimes, I felt so liberated I could just let anything out of the bag, as long as it still related to the character I was playing. Stories that I had absorbed years ago came to the forefront of my mind and became good fertiliser for my imagination, which was in full swing.

Richard III was now becoming more and more a fertile ground for some crazy meanderings. I attributed his frustration to the fact that the poor, unloved man – having no one to love or be loved by – since love had forsworn him in his mother's womb – had no war either in which to purge his frustration. Certain structures in society allow a villain to thrive – the military is one, politics is another, and the media is the third, where psychopaths, lunatics, and sadomasochists can pretend to be merely carrying out their duty while catering amply to their own dark agendas. Sometimes I went a bit further.

One night, Arnold Crook knocked on my door before the show just to ask how I was. A small alarm bell rang…

'Oh, I'm fine,' I responded, 'why, who's in?' I felt that he was just checking because there was some eminence in the house.

'Oh, nobody, just looking in to see how you are.'

I went on that night but he must have laid something in my subconscious. I was on high alert and was determined to do my best and had a smidgeon more confidence, and yet, at the same time, I was wary of a little warning note sounding in my head reminding me to keep myself steady and not go over the top as sometimes I was wont to do.

After the show, which had indeed gone well, there was a knock on my dressing room door and Arnold came in, and, while not beaming, he seemed quite satisfied with life.

'There's someone who wishes to see you.'

'Who?'

'The Prime Minister.'

Oh, how happy I was, how excited as I made my way into the little anteroom which leads off from one of the boxes. And there he was! In fact, he was lined up with Cherie, his wife, in the centre and another chap on her right. Arnold introduced me. Not only was I happy, but I was supremely confident of myself. Adrenaline was swarming through me, and I had just left the stage, the ring, the arena where I had faced hundreds of people, including Tony Blair and his wife. And so I burst in almost shouting, 'Tony… How wonderful to see you.'

Tony congratulated me and took my hand firmly, as did his wife and the third person, who may have been some kind of minder. He was fulsome and warm-hearted, as was Cherie, and I was glad I hadn't made too much of the comments of Richard III about how villains find their opportunities in politics – as was Arnold Crook! I'd just hinted about it, and that was enough. Tony joked about how much he had 'learnt' from the tales of villainy.

Of course, I was absolutely thrilled. I had performed to the prime minister of Great Britain, and he had chosen to see me out of all the plays on in London. He had singled me out, or someone had highly recommended me.

Nothing could be better than this; nothing could have confirmed my status as an actor more than this. And I had to share with no one else, not a writer, not a director, no other actors but me. I was the writer and – and – the Bard! I was walking on the proverbial air, and I could hardly pay too much attention to one of the Shaffer playwriting twins, who was ensconced in my room, and had also come to see me that night and to offer me a play to consider directing that he had written. I went home elated.

Soon afterwards I wrote to Tony Blair and received this reply, which I still treasure:

Dear Steven,

Thank you for your letter of 1 October. It was kind of you to write following our visit to the Theatre Royal in July to see Shakespeare's Villains. *Cherie and I enjoyed the performance enormously, particularly as it is difficult to find the time to fit outings of this nature into our diaries.*

Thank you, too, for your words of support. They are much appreciated. I will never forget your performance – a tour de force. Thank you for letting us see it!

Yours ever
Tony

***

Villains gave me the most ecstatic freedom – freedom to be independent, freedom to be totally creative, freedom from worrying about where the next idiotic job was coming from. Even when a job did come in and gave me the illusion that I was working, it did not usually fill me with pride. But now I had a specialist touring agent, and the dates were gradually flying in. Thanks to people's universal and everlasting interest in Shakespeare, it became a magic carpet that was to take me around the world.

I did a few gigs throughout the UK, then flew to the American East Coast universities, then to LA, Rio, São Paulo, Buenos Aires, Jerusalem, Rome, Florence, Liverpool – to the very same theatre where I had played *The Long and the Short and the Tall* in 1966 – the Liverpool Playhouse – and to the Gaiety Theatre in Dublin. Then we toured the entire continent of India, where we filled each date for nearly a month – fantastic as well as fascinating – and then Milan, Colorado, Cork (Ireland), Cyprus, Antwerp, Belfast, Madrid, the Opera House in Buxton, and then Liverpool once more. It felt like I was creating a fine web around the entire globe – all these great gigs simply earned by the world's fascination with the life and words of Shakespeare. At the end of this, I was booked for an eight-week tour of Australia which was quite astonishing, especially revisiting all the theatres where twenty-three years earlier we had played *East*.

***

The show was approaching the final dates of the tour when, out of the blue, I got a call from an unknown woman by the name of Melia saying she believed I was her father! During my Australian tour of *East*, I'd had a passionate night with an Australian nurse and Melia was the result of that wonderful night!

She said she didn't want anything but that she'd love the chance to meet me. She lived in Perth, about five hours away from Sydney by plane. Not exactly a quick flight, but still she insisted that she would like to visit me on tour. And naturally, being me, I dithered. I stuttered and mumbled something along the lines of 'Oh, I don't know, I'm not sure…' then because the tour was coming to an end '… maybe we could do it another time when I'm back?' It was such short notice, after all. We could plan it out better at a later date. With a 'heavy heart', I put the phone down.

But then I thought, *'Get some bloody guts, for Pete's sake! Call her back! Tell her to come!'*

So I picked up the phone and called her back. I told her to get a red-eye that night and I'd put her up in a hotel so I could see her the following morning. She said that would be perfect and off she went to the airport that very evening. The following morning came, and I went to the hotel room and knocked on the door. She answered it immediately. She was incredibly beautiful; it was so lovely to be able to speak to her. Thank God I called her back!

She told me about her life as a training instructor and I told her that it was my last performance of my one-man show in Sydney and asked her if she would like a ticket. She graciously accepted then after the performance, she visited my dressing room backstage. I introduced her as my daughter to the two producers and the rest of the stage management crew who were with me – they all just shrugged it off. Couldn't care less. Australians in the theatre business are used to anything.

Even so, I've kept in touch with Melia ever since and am so grateful that she got in touch.

***

I finished off the Australian tour in Tasmania. I usually travelled with just one efficient assistant who would plot the lights in each theatre and be the company manager/part-time companion; they would also organise our social hours by renting a car for our days off. In some cases, they booked flights, such as when we had three days off between gigs at the beautiful Raffles Hotel in Singapore and flew to Langkawi for some swimming and exploring. After Langkawi, and Singapore, I had a booking in South Africa, and after the show on Saturday night, we flew to Johannesburg. The contrast could not possibly have been greater. We performed at the celebrated Market Theatre and were most successful.

In fact, there were really few places where we were not performing, since the combination of Shakespeare and villains was an appealing mix. Before I forget, we also went to New Zealand, which was quite lovely, and what was most remarkable was meeting up with all the acquaintances from my distant past who had gladly fled London, or even Australia. I had the great privilege of playing *Shakespeare's Villains* on and off for twenty years, from 1997 to 2017. It was, however, after I completed my Aussie tour that my touring agent went her own way.

One of my last and most successful gigs was in New York at Joe's Pub, an addition to the performance spaces at the late Joe Papp's Festival Theatre, which was mainly to house one-man shows of a radical nature. I had just finished a few gigs on the East Coast and had decided to head downtown to Lafayette Street to visit the theatre. I spoke to the lovely old casting lady, Rosemarie Tichler, and while she said they had no spaces for a while, since they were mainly closed for the fierce winter weeks, she did mention that they had opened this small funky space which they called Joe's Pub and invited me to cast an eye on it. I did and was mightily unimpressed.

It had more of a sleazy nightclub feel – a small stage at the back of the room surrounded by a bunch of tables which still bore the entrails of the night before. After my tremendous gig at one of the West End's most illustrious theatres, the Theatre Royal Haymarket no less, this was a sadly abrupt comedown, but I strolled onto the pocket-handkerchief-sized stage, to see if it might be possible, then I abruptly left. They offered a three-week gig around Christmas. I thought about it and decided, '*Well, I'm sure it can't do me any harm.*'

After a pleasant rest in London, I flew to New York. The cab took me downtown and this time they had booked a small apartment where their touring actors sometimes stayed. However, I had no desire to stay in an old flat where they put up the guests, so I asked the cab to take me to where they usually put me up – the Gramercy Park Hotel – but an unhelpful slob on the desk claimed there were no rooms left for that night, so I trundled back outside to the waiting yellow cab and decided *faute de mieux* to return to that crappy flat.

I arrived at the building and asked the taxi to wait just in case they changed their minds after my earlier escape. I went in and one of your typical Yankee sleazebags wishing to exercise what limited power the slug had over the rest of the population kept me forever, asking 'What room have they booked for you?', 'What time were you meant to be coming in?', etc. In the end, I had had enough and was prepared to stay anywhere.

I walked out to find that the low-life taxi driver had driven off with my bags, script, clothes, medicine, notebooks – gone, all gone! Now I had no choice and told the rancid low-life on the desk that since he had deliberately taken so long, I had lost everything: the cab had just driven off, since his festering, carbon-stained brain had obviously forgotten my bags in the boot. I half-slept through the night and couldn't wait for the next day to come and wipe away all vestiges of the day just passed.

First thing in the morning, I took a cab back to the Gramercy Park Hotel, and now, of course, they found a room for me. I rang the Festival Theatre and told them the horrors I had been put through by their own rotten staff. I was glad to hear that the staff at the theatre were as disgusted as I was and that they promised to scour every corner of the yellow cabs' lost property offices. Meanwhile, I trampled through SoHo searching out the best men's boutiques and replaced my entire costume – my black shaped barathea pants and elegant loose black shirt and sharp black leather shoes.

I was back by 3 p.m. I was shown my dressing room among much solicitation and concern, then I changed into my new costume and walked onstage to block the lights and run all the cues. Suddenly, just by being on the stage, I did start to feel a little better. Later that night, I did a very rough run while constantly calling the theatre office for news. Then I gladly returned to my favourite hotel, the Gramercy Park, and ordered a delicious bowl of pasta and a glass of Beaujolais for my room.

The following day, I went in about 2 p.m. and at 3 p.m. did a final run-through. Afterwards, I walked down St Mark's Place and treated myself to a plate of sushi and bought a CD of beautiful Tibetan music. Then I walked back to the theatre and just sat waiting and playing my divine CD. I was the only performer in the entire building. I dressed, waited for the half-hour call, and then 'Beginners, Act One please.' I walked slowly onstage and began with Iago's first line. I felt strangely calm and with every minute was growing more confident. The audience were as quiet as mice. It felt more than OK, and at the end, the small house gave it an enthusiastic response, even a few cheers. Then I changed and wandered over to the small bar at the back of the room. I was determined to have a cocktail, and as I ordered, the barman said, 'On us, Mr Berkoff.' Oh, this was the better side of America! I never had that in any bar in any theatre I worked in in Britain. How charming! The margarita tasted quite heavenly. For the first time in days, I was happy. I walked back to the Gramercy Hotel, just over twenty minutes, and slept like the dead.

The next morning, I slipped out early before breakfast and purchased the couple of newspapers that were available – the show was given a rave review. The Public Theater called to present me with the good news that my baggage had been found! Realising that he still had my baggage, the taxi driver had just dropped it off at a yellow cab lost luggage on the outskirts of the city. The careful and dedicated hunt by the ladies at The Public Theater turned it up. Life was beginning to normalise. The show was successful, the hotel room was fine, and my precious luggage had been returned to me! *Alles ist in Ordnung.*

Since the show had gone so well in Joe's Pub, George Woolfe, the arts director of the theatre, suggested I come back in January for a six-week season in their main theatre, which is called The Anspacher Theatre. This was splendid news and the theatre was familiar to me, since I had staged *Coriolanus* there ten years earlier. They hadn't booked anyone in for the worst winter months and so I was rather proud to feel that I was keeping that theatre open. This time I'd be playing in one of their main theatres and we played to almost full houses each night of the six weeks.

It was a wonderful six weeks and gradually the acting fraternity were coaxed out of their warm winter snuggeries and traipsed over to The Public to view this relatively little-known Limey from London blowing up a bit of a storm with the Bard at The Public Theater. First, actor F. Murray Abraham stopped by and never have I met a more charming character and friendly man. Then Kevin Kline came and even executed a kind of mock genuflection by kneeling, which was probably a hyperbolic gesture to show appreciation of the show but at the same time gently mocking it.

In my show, I did for whatever reason throw in a few lines about famous actors doing Shakespeare and, of course, included Al Pacino, since he had recently directed a film about his performance of Richard III (a 1996 documentary titled *Looking for Richard*). As my show just had to include a heavy dose of satire, I rather let my creative imagination run away with me, which included my mimicking Pacino consulting a 'Shakespearean expert on verse'. It was funny and not at all mean. However, just before the show, the director George Wolf came by to alert me that Pacino was in that evening. Okay, I thought, I couldn't cut it since I was sure that Pacino might even see the humour of it. But I did rather lay it on with a trowel when 'praising' him in the intro.

After the show, I had a message to join him and his lady at a nearby eatery. I assumed then he must have liked the mention and not been at all offended. When I entered the café, I could see that he had rather a long face. He said that he was shocked, since, although his name had often been used before in movies, he had never heard it used on stage before a live audience. 'But Al,' I said, 'I wrote it with much affection. I also wrote about Olivier, Gielgud, McKellen, etc., and if there was a touch of irony, it was equally shared by all the others I mentioned. It was meant to compliment you!' His girlfriend chipped in that was exactly how she saw it and there was absolutely nothing remotely offensive in it. But I think Al felt somewhat self-conscious, as it was being said while he was in the audience. It was a couple of years before he spoke to me again!

Much later, I was doing my play *Massage* at the Odyssey Theatre in L.A. when he dropped in to see me and all sourness had been forgotten. We went to dinner round the corner in Abbot Kinney Boulevard. He had wanted me to direct him in *Salomé* but sadly it had not proved possible. I said it was imperative to have a short workshop first, but the director of the theatre said: 'You can just use my office for a read-through.' Then I realised that I couldn't work in this sloppy way. Anyway, when I performed it with my own company in New York, we were triumphant.

The reviews for *Shakespeare's Villains* were mainly very positive and my life at the Gramercy Hotel was very pleasant. I certainly got used to the environment on 23rd Street and had my morning cafés for breakfast well marked out. On the weekends, I had the great pleasure of going to Grand Central Station and taking the train to visit my ex-wife, Shelley Lee, in Croton, in Upper New York, just sixty miles from Manhattan. She lived the bucolic life surrounded by forest and stray deer. My time passed pleasantly and, on my night off, sometimes we would see some live theatre. We even went to a revival of *The Rocky Horror Show*, which was *so* horrific in a smarmy way that I was only too glad to escape.

CHAPTER 21

Into the 21st Century

One day around the year 2000, I had one of those rare but special calls from Stanley Kubrick; he had an idea he wanted to discuss with me… I was all ears. First of all, he asked me if I knew the eighteenth-century operetta *The Beggar's Opera*, and as it so happened I did. As I responded, another part of my mind was trying to determine his motivation in calling me… Yes, there's Captain Macheath, the inspiration for Bertolt Brecht's *The Threepenny Opera*. I listened further and Stanley went on, 'Do you know that at Pinewood Studios there is a beautiful small theatre where the restaurant used to be, which is seldom if ever used and would be perfect for the staging of it.'

I was still attempting to compute some sense from all this – why Pinewood and theatre? – when it came blasting into my head. Stanley, not actually being familiar with the theatre, wanted to try out *The Beggar's Opera*, to get the feel of it, before attempting to film it! How clever, but also how wise, as then he would get the chance to take the musical drama to pieces before getting involved in the massive costs of making an epic movie. I thought, '*Why is he confessing all this to me? Could he… could he possibly be thinking of me for Macheath?*'

Then he went on to ask me if I would possibly be willing to come down to Pinewood and audition for the role of Macheath!

'Of course I would, Stanley,' I replied.

'How's your singing voice?' he asked.

'Well, I will have a go,' I lamely responded, but I did love the music and the lyrics. Fortunately, I had seen a pretty good version at the previous year's Edinburgh Festival.

'OK, Steve,' he replied, 'we'll call you within the next few weeks to come down to Pinewood and maybe do an audition.'

'Absolutely, Stanley. Look forward to hearing from you.' I hung up. What an extraordinary call! I was overcome and made up my mind to work on my voice, but then again, I thought, it was just possible that he merely wished to work on it and I would be useful so that he could familiarise himself with the classical work.

About two weeks later – it was a Sunday evening as I remember, and I was just about to sit down to a lovely pasta dish prepared by Clara – the phone rang… I could have let it go to voicemail, but something just niggled me to answer it, being that it was a Sunday night and maybe it was something I should deal with. 'Hello?'

'Hello,' the voice responded, 'is that Steven Berkoff?'

'It is,' I said, wondering who on earth this person was calling me on a Sunday night with a very strong Australian accent, so thick you could cut it with a knife.

She went on to say that her boss, Stanley Kubrick, had given her my number and wanted her to arrange for me to come to Pinewood Studios to audition for *The Beggar's Opera.*

I felt I had been hit by a truck. Audition, for her, since she was directing the theatre show. I had, of course, conjugated a completely different interpretation and something didn't connect. Perhaps it was her accent – a female Aussie accent. Since I had recently spent a happy six months there, I normally had no problem with it, but that was in the past and this was now, and I had not only expected to hear the warm, friendly tones of Kubrick's Bronx dialect, I had also assumed that he would be directing. Not once had he told me that I was going to be directed by someone else. Obviously, the Aussie woman was putting it together for him to examine. This was, in my mind, a completely radical reinterpretation of how I had imagined it.

'So,' she said, 'when is it convenient for you to come down?'

'Sorry,' I replied, 'I can't do it.' A few more sentences and, just like that, my singing career was over.

I went back to supper. I thought much about it, especially after I received a brief handwritten note from Kubrick which started, 'Dear Steve, you are a weird dude,' and went on to berate me for letting him down. I immediately responded that he should be a little more understanding and that there was nothing I would not do for him, but he had never once mentioned that someone else was doing the production.

However, many years later he must have forgiven me, since I received a call from his hard-working assistant Leon Vitali (now sadly passed on) to say that Stanley was interested in me for a role in his latest bizarre movie *Eyes Wide Shut* – but in the end, that went to someone else. Shortly after, I learned that Kubrick's daughter was in fact an opera singer! Was this perhaps a workout for his talented but underemployed daughter? I was guilty of thinking too much! That was the last I heard of Stanley Kubrick before he passed on.

Messiah, Old Vic, 2003

In 2003, I directed a play of mine that I had been desperate to do for years. I called it *Messiah* since it was a dissertation on the crucifixion written several years earlier and partly based on a brilliant book called *The Trial and Death of Jesus* by Israeli Supreme Court Judge Haim Cohn. It is a most profound book on the subject which goes into the most incredible detail of the events leading up to the crucifixion. In the book Cohn makes the point that the Jews have never fully defended themselves against the charge of deicide and so he meticulously explores the historical records piece-by-piece. I thought this would be an incredible subject for a play, and I took many months to write it. At last, I decided it was time to direct it at the Edinburgh Festival.

I put together a company headed by a splendid Jesus, Rory Edwards. The role of Satan was played by Scottish actor Tam Dean Burn, who was quite brilliant. By now, I had found a producer, Christopher Malcolm, and at last I felt protected, since I now had an ally and friend.

The show won the Fringe Critics Award of the Week, but alas, on the last day, the wonderful Rory Edwards had a bit of a burn-out and had to drop out. Our ever-ready company manager, Mat Cullam, called me and, of course, I would never in the world let a show die on account of one actor's indisposition. I immediately booked a plane to Edinburgh first thing the following morning, and by 1 p.m. I was on the stage! It was a reading, but I gave it my all, as I did in the following and final performances. The cast were relieved to have me onstage with them, since they had regrettably been receiving some rather eccentric cues. So all was well.

As it happens, the management from The Old Vic had been to see the show and were impressed enough to invite us in for an eight-week season at the end of the year, which pleased us no end. Vidal Sassoon, the 'geometric' hairdresser, confessed to me that he would love nothing better than to see how directors and actors put a play together and if he could just be an assistant or gopher, he would invest £50,000. It was a sheer pleasure having Vidal come in and watch; he even moved to Docklands in London to be near rehearsals. Eventually, we opened and it went really well; this time, we found the best possible actor for Jesus – Greg Hicks.

The start of *Messiah* is visually striking, as Greg Hicks as Jesus spends an inordinate length of time on a symbolic nail-cross, stretching his muscles to the limit. While he does so, he is worshipped by his grieving mother, played by Helen Schlesinger. The life of Christ is largely recalled in retrospect, involving the condemnatory Pontius Pilate – Michael Jenn, the mercenary but loving Judas – Brendan Hughes and the headless John the Baptist – Jonny Coyne.

Philip Fisher's review in the *Glasgow Herald* understood well what we were trying to do:

> 'The production combines Berkoff's always excellent physical comedy, which shows remarkable imagination … with a relatively serious reinterpretation of biblical history. Even then, the always skilled Hicks is not allowed to remain serious for too long. In one of the funniest scenes in the play, he delivers extracts from the Sermon on the Mount, straight-faced, and instantly turns off the power, and becomes an actor during rehearsals.'

Now, just as we commenced our run at The Old Vic, the theatre announced that Kevin Spacey had been employed as the new artistic director! I would have thought that, as the new AD of The Old Vic, he might have graced us with a visit during our run, but we never saw or heard from him. Not a word, from the first to the last day, eight weeks later.

Shortly after this, I was attending a memorial for John Hurt, who had recently passed away. A member of the tabloid press begged for a word, a request to which I acquiesced by answering a few questions. Big mistake. For some reason, the reporter asked me if I'd like to run my own theatre company, continuing that since I had been at The Old Vic, would I be happy to work there as a director? To which I replied that 'the work being shown there now, under Spacey, might be a tad unadventurous, although I do respect Spacey very much as an actor.'

I had completely forgotten about the interview when I received a rather blistering screed from Mr Spacey himself. This was the very first time he had ever contacted me, expressing great disappointment in me, but for whatever reason another member of the press had picked up the story, and I received quite a nasty note from Mr Spacey. I wrote back immediately, offering to meet up for a friendly chat and even saying I would be most willing to offer advice or help. I did feel that since he had never felt inclined to see me during my tenure at The Old Vic, I may have felt less protective of him…

On the Waterfront, 2009

It was when I was casting my production of *The Trial* at the National Theatre that I was asked to use artistic director Richard Eyre's office. I was quite happy to do so, since it also had a beautiful view of the River Thames. During the morning's work, I could not help but notice, in his in-tray, a stage script based on the classic and iconic movie *On the Waterfront*. Now, bearing such a famous title, this script quite intrigued me and my very first thought was that this was a brave and bold enterprise for the National Theatre to attempt.

At the end of my casting session, I passed Richard Eyre in the corridor and felt I had to congratulate him, since I thought this was a very ambitious idea. However, he was quick to dislodge any such thoughts from my mind: 'No, this play is not for us,' he speedily responded, 'we've done a few too many movies to stage. But,' he went on, 'if you are interested, please take the script and read it.'

I read it and could see that the adaptation had many flaws, but I felt it was too dramatic a stage play to let pass (although I did let much time pass before I decided to do it, due to the poor adaptation).

One day, I decided to do a workshop on it and called together a group of my favourite actors. My God! As the actors lived those words, it came to life with a vigour that was outstanding. I found my perfect Terry Malloy (Brando's role in the film) in Simon Merrells, and a more than perfect priest in Vincenzo Nicoli while I took on the role of Johnny Friendly. The Boss Man was the late Alex Giannini, and we found a perfect lovely old guy, Sean Buckley, for Pop Doyle. Bryony Afferson played Terry's girlfriend, Edie Doyle, and Robin Kingsley was Charley the Gent. This team was outstanding.

We did a try-out at the beautiful old Hackney Empire, eventually touring to the Nottingham Playhouse, and then on to the Edinburgh Festival. And yet still our producers at the time were a little hesitant about risking bringing it into the West End so I had a word with the charismatic artistic director of the Theatre Royal Haymarket, Arnold Crook, who advised me on what to do next, and so eventually I joined forces with West End theatre producer Bill Kenwright.

Finally, we opened at the Theatre Royal Haymarket in 2009 for a four-month run and earned some of the best reviews ever. Author Budd Schulberg was flown over from New York for the first night and was of course invited onstage, to massive cheers from the audience. He came up onstage and said that this 'staged version' was by far the best he had ever seen. We were a happy team, and I became a friend of the great Budd Schulberg before he died. Shame that we were unable to get a New York gig; I felt it would have fascinated American audiences to see Limeys doing spot-on impersonations of New York dockers.

The Tourist, 2010

One day my agent had a call from American director Florian Henckel von Donnersmarck, who won the Academy Award for Best Foreign Language Film for his brilliant study of ghastly East Berlin politics in *The Lives of Others*. Now, for some reason, he was directing a potboiler, called *The Tourist*, with Johnny Depp and Angelina Jolie. I imagine that his well-recognised skill was thought to be ideal in turning something slightly less worthy into gold. I was never so proud to be chosen for a role as for the quasi-Russian villain Reginald Shaw. As it came straight after a tour of my stage production of *On the Waterfront* in Hong Kong, I had to dash offstage just before the curtain call, time being of the essence, to catch the red-eye to Venice. All very exciting.

Having arrived early in the morning, I was whisked to the hotel on the canal, then had a quick breakfast. So far so good. Florian himself then came to meet me – he was an extraordinary sight, at least six foot nine and utterly charming. He proudly told me that he was the tallest film director in Hollywood, which I did not doubt for one second. Florian had the script in his hand, and we went to the lobby to discuss it. The writing, as far as I could see, was dull and uninventive, so he invited me to rewrite all the scenes that involved me – I was glad to do so, and Florian was more than happy with the result. Then I went off to bed having not slept for 24 hours. The next day I met fellow actor Johnny Depp on the set. Being a bit of a fan of movie stars, I couldn't help but gabble my admiration. 'Oh, Mr Depp, I'm honoured to meet you,' I gushed, to which he charmingly replied, 'Oh, but I am honoured to meet you, Mr Berkoff.'

The film had a multinational cast, and Florian was able to give directions in every European language, including Russian. After my character arrives in Venice, we were straight into my first large scene with both Johnny Depp and Angelina Jolie. It started with myself and Ms Jolie, as I rather rudely interrogate her, yet it wasn't quite catching alight. So I suggested to Florian a few extra sentences which might warm the scene up a bit. He agreed and it worked very well. Then Johnny Depp came in. I, as Reginald Shaw, question him, and he answers in a most curious way; in the end, the entire scene seemed to go rather well.

However, when you are a major star in Hollywood like Ms Jolie, you are treated not only with kid gloves, but as if you are made of the most precious material, and after each take, figures dash out of the darkness to make their benedictions to you – make-up, wardrobe, 'Here's your cappuccino, darling,' etc. I realised that these were the benefits of such stardom. As an also-ran, you are certainly so much less important, and you are treated (or indeed neglected) accordingly. Ms Jolie herself was quite cool with me too – to the extent that she ignored me most of the time. Being a bit of a sensitive flower I took this quite personally. When I mentioned this to the director, he replied that it was 'quite natural as she is a method actress.'

Ah, yes. I thought. American! I had to realise that I was the enemy of Ms Jolie in the film, and if you are a method actress, you must not let go of this; you cannot be in one moment fearful and somewhat loathing and then chatter merrily after the scene is over, and I fully appreciated that. On the other hand, I found the scenes I did with Johnny Depp much easier to play, as he was very friendly and there was a certain mischievousness about him, and he had a much more laid-back and easy-going personality.

Filming went as well as possible, but I wouldn't exactly say that it was the thrill of my life – however I adored Venice.

Doctor Who, 2012

In 2012, I was offered this role of 'Shakri' in the BBC series *Doctor Who* which I found quite intriguing. The character was bizarre, highly theatrical, and in a strange way quite compelling. We were shooting in Cardiff, Wales, and I was only scheduled for one week with the incumbent 'Doctor Who' played by Matt Smith.

We had a good shoot, but my concern was that I would finish in time to enjoy my supper at the hotel, since the shooting days were quite long and the pay quite short. The director, acquiescing to my 'concern', promised that if I did the whole scene in one take, he would release me in time. As agreed, I did the whole scene flawlessly, but afterwards the director wasn't quite true to his word and wanted to keep me to do more takes. This created a touch of friction on the set until the producer stepped in and let me go – I was back at the hotel in time for supper. End of story.

The Birthday Party, 2014

One day, I had a call from the director William Friedkin (*The French Connection*; *The Exorcist*). He wanted to meet me to discuss playing Goldberg in Pinter's *The Birthday Party.* I happened to be in LA at the time, so it was quite convenient. Friedkin loved to think he was a dab hand in live theatre, even though he had already directed *The Birthday Party* for TV, with Harold Pinter playing Goldberg. I watched it and Pinter was very good. The play was somewhat dated and repetitious, but it still had a bizarre flair. But what a challenge, and to be reunited with Tim Roth, who was playing the mentally challenged son for whom his mother is creating a birthday party. In LA, William Friedkin took me out for lunch, and we had a very positive and engaging meeting. I decided to learn as much of the entire role as possible before starting work.

We were to open at the Geffen Playhouse, quite a prestigious theatre in Westwood, West LA. Frances Barber was playing the mother. Friedkin and I kicked off pretty well and he liked how I was progressing. I turned up on the first day and there was Tim Roth, whom I had directed in my adaptation of Kafka's *Metamorphosis* at The Mermaid Theatre in London twenty years earlier. He had certainly made it in Hollywood, and now here he was turning up with the mandatory Rolex. We all sat round the table and read right through the play. I felt comfortable in the role of Goldberg but, like all new productions, it would need some getting used to. A jovial Irishman played McCann, and we all gelled easily.

I had my usual motel flat in Venice Beach and the company had rented a black Thunderbird for me. I was called for my first blocking rehearsal, which we did swiftly, and I felt myself falling into character. I was just enjoying rehearsal and getting Goldberg halfway there; however, I could not help but notice, since I'd come from the same area as Pinter – Hackney, East London – that some of the East End patter was a tad dated and even self-conscious. After a few days, I was beginning to tire of Friedkin's way of directing. In fact, he didn't seem to have a 'way'. Much was just 'do it again… and do it again…' One morning, he was in his 'do it again' mood and this seemed endless, and I felt I had to stop it! So I just said, after I stopped rehearsal, that it might be better if he recast me. He took it remarkably well and merely said, 'Come into my office,' and we hammered it out.

Thankfully the meeting was without any rancour. I said to him, 'Mr Friedkin, when you are directing, get your stage manager to follow on the book' – Friedkin would hardly ever watch us perform since his attention was always fastened onto the script. He agreed and for the first time we were communicating and went back to work.

Now, our costume designer decided to get a suit made for me. I thought that as there were only a few thousand suits on sale on

Melrose Avenue just up the road, we could use one of those, but no – she decided that a suit had to be made, and so we drove for hours to the Valley to connect with a tailor whom she had obviously used in the past. It was a total waste of time. The next day during rehearsal, the costume designer decided to come into the rehearsal room to check out the actors. But after a drive of at least three hours, for some reason I couldn't bear to have her in the room, just so she could show she was doing something. I asked her very politely to leave while we rehearsed. Very wrong. Should have just ignored her and continued.

The next day when I came in, the first thing I did was to apologise to Friedkin, but that only seemed to encourage him to start a mini screaming fit. I repeated my apology, saying I was tired and felt exposed and didn't want somebody to come into rehearsals halfway through a scene, to which he replied very aggressively, 'And you are gonna get a lot more tired.' But this time, I just ignored him and got on with rehearsals, which were going quite well.

At this point in the play, McCann had a little trouble with an Irish word in the script, and I suddenly felt like being helpful and made a very mild suggestion to the actor, after having a brief discussion with Friedkin, as I was making the mildest of comments.

Friedkin suddenly started screaming like a banshee, 'DON'T GIVE THE ACTORS NOTES!' and then, screaming louder, 'YOU DON'T GIVE THE FUCKING ACTORS NOTES!'

Totally stunned by his insane outburst, I calmly explained my comments on the single word the actor was having a problem pronouncing. He then started screaming again.

He turned to the cast in the room and said, 'DOES ANYBODY KNOW WHAT THE FUCK HE'S TALKING ABOUT?'

Suddenly, I'd lost all feeling and purpose about what on earth I was doing in that room. I was being insulted and screamed at by an insane barbarian, and this wasn't where I belonged. For over thirty years, I had chosen to do my own work and been highly successful. Now, in joining the establishment, I realised what I'd missed all these years – being free of despotic directors and their utterly inflexible and dictatorial ways. I prepared to leave the room but not before saying, 'You've just lost the best Goldberg you'll ever have.'

He replied, 'Good', then, turning to his cast, he added, 'He's leaving of his own accord – you see? I haven't fired him.' I guess in the back of his reptilian brain he had to make that point so that I couldn't claim any compensation.

I walked out and the air had never smelled so fresh. Then I went to the parking area and happily drove home.

Over the next few days, he tried to recast me but couldn't, although he did try another actor, who also walked out, then another, but eventually the show was withdrawn! Friedkin seemed obsessed with *The Birthday Party*, having already filmed it with Robert Shaw as Goldberg. Maybe now he had shot his bolt. Apparently, he gave the theatre a cheque for a million dollars in compensation.

The Vikings, 2019–2020

Having never previously performed in a long running TV series, I was quite intrigued when my agent suggested me for the role of King Olaf in *The Vikings.* He was described as a shrewd and ambitious former King of Norway, which I felt was right up my street.

Best of all, it was being shot in a most picturesque area of Ireland just west of Dublin – you could not wish for a more exotic and beautiful location. And I had the best of both worlds, for I also loved Dublin and was spoiled in the best hotels of that extraordinary city. Naturally, I already had close feelings for Dublin since I had directed the first production in decades of Oscar Wilde's *Salomé* at the legendary Gate Theatre Dublin, which was then run by producer Michael Colgan, a few years earlier. The play had rave reviews and my production was destined to tour the world. I had played the role of King Herod, so the Viking King was my second monarch in Ireland.

Shooting Vikings was always exciting. The writing and research was utterly exemplary; scriptwriter Michael Hirst wrote every single episode – a Herculean effort – and yet the drama never lessened throughout the series. The scripts were taut, dynamic and constantly followed a clear dramatic line. I loved doing this work – it was demanding but intensely satisfying.

King Olaf ruled his domain with an iron fist and yet he was never reluctant to make a deal if he could avoid a bloody conflict – the role suited me and I was more than happy playing it. However, all good things have to come to an end, and King Olaf's demise came when he was captured and sentenced to death by Prince Oleg. I was chained to a post to be burnt slowly alive – a very tragic ending when he has to tell the young Prince Igor, who has been cruelly instructed to light the oil which will start the blaze, that he should be confident and light it. King Olaf, even from his appalling position, calms him by saying, 'It is alright, since I feel an invisible presence beside me that will be with me always.'

An awesome scene and I was proud to bow out of the series on that note.

Gender-Blind *Hamlet*, Windsor, 2021

Out of the blue, I received an offer to play Polonius in director Sean Mathias' 'gender-blind, age-blind' production of *Hamlet* that Sir Ian McKellen, as Hamlet, was to reprise. He had played Hamlet forty years earlier and now he was evidently keen to repeat the experience. This was quite an enterprise, bordering on the incredulous. However, to be offered work in a classical production of *Hamlet* was intriguing. It was a rare event and no doubt came from Sir Ian, with whom I have had a friendly association for a number of years.

Of course, I was very tempted, however, my initial instinct was totally negative since not only had I played Hamlet in London at the Roundhouse Theatre in 1980, in a production which I had also directed, but I had toured Europe and had even written a successful memoir on the production, published by Faber & Faber, called *I Am Hamlet*. I chose that title specifically as my reaction to a caustic review from critic Nicholas De Jongh, who said I was 'fatally miscast as Hamlet'. In fact, whoever plays Hamlet becomes Hamlet. It's one of those one-size-fits-all roles in a way. Also, having evolved my own style in direction, I just didn't think I would be able to survive being directed in a traditional or even conventional production.

So my first instinct was a definite rejection of their offer, but then, thinking more about it, I tried to draw out of my mind all the positives: it had all the ingredients to be an historic production, especially with McKellen at 82, so it did have just the right amount of bizarreness to make it appealing. The problem with being offered a part in a theatrical production is that after you weigh up the positives, the next day the army of negatives comes cascading down, but as soon as you have acclimated yourself to the negatives, then the positives come pouring in to take their place. This was my unfortunate mindset for several weeks.

One day, I called Julius Green, Bill Kenwright's efficient assistant, and confessed my latest decision, which was a positive, and I thought I'd make that decision known before the next day, when the negatives would come rolling back in. The positive was agreed to with much aplomb, but then of course I would spend the following day in fits of torment, figuring out how to summon up the courage to say, 'I've changed my mind.' But I didn't, I stuck to my positive decision. A small part of me felt some need to be wanted, to be asked for, instead of always hauling myself up to the mountaintop.

Now, this wasn't meant to be a woke production, and Julius Green eagerly called it age-blind and gender-blind at every possible occasion. It was a useful comment, through which one could avoid having to go into annoying detail. Rehearsals were to be at Windsor's beautiful Theatre Royal, and I turned up for the first reading full of the optimism of a new job and somehow inspired to do my utmost best. Polonius is usually a slightly dull and worthy role, but much can be done with it. I duly noted that my son, Laertes, was to be played by a young Black woman, Emmanuella Cole, but didn't dwell on that too much, since I thought it could be quite an adventure; after all, this was age-blind, gender-blind, and everything-else-blind. Claudius was being played by the splendid and highly sophisticated actor Jonathan Hyde. I recall seeing Hyde over thirty years earlier at The Old Vic in a Greek play directed by one of the up-and-coming fringe groups and being very impressed by him.

The lovely Francesca Annis was playing the ghost. Jenny Seagrove, who was Bill Kenwright's partner, was to give her Gertrude. We entered the theatre and all gathered in a circle eagerly clutching our scripts, and before we began our first read, Sir Ian very smartly asked everybody present to tell the assembled company if they had a special Hamlet in their memory. I thought that was a splendid idea, since nearly everyone had an anecdote and it would bring everyone out of their self-consciousness. When it came to Francesca Annis, she simply said a special one for her was Steven

Berkoff's *Hamlet*, and she would never forget it. I was both shocked and delighted and, even at that moment, began to congratulate myself for having decided to do Polonius. 'Thank you, Francesca.' The set had already been built as a kind of second stage where the audience would sit on the stage close to the action. I thought this would severely cut down the playing area, but Sean Mathias very smartly gave us a quick warm-up introduction which was articulate and persuasive.

What was strangest of all was the desire on the part of the management to film the production in advance, before we had even opened. However, I did find the filming part quite enjoyable, and it gave me the chance to bond with the rest of the cast, particularly Emmanuella. Apart from the odd hiccup, filming seemed to go very well, and Julius did pass on very complimentary comments on the rushes from Bill Kenwright.We spent three or more weeks on the filming, and to this day, some two years after the event, I have not seen a single frame of it, but word has passed down about how good it is and how it will probably 'drift into legend'.

At last filming was completed, apart from one or two scenes, and the company departed Windsor for two weeks to learn lines before the final rehearsal period for the stage version began. We were now largely sleeping over in Windsor, and since these were the days of the Covid-19 pandemic lockdown, the hotel would send out for food and supplied us with drinks. I had a pleasant room with a view looking over Windsor Castle and the only irritant I found was that if I was tardy getting down to dinner, I'd find the large central table packed with the principal actors and the director, while I scrabbled round looking for the table with the also-rans. Eventually, I tried to time my entrance to the dining room so that I would feel the pleasure of sitting with my peers. It does not take much to wobble my self-esteem.

I didn't waste time and swiftly made a decision regarding my costume and appearance. Polonius was growing by leaps and bounds as a truculent, pompous, saluting, boot-clicking, supercilious arse-licker of his superiors. It felt quite natural and I swung into action. After a few weeks, the young lady playing Laertes decided to leave the production and was replaced by a young man, Ashley Gayle, who was perfect for the role. It was easy to show affection to him and the key scene when Polonius gives Ophelia and Laertes sound advice had never been better.

But now I was taxiing to Windsor and back, which cost £300 per day, and if I decided to stay, since the hotel was in lockdown, you could only obtain sandwiches via room service. In the end, I decided that enough was enough. The show had by now opened, I had been on for two weeks, and the audience response to me was most satisfying.

Then, one morning, while in Windsor, I was given an out. Sean rang me up and enquired how I was. Despite my growing despondency, I responded that I actually felt quite alright since I felt that I'd given quite a good performance the night before. The audience had been very responsive again, and my scene had evoked much laughter.

'You seemed a little tired,' he said.

I paused. Suddenly I could see where this was going.

'Would you prefer it if I left the production?' I asked.

'Would you like to leave the production?' he replied.

I needed to be honest. I needed to confess that I would not be unhappy to put an end to all the travelling and hotels and, most of all, the loneliness. I replied, 'Does my understudy know my lines?'

Sean said, 'Oh, I'm sure that he does.'

I felt a glimmer of hope. 'In that case, I would be happy to leave the show, but when would be a good time for you?'

'When would you like to go?'

Then I blurted out, 'How about tonight?!'

Sean replied, 'Of course, if you wish.'

'And you're sure my understudy will be confident in the role?'

'Oh yes, I'm quite sure he is.'

I saw the gates of freedom tantalisingly open, and I was ready to bolt! Then I said something I had never before uttered to my director…

'Sean,' I said. 'I love you…'

The words just erupted out of me, and I was free. Thank god … I rushed out of my crappy hotel and dashed down to the theatre, picked up my bits and bobs from the dressing room, called a cab, and soon was whistling to everlasting freedom. And happiness!

I left the company without any rancour and felt that I had acquitted myself to my own satisfaction. This was, in fact, the second time that I had worked with Ian McKellen, the first being when he took on the immense role of Thomas More at the Nottingham Playhouse nearly sixty years ago, which was directed by Frank Dunlop. Ian played the ancient, saintly Thomas More very well for such a young man.

However, I couldn't have been happier to leave. As much as I did admire the actors in the company, and I was happy to have performed Polonius, I was now utterly convinced that working for others didn't sit comfortably with me. I'm just so glad that I found the right road for me and must learn not to take diversions – sometimes, though, you are tempted.

CONCLUSION

Coming up to my final working years, I am still able to create my own work, but now, without touring management, it has become more and more difficult to contract dates worldwide. In the interim, I became fascinated with the whole saga of Hollywood sex pest Harvey Weinstein and decided to research the whole mucky history. I sketched out another one-man show, which I simply called *Harvey*. I spent months learning it and finally played it for just three weeks at The Playground Theatre in 2018, a small fringe theatre in West London. I enjoyed it but couldn't always hold on to the lines! I announced the first week as a preview week and yet, in spite of this, two critics came on the very first preview and both decided to utterly destroy it! It seemed that they came with an agenda to scuttle my fragile craft, but I played on, growing stronger by the night. But after the limited run was over, I didn't pursue any further dates for it.

Looking back, I think I was becoming somewhat concerned about those odd flickers in my brain, since one sentence was a direct link to those that followed, and I found that when I 'dried', quite a normal thing for an actor onstage, it seemed to have dire consequences and even a fear that I might forget more of the play if I missed a critical link to it. So I thought I might give performing a rest for a while. I was perhaps hoping that the demons of dementia had found no willing sanctuary in my brain, damn them! But, when *Harvey* went well and I was in full throttle, it was an exciting evening.

The most welcome news was that a new theatre company had decided to revive my one-act play *Harry's Christmas* and planned to do it in December – and, of course, why not? As a kind of reflection of that period, I decided I should go with my wife, Clara, since she had seen me play Harry forty years ago and, at the time, I even used her name as one of the women I talk about in the play and am frantically and desperately trying to reach. Now forty years later, we were able to see it together. My relatively new agent said he wished to see it and we agreed to meet there. I saw the solo performance, and it was well played by a much younger man than I was. What astounded me was just how positive the reviews were.

The years since have been much quieter, since I no longer possess the same energy I used to have. It was almost my principle that, when I was sufficiently inspired to create a new work, I would seldom, if ever, depend on the goodwill of a producer, since that was far too uncertain a route to go down and disappointingly few would be bold enough to take a risk without a few trump cards, like a popular movie star for one of the leads. So, most times, I would fall upon my own resources and eventually witnessed the sheer joy of my fantasy coming to life. It is a totally euphoric experience. Also, I loved challenging myself no matter how long the odds; most times I would succeed and positively drool as the audiences started piling in without all the profits being syphoned off by a producer. Even to break even would be wonderful. But most of all, what is, in fact, paramount to me is the ability to be able to fulfil my dreams with something that has obsessed me for years. That is the greatest treasure of all. It justifies the very breath you breathe; it gives your life purpose.

I recall at the beginning of these memoirs that even as a child, I felt it was vitally important that I fulfil my fantasies in adulthood, that I hold those visions close to my heart and never relinquish them, no matter the trials and tribulations that may come my way. I confess that I have had many, but, in the end, I would push myself not to give up. Most of all, never give up the fight, even if at times you feel lost in the world.

So now, at my grand old age of 88, I look back and weigh my virtues in the balance. Did I achieve even a part of my dreams? I think so, since I pulled them down from the sky and brought them to life. I cannot say I failed by any means, although I might have benefitted from some encouragement from what we call the establishment.

I have, in the main, struggled alone... although yes, I will always be forever grateful to the Arts Council of Great Britain for the initial funding I so happily received in my early years. It was much-needed help. Also, to all the actors who believed in me and stuck by me and most of all shared my excitement.

To all of you, my deepest gratitude and love.

Tipping My Hat to Those Who Passed During My Journey on This Planet

Every age has its special heroes, artists, iconoclasts, and lunatics, and what unique events you will be privileged to witness depends on when you turned up on the planet. I considered it serendipitous to have been born in East London in 1937. How was the creative harvest in those years? Phenomenal! Laurence Olivier was striding the waves of drama, so even if I had just missed his *Oedipus* doubled with Sheridan's *The Critic*, a tour de force in 1938, I was a fully cognisant young adult when I saw his *The Entertainer, Rhinoceros, Othello, The Dance of Death, Semi-Detached,* and *Love for Love*. Sure, you can now see many of those performances on film, but what you miss is the awesome immediacy of the live event. It is unique. You saw him live as if you were witnessing a piece of history in the making – surely a privilege for any young, would-be actor.

Then, I shared the same air as Vivien Leigh and Peter Wyngarde in Jean Giraudoux's play *Duel of Angels*, which was unforgettable. Could any actor be as perfect as Peter Wyngarde – a dazzling conjurer with words and gesture, almost too perfect as he chiselled the very space in front of you? Can there ever be such a Mercutio again as Alec McCowan in Zeffirelli's breathtaking *Romeo and Juliet*? Or anything so good as Molière's *The Misanthropist* partnered with a perfect Diana Rigg? Then, I could also feast on Albert Finney in *Luther* by John Osborne or *Billy Liar* by Keith Waterhouse. Before that, I had seen his first exposure in London, which was an unusual piece of eccentricity called the *The Lily White Boys* by poet Christopher Logue in 1960. Let alone his amazing performance as a passionate young tearaway in *Saturday Night and Sunday Morning* with Shirley Anne Field and Tom Jones. All making such an impact in my young, impressionable youth.

Finally, the unforgettable Zero Mostel giving his Leopold Bloom from James Joyce's astonishing masterpiece adapted by Burgess Meredith, *Ulysses in Nighttown*, and the dazzling Patricia Neal in Tennessee Williams's *Suddenly Last Summer*, delivering the monologue detailing the cannibalistic sacrifice of her lover/poet that devastated the entire house. And then I had the good fortune of watching Paul Scofield's *King Lear*, directed by Peter Brook, which was the wonder of the age. Scofield was accompanied by Alec McCowan playing the fool, and I have to admit they were a superb pairing.

Over the course of my career, I have worked with or got to know so many people who are no longer with us. I would like here to pay tribute to them.

LAURENCE OLIVIER – Died 11 July 1989
I even used to dream of him; I was that obsessed. I think no one inspired me to become an actor more than he. When he died, Joan Plowright, his widow, cancelled her performance at the National Theatre to mourn. I took up this space with my own production of *Salomé*.

Laurence Olivier

PAUL SCOFIELD – Died 19 Mar 2008
Our relationship began after he wrote to me having seen my performance in my play *Decadence*. We kept up a regular correspondence over the years.

Paul Scofield

ALEC MCCOWEN – Died 6 Feb 2017
Impressed me like no other British actor and became a staunch ally and supporter. I was so flattered.

ELIZABETH SPRIGGS – Died 2 July 2008
Known in her younger days as a formidable actress at the RSC. First introduced me to Alec McCowan.

ALEXIS KANNER – Died 13 Dec 2003
A bravura Canadian actor, with red hair and stunning looks, who once worked for Orson Welles in his stage show, *Chimes at Midnight*, then went on to work for Peter Brook in his Theatre of Cruelty season. Limited but dynamic career. Was a great ally of Elizabeth Spriggs.

Alexis Kanner

JOHN DEXTER – Died 23 Mar 1990
Royal Court director. Directed me in Arnold Wesker's *The Kitchen*, which was renowned for its energy. This was my first and only performance at the Royal Court.

SIR ROBERT STEPHENS – Died 12 Nov 1995
Leading actor, awesome in his young years. Played the lead in *The Kitchen* by Arnold Wesker like an electric power source.

Sir Robert Stephens

ARNOLD WESKER – Died 12 Apr 2016
I played Raymond the pastry chef in Arnold Wesker's play at the Royal Court. Eventually, we became friends. He re-established the famous Roundhouse in Chalk Farm in 1964.

Arnold Weskler

BILL STEWART – Died 29 Aug 2006
Superb character actor whom I chose to play Joseph K in my first production of Franz Kafka's *The Trial.*

Bill Stewart

TERESA D'ABREU – Died 1995
Elegant and beautiful young woman who died far too early. Was in my very first production of *Agamemnon* and *The Trial* and then continued with a bravura performance in my version of Strindberg's *Miss Julie.*

SIR ANTONY SHER – Died 2 Dec 2021
I taught him at Webber Douglas School of Drama, then he played Joseph K in my second production of *The Trial* at the National Theatre in 1991.

Sir Antony Sher

BARRY PHILIPS – Died 2018
Dynamic young actor who first worked on my version of *Agamemnon*. He performed the role of Messenger and was an absolutely stunning tour de force. Then he played Les in the premiere of my first original play, *East*.

BRAD DAVIS – Died 8 Sept 1991
Mesmeric American actor. *Midnight Express*. Played the beetle in my version of Kafka's *Metamorphosis* at the Mark Taper Forum in LA. Shockingly, died young.

Brad Davis

T.J. MEYERS – Died 29 Mar 2012
Talented comedian who played the lodger in *Metamorphosis* on Broadway. Also was brilliant as the gardener in my production of *Richard II* at the Shakespeare Festival Theatre.

René Auberjonois

RENÉ AUBERJONOIS – Died 8 Dec 2019
Brilliant stage actor. Played the father, Mr Samsa, in *Metamorphosis* on Broadway.

LARS SCHMIDT – Died 18 Oct 2009
Produced *Metamorphosis* in French in Paris with Roman Polanski and on Broadway in 1990 with Mikhail Baryshnikov. Swedish producer. Widower of Ingrid Bergman.

Lars Schmidt

GEORGIA BROWN – Died 5 July 1992
Powerful ex-East End actress and blues singer. Played in my production of *Greek* at the Wyndham's Theatre. Died suddenly.

Georgia Brown

GARY OLSEN – Died 12 Sept 2000
Clever character actor. Played the lodger in *Metamorphosis* at The Mermaid in 1986.

JOE PAPP – Died 31 Oct 1991
Head of Shakespeare's Festival Theatre, for whom I directed *Coriolanus* in 1988 off-Broadway. Became a close friend and helped launch my career in New York. In many ways he was like a father figure – the father I'd always wanted. I was so touched when he wrote me this note, only a few months before he died:

Joe Papp

> *Hello, dear Steven, my jesting friend and yes, my son. I think of you always.*
>
> *Love, JP [Joe Papp]*

STELLA ADLER – Died 21 Dec 1992
Legendary American actress and teacher. Came to London to star in try-out of *Oh Dad, Poor Dad* in 1963, but sadly it flopped. Although she had a blazing reputation as an actress, I think her time was over. I played a bellboy.

Stella Adler

TERRY BEESLEY – Died 30 Nov 2017
Brilliant character actor who co-starred in my play *Acapulco* at the King's Head, Islington. Sadly, died by suicide.

KATRIN CARTLIDGE – Died 7 Sept 2002
Dynamic actress, ex-Complicité, starred in *Salomé* at the National Theatre in 1989.

Katrin Cartlidge

MARIA PASTEL – Died 23 Dec 2021
Brilliant character actress, starred in *Salomé* and *The Trial* at the National Theatre in 1989.

Imogen Claire

IMOGEN CLAIRE – Died 24 June 2005
Extraordinary actress/ex-dancer. Starred in *The Trial* and *Salomé* at the National Theatre.

CHRISTOPHER MUNCKE – Died 6 Apr 2022
American actor. Became my assistant director after I had taught him when he was a student at Webber Douglas Academy. He was a brave and helpful ally.

Jeremy Brett

JEREMY BRETT – Died 12 Sept 1995
Took over as lead from Robert Stephens in *The Kitchen* by Arnold Wesker at the same time as I was joining the company. A very sensitive actor and was a brilliant Sherlock Holmes on TV.

Christopher Plummer

CHRISTOPHER PLUMMER – Died 5 Feb 2021
Superb Canadian classical actor. Played Hamlet in the BBC TV production where I played the Player King, along with Lindsay Kemp. Last worked with him in *The Girl with the Dragon Tattoo* in 2011.

JO MAXWELL-MULLER – Died 30 Oct 2010
Engaging young woman who played Ophelia in the TV version of *Hamlet* opposite Christopher Plummer.

Leonard Rossiter

LEONARD ROSSITER – Died 5 Oct 1984
Superb tour de force actor. Played the title character in *The Resistible Rise of Arturo Ui*. I played the club-footed Givola.

DEL HENNEY – Died 14 Jan 2019
Liverpudlian/Irish actor. Played in *The Resistible Rise of Arturo Ui.*

Patrick Magee

PATRICK MAGEE – Died 14 Aug 1982
Powerful Irish actor in *A Clockwork Orange* and *The Luck of Barry Lyndon*, as was I.

STANLEY KUBRICK – Died 7 Mar 1999
American film director, for whom I worked in *A Clockwork Orange* and *Barry Lyndon.*

Stanley Kubrick

MICHELANGELO ANTONIONI – Died 20 July 2007
Italian film director. I played a small role in *The Passenger* in 1975.

JOHN MCENERY – Died 12 Apr 2019
British actor in Peter Medak's film *The Krays*, where I played George Cornell.

Sir Sean Connery

JAY BENEDICT – Died 4 Apr 2020
American actor. My partner in my final play, *The Actor's Lament.*

SIR SEAN CONNERY – Died 31 Oct 2020
I played a drugged-out victim in *Outland*, directed by Peter Hyams, in which Sean Connery played the lead. A most charming and civil man.

John McVicar

JOHN MCVICAR – Died 6 Sept 2022
Personable ex-gangster-turned-writer. In the film of his autobiography in 1980, I played character supposedly based on South London villain Charlie Richardson.

RONNIE BIGGS – Died 18 Dec 2013
Another robber-turned-writer. Film made of his escape from prison and exile in Rio de Janeiro. I played a Scottish copper out to capture him – not my proudest moment in film, but glad to have met the man himself.

David Bowie

DAVID BOWIE – Died 10 Jan 2016
Was a producer on *Absolute Beginners* in which I played the British fascist Oswald Mosley. I also wrote my fascist speech. Bowie did the music.

Prince

PRINCE – Died 21 Apr 2016
Directed me in the very weakly-received *Under the Cherry Moon* in 1986. Prince took over as director, and I took over the role gratefully from Terence Stamp.

Sir Roger Moore

SIR ROGER MOORE – Died 23 May 2017
I had the pleasure of working with this elegant gentleman in the Bond film *Octopussy*.

BILL KENWRIGHT – Died 23 Oct 2023
Supported me in my production of *On the Waterfront* at the Theatre Royal Haymarket in 2008. Also acted in the gender-blind *Hamlet* at Windsor.

Hugh Hudson

HUGH HUDSON – Died 10 Feb 2023
best known for the Oscar- and BAFTA-winning 1981 drama *Chariots of Fire*. His films include *Greystoke: The Legend of Tarzan, Lord of the Apes, Revolution, Lost Angels,* and *Finding Altamira.*

HAROLD PINTER – Died 24 Dec 2008
Renowned playwright, best-known for *The Birthday Party.* Winner of Nobel Prize for Literature. We both attended the same school: Grocers' Grammar School in Hackney.

Harold Pinter

DAVID LYNCH – Died 16 Jan 2025
A brilliant director whom I had the opportunity to meet in 1986. His films include: E*raserhead, Blue Velvet* and *Mulholland Drive.*

TERENCE STAMP – Died 17 Aug 2025
Was my fellow aspiring actor at drama school. His films include: *Modesty Blaise, Far from the Madding Crowd, Superman* and *Superman II.* For his role in *The Adventures of Priscilla, Queen of the Desert,* he earned BAFTA Award and Golden Globe Award nominations.

Terence Stamp

DONALD SUTHERLAND – Died 20 June 2024
Played Fortinbras in the 1963 TV adaptation of *Hamlet* that I was in. Films include: *M*A*S*H, Klute, Don't Look Now, The Day of the Locust, Invasion of the Body Snatchers, Ordinary People.*

Donald Sutherland

SAMANTHA EGGAR – Died 15 Oct 2025
Another fellow aspiring actor at Webber Douglas Academy. Not only ravishingly beautiful but had the talent to match it. Films include: *Doctor Dolittle, The Molly Maguires* and *The Brood.*

Samantha Eggar